VIET-NAM AND THE WEST

Viet-Nam and the West

by

RALPH SMITH

Lecturer in the History of South East Asia,
School of Oriental and African Studies,
University of London

HEINEMANN

LONDON

Heinemann Educational Books Ltd

LONDON   MELBOURNE   TORONTO
SINGAPORE   JOHANNESBURG
AUCKLAND   IBADAN
HONG KONG
NAIROBI

Published by
Heinemann Educational Books Ltd
48 Charles Street, London W.1

Printed in Great Britain by
Morrison & Gibb Ltd, London and Edinburgh

Contents

Maps

Preface

To write the history of one's own country, though never easy, is a relatively uncomplicated task: whatever the difficulties of source material and interpretation, one is at least writing about people and institutions belonging to one's own cultural tradition. To attempt to write the history of a country as different from one's own as is (for an Englishman) Viet-Nam, is an undertaking so difficult that it might even be called rash. For the subject of such a history must be viewed across a cultural gulf as wide as any that exists within the species of mankind. The problems are not merely those of language: they concern the whole framework of assumptions within which men live and have their being. For this reason, if for no other, the present essay sets out to be something more (as well as something less) than a mere chronicle of political decisions and their results. It seeks to bridge the gap between the study of politics and that of culture or civilization, and to relate the record of events to the framework of thought and belief, ideas and institutions, of the Vietnamese. Such an undertaking is as hazardous as, in the present state of the world, it is necessary. Whether one approaches the problem of cultural understanding as a diplomat or as an academic scholar, it remains one of the most difficult of all problems facing twentieth-century societies in their relations with one another. Especially is this the case between Asians and Westerners, and in the recent history of Viet-Nam there exists an opportunity to study the problem in all its complexity.

The present essay, though its arrangement is not strictly chronological, concerns the period from 1858 to 1963: slightly over a century, in which Viet-Nam moved from the last days of monarchical independence, on the eve of French conquest, to a situation of divided independence in which the two halves of the country were at war with one another. The war itself, whose origins go back to 1957 but which did not reach a level of great intensity until after 1963, must be the subject of another book. It is still much too early to attempt a detailed assessment of that war, which in all its cruelty and horror is still being waged as I write. But the question why such a war should have begun at all is one which men are already asking, and which can perhaps be given a tentative answer. It is inconceivable that either side at the start expected that it would be so bitter and intense as it became; nevertheless the war itself already existed in the logic of the situation of 1963. And from the point of view of the Westerner, the fact that the war had to be fought at all must count as a tragic failure, whatever may be the outcome of the conflict.

I am conscious that this essay does not do full justice to the subject: it does little more than scratch the surface of problems whose true complexity will only be appreciated when a vast deal more research has been done, and when many more minds are able to contribute to their elucidation. But a beginning must be made somewhere, and whilst there is some truth in the historian's dictum that 'interpretation must wait on scholarship', it is sometimes the case that interpretation will itself inspire scholarship.

The present study would have been impossible without the help and encouragement of a great many friends and colleagues. In view of the controversial nature of the subject, I shall not risk anyone embarrassment by recording his name in apparent association with points of view he may not wholly share. My gratitude is none the less deep for being expressed in general terms. I would mention especially my debt to colleagues at the School of Oriental and African studies; to those who participated in the China and the World study group at Chatham House between 1963 and 1967; and most important of all, to my Vietnamese friends in Paris and Saigon.

January, 1968   Ralph Smith

A Note on Vietnamese Names

VIETNAMESE, unlike most Asian languages, does not present serious problems of transliteration. Although it was originally written in characters similar to those of Chinese, a standard Romanized form was developed by Christian missionaries from the seventeenth century, and during the twentieth century this has become universally adopted by the Vietnamese. Very few people know the old characters.

It is not however possible, using English type, to reproduce all the diacritical marks which are necessary in the Romanized script of Vietnamese to indicate differences of tone. In the present work I have not attempted to do so, though I have included the circumflex mark where appropriate, whose purpose is to indicate vowel quality.

Nor is it possible to indicate the difference between the Vietnamese Đ and D. The name Ngô Đinh Diêm, for example, is pronounced Ngô Dinh *Ziêm* (in the Tongkingese dialect; the Cochinchinese pronounciation of the last name is something like *dYiêm*). The name Duy, often found as a middle name, is pronounced *Zwee*. It is impracticable to try to explain here all the subtleties of Vietnamese pronunciation, but one common name which often gives trouble is Nguyên: it should be pronounced *Ng-wi-en*.

In referring to one another Vietnamese normally use the third of their three names, which is the personal name. The only exception occurs in the case of a very distinguished person where it is appropriate to use the first (family) name with a special honorific title. Thus Hô Chi Minh (a pseudonym anyway) is never known as Minh; and while he lived Ngô Dinh Diêm was sometimes known as President Ngô. In order to avoid confusion I have (with the exception of Hô) adhered to the standard practice of using the personal name. No disrespect is intended to such revered figures as Phan Bôi Châu and Phan Châu Trinh, both of whom appear in Vietnamese writings as *cu* Phan.

ix

PROLOGUE

The Bodhisattva Mahasattva wrapped his body in divine garments,
bathed it in oil, made his last vow, and thereafter burnt his own
body. . . . And the eighty Lords Buddhas all shouted their applause:
Well done, well done, young man of good birth, that is the real heroism
which the Bodhisattvas Mahasattvas should develop; that is the real
worship of the Tathagata, the real worship of the Law.

Saddharma Pundarika (The Lotus Sutra).

Prologue

> On the twentieth day of the fourth month, in the year of the
> Cat, tenth of the decade, a monk named Quang Duc was
> covered with oil and burnt himself alive at Saigon.

THE traditional Vietnamese style of chronology, being cyclical
and lacking a continuous era, does not distinguish the absolute
uniqueness of events. Ten numerals and twelve animals allow
for a cycle of sixty years; then one must start again.[1] Consequently, described in this way, the self-immolation of Quang Duc
might belong to any of a number of years of the Cat, stretching
across several centuries: perhaps, for example, to 1363. The
occurrence of such an event in that year would not be of great
interest to most Western readers; only the student of the esoteric
would probe deeper. He would find that it was not without
parallel in the history of Asian Buddhism. In 1034, for instance,
two monks are said by the chronicles to have set fire to themselves
in the old Vietnamese capital of Thang-Long (the modern
Hanoi), their ashes being enshrined in a special temple by the
king Ly Thai-Tông. Again, in Bangkok a Buddhist monk
sacrificed himself in this way in 1791, and another in 1817. And
as recently as 1930 a Vietnamese monk burnt himself alive at
Biên-Hoa. Buddhism is a religion in which men seek to escape all
sense of attachment to a bodily self and a personal life, and
the complete destruction of his body by a monk is applauded
by several sacred texts. The monk who takes this extreme step
does so in the confidence that his rebirth will be into a higher
state of being. Ultimately he hopes to attain *Nirvana*, a state
so empty of existence in any sense materialist Westerners can
understand that it is neither 'being' nor 'non-being'.[2]

But the year of Quang Duc's self-immolation was not 1363,
it was six centuries later; and the event was not of merely esoteric
interest. Immediately it caught the imagination of a world which

3

was watching every detail of the political crisis then unfolding in South Viet-Nam. During the months which followed there was much debate in American circles about the significance of the 'fire-suicides' and the attitude to be adopted towards them. The opinion which prevailed at the time was that they signified a Vietnamese 'public opinion' near to breaking-point. Accordingly the government of the United States withdrew its support from President Ngô Dinh Diêm, and in November of the same year, 1963, he was overthrown by a military coup.

More recent, and more cynical, commentators have suspected that this interpretation may have been too simple.[3] Appalled at the chaos which followed the coup of 1963, they have detected in the situation of that year a clever political manoeuvre designed to make foreign journalists dramatize the Buddhist opposition to the government in Saigon, and so to encourage the Americans to take decisions which would ultimately benefit their enemies the Communists. They find evidence of a careful calculation of the effects the 'fire-suicides' would have on world opinion; and they point to the elaborate public relations system of the Buddhist organization, which ensured that whenever such a spectacle took place Western newsmen with their cameras were quickly on the scene. The sacred bonzes, it would seem, were not men totally withdrawn from worldly life, but clever politicians who new what they wanted and how to achieve it. The American diplomats and journalists fell into their trap.

To choose between the two interpretations is not easy; a characteristic Western reaction would doubtless be to suggest that the truth lies somewhere in between. But the truth is more complex. For neither of these views takes into account what must surely be the most important question about the immolations: that is, how a kind of action which if it happened six centuries ago we should regard as of purely religious significance, should in our own day and age come to be regarded as primarily political. Neither of the interpretations just outlined allows for the cultural significance of these events. Yet surely, whatever their political importance, these acts of self-destruction demonstrate more clearly than anything else the fact that culturally Viet-Nam is quite beyond the normal range of occidental comprehension. This fact is in itself of immense political significance.

Suicide is a deed not lightly undertaken, and in any society its occurrence will reflect fundamental themes of belief and culture. By Christian standards, to take one's life is a sin against the creator God, in whose sight every man should strive for living perfection on earth in order to be worthy of salvation in a life to come. The only view of suicide which such belief allows is that of an ignoble desire to escape: even the non-Christian humanist in the West condones suicide, he does not praise it. But in Viet-Nam, as in other countries of East Asia, to withdraw from the world is a means of proving virtue. Suicide can even be a way of proving superior virtue in face of a powerful but unvirtuous enemy. At that point, it can become not merely an escape but a weapon of considerable force. In 1963, a few weeks after the death of Quang Duc, another Vietnamese took poison in Saigon: the celebrated novelist Nhât Linh. He was about to be put on trial for opposition to the Diêm government, and his suicide was a more eloquent defence than anything he could have said in words. Quang Duc, as well as following a religious precedent, was speaking the same language as Nhât Linh. It is a language which most Westerners find utterly unfamiliar: so much so that in the summer of 1963 their first reaction to the fire-suicides was to over-dramatize them, and to exaggerate their significance. Inevitably this initial horror led in time to a reaction, and eventually many American observers came to conclude that fire-suicides have no significance at all.

But if the language of the suicides was unfamiliar, their context was even more so. The most important question for the Americans —journalists and policy-makers alike—was not *why* the monks were burning themselves, but how important the monks were in relation to the rest of Vietnamese society. It would seem that the Americans knew little about the nature of Vietnamese Buddhism before the crisis erupted; unfortunately it is not a subject which can be studied with profit at a moment's notice. It is not my purpose here to argue the question whether the American decision to withdraw support from Ngô Dinh Diêm was the right one, but merely to observe that it was taken almost in a cultural vacuum. Part of the tragedy of the American experience in Viet-Nam has been that a great deal in the political culture of the country and of its people is not readily intelligible to the Western mind. To say that this or that particular failure of cultural inderstanding has been of a decisive nature would be misleading. The self-immolation of Quang Duc is simply an illustration of a problem of communication which has pervaded the relationship between Americans and Vietnamese since 1954. The government of the United States has found itself becoming more and more deeply involved in the consequences of events whose causes or motivation it does not properly understand. That such a situation should befall the country whose boast is that its wealth and resources make it the most powerful in the world is galling indeed.

For Europeans to criticize Americans on this score however is not entirely appropriate. It so happens that in Viet-Nam the United States has become more deeply involved than any other Western power; but American involvement is only the most recent chapter in Viet-Nam's relations with the West. The current conflict there is the culmination of a developing relationship which began in earnest with the French attack on Da-Nang in 1858. It is in the complicated nature of that relationship, rather than in any specific decision of contemporary politicians that we must seek the origins of the present situation.

Like all other Asian countries, Viet-Nam has a quality and character of its own, which must not be blotted out under the weight of sweeping generalizations about 'the East'. It must be accepted as unique among the nations of the world. By European standards moreover, it is by no means a small country: taking North and South together it has a population of thirty millions, more than double that of Australia; and in surface area its extent is about equivalent to that of the whole British Isles including Eire. Its recorded history goes back as far as our own, to the first or second century before Christ. Even if it had not become the focus of an international crisis, it would be a country worthy of study in its own right.

True, Viet-Nam is not one of the great centres of creative civilization radiating impulses in all directions, like India or China or Greece. The Vietnamese character is poetic before it is analytical, and for ideas capable of becoming the basis of institutional organization the Vietnamese have tended to borrow from other areas of the world. In particular, down to the nineteenth century they borrowed from the Chinese; and the relationship of Vietnamese to Chinese culture is in consequence an extremely subtle one. During the thousand years before about A.D. 900, when Viet-Nam was the southernmost province of a Chinese empire, the peoples of the 'Indonesian' civilization which had previously flourished in the area were greatly influenced by the Chinese who came to inhabit and to govern their country. The position of those peoples in relation to their conquerors was not unlike that between the British and their Roman rulers at about the same period in time. The subsequent development of the relationship might also have been paralleled in the West, if the Roman Empire had recovered its unity after the fifth century but had never again succeeded in reconquering the British Isles.[4] But just as the Britons were never completely Romanized, so the Vietnamese were still not wholly Sinicized when, about A.D. 900, the break-up of the T'ang empire brought about their independence.

In the thousand years that followed, they created and defended a state of their own in the South, calling it first Dai-Viet (meaning 'Great Viet') and later Dai-Nam ('Great South'). From time to time they were threatened with incorporation into a reunified China, but on four occasions they succeeded in resisting or in quickly terminating Chinese attempts at reconquest. Although they sent periodic tribute to the Chinese capital, their king or emperor was ruler in his own right, making his own sacrifices to Earth and to Heaven. He and his officials continued to use the Chinese language for administrative purposes—and for classical literary composition—down to the nineteenth century: just as Latin was employed by clerics and lawyers in England and France long after the decline of Rome. The principles of Vietnamese government were based on those of the Confucian classics, and current Chinese literature was readily available to those who knew the characters.[5]

The parallel with England and France must not however be taken too far. The cultural gulf between Viet-Nam and the West, which became apparent in the nineteenth century, was much more than a gulf between 'traditional' and 'modern' societies. To think of traditional Viet-Nam as *culturally* comparable to medieval France or England would be a serious error. The nature of Western social and intellectual traditions made possible, from about the seventeenth century, developments which in time were to place European and Asian culture still farther apart: the 'scientific' and 'industrial revolutions'. Whether such developments could have ever taken place, given time, in

China or Viet-Nam is a question beyond our power to answer; for with Western expansion the traditional frameworks of East Asia were interrupted and forced to respond to Western influence. Conquest by France compelled the Vietnamese to turn away from China, at least for the time being, as their principal source of culture inspiration, and to turn towards the West. They accepted Roman script as a medium for writing their own language, and they were exposed to a wide range of new ideas and techniques in all spheres of activity.

Viet-Nam is possibly the most 'un-Western' of all Asian countries to have been conquered and ruled for a time by a European power. At the same time its colonial masters were probably the most eager of those powers to impose Western civilization on their Asian subjects. This coincidence has made Viet-Nam's relationship with the West culturally as well as politically dramatic. French rule has undoubtedly left its mark upon the culture and civilization of Viet-Nam, especially on those individuals who were so completely educated in French that they were accepted as virtually Frenchmen in France. Yet despite several decades of chanting 'nos ancêtres les Gaulois' there is no question that even the most Gallicized of them remain in essential respects Vietnamese.

In the past century or so, therefore, the philosophy of harmony derived from China was challenged by the philosophy of achievement brought by the Europeans. The encounter is not yet over, and those tempted to make too hasty a judgment of its outcome might do worse than to recall the reply of a Chinese scholar to a question about the effects of the French Revolution: it is much too early to say. But since we must live with this encounter, and some of us may have to die because of it, we ought to try very hard to understand it.

PART ONE

Our Great Viet is a country where prosperity abounds,
Where civilization reigns supreme.

Its mountains, its rivers, its frontiers are its own;
Its customs are distinct, in North and South.

Triêu, Dinh, Ly and Trân
Created our nation,
Whilst Han, T'ang, Sung and Yuan,
Ruled over theirs.

Over the centuries,
We have been sometimes strong, sometimes weak;
But never yet have we been lacking in heroes.
Of that let our history be the proof.

> Lê Loi's proclamation of independence
> after driving out the Ming, 1428.

I

The Vietnamese Tradition

THE temples and palaces of the 'Great Within' (the *Dai-Nôi*) of the imperial city at Huê are preserved as a national monument, much as the French Republic preserves Versailles and Fontaine-bleau. It is permitted to ordinary citizens, and even foreigners, to wander through pavilions and gardens once sacred and for-bidden. They may inspect the *Thê-Miêu*, the temple built by the second emperor of the Nguyên dynasty in veneration of the spirit of his father who in 1802 had united Viet-Nam under a single dynasty. They may visit the imperial throne hall, where emperors were first enthroned at the beginning of their reign and received the allegiance of their highest officials; prostration before the emperor on such occasions was abolished only in 1932. None of the buildings is impressive by its height, for the Vietnamese did not share the urge of the Indianized peoples of South East Asia to build upwards to the sky; but their spacious serenity reflects the search for harmony which pervaded all Vietnamese religion.

Not all however is preserved. When the visitor arrives at the centre of this inner city he will find no trace of the forbidden palaces of the imperial residence itself. At one edge of the area where they stood, the burnt-out shell of a minor pavilion bears witness to the destruction of the rest by fire. The destruction occurred early in February 1947, when the *Viêt-Minh* set fire to the palace before retreating in the face of reoccupying French forces. They had been virtually the government of this part of Viet-Nam for a period of eighteen months, since the seizure of power in Hanoi by Hô Chi Minh's provisional government. The last emperor of the dynasty, Bao-Dai, had abdicated on 25th August 1945; this destruction of his palace (and also, as far as is known, of the imperial seals) was a dramatic symbol of the transition from monarchy to republic.

The transition was not really so sudden, however. The Viet-namese monarchy had failed its subjects sixty years before in allowing the French to establish their 'protectorate' over Annam and Tongking. Although the French preserved the formalities of rule by a Confucian court and its officials, the reality of power lay with the Résident-Supérieur. Even those opponents of French rule who wanted, in the early decades of this century, to put on the throne a new monarch in place of the French nominee, recognized that it would not be enough merely to restore an independent Confucian regime. Their model was Japan, whose monarchy had successfully responded to the Western challenge by developing a constitutional government. As for those who, after 1911, looked to China for inspiration, their aim was to establish a republic of Viet-Nam and to have done with monarchy altogether.

The forbidden palace at Huê had thus ceased to be the focus of national life long before it went up in flames. Moreover this decline and final collapse of the monarchy was a spiritual as well as a political change, and it left a hole in traditional society far greater than the lacuna on the ground at the centre of the Huê citadel. The sanctity of the ruler had been central to that society. But it could not survive untarnished the disaster of material defeat at the hands of barbarian invaders. There was no sharp distinction between politics and other aspects of life in the Vietnamese tradition, and the Confucian monarchy had been the keystone of a cultural edifice whose very foundations were shaken by the victories of the West over the Middle Kingdom. The whole traditional conception of the universe was called in question by the failure of the monarchy, both in China and Viet-Nam, to respond successfully to the challenge of the West.[1]

The fundamental contrast between the traditional culture of Viet-Nam and that of the countries of Western Europe is readily apparent if one compares their respective views of the individual man, and their very different ideals of personal behaviour. In Viet-Nam, the complete self-abnegation of Buddhism was demanded only of the minority of people who entered that religion. But in the more 'secular' religions of Taoism and Confucianism, the ideal was still one of restraint and personal detachment. Vietnamese children were (indeed still are) brought up to regard it as very inferior behaviour to show any sign of their inner feelings in their relationships with others. The Confucian *quan-tu* (Chinese *chun-tzu*)—a word very inadequately rendered into English by 'gentleman'—was one who had penetrated the moral order that embraces both man and nature and so knew how to live in harmony with it. He was admired for his self-control, his ability to keep silent and at the same time to apprehend the reality of things. To show emotion was to lose face, to reveal a weakness unworthy of the cultivated man. Nor was this ideal limited to Confucianism; it was shared by the Taoists, who sometimes spoke of the *phong-luu*: literally a man who would allow water to flow past him, by implication one who would remain unperturbed.

The historical figures most admired by the Vietnamese include not only men of action, like Trân Hung Dao and Lê Loi whose heroism lay in defeating the Chinese, but also men who knew how to wait. Among the most celebrated of these men of inaction was Nguyên Binh Kiêm, who rose to a position of prominence as a successful young scholar, but then in 1542 retired from the court and refused to become involved in the conflict between the Mac usurpers and the clans who wanted to restore the deposed dynasty of the Lê. He lived for forty years in his 'refuge of the White Cloud', from time to time giving advice to the leaders of both sides; and when he died, having achieved only the peace of his own mind, a temple was erected in veneration of his spirit. Such a career recalls to mind the advice of the *Tao Te Ching*:

> Know contentment and you will suffer no disgrace. Know when to stop, and you will meet with no danger. You can then endure.[2]

This philosophy of withdrawal and of personal harmony is alien to the modern Western outlook, in which only positive achievement commands unstinted praise. Nor would it have been very much more acceptable to the medieval Christian: for despite its great diversity the Christian tradition has as its central theme belief in grace and salvation in the sight of a personal and omnipotent God, a divine legislator whose judgment is the ultimate reality. To obtain that grace, men must be actively good. It must not be imagined however that the Vietnamese tradition never allowed for any action at all. One might say rather that, by contrast with the Western tradition, it gave equal weight to the inner and outer spheres of human existence, to inner response and external activity. This was the essence of the Confucian philosophy which, as it developed over the centuries, became the foundation of both Chinese and Vietnamese society. The Confucian state was held together by the belief that when men act according to the universal moral order, virtue is sure to prevail; when they assert themselves against it, there is chaos. The *Great Learning*, one of the most important classical texts from the twelfth century onwards, says that:

> When things are investigated,
> then true knowledge is achieved.
> When true knowledge is achieved,
> then the will becomes sincere.
> When the will is sincere,
> then the mind sees right.
> When the mind sees right,
> the personal life is cultivated.
> When the personal life is cultivated,
> then the family life is regulated.
> When the family life is regulated,
> then the national life is orderly.
> When the national life is orderly,
> then there is peace in the world.'[3]

The person, the family, the nation. These were the three levels of existence, of participation in the moral order, which mattered to the Confucian scholar. The regulation and good order of all three were proof that universal harmony prevailed, and that Heaven would prosper the realm. The way to ensure this order was through the fulfilment of obligations: that of the son to his father, that of the pupil to his master, that of the subject to his ruler. It might have been possible to interpret the Confucian philosophy in a spirit of rebellion, for if the personal life of the emperor or of his officials was lacking in virtue and sincerity, then surely their fitness to rule was called in question. But in practice, Confucianism was essentially conservative. It was true that a ruler might lose the 'mandate of Heaven', but if he was then deposed it was less a matter of human choice than of an impersonal decree of Fate. There is nothing in the classics about the person as an individual, possessing inalienable rights. The universal moral order sanctioned only obligations.

The Confucian monarchy was nevertheless quite different from the Western conception of absolute autocracy. The foundation of the Confucian order was neither human reason nor divine authority: it was the very nature of the universe itself. The continued harmony of the universe depended upon regular sacrifices to Heaven: therefore there must be an emperor, and as the Son of Heaven he must be obeyed as the highest of all human beings. In the West on the other hand the traditional king was first and foremost a maker of laws, and he derived his authority from an analogy between the king in his kingdom and God in His Heaven. The whole attitude to action and achievement which characterizes Western civilization is rooted in the tradition of Christianity. Western man has tended to imitate his omnipotent God, and has sought to be both legislator over society and master of the natural laws which govern the physical world.[4]

The same conception of God did not exist in traditional China or Viet-Nam. To say that their tradition had no personal God at all would be misleading: it would be more precise to say that they distinguished (in practice, not in theory) between two levels of the supernatural, Heaven and the spirits. Personality was an attribute not of Heaven but of spirits, which were legion. Often they were the souls of departed men: in the cult of the ancestors it was incumbent upon every man to venerate the spirits of his own forebears, and any man who was unfortunate enough to have no progeny to perform rites for his soul after death would become a 'wandering soul', a burden to himself and to the world. Not all spirits were regarded as inevitably good; wandering spirits indeed were capable of positive harm to man, whilst the spirits of mountains and waters had to be correctly appeased or they would become wayward. Certain spirits however were especially beneficent, and men would appeal for protection to their wisdom and virtue. Every village had its protective spirit: sometimes an ancestor of one of the village clans, sometimes a famous hero with local connections. The kingdom as a whole was protected by the ancestral spirits of the imperial dynasty, in whose honour there were elaborate temples in the precincts of the capital. In addition there were special hero cults associated with the spirits of men like Trân Hung Dao or Nguyên Binh Kiêm, whose virtue in life gave his soul great power after death. Not surprisingly, people came to regard Confucius, or the mythical Lao Tzu, or the innumerable manifestations of the Buddha, as spirits of a very high order. The nearest the Vietnamese tradition came to a religion like Christianity was in the sects which venerated some spirit as supreme over all the rest. But they do not appear to have seen their protector as a judge: rather, his virtue made him infinitely compassionate, and salvation through him called only for devotion and faith. Such was, and still is, the nature of Amidist Buddhism, in which the spirit worshipped is that of the former Buddha Amitabha.

For the educated Confucian Vietnamese, however, the supreme position was reserved for Heaven, whose Way was the highest possible way of virtue. This supremacy, over spirits and men alike, was not that of a personal legislator, but of an impersonal moral force. Heaven was simply 'there', transcending all conflicts and activity, the source of infinite harmony, uniting in itself both the positive and negative elements of the universe. The decree of Heaven was not seen as a code of laws so much as a chain of Fate. Fate made sense of the experiences of the individual, and prevented the diversity and apparent contradictions of earthly life from interfering with his search for harmony.

In the medieval West of course, the power of making earthly laws was not that of the king alone: authority was divided between Church and State, in accordance with the doctrine of 'Render unto Caesar'. Conflicts between King and Bishop (or Pope) paved the way for a theory of limited sovereignty: it became natural for Westerners to think in terms of an authority that had more than one arm. This too was quite alien to the Confucian system: one might say that system was monolithic, whereas that of medieval Christendom was 'duolithic'. The contrast finds a curious symbol in the game of chess. In Western chess the centre of the board is shared by two pieces, the king and his consort; and power is divided between them. In Vietnamese (that is, Chinese) chess a single piece occupies the central position, the general flanked by his two scholar-advisers.[5] Yet there is irony in this comparison, for the general does not combine the power of both king and consort in the Western game. He stands alone, but he is confined to the eight points closest to his own spot. It was the West, and not East Asia, that produced the idea of absolute state power, in which the authority of Church and State were mercilessly combined. Perhaps the reason was that the Western king was forced to compete with the Church for the loyalty of his subjects. Eventually he would assert his own temporal power and deny the spiritual claims of the Church to be the guardian of absolute truth. When royal absolutism produced its own reaction, a new conflict developed between the totalitarian and the democratic views of the state: a conflict which is held by many to be the most important single theme in modern Western history. But it was a conflict which would have been utterly unintelligible to the traditional Confucian ruler or scholar.

Those who have sought to explain 'oriental despotism' in the same terms as occidental totalitarianism, of the kind practised by Hitler or Stalin, have failed to take account of all this, and also of the fundamental difference between Eastern (that is, Chinese and Vietnamese) and Western modes of logic.[6] The traditional mode of logic found in the West, from Aristotle onwards, has had as its fundamental aim the desire to arrive at some definitive truth: in other words, to eliminate contradiction. The archetype of the method is the syllogism, in which the apparent contradiction between two statements is resolved by a third. To say that the syllogism never occurred in traditional Chinese thought would be tendentious, and would beg a number of difficult questions about the interpretation of Buddhist and Mohist texts. But the syllogism was certainly not characteristic of Chinese and Vietnamese logic, and it is not found in the Confucian classics which were the staple diet of the scholar's education. The characteristic mode of logic there was 'conditional', embracing two statements rather than three: for example, in the text just quoted, '*when* things are investigated, *then* true knowledge is achieved'. It seems to have been generally true that when the Chinese or the Vietnamese scholar was faced with two ideas, he was always far more interested in discovering how they complemented one another than in exploring possible contradictions between them. Contradictions were resolved by Heaven: by man they must be simply accepted.

Thus Confucianism contained no philosophical basis for an insistence on the conformity of men's minds to one absolute truth. As a political orthodoxy Confucianism all but deified the emperor. But it did not compel him to defend and develop his power against a rival source of authority: nor did it lead him along the path of the modern dictator to seek control over his subjects' every thought and deed. The harmony upon which the supremacy of the emperor was based was the harmony of the universe, not a man-made harmony created by the elimination of contradiction from human minds. Being itself absolute, universal harmony had no need of absolutism.

Obligations to parents and to emperor were the cement of the Confucian order; but specific obligations were not hereditary. In this respect the Sino-Vietnamese tradition was much less severe on the individual than Hinduism, for there was no rigid caste system in Confucianism. In order to govern according to the universal moral order, the monarch had not only to be himself a man of virtue, but he had to choose virtuous men from all quarters of his realm to assist him. The measure of virtue was not birth, nor wealth, but learning. Consequently imperial officials were selected by means of regular examinations in the Confucian classics, to which all men of landowning families were allowed access. (And in a society where partible inheritance was the rule, a great many people had land.) The ownership of land in itself conferred nothing: to belong to the 'aristocracy' or 'gentry' of traditional Vietnamese society a man had to be educated and had to prove his education. Even in times when titles were sold by the court, the highest dignity and probably the highest offices were accorded only to those whose learning was genuine and who had passed the examinations.

The emperor and his hierarchy of scholar-officials took the place of both Church and State in traditional Vietnamese society. This left no room for any other 'established' religion, either Buddhist or Taoist. There was no officially recognized Buddhist *Sangha* such as existed in the Theravada countries like Burma and Siam.[7] Taoist 'masters' and Buddhist monks were either quite isolated from one another; or they were grouped into sects whose character was more analogous to the Vietnamese clan than to a Western Church. The master of the sect occupied the position of the clan-chief, and the duty of the pupil to his master was as binding as that of filial piety within the clan. Moreover, just as the clan would tend to divide into separate branches after a number of generations, so too a sect which prospered and grew was very likely to divide into two or more smaller sects after the death of its master. Thus Taoism and Buddhism lacked the kind of institutional framework of discipline that was necessary to hold together as one body all those who shared the same beliefs. And where there was no framework for orthodoxy, there was no problem of heresy.

Once again the contrast between East and West is very striking, for Christianity is very much a religion of orthodoxy. More, it is a religion of conversion and proselytizing, which means that it immediately identifies a man as either one of the faithful or not: Christian or pagan, orthodox or a heretic. Religion thus tends to define the community, and in medieval Christendom at least, it was the pastor and his cure of souls which tended to hold the local community of the parish together. In East Asia, on the contrary, it was the community which defined religious activity and there were many cults in which only a man born into the community (or initiated into it) could really participate. Thus the member of a clan had his own ancestors, the member of a village his own protective spirit to venerate. Likewise the member of a sect had his own teacher to follow, and acquired his beliefs from his master. There were many sects and there appears to have been no strong tendency for any one of them to claim the supremacy of a proselytizing religion. There was room for the eclectic attitude to religion which so often strikes the student of Chinese or Vietnamese society. 'Let a hundred flowers bloom, let a hundred schools of thought contend.' But the contention was not a matter of absolutes: the Vietnamese saw no philosophical necessity for one school to triumph over all the rest.

Thus there was no philosophical reason why Confucianism, the religion of the state, should find itself incompatible with the more personal religions of Taoism and Buddhism. There was nothing in the religions themselves to prevent a scholar from being a Confucian in his public life and a Buddhist or Taoist at home. A favourite Vietnamese illustration of the harmony between the religions, albeit one drawn from an early period, is the story of the emperor Trân Thai-Tong (1228–58). Wishing to escape the complexities of court politics and the heavy responsibilities of government, he left his palace one night early in his reign, and went secretly to the hills to become a pupil of the Zen master Truc-Lâm. But the aged monk advised him: 'Buddha is not in the mountains, Buddha is in the heart of man. When your mind is calm and clear, Buddha appears.' Summoned back to the capital, Thai-Tong returned to become both a Confucian

monarch and a patron of the Buddhism of the Bamboo Forest.[8]
The sphere of Confucianism was the external order of society;
the inner life of the person was left to the other religions.

But now we must face a paradox. For there were times when
religions other than Confucianism appear to have been persecuted
by the court. More than that, the whole history of Viet-Nam
shows a society often quite incapable of living up to its ideals of
good order and social harmony. It is a history full of dynastic
conflicts, rebellions and wars. Quite apart from wars against
external enemies—China in the north, Champa and Cambodia
in the south—there have been periods when the country has all
but disintegrated from within. Clan against clan, region against
region, the conflicts fill the chronicles of Viet-Nam from the
sixteenth to the nineteenth centuries. How is this paradox to be
explained?

Part of the explanation lies in the nature of the Confucian
hierarchy itself. In theory at least, the official career was open to
talent: therefore learning itself had to be open to talent. The
effect of the examination system in practice was that there were
always some men who had more education than responsibility.
Knowledge of Chinese characters and of political principles was
not the monopoly of a caste or sect, or even of a successful élite.
There were village schoolmasters who had once hoped to become
high officials. Worse still, there were sons of mandarins who
failed to attain the same level of scholarship as their fathers and
were thus prevented from inheriting their influence within the
state.

Of course there, was a compensatory distinction to be gained
in running the affairs of a clan or village. But for some that was
not enough. Sometimes they turned to religion, for in a religion
of small sects an ambitious individual might rise to a position of
some importance. In some sects it was necessary to become a
monk and to leave the civil life altogether; in others the priests
were hardly distinguishable from laymen, and the sect was
virtually a secret society with its own hierarchy of officials. It
is not easy to draw a hard and fast line between secret societies
whose character was fundamentally religious, and others whose
main concern was with politics or with banditry and crime.

The Heaven and Earth Society for example, which developed in China in the late seventeenth century, almost certainly had its roots in some kind of religious sect; but the story of its formal creation and early history is largely political since it became the vehicle of opposition in South China to the new dynasty of the Manchus. Later on, when its name and forms of initiation were taken overseas by the Nanyang Chinese in the nineteenth century, it became in many cases little more than an association of criminals and a protection racket. This same society had branches in Viet-Nam, and there were other societies of a similar kind.[9] If the leaders of such a society were truly religious, its character would be truly that of a sect. But if they were men of political ambition, they would make it into an instrument of political opposition; it might even sponsor an open revolt.

Beneath the surface of Confucian order therefore, there existed an underworld of secret societies and political revolt. Sometimes the opportunity for action was created by factions within the imperial court and bureaucracy: a crisis there might well be the signal for revolt in the country. In other cases the opportunity arose from the grievances of the peasantry, and a rebel leader might recruit a large following in a particular area, to create what amounted to virtually a private army. It was because secret associations were likely to become involved in this kind of activity that it was necessary for the Confucian court to keep a watchful eye on the sects of the Taoists and Buddhists.

From time to time decrees were issued insisting on correct principles in all branches of social life, and declaring that this or that sect should be suppressed. But what appears to us as religious persecution arose more often than not from political motives rather than from any desire to impose doctrinal orthodoxy for its own sake. From the seventeenth century onwards, Christianity was liable to be treated in a similar manner, and in the decades after 1825 the persecution of Christianity became a regular policy of succeeding emperors. But it was not the religion of the missionaries that was under attack. The Vietnamese court simply regarded the Catholics as a new kind of sect, with foreign priests taking the place of the Buddhist monk or the Taoist master. Their fear was not for Confucianism as a religion or a philosophy, but for their own position in power. If there had been a single religious Order or Church, of whatever beliefs, it would have been relatively easy for the emperor or his ministers to control it by disciplining its leaders. But the smallness of the sects, and yet the speed with which they could combine under an able leader, made periodic persecution the only way of dealing with them.[10]

The apparent contradiction between the philosophy of harmony and the reality of political conflict does not seem to have troubled Vietnamese scholars. To oppose the idea of harmony on the philosophical plane would have been almost to oppose Fate itself. Nor did successful rebellion lead to serious ideological conflicts. A new ruler who emerged from a rebellion, whatever its original religious character, would tend very quickly to take over Confucian institutions and would use the theory of the Mandate of Heaven to justify his new position. The period since 1500 has seen at least four occasions when rebellion and civil war grew out of the kind of circumstances just described, three of which led to the establishment of new dynasties.

To a Westerner the Vietnamese tradition seems to abound in paradox. It is perhaps necessary therefore to reiterate the importance of Fate as the unifying force of everything under Heaven. The Vietnamese conception of Fate is best revealed in the 'national poem', *Doan Truong Tân Thanh*, usually known as the *Kim Vân Kiêu*.[11] Its theme is the conflict between talent and Fate. Thuy Kiêu, a beautiful and talented girl of good family, falls in love with the equally gifted Kim Trung. But in order to save her father from the clutches of a cruel mandarin, she sells herself in marriage to a stranger. Her exemplary filial piety is rewarded with nothing but suffering for fifteen years; for she discovers that she has sold herself into prostitution. How could such a thing happen, the author asks? How could Heaven fail so conspicuously to reward virtue by success?

> Everything here below flows from the will of Heaven. It is Heaven which assigns to every human being his Fate.
> Why does it distribute favours as it does, giving to one person both talent and destiny?
> In order that he who has talent shall not use it to glorify himself.
> If a heavy *karma* weighs down our destiny, let us not accuse Heaven of injustice.

The root of goodness lies in ourselves.
Let us cultivate that goodness of heart which is worth more than
talent.

Kiêu's fate is that she must suffer for the heavy *karma* she has
acquired by her sins in a previous existence: Buddhist and
Confucian beliefs are accepted here as part of a single system
of morality. When Heaven is satisfied that she has expiated her
sin, only then is she allowed to return to Kim Trung. Heaven is
judge, but not in a spirit of salvation or damnation once and for
all: the chain of existence is virtually unending. Fate is unmoved
by human suffering, but it is not blind to human virtue; and there
is virtue in the very acceptance of Fate rather than in struggling
against it.

Nguyên Du, author of the poem, was a man who himself
suffered deeply. Having supported the unsuccessful Lê dynasty
of Hanoi at the end of the eighteenth century, he was condemned
by his own destiny to witness the triumph of the new emperors
of Huê, and to be forced to offer allegiance to Gia-Long. Rather
than rebel, he accepted the decree of Fate and retired to the
seclusion of his home village in Ha-Tinh province. Withdrawal
was not however the only answer to adversity or challenge of
which the Vietnamese were capable. It would be truer to say
that Fate, the arbiter between success and failure in any human
enterprise, was the deciding factor between action and inaction.
If Fate seemed unfavourable, it was better not to act: Nguyên Du's
withdrawal was characteristic of a man who felt himself defeated
by Fate. But a man who believed that destiny was on his side
would act with determination and courage.

This helps to explain the importance in traditional Vietnamese
society of geomancers and astrologers, and of spirit mediums.
Such people had special powers to enable them to discover what
Fate intended in any situation. The *thây-phap* (whom the French
called a 'sorcerer') was universally respected as a man who could
site houses or tombs in such a way as to protect them from evil
spirits, or who could calculate a man's horoscope so that he may
avoid unlucky encounters or unpropitious times to act. That
role extended moreover to politics. Rebel movements were very
often led by men who claimed supernatural powers, whether as
Buddhist monks or as Taoist masters, because men of that kind
had the best chance of convincing their followers that Heaven,

or the stars, or the spirits, were on their side.[12] In warfare too, armies would join battle only when one at least of the commanders was convinced that he was destined to victory; the horoscope of a supersititous general might play as important a part in his campaign as military skill. To risk a conflict against the will of Heaven was not only to court disaster but to act against the whole moral order of the universe.

When the French conquered Viet-Nam, the first reactions of the scholars were what one would expect from the nature of the tradition. Some followed the example of Nguyên Khuyên, a famous poet who withdrew to the seclusion of his native village in Tongking. Others, like Phan Dinh Phung, refused to accept that Fate was against them, and fought on for ten years and more.[13] But gradually a small minority of intellectuals came to see the French as something more than conquerors whose cause had been temporarily espoused by a cruel Fate. They began to see them as men of a new kind, whose success stemmed from a philosophy which rejected Fate altogether, and which therefore presented a challenge to the whole of Vietnamese civilization.

II

The Tradition Challenged

'OUR hearts are like iron and stone: they will never tremble.'
In those words the poet Phan Van Tri, writing in the 1860s,
defied the barbarians of the Western Seas. They occurred in the
course of a celebrated literary exchange between himself and his
contemporary Tôn Tho Tuong. Both men were natives of the
Vietnamese provinces which were ceded to France in 1862, but
whereas Phan Van Tri withdrew to his village and lived as a
schoolmaster after the conquest, Tôn Tho Tuong chose to serve
the French, and continued to do so until his death fifteen years
later. It was in order to justify this choice that Tuong wrote a
series of ten poems, to which Tri replied line for line.[1] The contrast
between their points of view was one which was to recur throughout the period in which the French ruled Viet-Nam. Tuong had
been to Europe, and saw the futility of attempting to resist a
foreign power which derived its strength from long lines of telegraph wires and from powerful engines emitting great clouds of
steam and smoke: he advised his countrymen to make peace for
the time being, in order to learn from their enemies. Tri, less
impressed by feats of technology, saw the issue solely in terms of
spirit: the only hope of eventual victory was to refuse ever to
admit defeat.

The two decades from 1860 to 1880, virtually the interval
between the first loss of Vietnamese territory to France and the
final establishment of a French protectorate over Tongking and
Annam, were a turning-point throughout East Asia. By 1870,
Japan had set out upon the road which led to a strong centralized
government and technological Westernization. In China too,
following the suppression of the Tai-Ping rebellion and other
disturbances, the 1860s saw the 'Tung-Chih Restoration' under
which men like Tseng Kuo-fan made their own attempt to
strengthen the country, but failed to establish sufficiently that
centralized control which was so important for the Japanese

success. In Viet-Nam, the reign of Tu-Duc (1848–83) was the one period when the traditional monarchy might there too have come to terms with the West, and possibly avoided the fate of being the only country in the Chinese-speaking world to be actually ruled by Europeans. Although that fate was not avoided, it is to this period that we must look in order to find the beginnings of the Vietnamese response to the Western challenge.

The first important embassy of the court of Huê to the courts of Europe—in fact to Paris and Madrid—was that led by Phan Thanh Gian in 1863. Its object, not achieved, was to secure the return of the three provinces ceded to France by treaty in the previous year. Its impressions of the West are recorded in the diary which Gian kept from day to day, and which has survived in the Huê archives.[2] The envoys were especially impressed by the concrete achievements of French civilization: the speed of travel by steamship and by railway, the artificial lighting in the streets at night, and the many kinds of factory that they were invited to inspect. But when one comes to the less material aspects of French culture and institutions, it is less easy to gauge their impressions. When referring in the diary to the dignitaries and officials of the Napoleonic court, they made no attempt to find a terminology that would indicate the differences between French institutions and their own. They used Vietnamese titles to designate the officials who received them, and they referred to the Church as the Ministry of Rites. Although the diary reveals hardly anything of the ambassador's innermost thoughts and reflections, its content does not suggest that he or his colleagues had any deep understanding of the institutions and ideas that underlay Western engineering achievement.

The Vietnamese of this period who were most likely to develop such an understanding were not the Confucian officials of the imperial government, but the Catholics who had received an education from the missionary priests. One such man, who in fact accompanied the envoys to Paris and Madrid in 1863, working as an interpreter for the French, was Petrus Truong Vinh Ky. He had studied in a Catholic college at Penang in the 1850s, and although he too was making his first visit to the West, he was going with some idea in his mind of what to expect, and some realization of the cultural differences between his own country and France. He stayed in Europe for several years, and

did not return to Saigon until 1867 when he took up a teaching
position in the French school for officials there. In a long series of
publications between then and his death in 1898 he took upon
himself the task of trying to explain Western knowledge to the
Vietnamese, and of providing more information about Viet-Nam
for the French. For example, in 1867 he produced (in French)
the first grammar of the Vietnamese language; and ten years
later the first French history of Viet-Nam.[3]

Truong Vinh Ky, like Tôn Tho Tuong, chose to work for
the French: their understanding of the West therefore, such as
it was, was not a factor in the affairs of Tu-Duc's empire. There
were however, others with some knowledge of Western learning
who chose to remain in the independent region of the country
and who from time to time pressed the government to make
reforms. Probably the most articulate of them was Nguyên Truong
Tô, a native of Nghê-An province and a convert to Christianity.
In 1859, at the age of about thirty, he was taken by his teachers
to Italy and France, where he spent several years studying a
wide range of Western subjects. He returned about the time of
the first loss of territory to France. Never having passed any of the
Confucian examinations (although he knew Chinese characters)
he was not eligible for any important office; his only political
position was that of private secretary to the governor of his native
province during the 1860s. Nevertheless during the eight years
preceding his death in 1871 he submitted to the throne at least
fourteen memorials advocating a variety of policies of reform. He
argued that to oppose France openly would lead only to disaster;
whereas to seek French assistance and friendship would allow
the Vietnamese to learn from the foreigners and eventually
strengthen their own country by imitating France. He proposed
that students be sent to France to learn new techniques in
agriculture and industry, and to master new methods of warfare.
He advocated policies to strengthen the economy by developing
trade and manufactures. He himself was especially interested in
mining and put forward detailed plans for developing the minerals
of central Viet-Nam. Some of his memorials reflect the same
attitudes as the proposals put forward in China during the 1860s
by Tseng Kuo-fan and Li Hung-chang, the most progressive of the
new generation of officials serving the Ch'ing dynasty.

Nguyên Truong Tô's plans were not entirely without result.

He appears to have won over the governor of Nghê-An to his project for developing mines, and was on the point of recruiting French technicians for that purpose when hostilities were renewed in Cochinchina in 1867.[4] But the chances of the imperial court as a whole being converted to his ideas were very slender. There was little hope of action to implement such proposals as that for a sweeping reform of the bureaucracy to eliminate corruption, or a reorganization of judicial procedures to separate the power of magistrates from that of administrators. The court of Huê was dominated at this time by an older generation of men, set in their ways and unlikely to accept any deviation from Confucian orthodoxy. The most powerful minister was Nguyên Tri Phuong, whose influence was brought to an end only by his death in 1873 whilst fighting the French at Hanoi. In other circumstances it might have been possible for Phan Thanh Gian to emerge as the leader of a reform party, opposed to Phuong; for he was a man of the same generation as the arch-conservative, as well as having first-hand experience of the West. But following his return from Paris empty-handed in 1864, the remainder of his career was taken up by further efforts to oust the French from Cochinchina. When he failed to prevent their seizing still more territory in 1867 he took poison; and the following year he was deprived by the emperor of all his official titles and distinction. The man who might have been the reformer became the scape-goat for something which timely reform might conceivable have prevented.

Nor was very much more done during the 1870s, after the death of Phuong. In 1873, when the French seized Hanoi for a time, a younger official named Bui Viên was sent to Hong Kong to make contact with some Western power other than France, and from there he went to the United States.[5] He appears to have been well received by the American President; but with the (temporary) disappearance of the French threat, the Vietnamese did not pursue the relationship. Bui Viên was appointed to be head of naval transport, and devoted his energy to the suppression of piracy in the hope of making the South China Sea safer for trade. It was not long however before French pressure was renewed. In 1882 a French administration more ready to expand the colonial empire set in motion the policy which led to the virtual annexation of Annam and Tongking. In 1885, after a Franco-Chinese war in which the victories were by no means all on one side, the Chinese surrendered to France their claims to the 'protection' of Viet-Nam.

The French conquest brought to an end the period in which it was meaningful to talk of the possible 'self-strengthening' of Viet-Nam within a traditional monarchical framework. For the next two generations and more, modernization would be intimately bound up with the problem of obtaining independence. But within the framework of colonial rule, or 'protection', the old questions still demanded an answer: what attitude ought the Vietnamese to take towards their conquerors? Could anything be gained by co-operation with the West, by seeking to learn from the West? And if so, what was the proper relationship between the culture and institutions of the past, and the ideas and institutions to be borrowed from the West? The exchange of poems between Tôn Tho Tuong and Phan Van Tri, and the opposition between the Nguyên Tri Phuongs and men like Nguyên Truong Tô, were merely the first round of a debate on the relevance of foreign culture for Viet-Nam which was to last throughout the era of French rule, and which is in a sense still not concluded today.

It was of course impossible that Viet-Nam should make no response at all to the Western challenge. The cause of Phan Van Tri was doomed, once colonial rule was firmly established. But his spirit did not die: throughout the French period there were those who believed that whatever the West had to teach there should be no compromise with the particular Frenchmen who were governing Viet-Nam. They were very often those who believed that Asians could supersede the achievements of the West by means of a revolution which Europe itself had not yet experienced: their heirs are the present-day Communists. Opposed to them were those Vietnamese who believed in an adaptation to the culture and institutions of the Europeans. They did not necessarily favour political subservience to the French government, but they saw in their relationship with the West an opportunity to develop Viet-Nam's own potential for progress. Although the various anti-Communist groups in South Viet-Nam today do not claim direct descent from the Westernizers of previous generations, their willingness to accept American aid stems from a fundamentally similar attitude towards the West.

One finds an analogy with this conflict between different reactions to occidental culture if one looks at China's experience in the same period (since, say 1860). Indeed, though it was never actually conquered by a single Western power, China faced many of the same problems as Viet-Nam, and given the Vietnamese habit of looking towards China for inspiration it is not surprising that some of the major Chinese thinkers of modern times have had considerable influence on the modern intellectual development of the Vietnamese. No apology is necessary therefore if we refer from time to time to the writings of those Chinese scholars, which are better known in the West than those of Vietnamese thanks to the efforts of American historians during the past few decades. Professor Levenson's study on the modern fate of Confucian China, in particular, draws together a number of conclusions of great relevance to Viet-Nam.[6]

What does Westernization mean in this context? The French colonial administrators, with their claims to a 'mission civilisatrice' and their philosophy of 'assimilation' (to be discussed in a later chapter), sometimes spoke as if they expected their Asian subjects eventually to become Frenchmen in all essential respects— though they provided educational facilities for only a small minority to do so in practice. But such a complete transformation of a whole population was out of the question; and in any case, with the exception of a tiny minority, the Vietnamese themselves did not want to become Westerners. What they wanted at the very most was to change, according to Western principles, the Viet-Nam to which they would always and inevitably belong. Westernization therefore involved some kind of interweaving of occidental and oriental cultures, not a wholesale replacement of one by the other.

Chinese Westernizers of the 1860s and 1870s, and perhaps too Vietnamese like Nguyên Truong Tô, saw the problem in simple terms. Their philosophy was one of *t'i-yung*: in Vietnamese *thi-dung*. They believed in imitating the West in matters of utility (*yung*), but in maintaining their own traditional values in matters of substance or essence (*t'i*). This was more reasonable than later critics of the philosophy supposed. The Confucian tradition had distinguished between the inner and the outer affairs of man, and had even allowed a man to be inwardly Taoist or Buddhist so long as he was outwardly a Confucian. Moreover, it was very much a tradition of pragmatism in material things, so that a man could be a Taoist at heart, a Confucian in politics, and still a very practical man in such fields as the building of dykes or the designing of gadgets. The type of man who was both a poet and a very practical administrator is well illustrated in nineteenth-century Viet-Nam by the career of Nguyên Công Tru (1778–1858). His poetry is full of the joys of living and the ephemeral nature of life. But in his career as an official under Minh Mang he was responsible for one of the major engineering feats of pre-colonial Vietnamese history: the bringing under cultivation of about 10,000 hectares of alluvial riceland in the coastal province of Thai-Binh.[7] If the techniques of irrigation were independent of belief in Taoist meditation or Confucian institutions, then why should not Western steam engines and telegraph lines be seen in similar light? Why should it have occurred to the Vietnamese (or the Chinese) of the Tu-Duc period that the material achievements of their new enemies were inseparably bound up with a cultural and institutional milieu totally different from their own?

It was towards the end of the nineteenth century that the Chinese, or at least a few of them, began to appreciate that the West presented a challenge to their institutions as well as to their technology. One of their reasons for doing so was the success of Japan, where technological and institutional reform went hand in hand. The *t'i-yung* philosophy did not adequately account for the relationship between institutions and material strength: were institutions part of the substance, or merely an aspect of utility? Confucianism was both a system of government and a framework of values: indeed its strength derived from the fact that it related institutions directly to the nature of the universe as a whole. This made it difficult to attempt a purely utilitarian reform of institutions without undertaking a complete re-evaluation of Confucianism.

It was in response to this difficulty that in 1897 the Chinese scholar K'ang Yu-wei published his treatise *A Study of Confucius as a Reformer of Institutions*. He tried to replace the established conservative interpretation of Confucius' teachings by one which would allow for change: to demonstrate that the essentials of the Confucian canon were in no way incompatible with reform, but even demanded it. In the following year K'ang and his disciples captured the ear of the young emperor at Peking, only to be hounded out by a conservative coup before they had time to make any serious reforms. Following the Boxer 'rebellion' the regime began—under the pressure of still greater Western interference in China—to attempt its own modernization. K'ang Yu-wei, still out of favour, watched the attempt from Japan or from whatever part of the world he was visiting. But when the Chinese monarchy finally collapsed he was too much of a Confucian to support the Revolution. His last appearance on the political scene was as one of the promoters of the vain bid to restore the emperor in 1917.

K'ang's leading disciple however, Liang Ch'i-ch'ao, was prepared to follow the logic of institutional reform beyond the Confucian framework altogether. His most important writings belong to the years 1899–1905, when he too was in exile in Japan or travelling around the world; but he continued to be an influential figure in Chinese thought down to his death in 1929, for he was willing to accept that the monarchy was not the only possible focus of political life.[8] Like many young Chinese in the 1890s, Liang had been enthralled by the Chinese translation of McKenzie's *Nineteenth Century*, a Spencerian tract of little importance in the West but one in which an Asian could find reflected all the assumptions and prejudices of the popular occidental belief in progress. Liang's conclusion was that if China was weak it was because her cultural tradition had been paralysed by complacency, so that she had failed to progress. Evolution was the result of incessant competition between the peoples of the world, of whom only the fittest could survive. But China had fallen into the error of supposing that no other people had any civilization at all: that the rest of the earth was populated by inferior barbarians. Naturally she was overwhelmed when other civilized people appeared at her gates. The question for Liang's generation was obvious: how can China begin again to progress? Whereas K'ang could see only the possibility of reform within the Chinese tradition itself, Liang began to study the history and institutions of the West, and to think in terms of deliberate imitation of countries like England and France. For the superiority of the West must surely derive from the nature of occidental progress.

Liang attached the greatest importance not only to institutions but also to the role of thinkers in influencing institutional development. He traced the origins of Western progress to the intellectual movement of the seventeenth century, which overthrew the authoritarianism of the medieval schoolmen and set the scene for the eventual overthrow of traditional conceptions of political authority as well. The true heroes of these developments were not great kings or politicians, but men like Luther, Bacon, Descartes, and Rousseau: men who asserted their right to think for themselves. China must follow their example and so emancipate itself from the strait-jacket of ancient authority. In identifying K'ang Yu-wei with Martin Luther, as leader of a Confucian Reformation, Liang may have seen himself in the role of a Chinese Descartes.

Liang's writings were almost certainly very influential in Viet-Nam, where they contributed to a new kind of national movement that began in the first decade of the twentieth century. Phan Bôi Châu, who went to Japan in 1905 hoping to get help for the Vietnamese reformers, returned home with copies of Liang's writings and distributed them widely amongst his friends.[9] We must explore the development of this and other Vietnamese movements in a later chapter: they did not all remain under the influence of Liang for long, but the initial impact of his ideas was irreversible. When it came to proposals for action, Liang was a constitutionalist: at first he wanted a reformed monarchy, though later he was willing to work under a constitutional republic. But for much of the time his concern was not with precise forms of government but with China's conception of its place in the world. China must see itself as a single nation, one amongst many in the world, or there was a danger that the penalty for claiming to be more than a state would be to become less than a sovereign nation. Liang himself was present at the Versailles conference when the official Chinese delegation refused to sign a treaty that appeared to tolerate Japanese aggression in Shantung. Twenty years before that, he had written an essay on patriotism in which he identified loyalty to the nation as one of the most important sources of Western progress. This was especially relevant for the Vietnamese, whose place in the world had been transformed by the French conquest. Ought not Viet-Nam also to strive to become a nation?

The concept of the nation supplied what the *t'i-yung* philosophy had lacked: a focus for institutional reform. It was of course in itself a borrowing from the West, and moreover even in the West it was of relatively recent development. It grew out of the conflicts of the sixteenth and seventeenth centuries in which the kings of a number of major states in Europe succeeded in replacing the medieval principle of papal suzerainty in spiritual affairs by the principle of *cuius regio eius religio*. That victory was of the greatest importance for Asia; for it amounted to a secularization of the state, without which Western theories of politics and law would not have been readily intelligible to Asians. The Vietnamese, for example, would have made little sense of political doctrines couched in terms of the duality of supreme authority, for as we have seen such duality was alien to their own tradition.

Also during the sixteenth and seventeenth centuries, kings were in many cases able to destroy what remained of the power of their feudal nobility, and to replace the feudal concept of lord and vassal by the modern notion of the state as consisting of a prince and his subjects. By about 1700 European political theory had begun to move in the direction that was to lead to the principle of the sovereign equality of nations in international law. That principle found its fullest expression in the creation of the League of Nations in 1919, and the enunciation of the Wilsonian doctrine of national self-determination. It was no doubt intended at the time to apply primarily to the post-imperial situation of Central and Eastern Europe. But inevitably it had great appeal for Asians in search of new concepts that might satisfy their increasingly ambitious aspirations. In the atmosphere of the Versailles Peace Conference the Chinese felt bold enough to refuse formal concessions to Japan. Earlier that year, a young Vietnamese tried to present to the same Conference a cahier of his own country's claims to greater justice, but was refused a hearing. As Nguyên Ai Quôc and later Hô Chi Minh, the same young man was to play a prominent role in the struggle to create a nation of Viet-Nam by less gentle means than the submission of demands.

The desire for nationhood became for the Vietnamese a focus for their borrowings from the West. They need not swallow occidental culture whole: they now had a criterion for deciding whether any particular idea was useful to them or not. Anything that served to help Viet-Nam to become an independent nation was of value; other aspects of Western civilization could be rejected. There were in fact two themes in modern European thought which were of especial relevance to this aim of nation-building: first, the development of what might be called economic rationalism; second, the increasing concern of political thinkers with the need to relate the system of government to the aspirations of the people.

By economic rationalism, I mean the tendency to make decisions about livelihood according to the best available rational opinion, with a view to getting the highest possible return for one's efforts: and to do this consciously, though not necessarily in relation to any theory or plan. On the level of the family or the individual enterprise, this is what Weber and Tawney referred to as the 'spirit of capitalism.' On the level of the state it has led to a variety of economic philosophies whose central feature was the desire to increase the wealth of nations. The Chinese Westernizer Yen Fu, who translated Adam Smith's *Wealth of Nations* into Chinese in 1900, believed that the most important of all factors in the rise of the Western powers was their spirit of economic enterprise.[10] On a more mundane level, one finds that Asians tend generally to regard materialism as an essentially occidental view of life. But their eagerness to strengthen their own countries has led many of them to become extremely materialistic themselves. It is a fallacy to suppose that twentieth-century Asia rejects materialism out of some vague respect for a religious tradition which in earlier centuries probably did limit some men's eagerness for wealth. The tendency to measure success, especially political success, in terms of material achievement was one of the most penetrating effects of the Western impact on Asia, and it has transcended most of the differences of opinion and policy that have divided Asian politicians during and after the colonial period.

Those differences are very much more apparent when it comes to questions about the proper relationship between government and people. When the Vietnamese, or indeed any Asians, asked themselves what political system had accounted for the triumphs of the West, Europe did not answer with one voice.

The arguments of Rousseau for example could be used to justify polities as different as representational democracy or totalitarian dictatorship. Whilst the ideas of Hegel about the importance of the nation-state led, by some strange logic, to the doctrines of Marx who regarded nations as of little import by comparison with the struggle between classes. In the twentieth-century European politics and international relations became increasingly dominated by struggles whose basis was to a greater or lesser extent ideological. How then were Asians to decide which Western theories to adopt themselves? It is not surprising that they sometimes found themselves transferring to their own countries conflicts which the West had seemingly failed to resolve. But in every emergent nation in Asia some kind of decision on issues of this kind was essential. The reform of institutions could not take place without raising the question of the place of 'the people' in the new political system.

Amongst the Chinese thinkers who addressed themselves to these problems of economic change and political development in the early years of this century, one of the most important was Sun Yat-sen. Whereas Liang Ch'i-ch'ao had concentrated on the nature of progress and institutional the development of the nation, Sun's principal concern was with the material development of China, which he believed could only be achieved through revolution. Sun was apparently introduced to the idea of revolution as a political method by the Russian *émigrés* whom he met in London in 1896.[11] It is very likely that they were Populists rather than Marxists, which may explain why Sun was not deeply impressed by Marxism at this stage in his career. Not sharing Liang's preoccupation with progress, he was not particularly receptive to the dialectical theory of history—though he appears to have been familiar with Marx's work at this time. Nor was he willing to accept that class warfare was a necessary phase of social development: conflict of all kind was something to be avoided, a necessary evil perhaps but certainly not the basis for political idealism. In Sun's view, the purpose of the Chinese revolution would be to avoid, rather than to fulfil the class war. He firmly believed that China could escape the internal tensions which had disrupted Western societies during their industrialization.

To that end he worked out a theory of how China should

industrialize, which was also a theory of political modernization. Of his 'three people's principles' (the *San-Min Chu-I*), the first stressed the solidarity and independence of the people; the second outlined the kind of constitution necessary for a proper balance between government and people; whilst the third related to the 'people's livelihood'. It was this which was Sun's real interest, down to about 1918. As early as 1894 he had stressed the importance of material improvement in a letter to Li Hung-chang, and incidentally had expressed a wish (never fulfilled) to study agricultural engineering in France. Eighteen years later, following the overthrow of the monarchy, he accepted a position in Yuan Shih-k'ai's government in which his chief responsibility was the development of a railway system throughout China. The plans for development which he worked out then and later deserve to count amongst the first serious essays in economic planning for developing countries. It was only with Sun's repeated failures to stay in power, after his flight to Japan in 1913, that he began to think out a new approach to politics and the nature of power. During the last seven years or so of his life (he died in 1925) he came gradually under the influence of Lenin's ideas about the role of the party in revolution, and the Soviet example of government by a revolutionary party.

Sun, like Liang, had a considerable influence on the development of political ideas in Viet-Nam, especially during the 1920s. The *Quôc-Dân Dang* party founded in 1927[12] had a programme based explicitly on Sun's ideas; but other parties at that period also owed some of their inspiration to the 'three people's principles'. The Chinese thinkers gave Vietnamese politicians an alternative source of ideas, quite separate from these of their colonial masters, which helped them to adjust to the situation in which Asians were dominated by Europeans. Some Vietnamese too, as we shall see, read the works of Rabindranath Tagore and M. K. Gandhi. We must explore in Part Two of this essay some of the political movements which resulted from their acquaintance with these new ideas.

The introduction into Vietnamese political thinking of such Western concepts as the nation, economic development, constitutional government, and revolution, represent a completely new departure. But political concepts cannot be set entirely apart from the cultural milieu of the men who use them. One may well ask how far the Vietnamese really understood Western modes of thought as a whole, and whether the concepts they borrowed could possibly have had the same meaning for them as for the Westerners who first produced them. It is interesting from this point of view to ask, for example, how far they really understood the ideas of a philosopher like Descartes, whom Liang Ch'i-ch'ao so much admired and whose writings were familiar to Vietnamese through their French education. Descartes would no doubt have agreed with Liang's assessment of his intellectual importance, for he was very conscious of being an innovator; and indeed his mathematical method for describing the universe was highly original. But was it Descartes the mathematician whom Liang was praising? If, as seems likely, it was the Cartesian spirit of inquiry rather than the content of his mathematical achievement that impressed the Chinese, then perhaps we should conclude that Liang greatly overemphasized Descartes' importance.

The 'scientific revolution' of the seventeenth century amounted to the drawing together of two previously separate elements in the Western intellectual tradition: on the one hand the empirical observation of phenomena, on the other the rational system of logic. Dr Needham has shown how much the former of these elements had in common with the empirical outlook of the Taoists;[13] what was not paralleled in the Chinese nation was the occidental mode of logic, which insisted above all on the elimination of contradictions. Whilst Descartes must be credited with having originated a new method within the framework of that logic, the mode itself is very much older. The principles of logic which the medieval schoolmen endowed with an absolute authority contained in themselves the seeds of intellectual growth, which in the seventeenth century overthrew that authority. Perhaps therefore the culture and mental gulf between traditional China and Viet-Nam on the one hand, and the modern West on the other, was greater than men like Liang supposed. It was ultimately unbridgeable, but its existence meant that only a very small minority of highly educated individuals would be capable of a complete understanding of the West. Even fewer perhaps would be capable of Westernizing themselves to the extent that they completely left behind all traces of the very different mentality of their own tradition. In speaking of the political movements of modern Viet-Nam therefore, we must be careful not to assume too readily that we are as familiar with Vietnamese ways of thought as the familiarity of terminology might at first suggest.

III

The Nation

UNLIKE some Asian peoples in the twentieth century, the Vietnamese did not have to invent a wholly new word for 'nation'. They had always thought of their country as the *quôc* (Chinese *kuo*), a word which can be translated as kingdom, country or nation. (Or sometimes they preferred the purely Vietnamese word *nuoc* which had almost exactly the same meaning.) But precisely because they did have a word of their own, one has to ask whether when they used it in its more modern sense it carried all the shades of meaning that the term 'nation' had for the Westerners from whom it had been borrowed. What *quôc* had meant in the past can only be understood by looking at the relations which traditional Viet-Nam had had with its neighbours, and especially with China.

After ten centuries of Chinese rule (*c.* 110 B.C.–A.D. *c.* 902) the Vietnamese were able in the tenth and eleventh centuries to establish an independent *quôc* of their own. In 1077, and again in the 1280s, they defeated Chinese attempts to incorporate Viet-Nam into the Sung and the Yüan empires respectively. In 1407 a third Chinese invasion was at first more successful; but after twenty years of rule as a Chinese province the Vietnamese once more found in Lê Loi a leader capable of driving out the Ming armies. One further attempt by imperial China to reconquer Viet-Nam occurred in the years 1788–9, but it too ended in defeat at the hands of the emperor Quang-Trung. Yet in spite of all these struggles Viet-Nam was not wholly independent of China in the sense of having what the Westerner would call national sovereignty. Its rulers regularly sent tribute to the court of Peking, and in return received Chinese diplomas of investiture and seals of gold and jade.

In this they were not alone. China also received tribute from many neighbouring kingdoms: from Korea, Burma, Siam, Mongolia and the lamas of Tibet: in fact almost all the countries on the fringes of the Chinese world at one time or another sent tribute in this way.[1] For the Chinese refused to carry on relations with any other state on a level of equality. As Son of Heaven, the emperor of the Middle Kingdom (the *Trung-Quôc*, in Vietnamese) performed sacrifices to Heaven which placed him on a higher plane than any other earthly ruler; and since China was also, in her periods of unity at least, stronger than any of her neighbours, this claim to superiority commanded respect.

Even in order to trade with China the kings of Siam and Viet-Nam had to offer tribute, and it may well be that many of the missions which they sent there had an economic rather than a political motive. At the same time, we must not suppose that in sending their tribute these lesser monarchs were recognizing any active obligation towards China, nor acknowledging a Chinese right to interfere in their internal affairs. The East Asian tributary system must not be mistaken for some kind of oriental feudalism on a grand scale. It is true that there were occasions in the early fifteenth century when a Ming emperor sought to arbitrate *between* tributary states, and there was an occasion in 1540 when another emperor of that dynasty threatened intervention in a conflict between two rival claimants to the throne of Viet-Nam. But on the whole China's superiority, or one might even use the word suzerainty, was passive rather than active. As such, it was accepted by lesser states as part of the natural order of the world.

In their own countries the rulers of Viet-Nam and Siam tended to imitate China in this respect, and to demand a like tribute from their own lesser neighbours. Thus Viet-Nam at different periods claimed tribute from the Lao principalities of Vieng-Chan and Chieng-Khuang, and from the king of Cambodia, as well as from the chieftains of hill-tribes entirely within the Vietnamese sphere. By the nineteenth century Viet-Nam and Siam were approaching the point where their simultaneous claims to tribute from Cambodia and from the Lao princes would bring them into serious and continuing conflict. Indeed there was a short war between them in 1835–6. The French settled the issue by establishing their own protectorates over Cambodia in 1865 and over Laos in 1893.

In both these cases the French used the Vietnamese claim to tribute as the basis of a policy which ended in concessions by the Siamese. This use of the tributary system by Europeans was however uncharacteristic. The general effect of the Western intrusion into East Asia was to destroy the system. As far as South East Asia was concerned, the flow of tribute to China was interrupted by the period of internal civil war which followed on the Taiping rebellion (1853–64), an event which would probably have caused disruption in any period. By the time the war ended, the Europeans had demonstrated their power to such an extent that China no longer seemed powerful enough to justify her claims to superiority. Moreover from 1842 onwards successive European victories over China drew an increasing proportion of her trade out of the tributary system into the Treaty Ports. In 1863 Siam virtually rejected a Chinese request for tribute, and in fact sent no more missions after that.[2] The Vietnamese, having experienced a direct European attack, may well have felt they had more reason to stay close to China, and continued to send tribute as late as 1883. But the practice was brought to an end two years later, after a war in which the French defeated China on precisely this issue: by the Treaty of Tientsin, the Chinese surrendered all claims of this nature to France. In the next two or three decades China painfully adjusted herself to the occidental theory of international relations, accepting her place as just one among many nations. Viet-Nam was prevented from making a similar adjustment; as far as international relations were concerned she was merely a part of France. Nevertheless in the longer term the French intrusion opened the way for the *quôc* to develop into something like a sovereign nation.

If the external situation of the Vietnamese *quôc* differed from that of the Western nation-state, the difference was even more true of its internal structure. On the eve of the French conquest Viet-Nam was a very much less coherent and unified state than might at first sight be supposed. The area of the present Viet-Nam had been ruled from Huê by a single monarch only since 1802. Before that the history of the country had been a long and complicated story of territorial expansion and frequent internal division.

The area which the Chinese had ruled down to about A.D. 900 did not stretch further south than the seventeenth parallel, and in some periods not even so far as that. The greater part of what

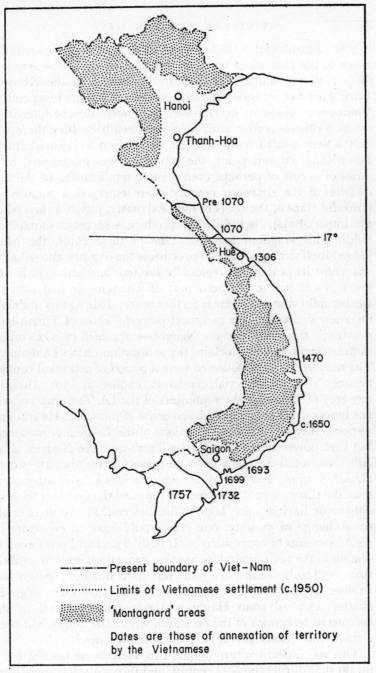

Map I: The Expansion of Viet-Nam (11th–18th centuries)

Labels on map:
Hanoi
Thanh-Hoa
Pre 1070
1070
17°
Hue
1306
1470
c.1650
Saigon
1693
1699
1757
1732

—·—·— Present boundary of Viet-Nam
·········· Limits of Vietnamese settlement (c.1950)
'Montagnard' areas
Dates are those of annexation of territory
by the Vietnamese

is now Central Viet-Nam belonged then, and for some centuries more, to the Hinduized kingdom of Champa; whilst the area still further to the south (Cochinchina) belonged to the Khmers. During the five centuries between 1000 and 1500 the independent Vietnamese kingdom of Dai-Viêt gradually absorbed territory on its southern border until by the sixteenth century there was only a very small Cham state left, centred on the district round Phan-Rang. At this point, the expansion was interrupted by a series of events of perhaps even greater significance. In the first quarter of the sixteenth century there emerged a number of powerful clans at the court of the Lê dynasty, just at a time when the imperial clan itself failed to produce a successor capable of holding his kingdom together. One of these clans, the Mac, judged itself strong enough to overthrow the dynasty altogether in 1527. But its power was regionally limited, and although it had great power in the northern part of Tongking it had a much weaker following in the areas further south. This was its undoing, for a few years later the two most powerful clans of Thanh-Hoa province—the Trinh and the Nguyên—combined to take control of those areas and to proclaim the restoration of the Lê dynasty. The sixty years which followed were a period of continual conflict between the two imperial claimants, ending in 1592 with the recovery of Hanoi by the supporters of the Lê. The emperor was not however restored in the fullest sense of the word. He still had responsibility for the ritual functions of the Confucian monarch, but real power now lay with the Trinh and the Nguyên. Had either one of these clans been all-powerful, the dynasty would almost certainly have been deposed. As it was, any attempt to seize the throne would have merely renewed the civil war without either side having much hope of final success. Before there could be a change of dynasty, one clan would have to eliminate its rival by means of court intrigue. If both clans had been forced to remain in the same capital for another generation it is not unlikely that the Trinh would have done just that. But the Nguyên had another alternative. In 1600 the chief of that clan (Nguyên Hoang) escaped from Hanoi and established himself in the conquered territories of the far south, where the family had been virtually hereditary governors for several decades.[3]

This was a decisive turning-point in Vietnamese history, for it meant that during the next century and three-quarters there were virtually two separate kingdoms, both formally recognizing the Lê dynasty but otherwise independent. Between 1620 and 1680 the Trinh made repeated attempts to recover control of the southern provinces, but in vain. Meanwhile the Nguyên resumed the southward territorial expansion of the Vietnamese. Towards the end of the seventeenth century they defeated the last Cham king and drove him into the hills. Already by then they were exerting influence from time to time over the kings of Cambodia, and in the century or so after 1658 they forced the Khmers to surrender most of the area which was later to become the 'six provinces' of Cochinchina. Gradually the conquered region was settled by Vietnamese migrants; it also became the home of Ming refugees, fleeing from the Manchu conquest of South China, who in the latter part of the seventeenth century settled at places like Biên-Hoa, My-Tho and Ha-Tiên. This Chinese element, as well as the assimilation by the Vietnamese of some of the Khmer inhabitants of the region, helps to explain some of the social and cultural contrasts between Cochinchina and other parts of Viet-Nam. The fact that it was the last area to be drawn into Viet-Nam and settled by migrants from the north is the reason why it is also far less densely populated than the rest of the country and is capable of producing a rice surplus.

The division of Viet-Nam into two kingdoms lasted for several generations; it came to an end when the more southerly one was itself overtaken by rebellion and a period of disunity. In 1773 a group of rebels under the name of Tây-Son, 'the men from the western hills', became increasingly powerful in the provinces of Qui-Nhon, Quang-Ngai and Quang-Nam, and even threatened the Nguyên capital at Huê. The Trinh ruler in Hanoi, seizing this unlooked-for opportunity, sent his own forces south in the following year, and it was to them that Huê finally fell. The Nguyên family fled or were killed, and in 1777 their dominions were virtually partitioned between the Trinh and the leaders of the Tây-Son. The latter were not content however with this territory, or even with the addition to it of Cochinchina. When the Trinh suffered an internal crisis of their own in 1786 the Tây-Son intervened in Tongking as well, and by 1789 they were in control of practically the whole of Tongking and Annam. The Lê dynasty was finally deposed, and the country was divided between the two brothers who had led the Tây-Son armies to victory. But in

Cochinchina, the sole survivor of the Nguyên clan refused to admit defeat and in 1788 succeeded in establishing himself at Saigon. Once again the Nguyên found themselves established in the most southerly region of an expanding Viet-Nam. But this time they went much further than defending their position. Between 1793 and 1802 the young Nguyên Anh conquered first Huê and then Hanoi, bringing to an end the Tây-Son dynasty and uniting for the first time under a single regime the whole of modern Viet-Nam. He took the imperial reign-title Gia-Long and secured recognition from the Chinese.

Given a long period of stability in its relations with other countries, and a succession of strong rulers, this newly created unity might have led in time to the growth of a much more centralized state in Viet-Nam than had ever existed there before. Under Gia-Long himself, the northern and southern regions of the new empire were left with considerable freedom from interference from Huê. But his son Minh-Mang (1820–41) was more ambitious. He insisted on having greater control over both Tongking and Cochinchina, and when those areas rebelled against him in the 1830s he reasserted his authority with great vigour. The Cochinchinese rebellion of 1833–5 was a serious affair, and for a time a Siamese army invaded in the hope of destroying Minh-Mang's influence in the region; but in time the invaders were driven out and the area was pacified, leaving the way open for the Vietnamese to assert their control also over Cambodia. After the whole country had been pacified, Minh-Mang undertook a reform of local government, and in 1836 ordered a complete revision of the village tax-rolls throughout Viet-Nam.[4]

When Minh-Mang died however, in 1841, he was succeeded by lesser men who proved unable to carry on and extend this work. Control of Cambodia was lost under Thiêu-Tri (1841–7), and under Tu-Duc (1847–83) the country became embroiled in the expansion of the West. A Franco-Spanish attack in 1858 led eventually to the loss of three, and then six, provinces to France; by 1867 the latter country was in possession not only of all Cochinchina but also of Cambodia, and the geographical balance of Gia-Long's empire was destroyed.[5] Moreover in the North and Centre there followed a series of rebellions, which made it the more difficult for Tu-Duc to govern effectively the areas of his empire which remained. The debate at his court about how to deal with the French took place against a background of endemic internal disorder. It is relevant perhaps to compare Viet-Nam at this time with Japan, where an essential preliminary to successful technological response to the West was a period in which (immediately after the Meiji restoration) the government established strong central control over its empire. In Viet-Nam, only a new and successful pacification of Annam and Tongking by the court at Huê could have saved those parts of the country from the same fate as that of Cochinchina. But by 1881, when the French decided to annexe the rest of Viet-Nam, nothing effective had been done. It was left to the French to restore order throughout their new 'protectorate'.

In time the Vietnamese began to ask themselves what was this 'France' which had so much power in the world? What was its driving force? Was it something peculiar to the French, or to Europeans generally, as a race? Or was it based on methods of organization and science which any race could learn? Could Viet-Nam perhaps become in time a nation powerful enough to drive out the French? Put succinctly these questions may appear in retrospect more logical and articulate than they appeared to Vietnamese at the time. But they reflect the direction of the thought of men like Phan Bôi Châu or Phan Châu Trinh. Slowly, hesitantly they were groping for some new approach to political life, and for a new sense of identity which would enable them once more to act effectively in the world.

The philosophy of social Darwinism which was abroad in Asia and in Europe alike at this period focused the attention of a great many politicians and thinkers on the question of race. The Vietnamese began to think of themselves not merely as a *quôc*, the people of one country ruled by one monarch, but also as a racially distinct 'people'—a *dân-tôc*. The racial distinction between themselves and the French was obvious enough. But they also became increasingly conscious of the racial difference between themselves and the Chinese. In this they were aided by the introduction of the Western study of archaeology. By the 1920s scholars of the Commission Archéologique de l'Indochine and of the École Française d'Extrême-Orient were beginning to piece together information about the ancient civilization which they associated with the bronze drums from Dông-Son, a site in Thanh-

Hoa province, and which had flourished in Viet-Nam before the coming of the Chinese.[6] The debate amongst Vietnamese scholars as to the relative importance of Chinese and 'Indonesian' elements in their culture still continues and will only be settled by painstaking research. But the political implications of the scholars' discoveries were felt long ago. A small but significant detail in a conversation between Nguyên Ai Quôc (the young Hô Chi Minh) and a Russian writer in Moscow in 1923 will serve to illustrate the point. The Vietnamese, whose nom de plume at that time meant literally 'Nguyên (who) loves his country', described himself—without any reference to Chinese affinities—as belonging to 'an ancient Malay race'.[7]

Another factor which helped the Vietnamese to distinguish between themselves and the Chinese during the early decades of this century was the reform of their language. Although they had long used classical Chinese as their formal court language, the Vietnamese had never allowed their own vernacular to die out completely. It was written down, in its own distinctive characters (*chu-nôm*), from the thirteenth century onwards; and as the language of poetry and fiction it seems to have had a role not unlike that of *pai-hua*, the popular language of China itself. The significant change which occurred under French rule was the Romanization of this vernacular, with the eventual consequence that the Vietnamese would come to regard Chinese as a language whose sound might be familiar but whose script was quite foreign to them. The method of writing Vietnamese phonetically in Roman script had first been invented in the seventeenth century by a group of Catholic missionaries who found *chu-nôm* too difficult for the translation of Christian texts. In 1651 Alexandre de Rhodes published in Rome the first Vietnamese-Latin dictionary, using the new script.[8] But down to the nineteenth century it was employed only for devotional literature and catechisms.

It was when the French took over Cochinchina in the 1860s that the new script began to be used as a language of administration. From about 1900 it was increasingly used in Tongking and Annam, and the trend was further promoted by the decision after 1916 to abandon the traditional examination system whose medium had been Chinese. But if the French hoped that the Romanization of Vietnamese would be a step towards the acceptance of their own civilization and the decline of Vietnamese culture, they were proved wrong. The Vietnamese had not lost touch completely with China, and they began to see in the spread of the Romanized script a parallel to the reform and modernization of language in China which was being undertaken under the leadership of such scholars as the American-educated Hu Shih. The new script of Vietnamese came to be known as *quôc-ngu* ('national speech') which paralleled the Chinese *kuo-yü*.

From about 1913 a number of periodicals were founded in Hanoi, which used the new script and sought to persuade the traditional scholars to abandon Chinese in favour of it. One of the most important of them was *Nam-Phong Tap-Chi*, founded by Pham Quynh and given the blessing of the French authorities, because they saw in it a means towards promoting a 'Franco-Annamite' culture. But out of it there developed in fact a Vietnamese literary 'renaissance' with younger writers seeking to imitate the forms of Western literature, but developing within those forms a content which reflected their own national aspirations. Something which the French had hoped would help to Westernize their colonial subjects became by the 1930s an element in their increasing sense of national identity. Novels, stories and poems in *quôc-ngu* became a focus of passive opposition to French rule.[9]

The sense of nationality will not in itself create a nation however. To borrow a phrase of Salvador de Madariaga, 'a nation is a psychological fact.' But also it must be an institutional fact, and it is not easy to develop national institutions where they did not exist before. The central problem of the Vietnamese in the twentieth century—and a theme which will be found through many of the chapters of this essay—has been that of translating their aspirations towards nationhood into a permanent institutional reality.

Merely to remove the French would not amount to a solution of this problem. The Confucian monarchy had, as we have seen, been fossilized as a result of French 'protection'. Of the traditional framework, it was the lesser institutions such as the clan, the family, the secret association, that survived into the twentieth century with the greatest vigour. To a remarkable extent, nationalism became focused on small associations with only a local following, rather than on the monarchy. There was, it is true, a movement for Constitutional monarchy during the period before about 1916; but it was overtaken in the following decade by more radical reformers, such as the Cochinchinese Constitutionalists, or by out-and-out revolutionaries. The latter operated in much the same manner as the old secret societies, and mutual suspicion between different groups of nationalists and revolutionaries made effective opposition to the French extremely difficult. This fragmentation of nationalism has been one of the most important factors in the unfolding of the Vietnamese tragedy.

In the circumstances, it was not inevitable that the whole of Viet-Nam would be drawn into a single national framework of institutions. The French divided the country into three parts: Cochinchina, which was a colony, and Annam and Tongking, which were protectorates. The two protectorates kept stronger links with one another than either had with Cochinchina, although there persisted within them a great deal of regional loyalty and suspicion of men from other provinces than one's own. Cochinchina, which was ruled for longer by the French and was more deeply influenced by Western culture and education, remained an area apart. Might it not, had circumstances favoured it, have become a nation quite separate from the rest of Viet-Nam? It has, after all, never in its history been ruled directly and completely from Hanoi.[10] There was even, for a while in 1945-46, a movement afoot in certain French circles to grant Cochinchina separate independence, but it came to naught. This possibility of two nations in Viet-Nam rather than one must be borne in mind when we come to look in more detail at events after 1946.

Yet in fact there has never been a Cochinchinese nationalism in the sense that the people (or for that matter the elite) of Cochinchina have felt themselves to belong to a Cochinchinese nationality. Vietnamese of all regions have tended to think of Viet-Nam as a single nation. What has very often divided them has been the difference between their respective views of how a single Viet-Nam ought to develop. For Northerners have tended to think of Hanoi as the only possible capital, and have regarded people of other regions as inferior; people from the centre have seen Huê as the natural focus for the Vietnamese nation; whilst the Cochinchinese have often looked no further than Saigon, which during the colonial period was both larger and economically more important than Hanoi. This is not the same kind of regionalism as that with which we are familiar in thinking about Western countries; it does not in itself amount to separatism. But it has nonetheless been a major obstacle to the development of a single national framework, or even a single national movement demanding independence.

PART TWO

France after the war proclaimed to the world the principles of law and democracy upon which her victories were founded. Should she not ask herself if her methods of colonization correspond to her ideals?

Alexandre Varenne, December 1925.

IV

Government and the Villages

THE French thought much more clearly than any other European power about the theory of colonial government, and their thought was pervaded by the notions of 'assimilation' and the 'mission civilisatrice'. Some colonial officials it is true, held to these notions more steadfastly than others, but none could escape the necessity of either implementing them or reacting against them. The thoroughgoing assimilationist was conscious of belonging to a France which had inherited the civilizing mission of the Roman Empire. He believed that just as Rome had civilized Europe, including ancient Gaul, it was now the duty of modern Gaul to civilize the barbarians of Africa and Asia. Often this sense of a civilizing mission was combined with faith in Christianity. But not invariably so, for there were other assimilationsists who saw themselves as heirs of the Enlightenment, and whose ideas of civilization centered around the 'principles of eighty-nine' and the creation of the Republic. The idea of assimilation was so deeply ingrained that it transcended many otherwise fundamental differences in French intellectual life.[1]

'Assimilation' had two rather different implications for colonial policy in practice. First, the 'mission civilisatrice' implied cultural assimilation: the education of native peoples and the inculcation of respect for French culture. But secondly, there were implications for administrative organization: the colonies must eventually be assimilated into the French Republic. Ideally French citizenship would be granted to all educated natives, the colonial communities would have full democratic representation in the National Assembly in Paris: and above all, these communities would be governed according to the laws of France, the Code Napoléon. It was the second implication which gave rise to the greatest difficulty. Cultural assimilation was inevitably a long-term aim, which required patient efforts over a long period: no one expected it to occur overnight. But the colonies had to be governed immediately, which meant that a large number of villages had to be controlled and administered from the French cities created at Saigon and Hanoi. Administrative assimilation was fine in theory, but it depended on cultural assimilation for its success: the Code Napoléon would be fully intelligible only to Vietnamese thoroughly educated in French. This practical difficulty was to lead in due course to the emergence of a new theory, that of 'association', which allowed for some measure of cultural independence on the part of colonial subjects. In the meantime, it was necessary for the administrators to adopt policies which recognized the greater familiarity of those subjects with their own traditions of law and custom.

At the level of the colony or protectorate (Cochinchina became a colony, whilst Annam and Tongking were protectorates), and even more at the level of the Union Indochinoise created in 1887, it was possible to introduce French methods immediately. But at the level of the village and the district, rapid change was less easy. In Cochinchina, annexed between 1861 and 1867, the conquerors were faced with the problem of running a country whose former officials had for the most part fled. They were able to use a number of Catholic-educated Vietnamese like Truong Vinh Ky, and also men of the 'failed scholar' class, like Tôn Tho Tuong. But for the rest they had to either administer the country directly, or educate Vietnamese in French methods of government to do it in their place. In Tongking and Annam, on the other hand, the imperial officials were hardly able to flee and it was possible for the French to take over the traditional administrative system at all levels. The emperor himself was left on his throne but under the close control of a Résident-Supérieur.

This meant that the French went further towards administrative assimilation in Cochinchina than in the rest of Viet-Nam, and also (since they had to educate officials themselves) that Cochinchina proceeded more rapidly towards cultural assimilation. Whereas Cochinchina had a French administrative college as early as the 1870s, the old imperial examination system was left in Tongking and Annam until 1916. And whereas the French began to reform the Cochinchinese village system in 1904, they did not make similar changes in Tongking until 1921, and in Annam the village system appears to have remained largely unchanged down to 1940.[2]

Even so, both in Cochinchina and in Tongking-Annam, the French impact on peasant life in the villages came very slowly, and the cultural assimilation which made fairly rapid headway in the metropolis of Saigon or Hanoi never completely embraced the countryside. In order to understand the role of the villages in the modern political development of Viet-Nam it is necessary to look closely at their normal traditional structure, and if possible to penetrate the formal records of their organization to learn something about the social and political realities within the individual village.

The village as an institution was probably even more important in the traditional life of Viet-Nam than it had been in the medieval West. It and the clan were the most basic of all institutions, together perhaps with the sects and secret societies whose activity was especially important at the village level. The basis of the clan was the veneration of ancestors, a cult which also ensured some sense of attachment to the village, for it required each family and individual to keep in touch with the place where their forefathers were buried. In traditional Viet-Nam it was most unusual for men to lose the sense of belonging to a particular village, even if they lived in a town or at the imperial court. When families migrated they would still retain the sense of having moved away from some earlier home.

The relationship between the clan and the village might sometimes be a very complicated one. In south China, especially in Kwangtung, it was not uncommon for all the members of a village community to belong to the same clan and in such cases the clan was the more important institution. The clan elders would constitute the effective local government and the ancestral hall would be the focus of village life. But in Viet-Nam this identity between lineage and settlement units seems to have been relatively rare, and the village was correspondingly a more important institution. Responsibility for local government would lie with the notables of the village, and whilst each family or clan in the village had its own ancestral altars, a more important temple was the *dinh* which contained a shrine to the protective deity of the village. Whereas the clan was held together by ties of filial piety, the cement of the village community was the sense of being protected by the same spirits, and probably also the acceptance of common administrative responsibilities imposed by the central government. The most important unit of village administration in Viet-Nam was called the *xa* (Chinese: *she*), or sometimes the *lang* (a purely Vietnamese word without Chinese equivalent). It is significant that the original Chinese word, *she* or *xa*, had two meanings: it might mean an association of people, or it might mean an altar to the spirits of the soil. At the same time the *xa* was the basic unit of local government.[3]

Each village had its own customs and rules of precedence, and there was considerable variation between regions and even from one village to the next. Thus in some places precedence at village meetings in the *dinh* was based on age; whilst in others it depended on scholastic attainment, so that students and scholars were given the highest place. There were also differences in terminology, and the subdivisions of the village were known by different names in different provinces. Even the appearance of the village was not the same in all parts of the country. In Tongking it was usual for villages to have thick bamboo hedges which provided an effective local defence against marauders, whereas in Cochinchina such defences are only rarely found. Generalizations based on the few studies of particular localities which have been made from time to time cannot therefore be regarded as in any sense definitive. Yet when one comes to compare what is known of these Vietnamese villages with our knowledge of traditional villages in England or France, it is possible to distinguish certain features which in a comparative sense may be regarded as typical of the villages in Viet-Nam.

To begin, the Vietnamese *xa* was not the property of any private individual or family, in the way that the English or French manor belonged to its manorial lord. It paid taxes, furnished men for the army, or performed corvée labour services, entirely by virtue of its obligations to the emperor; and if at a particular time the actual recipient of these dues was someone other than the emperor himself, that person derived his position entirely from an imperial grant. It was the custom for imperial officials to receive grants of the dues from certain villages for the duration of their official careers, but this did not amount to the creation of fiefs. Much land was of course owned by individual families, and a rich family might have a substantial estate and even tenants on it. But ownership never carried with it the administrative or judicial powers which pertained to feudal lordship. In Viet-Nam, village affairs were in the hands of a council of notables in each *xa*, whose principal officers were responsible for keeping order there and for ensuring the performance of the community's obligations to the state. They also looked after the village treasury, and administered the area of land which in almost all villages belonged inalienably to the *xa* as a whole, and which had to be regularly partitioned amongst the member families.

The formal rules governing village administration were determined partly by imperial decree and partly by local custom. Certain essential rules were laid down for the country as a whole: for the appointment of suitable officers and notables, for the regular revision of census and taxation rolls, for the procedures affecting division of communal lands, and so on. From time to time these rules would be changed or elaborated upon by an emperor anxious to reinvigorate the system or to render it better capable of meeting some new situation, and a long series of such decrees relating to Tongking from the eleventh century onwards has been preserved in a nineteenth-century administrative encyclopaedia.[4] In Annam and Cochinchina the *xa* system did not develop until rather later than in Tongking, for those areas were only settled by the Vietnamese from the fifteenth century onwards.

How far the decrees were acted upon in detail, and how far the administrative practices of Vietnamese villages were standardized as a result, are questions which cannot be answered without a great deal more documentary research. But it is thought that the fifteenth century was the period when the greatest degree of central imperial supervision over local affairs was maintained, at least in Tongking. During the seventeenth and eighteenth centuries there seems to have been some decline in the extent to which the details of village administration were supervized from above. By the nineteenth century provincial and district officials, both in North and South, seem to have interfered in village affairs much less regularly than had been the case in the fifteenth century. Perhaps that is the reason why the early French writers who described the *xa* in the years immediately after the conquest were so much impressed by the degree of autonomy enjoyed by the village notables. More recently Vietnamese writers have referred to this autonomy as evidence that their forefathers were familiar with the idea of democratic freedom at the local level long before the coming of the Europeans.

However, before we apply too readily such words as freedom and democracy to the Vietnamese village, we ought to pause to consider the original occidental usage of those terms. Within our own framework of ideas, the purpose of words like 'democratic' or 'autonomy' is one of contradistinction. That is, they imply the existence of the opposite concepts, 'autocratic' and 'centralization'. These other concepts imply in turn the notions of authority and sovereign power. But as we have seen, the Vietnamese tradition knew little of such notions; for its law was not based on authority and will, but on the recognition of universal harmony. In other words, the Vietnamese village was neither democratic nor autocratic, neither autonomous nor dictatorially controlled. The distinctions were irrelevant, even alien to the traditional system. Thus even in the fifteenth century, when the *xa* seems to have been subject to the traditional maximum of supervision from above, it would be wrong to assume that the nature of the supervision was precisely the same as what the Westerner means when he uses the word 'control'. The emperor made demands, and it was for the villagers to carry them out. But his guarantee that they would do so rested more on their sense of obligation than on an authoritarian system of coercion. Conversely when the villagers, who looked to the imperial officials as men who would guarantee their protection and good order, found that a local mandarin was corrupt or made unfair exactions, they could not appeal against him to the law: their only defence was either open revolt, or to leave the village and return when the official had gone.

This contrast between Vietnamese and Western European systems of local government has an important parallel in the sphere of political theory. In all parts of the world, the basic object of rural government may be said to be the same: to provide security. But on the question *how* security can best be guaranteed to ordinary people in their villages, there have been many different replies in human history: each cultural tradition has produced its own ideas. In the modern West men believed that the foundation of government was good law: a good system of administration and justice, in which officials were held more or less to the path of virtue by the rule of law. Thomas Hobbes, contemplating the turmoil of civil war in England, advocated as a solution a particular system of government: absolute monarchy. Other thinkers have tended to the view that what ought to be absolute is not monarchy but the law itself. Out of this tradition grew the Western theory of constitutional, democratic government. But in Viet-Nam, as in China, the traditional demand was not for good laws so much as for good men. 'With the right men', says the *Doctrine of the Mean*, 'the growth of good government is as rapid as the growth of vegetation in the right soil.' Rules were necessary of course; but if government seemed lacking in effectiveness the first thought was not to change the laws but to change the men. Law was deemed less important than virtue.

The formal regulations concerning the *xa* tell us only a little of what we need to know about rural society in Viet-Nam. Beneath the formal surface of administration there lay the reality of village politics. The formal organization as it is recorded in the imperial decrees hardly allowed for the possibility of conflict within the village. Open differences of opinion, and the provision of rules for settling them by debate or voting, were alien to the concept of social harmony. In any case, any system of formal opposition within an institutional framework would have involved loss of face for those Vietnamese belonging to the party that was overruled in any situation. Whatever the reality, decisions within the village council must at least have the appearance of a consensus.

That conflicts occurred in practice need not be doubted, but, since the regulations and decrees do not tell us about them, it is only rarely that the outsider has a chance to observe them. A valuable glimpse of the realities of village politics in Viet-Nam —in this case in Cochinchina—is afforded by an incident which occurred in Tân-An province in the years 1895–6, and which the French officials referred to as 'L'affaire de Môc-Hoa'. It is covered in great detail by a series of reports still preserved in the National Archives in Saigon.[5]

During the autumn of 1895, for reasons which are not recorded, a conflict arose between the leading notables of the village of Tuyên-Thanh and another group or faction within the village.

There may have been in the background a long-standing feud between members of two clans for control of the village, for the chief notables all belonged to the Vo family and their opponents to a family called Nguyên. Or possibly it was a case of a newly rising clan seeking to take over from an established one. Within the village itself the Vo were virtually the ruling clique, and since the custom of the village was that new notables should be elected by outgoing notables the group in office was in a position to perpetuate its control over affairs indefinitely. Their opponents on the other hand had influential friends at the level of the canton and of the province. The leading figure in the Nguyên group, Nguyên Van Nghi, held the office of deputy-chief in the canton of Môc-Hoa, within which the village lay; and he was on friendly terms both with the canton-chief, Lê Van Thu, and with a man called Hoc who had an influential post within the office of the French administrator of Tân-An province. Nghi, Thu and Hoc were in fact all Catholics, and on good terms with the French missionary priest at Tân-An. It may well be that Thu was the most important figure in the situation, for he had acquired great influence in many villages of the canton, and the crisis at Tuyên-Thanh may possibly have arisen partly from a conflict between the canton-chief and the Vo clique.

In December 1895, Thu and Nghi—with the aid of Hoc—were in a strong enough position to persuade the administrator of Tân-An to dismiss the ten Vo notables of Tuyên-Thanh and to hold a new election. They were also able to secure election in their place for several members of the Nguyên clan, and to enable the newly elected men to take over the highest offices on the council. The Vo leaders were thus ousted, and the new clique was free to pursue a policy of promoting Catholicism in the village. Nghi was said to have promised a place on the council of notables to anyone who was converted to the Christian faith. But the Vo were not so easily disposed of. The following February (1896) Vo Van Vang and his supporters presented a complaint against Nguyên Van Nghi and his friends to the Governor of Cochinchina at Saigon. An inquiry was ordered and the Vo party succeeded in gaining the sympathy of the French official in charge of it, Navelle. In May Navelle's report to the governor recommended the dismissal of Thu and Nghi from their offices in the canton, and the annulment of the recent election of new notables at Tuyên-Thanh. The Nguyên group were now placed on the defensive and had to find some way of discrediting their rivals in French eyes. On the night of the 11th June a fire in the village seriously damaged the house of a Catholic catechist, Antoine Quy, and the Vo were immediately blamed. About the same time the Catholic group organized the writing of a number of letters to the French authorities from various villages in Môc-Hoa canton, defending the virtues of Thu and Nghi. They began to hope that the advantage gained by the Vo might be reversed once more.

But to no avail. In late July or August, when the case of the fire was heard at a provincial court, the Vo were able to show that the house of Antoine Quy had been burnt down by the Nguyên party themselves in an attempt to incriminate their rivals. As for the letters supporting Thu and Nghi, the French officials declined to take them seriously. Towards the end of August a new election of notables took place at Tuyên-Thanh, in accordance with the old rules, and the Vo regained their ascendancy. Between then and the end of the year the ousted Nguyên group made as much trouble as they could for the Vo notables, with a series of petitions and complaints. But by this time the provincial authorities had made up their minds that the Vo were in the right and the new complaints against them were dismissed. The final fling of the Catholic group was a request—fully supported by the ecclesiastical authorities—for partition of the village. But that too was turned down.

To see this case as merely an example of tension between Catholics and Buddhists would be to miss the point. (Nor, for that matter, was it simply an instance of tension between the missionaries and anti-clerical officials amongst the French.) The central feature of the affair was the conflict between two rival factions, perhaps clans, for control over the village or even over the whole canton. It is not difficult to imagine comparable situations arising where all the people involved, including the provincial and central government officials, were Vietnamese. Indeed if the typical Vietnamese village was one which embraced more than one clan, such inter-clan feuding may well have been a very common feature of politics at this level. The existence of a great many secret associations would also contribute to conflicts of this kind. Nor need one assume the existence of a colonial government as a prerequisite for conflicts between canton or district officials and the notables of villages. A great deal of political manoeuvering must have gone on beneath the surface of formal village harmony.

However, the Môc-Hoa affair did involve Frenchmen, and it illustrates an important aspect of the relationship between Vietnamese villagers and their colonial masters under French rule. It so happens that in this case the details of the situation were brought to light by an administrative inquiry, but such a revelation was by no means inevitable. The initial success of the Nguyên party in securing the removal of the Vo notables depended on their connection with Hoc, the secretary and adviser to the French administrator at Tan-An. Hoc seems to have had considerable influence over decisions of this kind, and in other circumstances an official in his position might well have been able to hoodwink his superior so completely that no Frenchman would ever have realized the true course of events. In dealing with a country of many thousands of villages the French were always faced with the problem of knowing what went on amongst their Vietnamese subjects, for without that knowledge they were powerless to enforce their own regulations effectively. They had a police system, of course, and they could also sometimes (though hardly in a case like that at Môc-Hoa) obtain intelligence from missionary priests. But ultimately they were dependent on native informants or officials of one kind or another, and much could be concealed from them if the need arose. The French were not unaware of the problem, and became increasingly concerned at the difficulty of finding adequate personnel to manage village affairs. In a report of 1922 the Governor of Cochinchina complained that the notables of villages were 'for the most part very inferior to their task not only because of their barely elementary education, but even more because they bring to their work a routine spirit, hostile to every new idea'.[6] The fact was, the report continued, that fewer and fewer people wanted to become notables, so that good candidates rarely presented themselves for the office.

This need not mean that struggles for village election of the Môc-Hoa kind no longer occurred. What troubled the French was that they could not find notables with the degree of French education necessary for full co-operation between village and higher authorities. They should not have been so surprised at the difficulty. Only a small minority of children, even in Cochinchina, received a worthwhile education in French, and not unnaturally they aspired to something more than village work: for example to appointments in government departments at Saigon or Hanoi. Nor was this in itself a new development. Before the French came, it had been usual for the best educated people to seek imperial office, and for villages to be run by the less well-educated. What was new in the situation was the degree of reliance which a government of foreigners, whose command of the Vietnamese language was limited, placed on native notables for a service which the latter were probably very reluctant to perform. If the notables identified themselves with the French, they were liable to lose the confidence of the village; if they identified with the mass of the population and showed signs of being anti-French, they were liable to be removed. Not surprisingly many were content simply to pursue their own interests and to use their position for personal or family gain.

French fears were not unjustified. As we have seen there was a long tradition of secret religious and political activity in Viet-Nam in which the classic method had been for the leaders of opposition to the government to undermine the control of the centre over local communities. The French may have been right in thinking that all the ordinary peasants wanted was to be left in peace. But if they could not themselves guarantee that peace, the way was left open for the growth of secret anti-government associations to assert their own power in the villages. The kind of thing that could happen is well illustrated by events in Cochinchina during the years from 1905 to 1916, when a considerable number of what the French called 'les sociétés dites secrètes' flourished in a great many of the villages of the region.[7]

Sometimes they were no more than criminal gangs, terrorizing the countryside and living a life of robbery and violence. A well-documented example was the case of Mai Van Kiêm and about forty or fifty of his associates, who held sway over the villages round Trang-Bang (in the province of Tây-Ninh) for about eighteen months before their arrest in February 1916. Their first recorded act of violence was in September 1914 when they attacked a local man who dared to oppose them, and then set fire to his house. One man was imprisoned for three months after this incident, but the main culprits went unpunished: no one would give evidence against them and the local notables were too frightened to act. On another occasion, a few months later, a Vietnamese district official made an inquiry into Kiêm's activities, but the evidence was so distorted as to make it appear that he and his friends were the victims of a rival gang. When four notables were robbed one night, they were so intimidated that the court had no choice but to acquit the accused and set them free. It was not until the general crisis of February 1916 that the French authorities finally discovered the true situation and brought Kiêm's band to justice.

By that stage the French were far less concerned about mere criminals than about the political societies which had seemed suddenly to spring up in various parts of Cochinchina. In 1913 they forestalled a plot for open revolt in Saigon and Cholon, and possibly in some rural areas too, by arresting just in time a man called Phan Phat Sanh who dreamt of becoming emperor as 'Xich-Long' or 'Red Dragon'. Of Chinese descent, he had been associated at first with the overseas Chinese secret societies whose aim was to restore the Ming dynasty in China. But his own ambition appears to have been to use the secret society network of southern Viet-Nam to establish a throne for himself. To this end he had spent two years building up a following in Saigon and the province of Cho-Lon, and had found a retreat for himself at a monastery in the Cambodian border-province of Kampot. Whatever supernatural powers he claimed for himself, they failed him at the last. But he had followers, and his own organization was crude by comparison with that created by his leading supporters during the two or three years which followed his arrest. In February 1916 they planned to seize Saigon prison as the signal for a general Cochinchinese rising. The French again foiled the rebels before things got out of hand, but were alarmed when they discovered subsequently the extent and complexity of the network of secret societies involved.

Amongst the most notorious of the secret society organizers was a man known variously as Cao Van Long, Bây Do, and Ma-Vang. His career will serve to illustrate the nature of this network. Born in the province of Bên-Tre, he seems to have donned the priestly robe about 1910, and to have made his home thereafter at a temple or pagoda on a remote hillside in the province of Châu-Dôc. His retirement was not however that of a hermit. He spent much of his time wandering through the provinces of the Mekong delta organizing and encouraging silent opposition to the French. As he went, he distributed magic charms bearing the secret name of his temple, which were supposed to protect the recipient against all kinds of attack. His robe was thus more than a disguise, it was an essential element in his power over the rural population. When in 1917 he was arrested and sentenced to life detention, the Governor of Cochinchina commented:

> Thus ended the legend which had made a demi-god of this wretched apostle. His conviction will go far to destroying the prestige enjoyed by all such false bonzes and sorcerers amongst a naïve and credulous population.[8]

His optimism proved unjustified. A decade or so later new and more serious troubles were being prepared in Cochinchina, and elsewhere in Viet-Nam. If at that time there was less superstition amongst the populace, it was small comfort to the French to see the 'false bonzes' replaced by revolutionary and socialist politicians.

The pattern of conflict in the Môc-Hoa affair was between two factions of similar kind and similar social status. No doubt this kind of conflict was found later, even perhaps in the most recent period of Vietnamese rural strife. But with the political societies the conflict was between the villages and higher levels of administration, with the notables often taking the side of the secret societies or politicians. Or sometimes, in 1916, there was conflict within the village itself: between the notables and the rest of the population, or rather between the notables and the secret society leaders. In Bên-Tre province for example, an outbreak of violence near Mo-Cây early in February 1916 included attacks not only on Chinese shops but also on a village *dinh*, where many of the local archives were taken out and burnt. This kind of incident was still more common in the disturbances of 1930–31, especially in the provinces of Nghê-An and Ha-Tinh. As socialistic and Marxist ideas began to spread through the countryside the notables tended more and more to identify themselves with the French desire for preservation of the social order.

It is another serious limitation of the formal records concerning

the history and administration of the *xa* that they say very little
about the realities of social structure in the traditional village.
Only in the French period do we find the opportunity to analyse
Vietnamese social structure at all systematically, and by then it
had already begun to change under the western impact. Even
then, the subject is not an easy one to study in detail. Some
writers have drawn attention to the growing contrast between
patterns of landownership in Tongking-Annam and in Cochinchina; but this was not necessarily the most important fact about
Vietnamese agrarian society under colonial rule. That the
agrarian statistics collected about 1930 demonstrate such a
contrast is not in doubt. In Tongking and Annam the majority
of the peasants were owner-occupiers: fewer than $1\frac{1}{2}$ per cent of
the owners of rice land in Tongking (and 10 per cent in Annam)
leased out land to tenants. In Cochinchina the figure was 36 per
cent: much of the land had been still uncultivated when the
French arrived and had been brought into use under the French
system of large-scale concessions, with the result that by 1930
there were many places where the majority of the cultivators
were tenant-farmers. As much as 45 per cent of the land in
Cochinchina belonged to owners of fifty hectares or more, and
some of these were very large landlords. Yet to argue that this
made agrarian conflict more likely in Cochinchina than elsewhere
is to ignore the fact that the most important elements in peasant
discontent were poverty, credit, and heavy taxation. And the
poorest peasants in Indochina were very often those who owned
their own small parcels of land but simply could not obtain a
living from them adequate to meet such crises as a bad harvest
or a sudden rise in taxes. The most hated men in such a society
were often not the landlords but the moneylenders and the
officials who had to collect taxes.[9]

The political movements of twentieth-century Viet-Nam saw
in the grievances of the peasantry their greatest opportunity to
mobilize the rural masses against the French. In the towns,
politicians who were bold enough to oppose the French could be
watched, their newspapers censored, and if necessary their freedom
of movement curtailed. But in the villages, the French had to
overcome the basic problem of control. The nationalists could
spread propaganda more widely, and could escape arrest for
long periods; they could even organize revolt. They found it

difficult to coordinate their activities, and this explains why for many decades the French colonial officials could afford to treat their movements as of no fundamental importance. But the French never really solved the problem of local government in Indochina, and the time would come after 1945 when a political movement would be strong enough to raise a whole army by undermining the official chain of authority from Hanoi and Saigon down to the humble village, and by creating a rebel chain of command in its place.

V

Religion

RELIGION had often entered into politics in traditional Viet-Nam and secret sects had played their part from time to time in rebellions against the emperor. In the twentieth century, when the Confucian system was ceasing to command respect as a basis for political activity and when some other framework was needed for the expansion of nationalist feeling, it is hardly surprising that religious sects once again became prominent in politics. The tendency was strengthened by the fact that Asia generally was experiencing something of a religious revival in the late nineteenth and early twentieth centuries. It was a natural response to the challenge of the Europeans, and especially the Christian missions, that Asians should begin to re-examine their own religious tradition. Encouraged by the growth of interest in their religions in Europe itself, many of them came to the conclusion that in matters other than material technology, the East had often been at least the equal of the West.

In some parts of Asia, this religious revival has contributed a great deal to the growing sense of national identity, and has even sometimes provided an institutional framework for nationalism. In Viet-Nam too this has been the case to some extent. But given the country's tradition of sectarian religion, it was not to be expected that any single religious body would prove capable of uniting the whole country behind a single set of beliefs. The Vietnamese religious revival was consequently diverse, but none the less important for that.

The one religion which had attempted to become anything like an orthodoxy in traditional Viet-Nam was Confucianism. But it had been the monarchy that had made of Confucianism something more than a mere sect religion, and with the declining prestige of the monarchy under French 'protection' the possibility of that religion continuing to be both an established orthodoxy and a focus for national revival was considerably reduced. There was it is true a Confucian revival in certain quarters. Professor Levenson has shown how Chinese conservatives in the first two decades of the twentieth century tried to make of Confucianism a kind of state religion, even within the Republic. That movement found reflection in Viet-Nam, notably in the writings of Trân Trong Kim whose *Nho-Giao* ('Confucianism') appeared between 1920 and 1930. But when a prominent younger journalist called Phan Khôi criticized Kim's ideas in a newspaper of 1931, he evoked an echo of response throughout the country.[1] In so far as Confucian ideas survived amongst the generation of Vietnamese which reached maturity after 1920, it did so only as a set of ethical values, a way of living, and not as a movement capable of holding together an organized mass following. Nor, with the eclipse of the monarchy, was there great scope for Viet-Nam to develop the kind of religion that Japanese *Shinto* became in the twentieth century: a national cult held together by the rituals of the imperial court. The important elements in the Vietnamese religious revival therefore were Buddhism and Taoism, and the sects which sought to unite both religions (and even Christianity) into a single doctrine of the One.

Since the Vietnamese religious revival was one of sects rather than of a single orthodox 'Church', it is no cause for surprise to discover that it was as much influenced by limitations of region as were the nationalist political movements of the period before 1945. In Cochinchina, two religious movements dominate the scene: the *Cao-Dai* religion, and *Hoa-Hao* Buddhism. The former is the older movement, and may indeed have lost some of its early supporters to the latter. Caodaism could still claim at least half a million adepts in 1966; and the *Hoa-Hao* sect in the same year had about 550,000 members, mainly in the west of Cochinchina.[2]

To regard Caodaism as a kind of reformed Taoism may possibly give a better indication of the character of the religion than a description of it as reformed Buddhism; but neither term does anything like justice to its complexity. It belongs to the tradition, by no means new in China, of trying to draw together the three religions of Confucianism, Buddhism and Taoism into a religion of the One, or of the Way. An innovation of Caodaism is that it includes also Christianity, and claims to be heir to all the religions of the world. (The fact that Islam has played hardly any part in Vietnamese history is no doubt the explanation for

v.w.—6

its very peripheral part in Caodaism.) The new religion was officially established in the year 1926, but its roots go deeper than that, and in part its origins may go back to the sects or secret societies which organized the anti-French movement of 1916 in many parts of Cochinchina. Perhaps it should be traced even further back, to the sects of the *Dao-Lanh* religion which participated in the opposition to French rule in the 1870s. But we must return in a moment to the political role of the Caodaists, for to concentrate upon it to the exclusion of other aspects would be to forget the essentially religious character of the movement, which is to a large extent genuine.

The name *Cao-Dai* is that given by the religion to the Supreme Being, or God, whom it worships. It means literally 'high tower' (or 'high palace'), and is found originally as a symbol of the Supreme Being in a number of Taoist and Chinese Buddhist scriptures. It was also, though the fact may be of no relevance, used by early Protestant missionaries to translate 'Jehovah' when rendering the Bible into Chinese. In Caodaist temples, the *Cao-Dai* is represented not as a tower but as an eye: to this extent one can say that the Caodaist God is personal. But the symbol is still much less personal than that of Christ on the Cross.

The formal title of the religion is not Caodaism, however: that was merely a convenient French appellation. It is known in its own official records as the *Dai-Dao Tam-Ky Phô-Dô*, and the meanings of the three elements in this title tell us a good deal about its fundamental character. *Dai-Dao* means the 'Great Way': that is, the Way of Heaven, the Way of the *Tao Teh Ching* which governs the order of the universe and to which men must strive to conform. *Phô-Dô* means in effect 'salvation': literally, the crossing of the infinite, in the sense of being helped across by some greater Being. *Tam-Ky* means simply the 'Three Periods'. The *Cao-Dai* religion is therefore the 'Great Way of the Three Epochs of Salvation'. It is partly an apocalyptic religion, for it believes that the third epoch is shortly to begin and that it will be the epoch of great peace. But it is also a religion of purification, for it urges on all men that they should purify themselves in preparation for this third epoch. The Buddhist concept of *karma* enters into it as well. Thus it is more than a merely devotional religion, and makes greater demands on its adepts than the chanting of sutras: they must believe, and they must live upright lives.

The idea of three epochs allows for the introduction of all other religions into the Caodaist doctrine: for all are the result of attempts by God during the course of the two previous epochs to save mankind from materialism. The third epoch differs from all others because in that epoch all the religions of the earth will be united. In many of its features Caodaism is not unlike the *Tao-Yuan* religion which grew up in Northern China during the 1920s, and which aimed to unite all five of the religions of China: Confucianism, Taoism, Buddhism, Islam and Christianity. G. Goulet, writing in 1926, traced religions of this kind back to a much earlier sect in which the 'three religions' were united, for whose existence he found evidence in a Chinese text dated 1613.[3]

There is no necessity to explain Caodaism in terms of direct influence from outside during the 1920s. The fundamental urge to create a religion of the One lay deeply rooted in the Sino-Vietnamese tradition. But its revival at this particular time probably was due in large part to the new spirit that was abroad in East Asia following the European holocaust of the first world war. The death and destruction which the West brought upon itself after 1914 led Asians to question the superiority of Western values that they had previously taken for granted. They turned to spiritual values in reaction against the previously unchallenged materialism of their conquerors. Caodaism was the religious movement in which Vietnamese participated most fully in the universalist aspect of the Asian religious revival. Yet at the same time, even it had a nationalistic overtone, for the Caodaists emphasized with some pride that it was their country in which the Supreme Being had chosen to manifest himself to mankind anew.

The Caodaists were very conscious that their doctrines depended upon divine revelation. It is in their method of communication with the divine that they have found the greatest difficulty in persuading Westerners to take their religion seriously. For that method is frankly spiritualist. The most important adepts of the religion are the spirit mediums who speak or write messages from spirits at special seances. The Westerner, influenced by the Christian tradition if not himself a believer, finds it difficult to appreciate that in Viet-Nam this represents more than an activity of cranks; but traditional Vietnamese religion has always been spiritualistic, and Caodaism has made no major innovation in this respect.[4] Through the medium—using either the planchette or the beaked basket—the Caodaists communicate with a whole host of spirits, of whom the *Cao-Dai* is the greatest but not different in essence from the others. Many sacred Caodaist texts are derived not from the supreme being but from other spirits, including those of great poets and heroes of the past. One of the most important of these is the spirit of Li T'ai-po (Ly Thai Bach), an eighth-century Chinese poet famous for his habits as a tippler and for his skill in Taoist meditation. Another spirit who has played a part in the growth of the religion is that of the fourth-century general Quan-Công (or Quan Thanh-Dê), the Chinese God of War. It is on a comparable level that the Caodaists venerate the spirits of several Western heroes, notably Victor Hugo, and Jeanne d'Arc. Into their hierarchy of spirits the Caodaists have fitted all the great spiritual leaders of mankind: Confucius, Lao-Tzu, the Buddha, Moses, and Christ. To say that they venerate these spirits as 'saints' is to risk imposing too Western an interpretation on oriental reality. For the Vietnamese, the power of the protecting spirit is as much a part of spiritual reality as is belief in divine incarnation for the Christian.

The popularity of the new religion in the years after 1926 was immediate and considerable. Its involvement in politics was therefore almost inevitable. It is impossible not to see in the suddenness of Caodaist expansion a reinvigoration of the secret societies and sects which had been active a decade earlier. The continuity was not direct, and there is nothing to indicate any personal continuity of leadership; the men of 1916 were too discredited to try again. But the network of temples and relationships still remained. The Caodaists were not trying to create something utterly unfamiliar to the Cochinchinese peasantry. The new leadership was better educated than that of ten years before, most of the prominent Caodaists being former officials of the government who had been taught at French schools. It was also more specifically religious, for the Caodaist was not just a local *thay-phap* selling magical charms: he had a system of belief which could satisfy the growing number of country notables educated in local primary schools. Some of the leading people in the religion were indeed much more interested in religion than politics, notably the founder of Caodaism, Ngô Van Chiêu, and the head of the Bên-Tre Caodaists, Nguyên Ngoc Tuong.

Nevertheless for the politically minded there was an obvious opportunity to mobilize ordinary people and eventually to use the organization for political ends. The first important move towards such organization seems to have been the creation of three principal centres: at Cân-Tho or Bac-Liêu, at My-Tho, and at Tây-Ninh. The third of these has attracted the most attention, partly because it was the most articulate, partly because its leadership later co-operated with the French. The first Caodaist temple at Tây-Ninh was established in 1926, but since then it has been replaced by a much more lavish structure whose ornamentation has been described as gawdy by many Western tourists, but which manages to symbolize most of the features of a highly symbolic religion. In 1930 the highest dignitary of the religion, Lê Van Trung, invited adepts from all areas of Cochinchina to go to Tây-Ninh and settle there on a substantial acreage of land bought for the purpose. He may well have had in mind a Vietnamese imitation of Tagore's Santiniketan, or of the Gandhian *ashram*. But he was also thinking in terms of a state within a state. The Caodaist hierarchy was not only religious in character: it included a bureaucratic hierarchy also, within which Trung himself was a high minister. There was even some attempt to differentiate between legislative and executive power, but we have no means of knowing how effective it was in practice.

For a time, around 1930, it may have seemed possible that the whole movement could be directed from the one centre of Tây-Ninh. But as so often happens with Vietnamese organizations unity proved difficult to maintain. By 1932 rifts appeared in the leadership on issues that were sometimes personal, sometimes political, and sometimes religious. The relationship between the Western Caodaists (of My-Tho, Bac-Liêu and Cân-Tho) and those of Tây-Ninh had never been very close: the former groups now broke away and formed a number of branches on their own. A little later the Tây-Ninh group itself split up, and Nguyên Ngoc Tuong established his own 'holy see' at Bên-Tre, leaving Pham Công Tac to succeed to the authority (though not the title) of Lê Van Trung at Tây-Ninh. By about 1935 there seem to have been about ten different sects or branches of the religion, each with its own leaders and sometimes its own peculiarities of belief. The seriousness of the schisms should not however be exaggerated. For this was not a religion dependent on an apostolic succession and a conviction that there could be only one law-giving authority within it. A unifying authority was far less necessary to hold a religion like Caodaism together than it was in medieval Christendom. Although attempts to reunite the faithful in the late 1930s, and again in 1946, were not very successful, the adepts of all branches probably continued to feel a sense of belonging to the same religion.

Some of the Caodaists probably joined the *Hoa-Hao* sect when it emerged in Western Cochinchina in 1939.[5] *Hoa-Hao* Buddhism differs from Caodaism in that it does not claim to unite all religions into one, and in that it venerates the person of its founder, Huynh Phu So. His career, except that he was never a Christian, shows remarkable parallels with that of the founder of the Tai-Ping religion in South China in the 1840s. His spiritual education took place at a temple in the hills near the Cambodian border. Then in 1939, according to one account, in the midst of a great storm, he 'revealed' the principles of a new 'Buddhism of Great Peace'. He gathered around him a number of disciples, and his beliefs quickly spread. The religion which he revealed and preached is extremely puritanical, and is opposed to elaborate ritual of all kinds. It has a kind of spiritual centre in the village of Hoa-Hao (Châu-Dôc province), but it has no great temples comparable to those of Tây-Ninh or Bên-Tre.

During the 1930s, both the *Cao-Dai* and the *Hoa-Hao* sects became involved in the policies of the Japanese towards Indochina. It is said that Pham Công Tac was from the first a follower of the prince Cuong-Dê, whom the monarchist reform movement had chosen as its imperial candidate in 1904, and who had lived since 1911 in Japan. (He died there in 1951.) Certainly by the later 1930s Tac was in contact with Japan, and was prepared to collaborate with the Japanese. When the Japanese army occupied Cochinchina in 1942, by agreement with the French, the latter were afraid that the *Kempetai* would use the Caodaists as part of a base for a non-French government in southern Viet-Nam. Consequently they arrested a number of the leaders of the sect, and deported Pham Công Tac to Madagascar. The Japanese also tried to use Huynh Phu So and his sect as part of their plan, but seem to have decided that he was either not sufficiently well-disposed towards them, or that he was not capable enough as a politician to help them.[6]

This breach between the sects and the French authorities was healed after the Japanese surrender in 1945. The French were faced with the problem of recovering control of their former colony and of defeating the Communist-led *Viêt-Minh*; at that period, the religious leaders had to decide whether to come to terms with the French or to throw in their lot with the *Viêt-Minh*. The *Hoa-Hao* sect seems to have been generally hostile to Communism, and in 1946 its leader Huynh Phu So incurred the odium of the *Viêt-Minh* by trying to form a political organization of his own. For this he was murdered the following year (April 1947), whereupon his followers came to an agreement with the French which allowed them to administer the provinces where they were strongest, and virtually to maintain a private army. The Caodaists at Tây-Ninh also came to an agreement of this kind with the French, on the understanding that Pham Công Tac was allowed to return to Viet-Nam and resume his direction of the religion. Not all the Caodaists however supported the French: other sects within the movement joined forces with the *Viêt-Minh*. Information on this point is scarce, but it would seem that the group led by Cao Triêu Phat in Bac-Liêu province was pro-*Viêt-Minh* at least down to 1949.[7] Another Caodaist group later withdrew from Tây-Ninh, and indeed from the war, and posed for a time as a 'third force': this was the group of Trinh Minh Thê, who found a curious immortality in the pages of Graham Greene's novel, *The Quiet American*. These differences of policy between different groups are a reminder of the fact that although it is convenient to use such blanket terms as Caodaist or *Hoa-Hao* Buddhist, these movements in reality consisted of federations of smaller associations: the situation of 1945–54 in Cochinchina was considerably more like that of 1913–16 than some observers would allow.

The traditional pattern of sectarian opposition to government had not for the most part included any tendency for a successful rebel sect to make any ideological innovations. On taking power it would take over the whole Confucian system of administration and all its values, though it might have the strength to make things work better for a time. In the absence of (or rather decline of) the Confucian system in the twentieth century one might have expected the 'political' sects of that period to work out some new set of political ideals. But although the Caodaists made important religious innovations, they did not develop any new political theory which might have been the basis of a non-monarchical state. Some were Westernisers, but none produced a set of political ideas that was specifically Caodaist.

The sects so far described had their roots in Cochinchina, and apart from the communities of Caodaists at Da-Nang and Hanoi they did not make a great deal of headway outside that region. When we turn to the other principal element in the Vietnamese revival of religion, the Buddhists, we are dealing with a movement which had many followers in all three regions although it was perhaps strongest in Central Viet-Nam.

The Buddhists of the various Buddhist Associations that have flourished in Viet-Nam since about 1930 were conscious of belonging to the Buddhist revival in Asia as a whole: therefore they must be seen against the wider background of that revival, which has embraced both the Theravada and the Mahayana branches of the religion. In the Theravada world, the first modern movement for the reform of Buddhism occurred in Thailand in the 1840s, when Prince Mongkut created the Dhammayutika Order in Bangkok. Its influence outside Siam however was curtailed later in the century by the Europeans' annexation of Burma and Cambodia; Ceylon, the other traditional centre of Theravada religion, had been a British colony since 1798. The Buddhist revival which began to take place in those other countries towards the end of the nineteenth century was of a different kind, for it made Buddhism the focus of anti-colonial nationalism. In both Burma and Ceylon, in the 1890s, there grew up a movement for Buddhist schools and colleges, in imitation of—but also in competition with—the Christian missions. In Burma that was followed about 1916, by a more political move on the part of some younger Buddhists to make an issue out of the British habit of wearing shoes inside pagodas and monasteries. By the early 1920s this produced an even bigger movement, in which 'pongyi politicians' used their influence amongst the populace to stir up anti-British feeling. From that time onwards Buddhism was an established part of Burmese nationalism, and it continued to be so after independence was achieved. It derived much of its force from the memory that before British rule the Theravada *Sangha* in

Burma had been virtually a State Religion under royal patronage; and in 1961 Buddhism was once again elevated to be the country's State Religion.[8] In Ceylon the relationship between Buddhism and nationalism developed more slowly, but by the 1950s the religion was a major factor in politics there too, though not 'established' by the state. The Theravada countries saw a great intensification of Buddhist activity in the 1950s. The Sixth Buddhist Council was opened in Burma in 1954 (the Fifth having been held at Mandalay by King Mindon in 1871). And Ceylon led the celebrations for the 2,500th anniversary of the Buddha's attainment of Nirvana, in the Buddha Jayanti year of 1956.

The most important country in the twentieth-century revival of Mahayana Buddhism has been Japan. There too the first appearance of new vigour came about the turn of the century: Japanese Buddhism however did not become a focus for nationalism, since that was the almost explicit function of Shintoism. There were indeed occasions when Shintoism and Buddhism came into conflict. But since the end of the Pacific War there has been no more Shintoism, and Buddhism has played an important part in the nation's adjustment to defeat. The diversity of the religious revival in Japan has been considerable. At least four groups of Japanese Buddhists can be identified by even the most superficial observer, and a full exploration would show that within them there are many subdistinctions.[9] First, the *Zen* Buddhists, who seek sudden enlightenment through meditation under the direction of a master: they do not attach great importance to any of the scriptures. Second, the *Shingon* sect, whose beliefs include that of sudden enlightenment but are also to some extent tantric in character: their most sacred text is the Diamond Sutra. Third, the *Jodo* and *Shin* sects, which are Amidist: their Buddhism is devotional, based on the Amitayus Sutra, and they hope for salvation in the 'True Pure Land', the paradise of the former Buddha Amitabha. Fourth, the sects of *Tendai* and *Nichiren*, which are also devotional but whose path to salvation lies through the veneration of the Sakyamuni Buddha (Gautama) and the chanting of the Lotus Sutra. It is the fourth group which has been most active politically. One of its offshoots is the *Soka Gakkai* sect which honours especially the founder of the Nichiren sect. That movement claims about three million adherents, and as a political party has a number of representatives in the Japanese Diet.

In China, Buddhism was virtually eclipsed by the Communist take-over in 1949, but it had seen something of a revival in the first three decades after the first Revolution of 1911.[10] Shortly after the overthrow of the monarchy there was a debate on the question whether Buddhism should become the new State Religion, and although the idea was rejected the debate itself helped to produce increasing interest in the religion. During the 1920s, when many Chinese were becoming disillusioned with the Western superiority which they had formerly taken for granted, there grew up a Buddhist educational movement, leading to the foundation of a Chinese Buddhist Society in 1929. Seven years later it had nearly five hundred branches. The revival spread to the overseas Chinese communities in South East Asia, and in 1933 the Lotus Society was founded in Singapore, the forerunner of the Singapore Buddhist Federation created in 1950. In the Nanyang the trend was not halted by the Communist take-over as it was on the mainland, and in Singapore especially it continued to progress during the 1950s and 1960s.

After the second world war the gulf between Theravada and Mahayana Buddhism (the Lesser and the Greater Vehicles) began to be bridged. The World Fellowship of Buddhists, created in 1950, held its first congress in Ceylon and its second in Tokyo. However it is still necessary to make the distinction between the two Vehicles, and to remember that despite some interaction their twentieth-century revivals were separate movements. The most important difference between the two kinds of Buddhism has always been that of diversity of belief and organization. Theravada Buddhism has a tendency towards orthodoxy (albeit not always fulfilled) which finds expression in the *Sangha* organization, whereas the Buddhism of the Greater Vehicle is much more diverse and its characteristic institution is the sect. Thus in Thai Buddhism there are only two Buddhist orders, not widely different in belief: whereas Japan has a much larger number of sects, each with its own distinctive beliefs and practices. It is important to appreciate that Viet-Nam belongs (apart from its minority of Cambodians and a small number of Vietnamese who have imitated them) to the Mahayana tradition; and it is a mistake to suppose that its religious revival in recent decades has amounted to the introduction of Theravada Buddhism.

As in so many other respects, Viet-Nam was influenced by

China in its Buddhist revival; it was also deeply influenced by Japan. Vietnamese Buddhism began to follow the example set in these neighbouring countries when, during the years 1929–34, Buddhist Associations were created in various parts of the country, notably Saigon, Tra-Vinh, Huê and Hanoi.[11] Some of the associations were made up of monks (*tang-gia*), others of laymen who lived with their families but enjoyed a special religious status (*cu-si*). As time went on, some associations flourished, others declined. But in these early days none of them aspired to become anything like a nation-wide *Sangha*, and none of them acquired political prominence.

Twentieth-century Buddhism in Viet-Nam is almost entirely devotional, and of the four Japanese groups noticed above it is the third and fourth which have direct parallels in Saigon and Huê: the Amidists and the Lotus school.[12] The distinction between them is less sharply drawn here than in Japan, but it is possible nevertheless to identify certain pagodas as practising predominantly one or the other doctrine. The Lotus school is particularly strong in Central Viet-Nam. Zen Buddhism, which once existed in Viet-Nam, seems to have died out; as for the Buddhism of the Diamond Sutra, it is possibly still practised, but its pagodas are less prominent in national life than those of the Amidist and Lotus schools. One of the most important literary contributions to the Buddhist revival was an article written in 1932 by Trân Van Giap, a member of the École Française d'Extrême-Orient, on the development of Buddhism in Viet-Nam from the sixth to the thirteenth centuries.[12] That period was indeed the 'Golden Age' of Vietnamese Buddhism, to which present-day monks and *cu-si* look back for inspiration. (It was also, the reader will recall, the period of Viet-Nam's first emergence as an independent kingdom, and it saw some of the greatest victories of Vietnamese heroes over Chinese armies.) From the fifteenth century, as Confucianism became more formalized, Buddhism declined in importance as far as the court was concerned, with the result that less was said about it in the chronicles. But it would be a mistake to suppose that the religion declined to the point of virtual disappearance between then and the twentieth century. The revival of the 1930s was not entirely without roots in the past, even though it was to a remarkable extent a movement of the towns.

The history of Buddhism during the Japanese occupation of Viet-Nam (1942–45) is still unwritten. The Japanese presence may well have strengthened the revival, but any gains it may have made then were lost in the chaos that followed the Japanese defeat. It was not until 1948 that the Buddhist Associations began to recover from the conflicts of the post-war years. But by 1951 they were able to go further than they had ever gone before: at a Congress in Huê they succeeded in creating a single Buddhist organization for all three regions of the country, and declared their affiliation to the World Fellowship of Buddhists. The creation of that Fellowship in the previous year was no doubt one of the sources of inspiration for the Vietnamese Buddhists. But the emergence of the new organization at a time when the Communists were said to be infiltrating most organized movements in the country has led to doubts in some minds about the relationship between the *Viêt-Minh* and the Buddhist National Congress at Huê. The doubts still persisted in the early 1960s when the Buddhist campaigns against Ngô Dinh Diêm and his successors were under way.

Whatever may be the truth on that question, there can be no doubt that during those campaigns a certain section of Vietnamese Buddhists revealed a militancy that was partly religious and partly nationalistic. These were the Buddhists who organized street demonstrations, and burned themselves alive in order to emphasize their demands or their opposition to the government. Their activities are to some extent comparable to those of the Japanese *Soka Gakkai*, and on closer examination it turns out that they were in fact Buddhists of the Lotus school, rather than Amidists. Their greatest strength lay in Central Viet-Nam, and it is interesting that almost all the monks who burned themselves in the summer and autumn of 1963 were natives of that region, including Thich Quang Duc. Unlike the Caodaists and the *Hoa-Hao* Buddhists, the Lotus school concentrated their activities in the towns; they did not try to raise rebellion in the countryside. Nor did they—by contrast with the Amidists—succeed in winning much support for their activities in the Cochinchinese Delta. In 1963 they succeeded in making an alliance with the Amidists of the South, but it did not last long after the fall of Diêm.

The militant Buddhists became, for a time, an important factor in the political situation. But in their opposition to the war of the 1960s, and in their criticism of the governments in Saigon whose policy was to pursue the war, they did not enunciate any particular programme for political development. They did not put forward any set of ideas that was comprehensively and distinctively Buddhist. Perhaps one must conclude that Buddhism is such an essentially personal religion, concerned with the inner life of the individual rather than with the external life of society, that no such programme is possible. It is a basis for civilized moral values, for the virtue of the monk and the *cu-si*; but not for institutional reform. If so, then it is futile to look to Buddhism as such to provide a new political framework for the development of the nation.

A third major group in the Vietnamese religious revival were the Catholics: although their beliefs derive originally from the West, they have become the foundation of religious life for over two million Vietnamese. (Of the 2,290,000 Catholics in Viet-Nam in 1966, as many as 830,000 were still living in the North.) The first converts to Christianity in Viet-Nam were made by Jesuit missionaries in the first half of the seventeenth century who, having discovered that the country was a fertile field for their efforts, put into it much of the energy which in other circumstances might have gone into Japan. Later on, the place of the Jesuits was taken by the priests of the Société des Missions Etrangères, whose headquarters was in Paris. By 1682 there were said to be 200,000 Vietnamese Christians; and despite persecution the Church in Viet-Nam managed to survive at about that strength until the nineteenth century. Under French rule of course the missionaries were able to operate far more securely, and it was at that period that the greatest number of conversions was made.[13]

To the Vietnamese Confucian rulers the Catholics appeared as no more and no less than a new kind of sect, which had to be kept under some kind of control or it would become politically dangerous. Nor was that view wholly unjustified, if we consider Bishop Pigneau de Behaine's role in the politics of Cochinchina between 1785 and his death in 1799; or Father Marchand's participation in the rebellion of Saigon in 1833–35. But in their own minds of course the Catholics were very much more than a Taoist sect. Their more sophisticated organization certainly set them apart from other religious groups; so too, and on a more fundamental level, did their absolutist conception of the world as divided into Christians, who enjoy grace, and pagans or infidels who do not.

Politically this absolutist view has the importance that it has made the Catholics rigorous opponents of Communism in all forms, on grounds of doctrine and not merely of comfort. The fact that over 800,000 Catholics remain in the Communist-controlled North Viet-Nam suggests that they do not easily give way in such matters. The presence of twice that number in South Viet-Nam is even more important as a factor in the continuing struggle against Communism south of the seventeenth parallel. But when it comes to the question of positive political ideals, it may well be asked whether in the long run the Catholics have as a Church contributed any more to Viet-Nam's modernization than other religious groups. The most essential feature of Catholic political theory is that power should be divided between Church and State, because the authority on which these institutions are based has been divided by God. Under French rule it was possible, at least for the missionaries and for pro-French priests, to enjoy some form of recognition of spiritual authority, and to live in the hope that one day Viet-Nam would be completely converted to their faith. But in the context of an independent Viet-Nam such a position is less easily maintained. For a while, during the war years of 1946–54, it was possible for some Catholic clergy to hold out against the *Viêt-Minh* and at the same time to be virtually independent of the French. Thus the Bishop of Phat-Diêm, Lê Huu Tu, was able for a time to defend his bishopric on a basis not unlike that of the Caodaists at Tây-Ninh. But such circumstances could not last for ever, and in the end he had to flee to Saigon. The Catholics in an independent Viet-Nam are bound to face up to the fact that they are a minority of the population, and therefore cannot impose an absolutist doctrine of divine authority. The most they can hope for is toleration.

To sum up therefore, one can say that although the Vietnamese religious revival has had a considerable impact on politics, the character of the religions concerned—Caodaism, *Hoa-Hao* Buddhism, Amidist and Lotus School Buddhism, and Catholicism —has not been such as to lead to the growth of any new political theory out of the religious revival. And what Viet-Nam needed to replace its old Confucian orthodoxy was a political theory. Nor has any single one of the religions succeeded in uniting the whole country behind its own faith. In this respect religion has played a very different role in the modern development of Viet-Nam from that which it played in certain other Asian countries, notably those of the Islamic world. In that, perhaps Viet-Nam has been fortunate: for its sufferings in the twentieth century have not included communal violence between religious groups. Although some journalists tended to characterize the movement against Ngô Dinh Diêm as a struggle between Buddhists and Catholics, it was in fact much more complicated. Viet-Nam has never (since the persecutions of the reign of Minh-Mang) seen religious violence comparable to that which occurred, for example, in British India at the time of partition.

VI

Constitutionalism

BETWEEN Viet-Nam and China there was a long-standing cultural affinity which makes it natural to compare the ideas and institutions of the two countries, both traditionally and in the modern world. But when in the nineteenth century Viet-Nam became the one country of the Chinese cultural world to be conquered and actually ruled by Europeans, their experiences began to some extent to diverge. Viet-Nam came to have something in common with other areas of Asia which she did not share with China, for example with British India.

India is the most striking example of an Asian country which borrowed ideas from its conquerors in order to overthrow them, and in so doing achieved a fusion of Eastern and Western thought. Having been brought under British rule by stages during the century and more before 1857, India had a much fuller experience of Western culture than China, and a longer period in which to work out a *rapprochement* between its own tradition and that of the West. Viet-Nam's period of European rule was much shorter, but its relationship with France was similar in kind to that of India with Britain, and the French had if anything a deeper cultural impact on most of their colonies than did the British. A comparison between India and Indochina during the colonial period might therefore be expected to contribute towards our understanding of the modern development of Viet-Nam.

The political solution to their problems which the Indians adopted had as its pivot the conception of government by constitional means, It might conveniently be termed, though the word was one more likely to be used in French than in British possessions, constitutionalism. In the latter part of the nineteenth century constitutional government was widely regarded as an integral factor in Western success throughout the world. In countries like Japan and Russia those people who demanded the

86

modernization of government and law usually evisaged a constitution as a necessary part of the process. Japan formulated a
constitution in 1890, which worked successfully until the rise
of military power after 1930. The Chinese too looked upon the
idea as one which they would adopt as soon as a reforming or
revolutionary regime could be installed: Liang Ch'i-chao, an
admirer of England, and Sun Yat-sen, who was more impressed
by France and the United States, both agreed on this.

But newly created constitutions were not always successful in
practice. In Russia the parliamentary system that was hesita-
tingly set up in 1905 proved too fragile a plant to survive. In
China, after the overthrow of the monarchy in 1911 a constitution
was inaugurated but was never allowed to become the effective
focus of government and legislation. Power passed to the generals,
who refused to accept rule by an elected assembly or a civilian
president. It is the more remarkable therefore that in India
constitutionalism took deep root. The National Congress, which
was already holding its first meetings in the decade that saw
the French conquest of Annam and Tongking, was a movement imbued with respect for English principles and conduct.
Even when its objectives became more extreme, including
total independence for India, it did not abandon completely
the principles of the rule of law and of representative government
which had been learnt from the British. After 1920 it preferred
non-violent passive resistance to action entirely within the
law, but even in that there survived something of Gandhi's
early respect for the British idea of fair-play. When independence
was finally obtained, albeit in a climate of religious tension,
the constitution adopted by the Republic of India reproduced
the essential features of British parliamentary democracy.

Turning to Viet-Nam, one is led to wonder why French
colonial rule there did not produce results similar to those of
British rule in India. Why should Viet-Nam, despite its experience of colonial domination, have remained much more like
China than India? Why was it that when the country eventually
achieved independence in 1954, it came only after a long and
bitter conflict in which constitutionalism was virtually squeezed
out by the extremes of colonialism and revolution? Part of the
answer lies in the nature of French policy; but we must also give
some attention to the actual development of a constitutional

movement in Viet-Nam, which most writers on Vietnamese history in the twentieth century have tended to ignore.[1]

French colonial policy has to be seen in terms of the intellectual debate about the merits of 'assimilation' and 'association' which developed during the 1880s and which was still not really settled when France lost control of Indochina. It must be seen too in terms of the problems (and administrative inertia) involved in the actual running of a colonial territory. As far as Viet-Nam was concerned, complete assimilation was never a practical possibility. As early as 1885 Paul Bert was proposing an administrative policy which, in its frank use of village traditions, would amount to a kind of 'association'. Bert died before he had been governor in Tongking for as long as a year, but his ideas survived him and became the basis of a more systematic theory of association. By 1900 writers like Chailley-Bert (son-in-law of the former governor) and Joseph Harmand were advocating a colonial policy based on the association of rulers and ruled in an enterprise which would be to the advantage of both.[2] This new theory owed something to the growing French admiration for British and Dutch colonial methods; and in particular to their practice of 'indirect rule'. It recognized, too, that in a country like Viet-Nam the people were not mere savages before French conquest, but had a culture of their own which they might wish to keep. Thus the assimilationist idea that the natives should be transformed into Frenchmen with the maximum possible speed gave way, in the minds of the associationists, to a greater respect for native institutions and traditions.

The new philosophy fitted in well with the growing concern amongst both colonial officials and politicians at home, that the colonies should be made to pay their way. In 1884 Jules Ferry had justified his policies in Tongking and elsewhere by the argument that 'for all the great nations of modern Europe, once their industrial power is formed, there is posed the immense and formidable problem: the question of the market . . . all the great industrial nations came in turn to the colonial policy'.[3] By 1900 the debate on whether colonies ought to be acquired or not had given way to one about how they could best be exploited, or their 'mise en valeur'. The original economic aims of colonization, which were commercial more than anything else, were supplemented by the additional desire to make colonies profitable in themselves by investing capital there. It was in this context that the associationists looked forward optimistically to a future in which the colonies would develop economically, on the basis of Western capital and native labour, both sides benefiting from the result. Cultural assimilation, and the 'civilizing of the natives', began to seem less important than the reaping of economic gain. The most important problem to which the new attitude gave rise did not become apparent until a rather later period (after about 1917), when the Vietnamese themselves began to ask whether association had any political implications.

'Assimilation' and 'association' did not coincide with any precise division of thought amongst the Vietnamese themselves. One might think, on first acquaintance with the two theories, that the colonized people would themselves prefer association. But in practice the latter theory had a variety of different interpretations. Sometimes it was thoroughly conservative in its implications: Lyautey for example, one of the most famous associationists, was at heart a monarchist who believed in using traditional institutions as a means to better control over colonial peoples. In Viet-Nam such an approach meant the preservation intact of the Confucian system and all its traditions; and indeed to a remarkable extent this is what actually happened under the Résidents-Généraux in Tongking and Annam (especially Annam). But as we have seen, the more progressive Vietnamese politicians by the first decade of the twentieth century were dissatisfied with traditional Confucianism. They wanted either to modernize the monarchy, or to do away with it altogether.

It was the interpretation placed on 'association' by later, more progressive Governors-General (notably Albert Sarraut and Alexandre Varenne) that had some appeal for the Vietnamese elite. Sarraut and Varenne both alarmed the comfortable colons of Saigon and Hanoi by making speeches which raised the hopes of the more 'moderate' Vietnamese nationalists. (The quotation at the beginning of Part II is from one such speech by Varenne.) They dared to think in terms of political as well as of economic association. Their kind of association did not emphasize the value of traditional institutions: it concentrated on the development of education and economic growth. Sarraut, for example, founded the University of Hanoi in 1917—about the same time as he abolished the imperial examination system that had been allowed to survive in Annam and Tongking. Ironically, he promoted in the name of association a new phase of cultural assimilation. But he envisaged eventual Vietnamese independence; the assimilationists had never admitted the remotest possibility of an independent, or even 'associated', Vietnamese nation. The new theory of association both opened up that possibility and enabled moderate Vietnamese to regard a spirit of nationalism as not wholly incompatible with a Franco-Vietnamese cultural *rapprochement*.

Constitutionalism in Viet-Nam had two principal roots. One was this new concept of association, as interpreted by Sarraut and Varenne from about 1917 onwards. The other was the movement for constitutional monarchy which had grown up during the first decade of the twentieth century, under the influence of Liang Ch'i-ch'ao and his admiration for Japan.[4] As a Vietnamese movement, one may date the beginning of this early constitutionalism from the secret conference held by a group of younger scholars in the province of Quang-Nam in 1904. Among those present were two of the most famous of all Vietnamese nationalists, both of whom belonged to roughly the same generation as Liang Ch'i-ch'ao: Phan Bôi Châu, a native of Nghe-An province in northern Annam; and Phan Châu Trinh, whose home was in Quang-Nam. Phan Bôi Châu was later to desert the cause of constitutional monarchy, under the influence of Sun Yat-sen's programme for revolution. Phan Châu Trinh was more firmly constitutionalist, and more willing to learn from the French. His letter of 1908 to the Governor-General of Indochina marks the beginning of Vietnamese hopes that they might improve their lot by simply demanding reforms from the French.

The outcome of the meeting of 1904 was the creation of a new political society, the *Duy-Tân Hôi* ('Reform Association'), whose object was an independent Viet-Nam and a reformed monarchy. To that end the association selected as its 'pretender' to the throne a prince who claimed descent from the emperor Gia-Long (through the eldest son who had predeceased that monarch). The prince, Cuong-Dê, was smuggled out to Japan, and remained an exile until his death in 1951. The reformers appear to have had some part in almost all of the anti-French activities of the years 1904–8, which was the period when the colonial rulers first had to deal with opposition of a 'modern' kind. Three of these movements deserve mention.

The movement known as the *Dông-Kinh Nghia-Thuc*, which was centred mainly on Hanoi but had the support of people from Annam and Cochinchina, was educational in purpose being organized to help young students to escape from the country and go to Japan. The French were able to put a stop to this by an agreement with the Japanese authorities in 1909. In the meantime, the colonial authorities launched a university of their own in Hanoi but closed it down within a year owing to student unrest. Secondly, at about the same period there was a group in Cochinchina led by Gilbert Trân Thanh Chiêu (a French citizen) which planned to develop a textile industry in the area; possibly it was influenced by the Indian *Swadeshi* movement. It sought French assistance to this end, but without any success, and in 1908 the authorities in Saigon suppressed the group on the grounds that it was using its industrial venture as a cover for political opposition. In 1908 too, there arose a peasant movement in Central Viet-Nam (especially in the province of Quang-Nam) against high taxation and heavy corvée labour. It involved little violence, and fairly soon subsided; but it seems to have had the support of the *Duy-Tân* association, even if it was not actually promoted by it. This was the first major peasant demonstration against the French in which specific grievances were raised in the hope of persuading the French to modify their policies. Neither Châu nor Trinh appreciated at this stage the wider possibilities of such a peasant movement, which were later to be exploited by the Communists. The reformers of this time were in fact groping in the dark, trying to find a way of opposing their colonial masters without bringing down upon themselves the kind of military suppression which had been used to quell the risings of Phan Dinh Phung and others in the period immediately after the conquest.

The trouble of 1908 did in fact lead to oppression. One leader, Trân Quy Cap, was executed immediately. Phan Châu Trinh himself was arrested and sentenced to life imprisonment on Poulo Condore; however in 1911 he was released and exiled to France, where he continued his campaign to win over French leaders to a more constructive policy in Indochina. Phan Bôi Châu escaped to Japan, and subsequently became a disciple of

Sun Yat-sen. The *Duy-Tân Hôi* however made one further attempt to impose its ideas on the French, in 1916. It launched a plan to abduct the young emperor—whose title was, somewhat surprisingly, Duy-Tân—and to raise a revolt in the provinces of Quang-Nam and Quang-Ngai. The emperor was in fact spirited away from his palace one night, but the French discovered him in a nearby temple two days later, before the revolt could begin. Duy-Tân himself was exiled to the island of Réunion, and the rebel leader Trân Cao Van was executed. That was virtually the end of the Reform Association, though there continued to exist in Quang-Nam a group of people ready to look to Japan as a model: it was their political heirs who twenty-five years later formed the pro-Japanese *Dai-Viêt* party in Central Viet-Nam.

The most important constitutionalist party which Viet-Nam produced under French rule, which was constitutionalist in its methods as well as in its aims, was that founded in Cochinchina about 1917. Its origins are to be found in the movement for French education known as the Société d'Enseignement Mutuel, originally created by Frenchmen before 1900. By the second decade of the twentieth century that society had a great many French-educated Vietnamese members, especially in Cochinchina, and there was a considerable sense of camaraderie amongst Cochinchinese who had attended the Collège Chasseloup-Laubat in Saigon. In 1917 a group of them formed the Parti Constitutionaliste and established a newspaper, *La Tribune Indigène*.[5] They were able to act somewhat more openly than political groups in Annam and Tongking, since some of them were French citizens and it was permissible for a Frenchman to publish a political newspaper in the French language. Besides their interest in education, they had two principal motives. One was to persuade the French to grant more freedom to Vietnamese in the colony; the other to create an *esprit de corps* amongst the Vietnamese themselves in the hope of reducing the hold which the overseas Chinese had over the Cochinchinese economy. Their first venture into organized activity was in fact economic, not political: an attempted boycott of the Chinese in 1919. It was not very successful, but it enabled the organizers to gain valuable political experience.

The most important individual in this group was Bui Quang Chiêu, a native of Bên-Tre province, who had been born in the same year as Liang Ch'i-ch'ao (1873). He received a French education, and then went to Paris to study agronomy—an aim which, incidentally, Sun Yat-sen expressed at about the same time but was never allowed to fulfil. On his return in 1897 Chiêu entered the government service of Indochina and for thirty years or so devoted his working life to the promotion of sericulture. At the age of forty he was a recognized expert on his subject, and by the time he retired he was a deputy director of the agricultural services for the whole of Indochina. But he was not content merely to serve in a colony where only a tiny minority of his compatriots were allowed the kind of opportunity which he himself had had. He was a founder member of the Parti Constitutionaliste, and within a few years he emerged as its leader, along with Nguyên Phan Long. His political philosophy, and that of the party generally, is indicated by the articles which appeared in the *Tribune Indigène* between 1917 and 1924, and in its successor the *Tribune Indochinoise* after 1926. A summary of the Constitutionalists' demands written towards the end of 1924 concentrated on four points: educational expansion, including the creation of a real university at Hanoi; reform of the judiciary, and the appointment of native *juges de paix*; changes in the naturalization laws, to enable more people to acquire French citizenship; and the creation of a really representative council or parliament based on a wide franchise. Ironically, all but the last of these points could have been put forward by a French idealist who really believed in assimilation. But it was the last point which counted, for what Chiêu wanted in the end was a Viet-Nam run on modern lines by Vietnamese.

The fact about the Constitutionalist Party which most distinguishes it from all other groups in Viet-Nam at this (and later) periods is its emphasis on representative institutions. The French as we have seen, were slow to introduce their own constitutional principles into the government of their colonies, and many educated Vietnamese learnt of the virtues of democracy from the writings of Rousseau and Montesquieu long before they had any chance of voting in an election themselves. Nevertheless the French did make some attempt to introduce representational institutions in Viet-Nam, though they never allowed them any genuine legislative power. Advisory councils at the provincial level, elected on a narrow franchise, were created in Cochinchina in 1889 and in the other regions in 1913. Municipal councils were also established, again with limited electorates, in Saigon and Hanoi. But only in Cochinchina was there an elected council for a whole region of the Union. When it was created in 1880 the Conseil Colonial of Cochinchina had ten French members and six Vietnamese, and the latter were elected by a mere few hundred people. Thanks partly to the efforts of the Constitutionalists the number of Vietnamese members was increased to ten in 1922 and the native electorate allowed to expand from a mere 1,500 to over 20,000. But this was still a small number of voters in a population of six million, and not surprisingly Chiêu and his colleagues saw it as merely a small step in the right direction.[6]

It was the Conseil Colonial which gave the Constitutionalists of Cochinchina their opportunity to learn about representative opposition. Nguyên Phan Long became vice-president of the council in 1922 and used his position to press for a genuinely 'Franco-Annamite' approach to policy. In November and December of the following year he led a campaign against the proposal of the French to create a virtual monopoly over the port of Saigon and to grant it to a French concern. The campaign failed; only seven of the ten Vietnamese members voted against it, and even if all of them had done so they would not have amounted to a majority for there were now fourteen French members. Even so, the Constitutionalists succeeded in rallying a good deal of opinion in Saigon behind their cause, and they began to see more clearly the possibilities for organized protest against the government. In 1926 they reached the height of their influence. In the early months of that year, Chiêu visited France and publicized the ideas and demands of his party there. Then in October, at the elections for the Conseil Colonial, the list of candidates of the Parti Constitutionaliste swept the board. It was at this stage that Chiêu himself was elected to the Conseil, and immediately he became vice-president.

Their success did not last however. Had the French at this point decided that by encouraging the Constitutionalists they would stave off the rise of a more extreme opposition, had they chosen to grant Cochinchina some kind of constitution, it is just possible that Chiêu could have gone on to build up a party comparable to the Indian Congress Party, smaller in scale but capable of uniting into a single movement the majority of the colony's moderate politicians. But the French saw no danger of extremism at this period, and showed no inclination to give even a small amount of real responsibility for decisions to the elected councillors. Moreover they refused to allow the Constitutionalist movement to spread to the other regions: in the summer of 1926 Pham Quynh proposed the formation of a Constitutionalist Party in Tongking, but the Governor-General was not willing to grant it the legal recognition which Chiêu's party by now enjoyed in Cochinchina. Nor were any steps taken to introduce the principle of election into the advisory councils of Tongking and Annam. Unaware of the historical significance of the moment, the French allowed an opportunity to slip by which would never return.

Frustrated by its lack of real progress, the Constitutionalist party began to break up. By 1930 it had split into about three factions, and although between them they still controlled most of the native seats in the Conseil Colonial, they had lost much of their buoyancy of a few years before. In the colony at large they had to watch the political initiative pass to more extreme leaders, forerunners or allies of the Communists. 1930 was the year in which Cochinchina once again experienced the upheaval of a rural revolt based on secret societies. It seemed to a great many young Vietnamese that to spread propaganda and discontent in the villages was the only way to get what they wanted. True, in the 1930s there were Marxists like Ta Thu Thâu, who would gain election to the municipal council of Saigon and stand in elections for the Conseil Colonial. But never again would a single party enjoy the confidence or the electoral cohesion achieved by the Constitutionalists in 1926. Bui Quang Chiêu himself, moreover, was drawn away from his homeland for most of the period between 1933 and 1941, in order to serve as Vietnamese representative at the Ministry of Colonies in Paris. By the time he returned home, to a country about to be occupied by Japanese forces, the time for a constitutional movement had passed. In that very year, 1941, the *Viêt-Minh* front was established by a small band of Communists in the Chinese province of Kwangsi.

The Parti Constitutionaliste differed from other Vietnamese political groups in this period (except possibly the Communists) in being remarkably cosmopolitan. It was not merely that the

French education on which they placed so much emphasis opened up for them a vast new range of cultural experience. They were also conscious of belonging to a generation in which the whole of Asia seemed to be waking up. Whilst many of their fellow Vietnamese had their eyes exclusively on China and Japan, the Constitutionalists also looked towards India, and were greatly impressed by the example of Gandhi and Rabindranath Tagore. In 1929, Bui Quang Chiêu and his friend Duong Van Giao visited India and made a pilgrimage to Tagore's experimental school at Santiniketan. Later the same year, they persuaded Tagore to call briefly at Saigon during one of his Far Eastern tours. In his speech of welcome on that occasion, Chiêu expressed an idealism which he felt that he and his followers shared with their visitor:

> Far from being hostile to the civilization of the West, our illustrious guest from Santiniketan wishes with all the vigour of a poet to reconcile the civilizations of East and West, in order to bring to the world the beauty and goodness which they can generate together.[7]

The Cochinchinese leader was perhaps ready to embrace in his own philosophy a larger element of occidental civilization than were Gandhi and Tagore, and his main source of western values was France rather than England; but he believed his spirit to be the same as theirs.

The reconciliation of civilizations was a function of education, and one of the most persistent demands of the Constitutionalists was for the expansion of schools by the French. In their eyes one of Sarraut's most valuable contributions to Vietnamese development was his creation of the University of Hanoi in 1917, followed a little later by the final abolition of the traditional system of imperial examinations at Huê. But the standards of the new university were never so high as those of French metropolitan universities, and the Constitutionalists would not rest content until there was a proper higher educational system established in Cochinchina. Even more urgently they called for the expansion of primary and technical education. Something was done, but not enough. Impatiently, in the 1920s both Bui Quang Chiêu and Nguyên Phan Long founded their own private schools in Saigon during the 1920s. Meanwhile in Tongking a comparable movement for educational expansion was started by Pham Quynh.

Unfortunately, despite their claim to be 'civilizing' Asia, the French were too afraid of the political consequences of education to embark upon a thoroughgoing expansion of schools and colleges. Most unfortunate of all was their failure to educate the rural population, which tended to produce a cultural gulf (even within family groups) between the French-educated elite of Saigon and the people of the villages. A similar gulf existed of course in India; but in Viet-Nam, as in China, its consequences were much more serious because there the cities had never dominated the countryside to the extent they did in India and other parts of Asia. The most educated Vietnamese were therefore bound sooner or later to loose their leadership of the rest of society, unless they themselves could succeed in educating it before it was too late.

The generation of Asians which included Rabindranath Tagore, Liang Ch'i-chao and Sun Yat-sen, and also Bui Quang Chiêu and Phan Châu Trinh, brought about what some have called an Asian Renaissance. A more appropriate term might perhaps be an 'Asian Enlightenment'. It combined recognition of the power of reason with the desire for human progress, in much the same way as had the Enlightenment of eighteenth-century Europe, and in so doing it generated a comparable optimism and sense of universal values. But if the European Enlightenment was doomed to the disillusionment of revolutionary violence in the decades after 1789, the Asian Enlightenment likewise ended all too often not in the triumph of intellect but in the violence and bloodshed of civil war. In Viet-Nam the tragedy was especially great, and the war exceptionally long and bitter. It destroyed, for a generation at least, the possibility that an enlightened elite would lead the country smoothly to independence and further progress. The fate of Bui Quang Chiêu is a symbol of the tragedy, for he was a personal victim of its violence: in late September 1945, he was taken from his home by the Communists and killed.

Revolution

'IF the colonials are obstinate in refusing to the Annamites elementary liberties, the latter will not be able to disown the violence of the masses and the action of the *émigrés*.' The warning was given in 1925 by a young Cochinchinese, Nguyên An Ninh, who a few years earlier had joined the increasing number of Vietnamese students in Paris, and had then returned home to plunge into nationalist politics (such as they were) in Saigon.[1] It appeared towards the end of a pamphlet in which he expressed hopes for Franco-Annamite understanding and co-operation, setting forth many of the same demands as the Parti Constitutionaliste.

But Ninh was nearly thirty years younger than Bui Quang Chiêu, and considerably less patient in his attitude towards the French. Born in the province of Cho-Lon about 1900, he came of a family which had supported the reform movement of 1907–8 and he had inherited his father's distrust of the colonial regime. In Europe he became even more acutely aware of the contrast between the standards of liberty and equality which the French upheld in their own country, and their disregard of such standards in Indochina. If the 'principles of eighty-nine' were valid in Paris or Marseilles, then why not in Saigon? He returned home imbued with the ideals of socialism and liberty, but very quickly reached the conclusion that the French would never make any real concessions to the Cochinchinese subjects unless they were forced to do so. Late in 1926, or possibly earlier, Nguyên An Ninh began to form a sort of secret society, calling it the 'Hope of Youth' party; he recruited to it people in the countryside as well as in Saigon, and as was inevitable sooner or later, it attracted the attention of the Sûreté. Quite what he intended to do with the party at this stage never became clear, for in the latter part of 1928 he was arrested and imprisoned for several years. His followers, as we shall see, were taken over by the Communists;

and he himself by the time of his release from prison sometime before 1936 was converted to Communism in some form. In that year we find him acting in association with the Trotskyist group of Ta Thu Thâu which ran the newspaper *La Lutte*. But in 1937, after his attempt to create a new secret movement and to organize an All-Indochina Congress (which would have been a left-wing front rather than a copy of the Indian Congress), he was once more imprisoned by the French. He died on the island of Poulo Condore in 1943.

This was a career typical of the more impatient members of his generation: a generation, moreover, which included several of the present leaders of the Democratic Republic of Viet-Nam. It was in the mid-1920s that such people began to turn away from constitutional and Franco-Annamite ideas, and towards the concept of revolution. Some, like Nguyên An Ninh, looked to French history and the revolutionary tradition of their colonial rulers. Others, probably the majority, looked towards China where in 1925 the *Kuo-Min-Tang* and the Communists began what amounted to a second revolution, centred upon Canton. In this they were following the lead of an older man, Phan Bôi Châu, who had begun to think of revolution about 1907 when he first came into contact with Sun Yat-sen.

Phan Bôi Châu had himself tried to imitate the methods of Sun Yat-sen's early career: terrorism in the towns and subversion in the army. Sun's importance in Vietnamese eyes was no doubt increased by his brief sojourn in Indochina in 1907–8, between his expulsion from Japan and his deportation by the French to Singapore; for during that time he launched at least two attacks into Yunnan and Kwangsi from the territory of Tongking. About the same time, as the more moderate Vietnamese nationalists were organizing the movement to encourage students to go to Japan, Phan Bôi Châu began to plot an armed rebellion of his own in Tongking. The success of the first Chinese revolution in 1911 gave him added confidence, and in the following year (at Canton) he founded the *Viêt-Nam Phuc-Quôc Hôi* ('Viet-Nam Association to Restore the Nation' sometimes called the 'Vietnamese Independence Association'). It flourished for several years, finding recruits in Tongking and Annam as well as amongst Vietnamese communities in Kwangsi, Yunnan and Siam. But Phan Bôi Châu does not appear to have succeeded in creating a network of rural secret societies such as grew up in Cochinchina at about the same time (1913–16). He persuaded the veteran leader Hoang Hoa Tham to set up a remote stronghold in upper Tongking, which held out until Tham himself was killed in 1913. But beyond that the activities of the Association did not go far beyond the throwing of bombs from time to time in Hanoi and other urban centres, and the plotting of some kind of mutiny in the army. When the latter finally occurred at Thai-Nguyên in 1917, it was quickly suppressed.[2] For the next eight years or so after that event, the Association did hardly anything.

Nevertheless its principal achievement was to create a link between Vietnamese nationalism and Sun Yat-sen, which was to prove of the greatest importance in the 1920s. By the time of his death early in 1925 Sun had been converted to the Leninist conception of how a revolutionary party should be organized. It was in the wake of the Soviet mission to Canton, led by Michael Borodin, that there arrived on the scene late in 1924 the Viet-namese Marxist Nguyên Ai Quôc. Whilst Borodin was directing the revolution of the *Kuo-Min-Tang*-Communist alliance, his Vietnamese colleague was left to create a comparable revolutionary machine in Indochina.

'Nguyên the Patriot', at this time a man of about thirty, was a native of the same province as Phan Bôi Châu: Nghê-An (in North Annam).[3] The son of a minor official who had retired about the time of the 1908 revolt, he had been educated first in Chinese characters and the Classics, and then sent to Huê to study French. Before the age of twenty he had gone to sea as a deck-hand, and after a period of wandering had settled in Paris. During the first world war he became a prominent figure in the Paris community of Vietnamese students and political exiles, and there is a story that in 1916 he and Phan Châu Trinh were imprisoned in the Santé at a time when the French government feared attempts by Germany to aid a Vietnamese rebellion. It was at this time that he took the pen-name 'Ai Quôc' by which he was best known until he adopted that of Hô Chi Minh in 1942. He became an ardent socialist as well as a nationalist, and in December 1920 he was amongst the founders of the French Communist Party at the Congress of Tours. Unlike Nguyên An Ninh, however, he showed no inclination to return to Viet-Nam to start a revolutionary movement amongst the peasantry:

he probably accepted the orthodox Marxist position at this time, that the revolution must depend on the proletariat. And in the context of the world as a whole there seemed more likelihood that the Soviet Revolution would spread to France than that there would be a real revolution in Viet-Nam. Yet he cannot have been wholly blind to the importance of the peasantry, for in 1923 he went to Moscow as a delegate to the first congress of the Peasant International. And from there he went on to Canton. His task now was to spread the Communist movement to Viet-Nam, and by the middle of 1925 he had organized the *Viêt-Nam Cach-Mang Thanh-Niên Hôi* (usually known by the abbreviated name of *Thanh-Niên*, the 'Viet-Nam Revolutionary Youth Association'). Recruiting first a number of younger followers of Phan Bôi Châu, it gradually spread its net wider, and by 1929 it was reckoned that the Association had about a thousand sympathizers or members in Indochina itself, of whom a fifth had made the journey to Canton in order to be trained at the Whampoa academy in revolutionary and military tactics.

The problem which Sun Yat-sen had found difficult, that of effective organization, was one which also faced the Vietnamese revolutionary groups. The Vietnamese had first to organize an opposition movement that would be capable of bringing them to power. Secrecy was essential, and it is hardly surprising that they adopted the traditional secret society and its sworn brotherhood as their first method of organization. For whereas the French would tolerate Constitutionalists, at least in Cochinchina, they were determined to root out the advocates of revolution by all means at their disposal including the secret police. The swearing of oaths was to some extent a guarantee of loyalty in such circumstances, though it was not invariably effective and the Sûreté often knew a great deal about what was going on. One of the most valuable things the Vietnamese revolutionaries acquired from the Soviet example was the cell-system which enabled a secret party to function without all the members knowing one anothers' identity.

The need for secrecy blended with an important element in the traditional Vietnamese character: inherent caution and a preference for inaction. In 1909 the Governor-General of Indochina summed up the Vietnamese personality as he had observed it:

> The Annamite is of an observant and prudent disposition; he conceals and dissimulates his impressions; he knows how to wait; his temperament does not make him act except after careful deliberation; which is to say that he never excites himself without a motive, and that any demonstration of opinion of a serious nature is always the fruit of long and silent preparation.[4]

Often the caution was so great that action never followed preparation at all. One is reminded of the Vietnamese would-be terrorist who in 1912 went all the way from Kwangsi to Nam-Dinh, with a bomb which he planned to throw at the Governor-General at a feast to honour laureates of the examination, and then failed to throw it and took it all the way back to Kwangsi. Such caution accounted for the natural reluctance of revolutionaries to confide in one another, and was an additional factor tending to make revolutionary associations small societies rather than (at this stage) mass parties. A small group could never on its own hope to achieve a country-wide revolution. Federations and alliances of small associations were essential, and they were often formed at moments when the tide of revolution seemed to be rising to its height. When times were hard, disagreements would develop and the alliances would break up, although the differences were very often not so deep as to prevent any further collaboration at a later date. Being small moreover political associations tended to be limited geographically, drawing most of their members from a particular region or province. This did not mean that in any one region there would be only one society: before it could dominate even a single province, a group had to compete with its rivals and somehow eliminate them. But it meant that if there was to be an effective revolution there would have to be not only co-operation between small groups, but also co-ordination between regions.

When it was founded in 1925 therefore, the *Thanh-Niên Hôi* was just one amongst many organizations, and there was no inexorable logic which would ensure its eventual domination of the scene: no reason why it, rather than the party of Nguyên An Ninh for example, should lead the Vietnamese revolution. It owed its eventual success partly to the organizational methods it learnt from Moscow, but very largely to the skill and ingenuity of Nguyên Ai Quôc. Its first problem was to get some sort of footing in Viet-Nam itself, and then to expand so that it covered all regions of the country. Its method was either to make alliances with existing groups or to undermine them by absorbing their membership. Often it would do both. The method is somewhat reminiscent of the 'take-over bid' in the competition between rival firms in Western countries.

Insight into how the method worked on the ground is provided by the story of the relationship between the *Thanh-Niên* Association and the *Cach-Mang Dang* between 1926 and 1929, as it was subsequently told to the Sûreté by a former member of the latter organization.[5] The *Cach-Mang Dang* ('Revolutionary Party') had been founded in 1925 by a group of former adherents of the *Phuc-Quôc* movement, and its principal centre of strength lay in Nghê-An and the neighbouring province of Ha-Tinh. In time it established branches in Thanh-Hoa and at Huê, as well as at Hanoi, and it entered into an alliance with a party called the *Tân-Viêt Dang* in southern Annam. Its programme was republican and revolutionary, but not Marxist. Because of its strength in the home province of Nguyên Ai Quôc (and of other founders of the *Thanh-Niên*) it was a natural target for a 'take-over bid' by the latter association. In fact it was the *Cach-Mang Dang* which made the first move, in 1926, by sending some of its own members to Canton to open relations with the new organization there. They became converts to the *Thanh-Niên* cause, and when they returned home they suggested to their former leaders an alliance between the two parties. In the next two years a series of conferences between representatives of the two sides was held, but no agreement was possible because the leaders of the *Cach-Mang Dang* refused to virtually submerge their own party in the other, and to accept the discipline of the leaders in Canton. But as time went on the ground was cut from under their feet, one after another their followers being secretly lured away by the *Thanh-Niên Hôi*. By the middle of 1928 the *Cach-Mang Dang* had lost almost all its members in northern Annam, and the remnant moved to Huê where the society was reorganized as the *Tân-Viêt Cach-Mang Dang* under the leadership of Dao Duy Anh. The first round had gone to the Communists, but the society still had a body of members in southern Annam. But the rivalry continued, and when the

Tân-Viêt leaders were arrested in July 1929 the *Thanh-Niên* seized its opportunity to make further gains. By the end of 1929 they were the most important movement in Central Viet-Nam, although they probably did not have complete discipline over all their new members.

Characteristically however the *Thanh-Niên* Association itself split into two rival branches at a congress in Hong Kong in May 1929, on the issue whether to adopt an overtly Communist title and programme. The two sides were in competition with one another for the rest of the year, and the breach was not healed until February 1930, when Nguyên Ai Quôc (who had had to leave Canton in 1927) was called on to return and created a unified Indonchina Communist Party. It is from that time that the present *Lao-Dông* Party in Hanoi dates its foundation.

In Cochinchina and Tongking the Communists were less immediately successful, though they had established cells in Hanoi, Haiphong and Saigon by 1928. In Chochinchina, real progress probably began for them with the imprisonment of Nguyên An Ninh towards the end of 1928, for the Communists seem to have won over many of his followers, or at least made an effective alliance with them. It was probably a little later that they also began to win a following in the area round Cao-Lanh on the Mekong. But large areas of the South were not affected by Communism at this period. Many areas of Cochinchina remained under the influence of various branches of Caodaism, whilst many village notables who might elsewhere have been won over to revolution continued to support the Constitutionalists.

In Tongking, the most important political party down to 1930 was one whose programme and methods were closest of all to those of Sun Yat-sen and the early *Kuo-Min-Tang*. It called itself the *Quôc-Dân Dang* ('National People's Party'), and its main links with the Chinese seem to have been through Kwangsi or Yunnan. Founded in 1927, it followed Chiang Kai-shek's example of refusing to co-operate with the Communists, so that although the *Thanh-Niên* may have infiltrated its membership there was no question of a merger. Its members were mainly officials, school-teachers and soldiers, and its main strength seems to have been in the country to the north and east of Hanoi. But there is little evidence that it sought a large peasant membership, or tried to mobilize the countryside against the French. Its

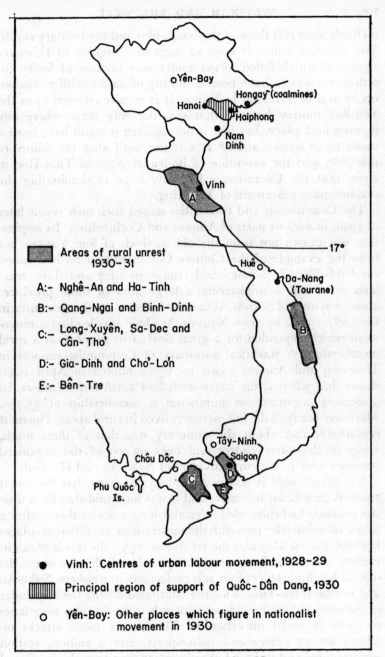

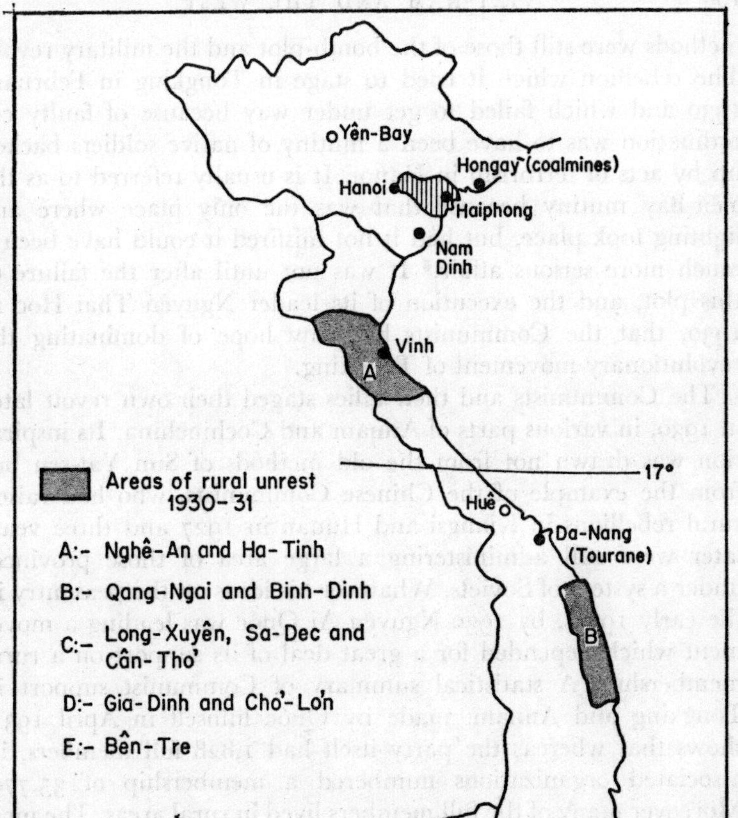
Yên-Bay
Hongay (coalmines)
Hanoi
Haiphong
Nam Dinh
Vinh
A
17°
Huê
Da-Nang (Tourane)
B
Tây-Ninh
Saigon
Châu Dôc
C
D
E
Phu Quôc Is.
Areas of rural unrest 1930-31
A:- Nghê-An and Ha-Tinh
B:- Qang-Ngai and Binh-Dinh
C:- Long-Xuyên, Sa-Dec and Cân-Thơ
D:- Gia-Dinh and Chơ-Lơn
E:- Bên-Tre
Vinh: Centres of urban labour movement, 1928-29
Principal region of support of Quôc-Dân Dang, 1930
Yên-Bay: Other places which figure in nationalist movement in 1930
Map II: Political Unrest in Viet-Nam *c.* 1930

methods were still those of the bomb-plot and the military revolt. The rebellion which it tried to stage in Tongking in February 1930 and which failed to get under way because of faulty co-ordination was to have been a mutiny of native soldiers backed up by acts of terrorism in Hanoi. It is usually referred to as the Yên-Bay mutiny because that was the only place where any fighting took place, but had it not misfired it could have been a much more serious affair.[6] It was not until after the failure of this plot, and the execution of its leader Nguyên Thai Hoc in 1930, that the Communists had any hope of dominating the revolutionary movement of Tongking.

The Communists and their allies staged their own revolt later in 1930, in various parts of Annam and Cochinchina. Its inspiration was drawn not from the old methods of Sun Yat-sen but from the example of the Chinese Communists, who had raised rural rebellions in Kiangsi and Hunan in 1927 and three years later were still administering a large area of those provinces under a system of Soviets. Whatever his ideas on the peasantry in the early 1920s, by 1930 Nguyên Ai Quôc was leading a movement which depended for a great deal of its support on a rural membership. A statistical summary of Communist support in Tongking and Annam, made by Quôc himself in April 1931, shows that whereas the party itself had 1,828 full members, its associated organizations numbered a membership of 35,770. Moreover many of the full members lived in rural areas. The most remarkable fact about the summary was that of these totals, 1,332 of the party cadres and over 33,000 of the organized peasants were in the two provinces of Nghê-An and Ha-Tinh.[7]

Not surprisingly it was in those two provinces that the revolt reached its greatest intensity, and it was later said that for a time the peasants had succeeded in establishing a Soviet there. After a series of relatively peaceful demonstrations in different places between the 1st May and the 1st August 1930, the revolt began in earnest about the beginning of September with attacks on the official headquarters of four sub-prefectures in southern Nghê-An and northern Ha-Tinh. Violence continued during the remainder of the year, and the French used not only troops but also aeroplanes to quell repeated disturbances. There were more attacks on administrative offices and police-posts, and a railway station was occupied and sacked; but attempts to march on the provincial towns of Vinh and Ha-Tinh were halted by the police or troops before they could become serious threats. About the middle of December the situation calmed down, but further disturbances broke out the following March and lasted till August (1931). Meanwhile from November onwards there was trouble of a similar nature in Quang-Ngai, the province which seems to have been the original centre of the *Tân-Viêt Dang* (by 1930 an affiliate of the Communists), and also the only other province where Quôc's survey noted a substantial peasant association. The fact of organization appears to be the main reason why these three provinces rose whilst others remained quiet. The suggestion of a contemporary journalist that Thanh-Hoa, whose calm stood out in sharp contrast to the turbulence of Nghê-An, was quiet because its peasantry was materially better off would seem to be only a subsidiary factor in the explanation.

In Cochinchina too the trouble was probably greatest in the provinces where the Communists had found most recruits. In Long-Xuyen and Sa-Dec, on the Mekong, and in Cholon and Gia-Dinh provinces close to Saigon, the most serious trouble occurred between May and October 1930. It was directed initially against heavy taxation, but in many places it became more specifically Communist as time went on. In the province of Bên-Tre, where evidence of Communism was most conspicuous, the unrest reached its climax a little later, in February and March 1931. The lack of co-ordination in timing, between the different areas of Annam and Cochinchina, cannot however be adduced as evidence in itself that they were not all part of a single revolt. It is highly likely that there was a lack of co-ordination within the Communist movement itself, an inevitable consequence of the character of an organization consisting of many small groups strung together. Those who believe that the whole revolt was organized in detail from Hong Kong by Nguyên Ai Quôc find some support in the fact that it did not long outlast the arrest of the Communist leader in June 1931.

'The violence of the masses and the action of the *émigrés*' were complementary phenomena, and without a peasantry willing to be organized by leaders from outside there could have been no revolt. The French authorities never lost control of the situation, in that none of the threatened administrative centres was actually occupied by rebels. Nevertheless the persistence of the peasant organizations was remarkable, and from beginning to end the disturbed state of the country lasted for over a year. In this the Communist revolt was of a character very different from the Yên-Bay mutiny, and in the long run its implications were much more serious. Unlike Mao Tse-tung's followers in Hunan and Kiangsi the Vietnamese peasants were not organized as an army and were not particularly well armed. But their very endurance gave an indication of what might be possible if the whole rural population were mobilized on the side of an armed independence movement. The lesson was not lost on their leaders.

The regional limitation of the Communist-led rebellion of 1930-31 shows that despite its successes of the previous two or three years, the Indochina Communist Party was still not a truly nation-wide organization drawing support from all parts of Viet-Nam. It was not until 1945-46 that they were finally able to gain effective ascendancy within the revolutionary movement, and to control a front organization capable of uniting behind them a large enough section of the people to wage a successful war against the French. Even then they did not draw every nationalist group into their orbit, and as late as 1954 they still had not dominated the whole of southern Viet-Nam.

The difference in this respect between Cochinchina and the North and Centre of Viet-Nam deserves to be borne in mind in any assessment of the eventual division of the country into two halves. We have seen that administratively Cochinchina's experience of French rule differed considerably from that of the Protectorates of Annam and Tongking; and that in consequence French cultural influence was much deeper than elsewhere in Viet-Nam. Economically too there was a marked contrast between the areas: Cochinchina had enough land to export large quantities of rice, and the port of Cholon became a major centre of the trade. It attracted a large number of Chinese immigrants, and this affected the general character of Cochinchinese society. Secret sects and societies flourished to a much greater extent there than in the North, and out of them there eventually grew the new Cochinchinese sect-religions of Caodaism and *Hoa-Hao* Buddhism. The Communists thus had to contend in Cochinchina with both a more thoroughly French-educated elite (including Constitutionalists) and a number of religious movements which were not very receptive to atheistic Marxism.

But there was yet another reason for the weakness of Communism in the South, if by Communist we mean Stalinist: that is, the branch of the movement which gave its allegiance to the Third International in Moscow. Cochinchina was one of the two areas of Asia (the other was Ceylon) to produce a Trotskyist movement in the decade following Trotsky's expulsion from the Soviet Union. There were indeed two Trotskyist groups in Saigon in the 1930s: one led by Hô Huu Tuong, the other by Ta Thu Thâu (who before his departure for Paris in 1928 had been a teacher in the school run by Bui Quang Chiêu). In addition, it is probably fair to say that Nguyên An Ninh was at that period closer to the Communism of Trotsky than to that of Moscow. From 1933 to 1937 the Trotskyists and the Stalinists in Cochinchina (the latter led by Duong Bach Mai and Trân Van Giau) collaborated in a united front and in the production of a newspaper, *La Lutte*.[8] The influence of the Trotskyists steadily grew, and when the front broke up in 1937 it became clear that Ta Thu Thâu and his friends were by far the stronger component of the alliance. In the elections for the Conseil Colonial in 1937 the three Trotskyist candidates won their seats easily, in competition with both Constitutionalist and Stalinist opponents. It was the nearest any single organized group had come to dominating such an election since the success of the Constitutionalists in 1926. But with the coming of the second world war the Trotskyists, like the Stalinists, were subject to repression and the opportunity for further progress as a legal movement was lost. Nevertheless their presence and popularity severely restricted the growth of Stalinist Communism, and this had its effects in the years after 1945.

In order to understand how the alignments of the period between 1945 and 1954 developed, we must look very carefully at events during the years 1945 and 1946. The Japanese occupation of Indochina, which began in earnest in July 1941, was initially only a military occupation: responsibility for administration was left in the hands of Decoux, the French Governor. But in March 1945 the Japanese finally took full political control and established an 'independent' Vietnamese government under the leadership of the pro-Japanese Trân Trong Kim. It was supported

by a number of groups which had been willing to work with the
Japanese, including the *Dai-Viêt* party which had been created
in 1942.[9] But it proved too weak to survive the Japanese surrender
later in the year, and when the Japanese lost the war it collapsed.
It had been agreed at Potsdam that when the surrender took
place, Indochina would be occupied by Chinese (*Kuo-Min-Tang*)
forces in the north and by British troops in the south, the dividing
line being at the sixteenth parallel. But neither army was given
any political authority in Viet-Nam, and consequently the
Japanese surrender produced a political vacuum. It was this
which gave the *Viêt-Minh* Front its opportunity.

The *Viêt-Nam Dôc-Lâp Dông-Minh* ('Viet-Nam Independence
League', the full name of the *Viêt-Minh*) had been created after a
conference of the Indochinese Communist Party at a place called
Chin-si just over the border of Kwangsi, in May 1941.[10] Its
secretary was Nguyên Ai Quôc, who had been in Russia for much
of the time since 1933, and its membership was predominantly
Communist. But its programme was simply defined as the liberation of the people and the salvation of the nation. It aimed to
become a union of patriots, working ultimately towards 'new
democracy' under its own leadership, but hiding its real ideological nature until such time as independence had been won.
South China was not however at that time a hospitable place for
Communists, and the new movement could not expect a great
deal in the way of support from the *Kuo-Min-Tang* authorities
there. In fact, Nguyên Ai Quôc spent all of 1942 and the first
month of 1943 in a Chinese prison. Whilst he was there, in
October 1942, the Chinese strongman of Kwangsi (Chang Fa-
kwei) took the initiative towards creating his own league of
Vietnamese independence movements, the *Viêt-Nam Cach-Mang
Dông-Minh Hôi* ('Viet-Nam Revolutionary Alliance'). Although
the *Viêt-Minh* were allowed to participate in this alliance, the
predominant group within it was the *Quôc-Dân-Dang*: that is, the
branches of that party which had survived the suppression of
1930 by living in Yunnan and Kwangsi. The other principal
group which entered the alliance was the pro-Japanese *Phuc-Quôc*
movement, also a party of men who had long been in exile.
However, by a remarkable piece of diplomacy Nguyên Ai Quôc
managed to convince Chang Fa-kwei of his willingness to join in
this new organization, and was released from prison under the

name of Hô Chi Minh. He became the most influential man in the new movement, which because it included the *Quôc-Dan Dang* was given whole-hearted support by the Chinese. Between the winter of 1943 and the spring of 1945 he was able to use this position to establish for his *Viêt-Minh* followers a base-area in the province of Cao-Bang. When the Japanese surrender came, he was ready to act. On 13th August 1945 the *Viêt-Minh* formed a 'National Liberation Committee' and decided on the plan to seize power in Hanoi. By the 20th they were in control of Hanoi, and had become virtually a provisional government. On the 25th they secured the abdication of the Emperor Bao-Dai. And on the 2nd September Hô Chi Minh read the 'Declaration of Independence of the Democratic Republic of Viet-Nam' in Hanoi.

The sense of independence was general, throughout the country. But Communist power was by no means so universal. Viet-Nam was not the kind of country in which a coup in Hanoi could confer on a government or party immediate control over the whole nation. If the *Viêt-Minh* was eventually to gain political control over the newly independent republic, it had to work very hard to make itself the dominant party in every region and every province. It began by eliminating potential constitutional leaders: Bui Quang Chiêu, Pham Quynh, Ngô Dinh Khôi (elder brother of Diêm) and Ta Thu Thâu were all murdered by the Communists within a month or so of the 'August Revolution'. But the other revolutionary groups could not be so summarily dealt with; nor could the Cochinchinese sects.

In the first half of September Allied forces occupied key points in Viet-Nam as previously arranged: the Chinese in Hanoi, the British in Saigon. This gave the Communists yet another factor to contend with, for they knew well enough that both the occupying forces were vigorously anti-Communist and would not acquiesce in the creation of a Marxist-Leninist government in either of their occupation zones. In the South the occupation was to prove an insuperable obstacle, for when fighting broke out in Saigon towards the end of September the British rearmed the French troops in order to restore order. By early October the British were co-operating fully with the French in an operation which led to the latter recovering control over the greater part of Cochinchina by the end of the year.

In the North on the other hand Hô Chi Minh was able to play a clever game of bluff with the Chinese general Lu Han, by pretending to co-operate with the *Quôc-Dân Dang*. In November he dissolved the Communist party altogether (that is, as an open organization), and the following month he agreed that seventy out of the 350 seats in the forthcoming elections for a national assembly should be reserved for the nationalists. By so doing, he was able to persuade the Chinese to allow the elections to be held in January 1946, and so to add to the *Viêt-Minh* dominated provisonal government an elected assembly in which the *Viêt-Minh* had a majority. Also during this period, the provisional government had to organize famine relief to cope with the consequences of the loss of most of the Tongking harvest of 1945. It was only in February 1946 that Hô Chi Minh was brought face to face with the problem against which these tactics proved unworkable: the government in Chungking made an agreement to hand back the northern half of Viet-Nam to France, in return for the termination of French extra-territorial privileges in China itself. In March, the *Viêt-Minh* had to accept a compromise with the French. A long series of negotiations continued, which eventually produced a supposedly more lasting compromise. But by the end of 1946 Hô Chi Minh was convinced that only war would give Viet-Nam real independence under a *Viêt-Minh* government, and after a serious clash in Hanoi on the 19th December the provisional government withdrew from the capital and began its protracted 'resistance' struggle. In the meantime, for much of that year Vo Nguyên Giap led *Viêt-Minh* forces in a campaign to eliminate the *Quôc-Dân Dang*, whose protection had been the presence of Chinese troops and which was left in a weak state when they withdrew. The *Quôc-Dân Dang* had allies, in the *Dai-Viêt* and other non-Communist revolutionary parties, but it was unable to stand up to the Communist attack. If one thinks back to the situation of 1925–9, one can perhaps see in the conflict of twenty years later the same kind of 'take-over bid' as before, but on a larger scale and with arms.

In the events of 1945–6 one can identify something like the 'Vietnamese Revolution'. Its effect was to kill the possibility of a smooth evolution towards constitutional independence such as occurred in India. But beyond that, its outcome was still not predictable at the end of 1945. The Communist Party played a very prominent role in the events of that year, but its eventual domination of the situation was by no means a foregone conclusion. It was only with the French decision to reimpose some kind of colonial rule on its former possession that the pattern of conflict began to crystallize into that with which we are familiar today.

VIII

War and Partition

WAR and Communism have shaped the pattern of Vietnamese history since 1945: the first was indeed the opportunity of the second. If the French had not decided after the Pacific War to recover control of their former colony by force, it is by no means certain that the Communists would have emerged as the strongest contender for power in an independent Viet-Nam. It was only the war of 1946–54 that enabled them to establish their hold on the North, and part of the Centre, of Viet-Nam; and only with the renewal of the war after 1958 that they became a powerful force in the South.

The fragmentation of nationalism during its formative years made some kind of internal conflict inevitable after 1940. But down to that time none of the movements in opposition to the French was in possession of anything like a regular army, not even the Communists. It is instructive to compare the situation of the Vietnamese Communists at this date with that of the Chinese Communist party. Mao Tse-tung's followers had begun to arm themselves as early as 1927, and had preserved a considerable measure of their armed strength by means of the Long March of 1934–5. During the years that followed, Mao ensured that his party became thoroughly militarized and educated them in the theory of 'guerrilla strategy', which was used to great effect against the Japanese invaders. Moreover, during the decade after the Long March the Chinese Communists were virtual rulers of an extensive Border Region with its capital at Yenan. By 1946 therefore they were well prepared to sweep across China and to drive out the *Kuo-Min-Tang* army by sheer force.

The Vietnamese Communists were very far from being able to imitate such victories in the years before 1946. At the time of the Long March most of their leaders were in prison or in exile, and it was only a French amnesty that enabled some of them to revive the party network in the late 1930s, and then to escape to Kwangsi when the colonial government again clamped down in 1940. It is true that by the beginning of 1947 both Hô Chi Minh and Truong Chinh (secretary-general of the Communist Party) were publishing articles on guerrilla strategy, but neither of them had the experience of a Mao or a Chu Teh behind him. Both were much better at politics than at war. By that time too (indeed as early as 1944) the chief military leader of the Vietnamese Communists, Vo Nguyên Giap, had established a 'base-area' in the province of Cao-Bang: but it was hardly comparable to the Yenan Border Region.

At the start of the war against the French the Communists were not even powerful enough to fight under their own banner. At most Party membership was around twenty thousand; possibly less. They therefore needed a patriotic front organization. Having formed the Viet-Minh in 1941, which was itself not openly Communist, they created an even wider front movement in May 1946: the *Liên-Viêt Quôc-Dân Hôi* ('United Vietnamese National Association'). The Indochinese Communist Party was even formally dissolved in 1945, and it was not until 1951 that its leaders felt strong enough to bring it formally back to life, from its clandestine existence, under the name of *Dang Lao-Dông* ('Party of the Workers'). In the interval the Communist ambitions of the *Viêt-Minh* leaders were carefully concealed behind patriotic slogans. (Which is not, of course, to deny that the Communists were to a very large extent patriots themselves, who espoused Communism as a tool of nationalism: the argument that one cannot be both nationalist and Communist is surely no longer tenable, for being a nationalist does not preclude a man from participating in an international movement.)

Under cover of these front organizations, the Communists made it impossible for any rival nationalist party to function in those areas where its own control was firm: in particular, Tongking and the northern provinces of Annam. By 1954 they had a firm grip on the rural population of those regions, and in some places had begun to consolidate it by means of the land reform campaign, to be described in a later chapter. Their methods were by this time somewhat more brutal than those of the twenties, when the *Thanh-Niên* association had demonstrated its mastery of the 'take-over bid'. They had learnt the truth—if that is the word—

of the principle which Mao Tse-tung had enunciated in an oft-quoted statement of 1938:

> Political power grows out of the barrel of a gun. Our principle is that the Party commands the gun, and the gun will never be used to command the Party. But it is also true that with guns at our disposal we can really build up the Party organization. . . . We can also rear cadres and create school, cultural and mass movements. Everything in Yenan has been built by means of the gun.[1]

As the war progressed, the Vietnamese Communists used their own command of the gun to strengthen their party.

When the French embarked upon the reconquest of northern Viet-Nam in 1946 they had little conception of the kind of war they would have to fight there. Previously they had faced only the problem of keeping a civilian population under control; and though they had never been totally successful even in that, they had been strong enough to prevent emergencies like that of 1930–1 from getting seriously out of hand. But now they had a dual problem: to recover and maintain control of the population in the villages, and at the same time to defeat a 'rebel' army. Whilst that army was small at the beginning, it was using the methods it had learnt from Mao to become stronger every year. The initial advantage of the Communists over other opposition groups in the field was that they alone had a technique for fighting the only kind of war that was likely to succeed against the military superiority of the French. Whilst they owed it in large part to the Chinese example, they were able to apply it successfully to the somewhat different circumstances of Viet-Nam; and they made their own formulations of the method in such works as Truong Chinh's *The Resistance will Win* (1947) and Vo Nguyên Giap's *People's War, People's Army* (1959–60).[2]

The two ideas which stand out in those essays are that the war must be a 'protracted war' and that it must be a 'people's war'. Truong Chinh wrote that 'the guiding principle in the strategy of our whole resistence must be to prolong the war'. The crucial phases of the protracted conflict were those in which the emphasis was on guerrilla strategy and 'mobile' war. In neither of these phases was there any definable battle front: actions were to be fought by the *Viêt-Minh* only when they had a local superiority of strength and were certain of victory: at other times they would fade away rather than engage superior numbers. To the French professional soldier, for whom virtue consisted in fighting to the last man, this may have seemed a policy of cowardice; but it accords very well with the traditional Vietnamese belief in Fate, and the notion that likelihood of success should be the criterion for any decision between action or inaction. As for the overall strategy of the war, its prolongation meant wearing down the colonial power, rather than making a frontal assault on it. The late Professor Fall suggested that it was General Giap who first appreciated that in a very long war the French parliament (and the French taxpayer) would ultimately be one of the best allies of the *Viêt-Minh*. As things turned out, it was never necessary to make a frontal assault on Hanoi at all: the city was won through negotiations, brought about when the French finally acknowledged that Fate was not on their side, and gave way.

The principal objective of the Communists during the first two phases of the war was not to capture or defend territory, but to win over the rural population. It was in this sense that their strategy was one of 'people's war'. Truong Chinh found a phrase which appealed to the Vietnamese poetic imagination in the Maoist slogan: 'The people are the water, our armies the fish.' The reality was sometimes rather more harsh. In order to mobilize the people in support of the struggle, it was necessary to educate them to hate both the French and the 'pro-French' Vietnamese: it might sometimes also be necessary to make ordinary villagers fear the rebels more than they feared the government, and this accounts for the brutality of which the Communists were sometimes guilty. By whatever means, they succeeded in ensuring that large numbers of people withheld their co-operation from the colonial authorities and took the risks involved in supplying and protecting the *Viêt-Minh* army. Thus the French administrative machine was undermined so that whoever might have formal responsibility for a particular area, the real power lay with the *Viêt-Minh*.

This concentration upon winning over the mass of the people was fundamentally Marxist in character, though Marx had not foreshadowed the method. But in many other respects the kind of revolutionary warfare devised by Mao Tse-tung had roots which

were less ideological than cultural and historical. Dr Jerome
Ch'en has remarked how much of Mao's thought derived from
his study of Chinese history, and in particular of great rebellions
like that of the Tai-Ping. A similar element of historical inspiration was evident in the military thinking of the *Viêt-Minh*, whose
leaders looked to the example of Vietnamese heroes who defeated
Chinese armies in the past: Trân Hung Dao, Lê Loi, and the
Tây-Son emperor Quang-Trung.[3] On several occasions the
Chinese captured Hanoi but subsequently failed to control the
country as a whole in the face of guerrilla resistence. In this
respect Vietnamese experience contrasts strikingly with that of
other countries of the Indochinese Peninsula: in the wars between
Burma and Siam for example the fall of the capital city usually
meant the loss of the whole kingdom. Control of Hanoi was never
the key to control over Viet-Nam, as the French found to their
cost in the years after 1945.

Another military figure from the Vietnamese past whose
reputation and skill may have influenced the Communist
guerrillas was the seventeenth-century general Dao Duy Tu. It
was Tu's reorganization of the southern army, and his construction of the fortifications of Dông-Hoi, that saved the Nguyên
principality from annexation by the Trinh in the first of the wars
between the two 'states' about 1630.[4] Those fortifications are
situated in Quang-Binh province (Northern Annam), which was
the home of Vo Nguyên Giap: the twentieth-century general
therefore would be sure to know the story of their creator and his
campaigns. (The inspiration may be even more important for
Giap, since unlike many of the other *Viêt-Minh* leaders he was a
man of humble birth, and he may well have found encouragement
in the career of a great general who had once been debarred from
the civil examinations because his father was an actor.) The
whole story of the Nguyên survival in the wars of the seventeenth
century was a lesson for the Communist army, in that it was a
striking example of soldiers defending their homes proving more
effective in battle than an army fighting far from home in the
interests of 'feudalist' commanders.

The French army, also fighting far away from home, was
forced in the end to admit defeat. The colonial authorities found
themselves caught in a vicious circle: they could not re-establish
an effective rural administration unless they could defeat the

People's Army; but they could not win permanent military victory unless they had sufficient control over the countryside to prevent the peasantry from joining or supplying that army. The sad story of the French effort to escape from the closed circle has been ably chronicled by the late Professor Fall.[5] It was a story of repeated attempts to convert the war into a more conventional one, and to bring the *Viêt-Minh* forces to pitched battle. It ended in the bitter irony of Diên Biên Phu, where the one important set-piece battle was won by the Vietnamese. But it was not simply the loss of Diên Biên Phu that defeated the French, so much as the fact that their only method of dealing with the whole situation was one that required well-nigh inexhaustible supplies of men, materials and money. The French gave up because they could not afford to go on.

Their defeat was not however so overwhelming that they had to withdraw unconditionally. The *Viêt-Minh* was very strong in the North and in many parts of Central Viet-Nam. But in Cochin-china, and some parts of Annam, they had failed to eliminate all rival nationalist groups. In Cochinchina there were some provinces where the most powerful group was not the Communists (who were by this time the acknowledged leaders of the *Viêt-Minh*), but one of the politically active sects; and around Saigon the most powerful organization was the *Binh-Xuyên* secret society, which controlled both the police and the underworld of Saigon. The more openly the Communists revealed their rigid ideological approach to the future of Viet-Nam, the less chance they had of absorbing these groups; and in Cochinchina their command of the gun was not yet great enough to eliminate their rivals by force. This contrast between the North and the South of Viet-Nam was of the greatest importance in making possible the partition of the country at the seventeenth parallel.

Another factor making such a partition possible was the creation by the French of the Associated State of Viet-Nam in 1949, which was recognized as an independent state by the Western powers in 1951 (although its independence was very, very limited). In other circumstances, the creation of such a state might have been regarded as a major step forward to a genuinely associationist policy on the part of the French; as it

was, it came too late to rally all the nationalist leaders behind a
constitutionalist movement. Nevertheless, some Vietnamese
leaders (especially Cochinchinese) were willing to co-operate,
and Bao-Dai was persuaded to desert the *Viêt-Minh* and become
Head of the new state, on condition that in due course it would
become completely independent. The actual arrangement of the
partition of Viet-Nam was the work of the great powers at
Geneva. But without the existence of both a substantial non-
Communist element in the southern part of the country, and of
the beginnings of a non-Communist state framework, no decision
of the powers would have led to the kind of partition which in fact
occurred. In view of the fragmentation of Vietnamese nationalism
throughout the colonial period, the partition was not without a
certain logic.

To speak of partition at all is to risk serious distortion of what
actually happened in 1954. The events of that year did not bring
into existence two distinct states or nations by any straight-
forward agreement to that effect. Nothing that happened at
Geneva in the summer of 1954 affected the sovereignty of Viet-
Nam: at least, not intentionally. The substantive element in the
Geneva Agreement on Viet-Nam, that is the document signed by
the military representatives of the French High Command and
the *Viêt-Minh* Command, was purely military in scope. The
partition into two zones which it laid down was a purely military
one, as a means to enable the opposing armies to be re-grouped,
and no foundation of authority was accorded to either of the two
parties administering the respective zones. The only mention of
political arrangements was a reference to the elections which
would eventually decide on unification of the zones. As for the
(unsigned) 'Declaration' of the Geneva powers, made on the
day following the cease-fire, it too was at pains to insist that no
final political settlement had been made: 'the military demarca-
tion line is provisional and should not in any way be interpreted
as constituting a political or territorial boundary'.[6] The nearest
this Declaration came to any political pronouncement was in its
statement that:

> So far as Viet-Nam is concerned, the settlement of political
> problems, effected on the basis of respect for the principles of
> independence, unity and territorial integrity, shall permit the

Vietnamese people to enjoy the fundamental freedoms, guaranteed
by democratic institutions established as a result of free general
elections by secret ballot.

The elections, that is, which were to have been held by July 1956.

Whatever might be said to have been the 'real' intention of the
powers, the Geneva documents themselves include nothing that
any international lawyer could interpret as a transfer of sovereignty,
and certainly no statement that the sovereignty of Viet-Nam
should be partitioned. The independence of Viet-Nam is enshrined
in two other sets of documents, whose contents and effect are
totally incompatible with one another. According to the Communists, that independence derives from the events and declara-
tions of the 'August Revolution' of 1954: the abdication of Bao-
Dai in favour of the Democratic Republic, and the declaration of
independence which Hô Chi Minh read out in Hanoi on 2nd
September.[7] If these two documents are accepted as valid, then
everything the French did thereafter in relation to Viet-Nam was
illegal, because France was no longer the sovereign authority.

This interpretation can be challenged, and if one is to argue
that South Viet-Nam is in any sense a sovereign state, it must be
disproved. The only possible alternative interpretation depends
not on the Geneva Agreements but on the treaty signed in Paris
on 4th June 1954 between the government of France and a
representative of the Associated State of Viet-Nam.[8] This interpretation assumes that there was in fact no interruption of
French sovereignty between the signing of the treaties of 1883–5
and that of 1954, except for the granting of partial independence
to the Associate State by the Élysée Agreement of 1949. It
requires that one dismiss the events of August–September 1945 as
illegal; and also the agreement of March 1946 between the
Viêt-Minh and France on the grounds that it was invalidated by
the subsequent outbreak of hostilities. (Cochinchina had in any
case not been involved in the agreement of 1946, but had been
allowed a nebulous 'autonomy' between that year and 1949.)
It was on the basis of this second interpretation of the way Vietnamese independence came about that the Diêm regime refused
to accept that Viet-Nam had been permanently divided, and also
rejected the Geneva Declaration within a year of its being made.

Thus at the time when the Geneva Conference decided to

create two military zones in Viet-Nam, there already existed two governments, each claiming to be the sole sovereign authority in Viet-Nam. The real importance of the cease-fire agreement was that it created conditions in which both of them could continue to exist, one in Hanoi and the other in Saigon. The decision that elections should not be held for two years, moreover, gave both governments (even assuming they accepted the Declaration in full) a long breathing space in which to consolidate their hold on their respective zones. The decision to allow migration from one zone to the other within three hundred days of the cease-fire tended to reinforce this possibility. The fact that nearly a million non-Communists actually left Tongking for the South lent colour to the claim of the Saigon regime that it was the responsible government for all Vietnamese who were not actively Communist. Every day that passed from the time the fighting stopped would increase the likelihood that Viet-Nam would become virtually two states despite the insistence at Geneva on her theoretical unity. When July 1956 arrived, there were no elections.

PART THREE

The task is nothing less than to enrich the hopes and existence of more than a hundred million people. And there is much to be done. The vast Mekong River can provide food and water and power on a scale to dwarf even our own Tennessee Valley Authority. The wonders of modern medicine can be spread through villages where thousands die every year for lack of care. Schools can be established to train people in the skills that are needed to manage the process of development. And these objectives, and more, are within the reach of determined and co-operative effort.

President Lyndon B. Johnson,
April 1965.

IX

The Quest for Modernity

VIET-NAM in 1954 was very different from the country it had been, on the eve of French conquest, a hundred years before. When the French were defeated at Diên Biên Phu it seemed as if the wheel had turned full circle. France, despite her continued superiority in wealth and technology, had failed to recover control of territories which her armies had conquered with relative ease in the decades after 1860. The *Viêt-Minh*, without being able to equal French fire-power, appeared to have found a way of rendering the Western technical advantage of no account. Moreover their political philosophy was one which not only rejected the claims of Western civilization to be the highest point in human evolution, but asserted the counter-claim that by means of Marxist revolution an Asian country could actually supersede the West in the dialectical chain of historical development. In time, according to this same philosophy, Europe and America themselves would experience a comparable revolution—though that was not a matter of central concern for Vietnamese Marxists, whose primary interest was in the progress of their own country.

The French withdrawal in the face of such an enemy seemed like a permanent defeat for the West in Viet-Nam, as well as a disaster for those Vietnamese who still had faith in some form of Westernization. But precisely because there were such Vietnamese and because the United States at least was prepared to assist them, the Communist victory turned out to be incomplete. The Americans regarded Diên Biên Phu as a defeat for French colonialism, but not for Western civilization in general. They recognized that the success of the Vietnamese in defeating France owed much to one idea at least which Viet-Nam now shared with the West, that of the nation and its right to independence. They attributed the Communist nature of the victory to an accident of history which had given the leadership of the independence movement to the Communists; but now the struggle was over, they believed, a great many Vietnamese would reject Communist ideology and would prefer continuing friendship with the West. The fact that many Vietnamese did prefer it, combined with American willingness to help them, led to the attempt to create in South Viet-Nam an independent pro-Western state.

Thus in the years after 1954 the two halves of Viet-Nam were able to choose two very different roads towards modernization. The international repercussions of the ensuing conflict between the two 'states' have tended to obscure the fact that the real issue, for the Vietnamese themselves, is whether one of these roads to modernity should prevail over the other. The ideal of economic development set forth in such statements as President Johnson's Baltimore speech of 1965 is one shared by both sides.[1] The issue is how the ideal is to be attained: what kind of policies should be adopted, and how the economic system ought to be related to other aspects of Vietnamese social development. For the great powers the broader international issues are perhaps the most important: but since our primary concern in this essay is with Viet-Nam itself, let us for the moment take Communist and American idealism at their face value, and consider the social and economic implications of the alternative lines of development.

Before the French conquest the economy of Viet-Nam was, by comparison with that of the industrial countries of the West, under-developed. It was not however completely *un*-developed; nor was it totally isolated from the wider economy of East Asia whose most developed regions were in China and Japan. Viet-Nam was exporting both raw and manufactured silk to Japan for example, during the second half of the seventeenth century. We know this because for a while Dutch merchants participated in the trade, being the only Europeans at the time admitted to Japan.[2] The actual volume of Vietnamese exports at that period (or any other before the nineteenth century) cannot even be guessed, for the greater part of it was in the hands of Chinese merchants who have left no record of their activity. But the trade certainly had an impact on the Vietnamese economy, and by the mid-eighteenth century we find silver bars being used as currency where formerly only copper coins had been acceptable. Moreover the fact that the exports included manufactured silk indicates that this was more than merely commerce in primary products. In some provinces there was probably already a cottage textile industry.

Marxist historians writing in Hanoi in the 1950s have sought to identify something like a nascent capitalism in the economic developments of the Trinh-Nguyên period (the seventeenth and eighteenth centuries) and have even gone so far as to interpret the Tây-Son rebellion which brought that period to an end as a social revolution growing out of economic change. But in fact both Chinese and Vietnamese society were so different in character from the Western societies which produced the beginnings of industrial capitalism at a similar period, that it is misleading to describe anything in the East Asian countries before the nineteenth century by using the word capitalist. As far as Viet-Nam was concerned, industrial production must have been on a small scale, carried on by craftsmen working in cottages; the opportunities for profit, such as they were, lay not with the manufacturers but with the traders who were in most cases foreigners. The emperor taxed the trade, and his officials no doubt took their pickings, but this meant only an inflow of silver into those sections of society whose interest was in temples, wars and conspicuous consumption. Moreover, it was a section of society completely dominated by the imperial court. An Englishman who spent some time in Tongking in the later years of the seventeenth century, when both the English and the Dutch had factories at Hanoi, complained of the way in which the Vietnamese rulers oppressed the mercantile community. 'It is one of the policies of the Court', he observed, 'not to make the subjects rich.'[3] There were no Vietnamese independent of the Confucian hierarchy who ever had enough capital to invest in trade or industry on a large scale.

Even in China, where this was less true, nothing like an independent merchant class was able to establish itself and dominate the economy. There too the complete ascendancy of the Confucian court was never challenged by a 'bourgeoisie' in the literal sense of the word. At a time when European kings and princes were borrowing money from urban financiers—at interest —Chinese and Vietnamese monarchs were still in a position to demand what they wanted from their rich subjects, and to take it. Equally significant was the fact that money was never in itself a path to political advancement. Only landowners could enter the imperial examinations, or even buy their way to official titles, so that even the peasant who owned some land was nearer to the top of society than a merchant who had yet to purchase an estate.

Given the cultural and institutional framework of Viet-Nam on the eve of European conquest, which in spite of the Tay-Son 'revolution' was not greatly different from what it had been two centuries before, there was little chance of the country achieving any major economic development along new lines without the infusion of some new and challenging factor. It may be that eventually the mere pressure of population growth might have created such a challenge, without any foreign intrusion. But in actual fact, the Europeans arrived first, and they were the source of challenge. It was the French who took Viet-Nam its next step along the road of economic change.

Jules Ferry had justified the acquisition of colonies, before a reluctant public opinion, by arguing that they were an economic necessity. His successors were faced with the task of making them yield an actual economic gain, not necessarily to the government itself, but certainly to the French nation as a whole. In the early decades of the twentieth century the debate about forms of government gave way to a discussion of 'mise en valeur'. An important aspect of the work of Paul Doumer, as governor of Indochina from 1897 to 1902, was that he balanced the colonial budget and made the country a promising place for the investment of capital. He did not however solve the problem once and for all. His successors were less capable men than he in the financial field, and by 1910 there was once more an outcry in the French Assembly about the cost of administering colonies which ought to be able to pay their way. After the war of 1914–18 in Europe, Frenchmen had an even stronger motive for looking to the colonies to yield profits: the metropolitan economy needed every possible financial support for its own reconstruction.

Down to 1914, the principal results of the application of French capital in Indochina were in the fields of communications and mining.[4] Two small sections of railway were built in Cochinchina and in northern Tongking during the first years of the protectorate, but it was Doumer who inaugurated the first thoroughgoing programme of railway construction, with his plan for 1,700 kilometres of track. By 1914 the Yunnan and Kwangsi railways had been completed (including a large bridge over the Red

River named appropriately after Doumer himself), and long sections of the line that was to link Hanoi with Saigon were in operation. The system was further extended in the 1920s and 1930s, so that on the eve of the Pacific War Indochina had nearly 3,000 kilometres of railway. Meanwhile, the development of mining on a substantial scale had also begun in the early years of the twentieth century, with the opening up of new coal-mines in the Quang-Yên basin and the beginnings of zinc and tin extraction in northern Tongking.

In the two decades between the first and the second world wars, these lines of development continued. Mining and railways were further expanded; in addition, rubber production became an increasingly important element of the economy. Large areas of land to the north and east of Saigon were brought under this and other plantation crops, and the rise of the automobile industry in America and Europe created a rising demand for both rubber and tin.

These developments affected mainly the protectorates of Tongking and Annam, and the northern upland areas of Cochin-china. In the flat delta lands to the south of Saigon the most important change that took place under colonial rule was the expansion of the rice industry. The French undertook some important irrigation works which enabled an expansion of the cultivated area, and on the whole it was this rather than any major improvement of techniques that accounted for the growth in production. Most of the farmers and landowners were Vietnamese; but the opening up of the export market depended on the activity of Chinese immigrants to the area. Cholon became the focus of the trade, and it was the Chinese community there— and also the Indian money-lenders of Saigon—who took the lion's share of the profits.

Inevitably the general economic slump after 1929 was a setback to economic development, and it led many of the Chinese who had migrated to southern Indochina to return home. But the setback was only temporary. By the later 1930s the flow of trade, of capital, and also of Chinese, had resumed their previous levels. When Professor Charles Robequain published his study *L'Evolution Economique de l'Indochine Française* in 1939, he was able to record a long series of achievements over the previous six decades, and to express—as well as serious criticisms—a certain measure of optimism about the future of the country provided its immediate problems were overcome.

As Robequain well appreciated however, the French policy of 'mise en valeur' had not been designed to develop the Indochinese economy for its own sake. That indeed was his main criticism. The cultural idea of 'assimilation' had its economic counterpart in the doctrine of colonial protection and preference; and whilst the associationists had some success in revising 'assimilation' in the cultural and political fields, in economic matters it was usually the protectionist line that dominated policy. The first measure of French colonial preference was the act of 1892 which differentiated between French trade in Indochina and the trade of all other people there: the former being made free of the duties to be charged upon the latter. The policy reached new extremes in the 1930s with the result that by the time of the Pacific War France completely dominated trade with her Far Eastern possessions.

From the protectionist point of view it was equally important to limit colonial development to those fields which would complement production in the metropolitan country, and to prevent the growth of Indochinese industries that might eventually rival those of France itself. Apart from the establishment of textile factories at Nam-Dinh, the French did little to promote the modernization of manufacturing industries in Viet-Nam; they preferred to see the Vietnamese use manufactured goods imported from France. After 1930 they even allowed the traditional Vietnamese activities of sericulture and silk-spinning to decline. It was only with the coming of war, after 1941, that the rupture of sea transport between Indochina and France began to necessitate some improvement in the manufacturing capacity of the colony.[5] But even then the long-term interest of the Japanese, who for the time being replaced the French as the dominant power in relation to Viet-Nam, was to make Indochina part of their 'Co-Prosperity Sphere' not to industrialize it.

A further problem which troubled Robequain, and which the French had failed to approach from a Vietnamese point of view, was that of population. The density of population in Tongking and parts of Annam was already great by the end of the nineteenth century. By the 1930s there were districts where it was as high as 2,000 per square mile.[6] Yet in Cochinchina there was plenty

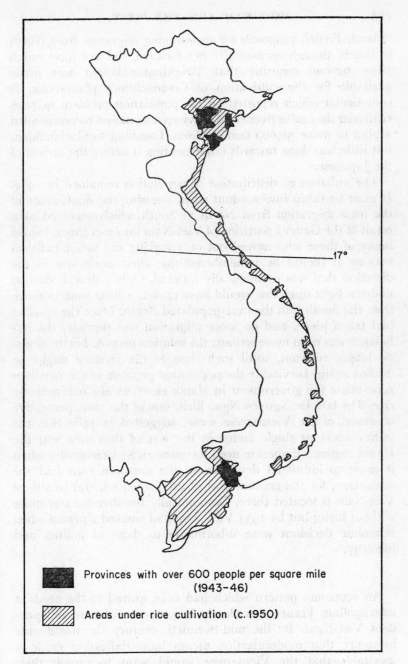

17°

Provinces with over 600 people per square mile
(1943–46)

Areas under rice cultivation (c. 1950)

Map III: Population Density and Rice Land in Viet-Nam *c.* 1950

of land. French proposals for encouraging migration from North to South, though occasionally put forward, did not have much effect beyond ensuring that Tongkingese labour was made available for the cultivation of Cochinchina's plantations. A commission which reported on the population problem in 1936 criticized the ineffectiveness of previous action, and recommended a plan to move 50,000 families from Tongking to Cochinchina. But little was done towards implementing it before the arrival of the Japanese.

The unbalanced distribution of population remained in 1954. It must be taken into account when assessing the significance of the mass migration from North to South which occurred as a result of the Geneva partition of Viet-Nam into two zones. Whilst many of those who moved out of Tongking did so for political reasons, it should be remembered that their move was in the direction that was economically rational. Only political idealists under a tight discipline would have chosen at that time to move from the South into the over-populated North. Once the division had taken place, and no more migration was possible, the imbalance was even more serious; the solution proposed in 1936 was no longer relevant, until such time as the country might be unified again. Inevitably the population problem of the northern zone made the government in Hanoi covetous of Cochinchinese rice. The late Dr Nguyên Ngoc Bich, one of the most perceptive observers of the Vietnamese scene, suggested in 1962 that the most important single factor in the war of that time was the Hanoi regime's desperate need for more rice.[7] Conversely, when it came to industrial development the northern zone had the advantage, for the greatest part of the known mineral wealth of Viet-Nam is located there. Economically the division was quite without logic; but by 1954 Viet-Nam had entered a period when economic decisions were subordinate to those of politics and ideology.

An economic pattern which had been geared to the needs of metropolitan France was clearly inappropriate for an independent Viet-Nam. By the mid-twentieth century the world-wide insistence that modernization means industrialization made it inevitable that the Vietnamese would want to exploit their industrial as well as their primary resources. This demanded a new approach, and possibly an element of planning. Where should they look for inspiration? To the West? To the Communist countries? Or to other areas of Asia, not Communist but not yet industrialized either? Even after they had rejected European rule, the Vietnamese were still faced with the old question: could they learn anything from the West, which would enable them to develop more rapidly or more successfully than if they turned their backs on their former masters? Once again there were opposing schools of thought, but this time the opposition became crystallized into a political conflict between two 'states'.

Both France, and to an even greater extent America, were already far along the road of industrialization when Viet-Nam became independent. To imitate them directly and immediately, to hope for a comparable achievement in a single generation, was out of the question. Moreover those countries had not only taken many generations to reach their existing level of investment and consumption; they had been able to do so without facing the contemporary Asian problem of a population growing faster than the rate of capital accumulation. The question arises, in relation to Viet-Nam and in relation to Asia generally, what does commitment to the 'Free World' (that is, to the West) imply when it comes to a model for economic modernization?

Professor Walt Rostow has paid special attention to this problem in his essay *The Stages of Economic Growth: a Non-Communist Manifesto*, published in 1959 a few years before he became prominent among Washington's 'hawks' as an advocate of the hard line policy in Viet-Nam. His approach, like that of Marx, combines the methods of history and of economic analysis; and his first concern is to trace the stages by which Western countries (and also Japan) reached their present level of industrial achievement. As far as most of Asia is concerned, the important parts of the essay are those relating to what he calls the 'take-off': the point at which an agrarian society embarks firmly on the road to becoming an industrial one. In seeking to identify the social and political conditions necessary for any society to reach that point, Professor Rostow emphasises especially the character of the social group in whose hands wealth is concentrated. What is necessary above all is for spending capacity to be 'shifted into the hands of those who will spend it on roads and railroads, schools and factories, rather than on country houses and servants, personal ornaments and temples'. Putting the same point in another way, he argues the need for a new elite: 'it is essential that the members of this new elite regard modernization as a possible task, serving some end they judge to be ethically good or otherwise advantageous.'[8]

But who is to constitute that elite in Asia? Within the definition offered, they might be colonial administrators like Doumer and Varenne: but in the post-colonial world that kind of elite is no longer appropriate. Another group which might answer to the definition is the revolutionary political party, with sufficient power over both economy and society to plan their development according to Marxist-Leninist doctrines. But the whole point of Professor Rostow's work is to argue that an elite of that sort is both socially harmful and economically unnecessary. He dismissed Communism as 'a disease of the transition'. Taking into account his desire for economic growth 'on a political and social basis which keeps open the possibilities of progressive, democratic development', one is tempted to suppose that in practice the elite he has most in mind is that body of men imbued with the Weberian 'spirit of capitalism' who brought Europe, and later America, to their own point of 'take-off'. But what are the implications for Asia if, as Weber suggested, that spirit was an essentially occidental phenomenon? It was only in the West that such an elite grew spontaneously out of the traditional framework of society.

Perhaps what Professor Rostow really means is that the best hope for Asian economic progress is through the creation of an elite which has been educated in Western ways, and is capable of implementing policies based on Western economic theory. Certainly American policy in South Viet-Nam would make no sense without the existence of such an elite. It is unfortunate that neither Professor Rostow nor any of the Western economists who fundamentally agree with him (though not necessarily with all the details of his economics) has so far made a thorough study of the cultural implications of his theory.

Even supposing that a thoroughly Westernized elite can survive in Viet-Nam, the question of sources of capital still has to be answered. To pretend that a transfer of income from traditional landlords to a Westernized middle class is all that is necessary for sudden economic growth would be utterly unrealistic, especially when it is assumed that everything must happen within a political system based on law and democracy. In a country like Viet-Nam the function of the elite, within the terms of Professor Rostow's theory, is not simply to invest the capital accumulated within the country, but also to spend large sums of money granted by the Western powers in economic aid. When he speaks of the challenge of creating a partnership, he is speaking of a challenge as much to the West as to Asians themselves. In a Marxist-Leninist framework, the emphasis is on capital accumulation; in a Rostovian framework the emphasis must be on aid. Without aid, there is no point in Viet-Nam turning to the West for economic inspiration. And aid means, sooner or later, tying the Vietnamese economy to those of the West, and in particular that of the United States. What the West has to offer is not an explicit model for growth, but merely a set of principles and a world market. Those who would dismiss this as inadequate should ponder on the history of Western development itself. In the growth of European industry, the movement of capital from one country to another was an integral part of the process: even Britian owed finance capital to the Netherlands in the eighteenth century. And America's own industrialization would hardly have come about without large scale capital investment from Europe. Americans are in effect inviting Asians to do what they have done themselves.

What is the alternative? In practice those Asians who reject Western aid find themselves turning in the end, if not in the beginning, to the models of Russia and China. For the Vietnamese to turn to China also lay in the logic of their history, though that need not mean that it was right for them to do so at this particular point in time. In fact the older generation of Vietnamese Communists learnt their Marxism from Russia or Europe, not from China. For many of them—despite the earlier translations of Adam Smith—contact with the writings of Marx and Lenin may well have been the first direct acquaintance with any theories about economic development. In Lenin's concept of imperialism moreover, they would find an economic view of the world which fitted in extremely well with their over-riding eagerness for independence.

By the time that the Vietnamese Communists began to gather

strength in the years after 1945, the leading thinkers of the world movement had already to a considerable extent disposed of the objection that the original theories of Marx did not apply to a pre-capitalist agrarian society. Whereas European Marxists have tended to emphasize the *effect* of new economic developments on political life, Communists in Asia have seized upon the interpretation of Marx (perhaps equally valid) that revolutions open the way to economic change. Their view is adequately summed up by Trân Van Giau in his introduction to the textbook on Vietnamese history which was prepared for use in the university of Hanoi:

> Only by passing through the class struggles of countless thousands of workers will it be possible to improve the old relationships of production, which have impeded the development of the forces of production a stage further.[9]

From this re-interpretation of Marx it is but a small step to the argument that a revolution in a predominantly agrarian society might in practice open the way directly to the creation of a socialist system of production. In a speech in the early 1960s for example, one of the leading theorists of the *Lao-Dông* party (its first-secretary, Lê Duân) proclaimed as much:

> The fundamental characteristic of the social revolution in our country is to advance towards socialism without going through the stage of capitalist development.[10]

There is an interesting resemblance between this objective and the ideas of Sun Yat-sen. Lê Duân's methods however were those which he had learnt from Chinese and Russian Communism. In that same speech he stressed the need for what he called socialist accumulation (of capital). Whilst admitting the value of 'the assistance of brother socialist countries,' he insisted— as have all Asian Marxist-Leninists—on the necessity of 'accumulation made in our own country'. This would inevitably mean sacrifices by the mass of the population. Though he paid lip-service to the need for a rising standard of living, Lê Duân spoke much more forcefully about the 'high sense of economy' that was required of the people. The real purpose of the speech was to justify the sacrifices implicit in the Communist method of economic growth: sacrifices based not on exhortation alone but also on discipline.

It was the methods of the Communists not their aims which antagonized the Western-educated elite of Viet-Nam. For these methods meant in practice the rejection of the West, as well as of traditional culture. In the long run it was impossible to divorce opposing views of economic development from much deeper questions concerning the whole development of society and its values. As it turned out, these deeper questions, and the political implications of opposing answers, came to occupy the forefront of men's thoughts. In comparing the development of the two halves of Viet-Nam in the period between 1954 and 1963, we must examine their political and social life as a whole.

X

Communism

THE division of Viet-Nam into two regions controlled by separate and conflicting governments was not without historical precedent. As we have seen, such a division occurred in the early seventeenth century and lasted for about a century and a half. But that earlier division was merely political. What was quite unprecedented in the situation created by the Geneva armistice was the existence of two competing governments opposed to one another on ideological as well as political grounds. A divided country in a world separated ideologically into 'two camps', Viet-Nam became one of the foci of international conflict. This most recent phase of its history will not be intelligible to us unless we inquire more closely into the significance for the country itself of ideological partition.

Ideology, as a factor in politics over-riding all others, is a product of the Western insistence on the elimination of contradiction in philosophy and on the establishment of absolute good in society. It first entered seriously into European politics at the time of the Reformation, when kings and princes went to war on issues of religion as well as in pursuit of power. It re-emerged, with greater intensity, during the period following the French Revolution. And it reached still greater heights in the many-sided conflicts that resulted from the Russian Revolution and the rise of German Nazism.

The quest for the absolute, either in philosophy or in politics, was quite alien to the Vietnamese tradition; so too, therefore, was the ideological basis of political conflict. The Confucian and Taoist philosophies, in contrast to Christianity, were pervaded by the notion that opposites not only can but must be reconciled: indeed that the continuation of the universe depends on the harmonious interplay of positive and negative forces. Even Mao Tse-tung, in his essay *On Contradiction*, begins by defining 'the law of contradiction' as the 'law of the unity of opposites in things'.[1] Tradition dies hard.

138

In so far as educated Vietnamese began, after 1859, to be influenced by French civilization they came into contact for the first time with the attitudes of mind that were capable of producing ideological conflict. Some were converted to Catholicism and accepted the authority of the Pope, in an age when papal infallibility was just beginning to be defined. Catholicism apart however it is probably fair to say that the first major intrusion of ideology into Vietnamese political life came after 1920, with the discovery of Marxism-Leninism. In Communism the Vietnamese—or rather a small number of them—found for the first time a coherent political philosophy which declared itself totally incompatible with the old orthodoxy of Confucianism. Hitherto the traditional philosophy of government had never been completely rejected in Viet-Nam except by foreigners. Even the Cochinchinese Constitutionalists, who rejected or ignored the monarchy, did not oppose the ethics of the Confucian system. Bui Quang Chiêu would probably have described himself as still a Confucian.

But Communism was opposed to tradition in all its forms. It dismissed all established ideas and institutions as belonging to past stages of historical development whose values were about to be superseded. Just as in France or England democracy was 'bourgeois', so in China and Viet-Nam Confucianism was 'feudal'. The advent of this new iconoclasm meant that it was no longer possible to hold that *all* ideas could ultimately be reconciled with one another. Confucianism had persecuted the sect religions only in so far as they were political; beyond that, it had let them be. But this new sect religion was nothing if not political. The Communists had only one aim: power, on their own terms.

For those who espoused the new theory of society, it provided a sense of meaning and of purpose which seemed to be denied to those who remained outside. Confucianism had proved itself politically ineffective against the French, whilst the Westerners had—it seemed to them—failed to give the Vietnamese any coherent set of values (other than the hated colonial system) by which to replace it. Vietnamese Marxists have not, any more than the Chinese or for that matter the Russians, taken over every statement of the Marxist canon and made it an axiom of belief. Much that Marx wrote, especially in his analysis of

capitalist societies, is irrelevant to Viet-Nam and is recognized by
the Vietnamese Communists to be so. The importance of Marxism
for them lies not in its details but in its spirit. What has appealed
to them most about Marx's writings is that aspect which is
summed up in his dictum (in the 'Theses on Feuerbach'): 'The
philosophers have only interpreted the world in various ways.
The point however is to change it.'[2] This was the antithesis of the
traditional belief in Fate. The Vietnamese word for revolution is
cach-mang, which literally means to 'change Fate'; but it can also
mean to overthrow it. What Marx provided in his science of
revolution was a positive alternative to the old acceptance of
Fate, at least on the level of political systems. Truong Chinh
once turned the whole philosophy of the *Kim Van Kiêu* on its
head by translating one of its lines to mean 'the will of man
triumphs over Fate'. The Communists still apparently enjoy
reading the sentimental story of Thuy Kiêu, but their formal
interpretation of it differs completely from that originally intended:
they see it primarily as a story of the tribulations suffered by a
young girl because of the cruelty of a 'feudalist' mandarin.

On a philosophical level Marxism has provided its adepts
with a set of beliefs and ideas which answer many of the questions
most puzzling to twentieth-century Vietnamese. That is part of
the reason for its success. But no philosophy can make much
headway without influencing institutions. The really important
factor in the rise of Communism in Viet-Nam as elsewhere has
been the disciplined organization of 'the Party'.

The Vietnamese Communist organization which was founded
in 1930 was in some respects very similar to the secret societies
which had led rebellions in the past, both against Confucian
emperors and against the French colonists. Its cell system and
its method of organizing the peasantry in associations separate
from the party itself, were factors which enabled it to operate
on a broader geographical basis than many earlier societies:
but in that, its organization was merely an elaboration of old
methods. What was new was the fact that long before it obtained
power the party had a political philosophy, on the basis of which
it intended to make sweeping changes in the system of administration and in society. No previous secret society that had success-

fully rebelled made radical changes in the framework of government and social relationships. But when the Communist party came to power, in North Viet-Nam, it was able not only to take the place of the Confucian hierarchy but to embark on a policy of social change.

The way in which the *Lao-Dông* party worked towards this social revolution, following its resurrection in 1951, is vividly revealed by the nature of the land reform campaign of 1953–6. The confiscation and redistribution of large estates had been an essential element in the Russian Revolution of 1917, and the preliminary to the eventual collectivization of land a decade or so later. In China too, land reform had been a part of Communist party policy since the 1920s, and as the Communist armies gained control of all China between 1947 and 1950, a thorough programme of land reform was inaugurated. By 1952 the stage of confiscation was virtually complete in China, and during that year there were experiments with the next stage, co-operativization. Thus by 1953 the Vietnamese had two major precedents within the Marxist-Leninist world for the reform they were about to begin.

They had precedents too, though it is difficult to know if they were conscious of them, in the policy of certain traditional governments in Viet-Nam: for on several occasions in the past there had been imperial decrees limiting the amount of land that could be owned by any subject who was not either a prince or a high official. The background to such a decree in 1711 is well-documented. A situation had arisen in which, as a result of bad harvests and high taxes, people were beginning to leave their own holdings and becoming tenants or labourers on large estates, as a result of which the government was losing its taxes. Reductions of tax had been announced on several occasions in order to entice them back to their homes, but then in 1711 it was ruled that no one could be allowed to create a large private estate. Some centuries earlier, in 1397, there had been a decree forbidding anyone outside the imperial clan to own more than 10 *mâu* of land (less than ten acres).[3] The original inspiration for such measures seems to go back to the land-equalization policies of T'ang China, and the notion of an ordered society in which every man had his fields. The Communists of course wanted to go much further than that, for they wished to abolish individual ownership altogether. But their first step was along the same lines as those traditional regimes: to prohibit or confiscate large estates. Therefore they had to face the same problem as those earlier governments: how to get their decrees enforced.

It was not the Communist method, following Soviet and Chinese precedents, to leave such matters merely to decrees. For the enforcement of decrees would depend on those who were already in control of village administration and who in all likelihood were the principal owners of land. The Communists aimed at a complete social revolution in the village, and to this end they sent Party cadres into every locality to ensure that land reform was enforced regardless of the wishes of the notables. Those people who were held to have too much land were 'tried' and condemned by public accusation meetings, losing both face and livelihood in the process. Some were still more harshly treated, being executed for their economic crimes. To some extent the realities of the campaign depended on politics rather than social structure: many of those killed were probably suspected anti-Communist politicians. But to the extent that the motive was simply to 'liquidate' a class of men whom the Communists believed undesirable, the method of village trials ought to have been quite effective.

So it would have been, perhaps, if it had been based on a thorough investigation of the patterns of ownership, and if the situation had been one in which there were a great many large estates whose owners could unmistakably be classified as landlords. But no such investigation seems to have taken place: consequently no allowance was made for the fact that in Tongking and Annam the amount of land in the hands of large landowners was very much smaller than in China. There were of course some landowners with substantial estates, but estates of over fifty hectares were much rarer in the North than in Cochinchina. The great majority of the population would appear, from the statistics of 1930 referred to earlier, to have been peasant-proprietors. Many were no doubt rich peasants, in Lenin's sense of the term: that is, they had enough land to need the labour of others to help them work it; but a rich peasant is not a landlord, even if he is anti-Communist. Mr Hoang Van Chi, in his highly critical study of the Communist revolution in North Viet-Nam,[4] pointed out that the method followed by the

Party in practice was not that of classifying the population on the basis of statistical information collected in Viet-Nam itself: it consisted of establishing quotas for different classes, based on information drawn from Chinese Communist programmes, and then filling them by identifying a given proportion of the inhabitants of each village as landlords, another proportion as rich peasants, and so on. Not surprisingly, many people found themselves being classified on a higher level than purely economic criteria warranted. Or they found themselves being classified as landlords because of their movable possessions. Many of those who suffered as a result were party-members: no one was safe from the 'land reform battalions' when their activity was in full swing. That the suffering caused by their extremism is not merely a figment of the imagination of unsympathetic Western opponents of Communism is suggested by the subsequent admission of the party leadership that in the course of the campaign a great many mistakes had been made: and by the accounts of particular instances of injustice in the North Vietnamese press during the 'Hundred Flowers' period of apparent liberalism in 1956–7.

The course of the land reform can be divided into two parts. The first, inaugurated by the publication of the Agrarian Reform Law and Truong Chinh's speech to the *Lao-Dông* Party Congress of November 1953, came to an end with the Geneva Agreement, which permitted the exodus of hundreds of thousands of Northerners to the South between July 1954 and April 1955. The second, more extreme phase, began with an Agricultural Production Conference in Hanoi in November 1955, at which Truong Chinh was again the leading spokesman. In the next two months the pace of accusation and confiscation reached its peak, and by early in 1956 it was becoming clear to less fanatical members of the party leadership that the country could not stand such a pace of change for long. In April of that year Truong Chinh was relieved of his position as general secretary, and the following autumn his rival Vo Nguyên Giap was the principal spokesman at a central committee congress which admitted the 'errors' of the campaign and inaugurated a programme of 'rectification'. Many of those who had been imprisoned appear to have been released, and probably some of the more extreme decisions of the previous year were reversed.

Politically however the campaign had achieved results which

were irreversible, and which no one in the party's politburo can
have seriously wanted to change. The terror had enabled the
party to establish its power at the village level in most parts of the
country, which was essential if it was to enjoy real control of rural
areas. The firmness of this control in the villages helps to explain
why the rising tide of discontent during the second half of 1956
did not get out of hand. During those months the new government
gave free rein to the intellectuals, in accordance with its policy
(borrowed from China) of allowing 'a Hundred Flowers' to bloom
in apparent freedom. The culmination of this policy was a sudden
clamp-down and a re-education programme; but the period of
liberty would surely not have been permitted at all if the rural
areas had not by then been under firm Communist control. On the
one occasion when there was a serious rural revolt, in the predominantly Catholic district of Quynh-Luu (Nghê-An province),
it proved easy for the government to contain and to suppress it.[5]

Having established itself in power, the regime was free to
embark upon a plan for economic development. Under the Three
Year Plan of 1958–60, and in the early years of the Five Year
Plan which began in 1961, some progress was made towards
industrialization, though the form in which the statistics were
presented made it difficult to estimate from outside how much
was really achieved. But the food problem meant that agriculture
continued to be the central concern of the North Vietnamese
planners. In an area that was already overpopulated in 1954,
population continued to grow; and food scarcity was endemic.
In view of that scarcity, the government was naturally reluctant
to resume the pace of agrarian change that had characterized the
land reform period.

Western observers of the North Vietnamese scene have
frequently asked whether Hanoi veers towards China or towards
Russia in its policies of social and economic development. Whilst
the question of the Hanoi government's relationship with the two
competing Communist giants is clearly of the greatest importance
in the sphere of diplomacy, as far as economics are concerned it
is perhaps somewhat artificial. The Sino-Soviet conflict did not
begin to raise issues of economic policy until the time of the
'Great Leap Forward' of 1958, when China began its experiment
with 'people's communes'; but it was not until that same year
that North Viet-Nam seriously began to create even 'low-level'

co-operatives. Only in 1961 was it reported that 88 per cent. of peasant households had been brought into co-operatives of that kind, and 24 per cent into co-operatives of a more advanced type. Thus the agrarian programme of the Vietnamese Communists was so far behind that of China that there could have been no possibility of their imitating the 'people's communes' on a grand scale in 1958.[6] From such evidence as is available, it would seem that the stage of collectivization completed in China by 1957 was still incomplete in North Viet-Nam as late as 1963. In the succeeding years the war in the South reached proportions that compelled the Hanoi leaders to postpone further agrarian change. With the commencement of the American bombing of North Viet-Nam in 1965, it was probably as much as they could do to keep the existing structure from falling apart.

As a social philosophy, and a method of social organization, Communism has set out to replace Confucianism in Viet-Nam. But more than that, it has set out to replace *everything* in the Vietnamese tradition: its aim is not merely a political and economic but also a cultural revolution. That is, it wishes not merely to change society but also, whether they like it or not, the minds of individuals. Thus the campaign for land reform was not merely a movement to change the pattern of land-holding, or even to transform the rural balance of power. To the Vietnamese Marxist the term 'landlord' is not merely an economic category: it has many of the cultural overtones which have come in the West to be associated—and not only by Marxists—with the epithet 'bourgeois'. In the eyes of Truong Chinh, a landlord was not simply a man who had so many hectares of land or so many tenants and labourers on his estate. He was a certain kind of person, imbued with traditional values and representative of the 'feudalist' class whose way of life had dominated Viet-Nam for centuries. The aim of the revolution was to uproot that class, and to destroy its values. Since in purely Marxist terms the relationship between the 'feudal' way of looking at things and the feudal pattern of economic life was one of simple causality, all that was needed to destroy the traditional outlook in theory was to rearrange the pattern of ownership. But in reality the cultural tradition was not so exclusively dependent on economics, and was unlikely to be uprooted by purely economic change. Whatever might have been true in Europe, in Viet-Nam 'class' could not be measured precisely in terms of income and quantities of land. Its liquidation therefore required the additional element of terror.

For the Vietnamese the central questions about Communism do not revolve around such abstractions as economic analysis or the interpretation of history, nor even around the problem of rural social structure. They relate to the conflict between revolutionary and traditional values: between the claims of the party and the aspirations of the individual. The traditional Vietnamese· view of the individual was very different from that of the modern West. There was no sense of a contradiction between the rights of the individual and the claims of society: such concepts did not exist in Confucianism or Taoism. But neither was there any political theory of absolutism, requiring that the individual subject his every desire to the demands of Confucian orthodoxy. If there was no antagonism between individual and society, the growth of harmony between them depended on the full development of both. Thus the ideal of the *chun-tzu* was one which could only apply to the individual, and it was held that if the life of the family and the nation were to be orderly, then the personal life must be cultivated. As well as his sense of harmony with the world, the Confucian-Taoist scholar had an ideal of personal detachment and inner certainty of himself.

French education brought the Vietnamese into contact with a new kind of individualism, but one which had considerable appeal for many of them. In Rousseau's *Contrat Social* they found a theory which reassured them that, even in modern society, a balance would be possible between the aspirations of individuals and the authority of the state: societies should be organized in such a way as to ensure for each individual the maximum of legitimate freedom. As for the more mundane effects of French culture on every-day life, it introduced the Vietnamese to new attitudes to personal freedom and responsibility. During the 1920s and 1930s there was a growing desire amongst young Vietnamese, especially in Saigon and Hanoi, to escape from customary obligations and above all from the discipline of the family. In literature this found reflection in something like a Vietnamese romantic movement.[7]

There had always been a romantic strain in Vietnamese poetry and novels, but love had been traditionally hedged about by

Fate, and the dominant mood was nostalgia rather than defiance of Heaven. In the twentieth century Fate was less completely supreme: or, at least, it did not always reinforce convention. The first Vietnamese novel in *quôc-ngu* prose, *Tô-Tam* published in Hanoi in 1925, was the story of a young girl who fell in love with a fellow-student, only to face the inevitable dilemma when her parents arranged for her to marry someone else. She evaded the issue of filial piety by committing suicide. But ten years later the reading public was taken by storm by a much more ambitious novel, *Doan-Tuyêt*. In that novel too the story began with the love of two students, but in this case the girl chose to obey her parents and accept an arranged marriage, whilst her lover went off to become a radical politician. Later on however the ill-treatment and neglect of her husband led her to rebel and to leave him (an unthinkable thing in itself); and when he tried to prevent her going, she killed him. This set the scene for a trial in which the pleas of the defence achieved an acquittal, and the heroine was then permitted to flout orthodox conventions completely by becoming first a school-teacher and then a journalist. The author of this novel, Nhât Linh, was one of the most prominent of the new writers in Hanoi in the thirties, and leader of a literary group which called itself the *Tu-Luc Van-Doan*, the 'self-strengthening literary circle'.

The individual of the Taoist-Confucian was regarded by the Marxists as 'feudal'; that of the Hanoi romantics and their public as 'bourgeois'. The Communists declared war on them both. Nhât Linh (whose original name was Nguyên Tuong Tam) was in fact an anti-Communist politician, associated with the *Quôc-Dân-Dang* and then with the *Dai-Viêt* parties; he himself left Hanoi in 1954 and went to Saigon where he took his own life nine years later. But the individualism for which he stood as a writer was not the property of any particular party; it was a part of the climate of opinion with which the Communists had to contend if they were to revolutionize society along Marxist lines. It was an attitude of mind which many of those who fought for the *Viêt-Minh* in the period 1945–54 shared, for only the thoroughly indoctrinated members of the Party saw it as incompatible with socialism and independence. By 1954 however it was the fervent Marxist-Leninists who controlled the northern zone of Viet-Nam and the individualists found themselves under attack.

The Communists' counter-ideal also had its literary manifestations, one of the best examples (which has been translated
into English) being the novel which Huu Mai wrote in 1961,
recalling the heroism of Diên Biên Phu: *The Last Stronghold*.[8]
The most important hero of the story is a young officer called
Quach-Cuong, whose bravery is unsullied by fear and whose
ideological purity is unblemished by doubt. A fitting model for
emulation by the ordinary Vietnamese in peace and war. It is
not merely submission that the all-powerful party demands
from its followers, but strenous effort directed towards the goals
selected by the party; in this case the capture of a key position
within the fortified complex of the French encampment. Other
characters, whose performance is equally praised by the author,
are shown having to struggle with their own fear, and overcoming
it only with great difficulty. Such is the political commissar of the
novel, Tuân, who takes time to accustom himself to the dangers of
the battlefield and to earn the trust which is placed in him by the
officers on account of his party position. Others grapple with
their fears less successfully, and some turn out to be hopeless
cowards. There is a tendency to see individualism as the cause
of cowardice, and to relate failure on the battlefield to class
origins in the bourgeoisie: significantly only officers are shown
as suffering from it. But it is interesting to find that the author
does not frown upon sentimentality in itself, or upon love, as
bourgeois failings. Even the Communist must make some con-
cession to the poetic sentiment of the Vietnamese, so long as it
does not interfere with politics.

Huu Mai's portrayal of the party and the people's army in
action is however, somewhat idealized. The *Lao-Dông* leadership
has not limited its encouragement of the new virtues of self-
sacrifice and heroism to the publication of novels. It has made
more positive attacks on individualism by means of re-education,
or campaigns of 'rectification': in Sino-Vietnamese, *chinh-phong*.
The model for such campaigns was that conducted by Mao
Tse-tung in the Chinese Communist Party at Yenan in 1942; and
the Chinese have repeated the exercise on a number of occasions
since then, notably in 1957. 'Rectification' was one of Mao's
major contributions to the theory and practice of Communism,
and has had no precise parallel in the Soviet Union. One of
Mao's aims was to make his followers aware of their Chinese roots,

and to encourage pragmatism amongst them in borrowing from foreign theorists; the other was to 'remould' them, to make of them truly proletarian party-members, capable of subjecting their own inclinations to the discipline of the party.

The first Vietnamese attempt at a full-scale rectification campaign came in 1953, on the eve of land reform.[9] It followed the principles which Mao had laid down in relation to the second of his aims, and was very clearly an attempt by the strongly pro-Chinese elements in the *Lao-Đông* party to bring their practice in line with that of China. A second rectification campaign followed in 1958, after a short period in 1956–7 when intellectual criticism of the party had been encouraged. It was at this stage that the *Lao Đông* leaders had their showdown with the intellectuals who had chosen to stay in the northern zone rather than flee to the South several years previously. To a large extent the issue turned on individualism in art and literature.

The leading spokesman amongst those intellectuals whose opposition to the regime was strongest was a seventy-year-old veteran of Vietnamese nationalism, Phan Khôi. A native of Quang-Nam, he had begun his political career as a follower of Phan Châu Trinh, and had never been deeply influenced by Marxism. But in 1954 he chose to stay in Hanoi. In September 1956 he was encouraged by the mood of apparent liberalism in Hanoi to begin publishing a review, *Nhân-Van*, in which he and his friends openly attacked the excesses of the party and its cadres. Three months later it was closed down, and in April 1958 he and his colleagues were arrested; Phan Khôi himself died in prison just before he was to be put on trial. The tone of *Nhân-Van* was not completely uncompromising towards the Communists and their ideals; had its writers felt great antipathy towards Marxism as a political theory they would not have stayed in the North. They did not even resent the exhortations of the party to intellectuals and artists to gear their works to the needs of the revolution: what they resented was the total lack of freedom to express their feelings as they wished. In particular they were disgusted by a system of censorship which entrusted to half-educated party hacks the task of dictating to writers what they may write. 'Art is a private sphere,' wrote Phan Khôi, 'politics should not encroach on it'. And again:

It is true that arts and letters, being at the service of politics, must naturally be led by the latter. But may I ask one question? If the politicians want to reach their goal, why don't they use banner slogans, instructions and communiqués? Why the necessity of using arts and letters?'[10]

The fundamental difference between the Vietnamese Communists and their opponents is that to the former these questions seem quite as unreasonable as to the latter they seem unanswerable. And this too is the difference between Communism and Confucianism as orthodoxies. It was possible to be both Confucian and Buddhist or Taoist without any outstanding inconsistency. If one is Communist, there is no room for any other belief, for all other ideologies are superseded.

XI

Non-Communism: The South

COMMUNISM was one possible solution to Viet-Nam's need for a new social framework to replace the traditional Confucian system. But for some Vietnamese—a large enough number for it to matter—the price of accepting this framework was too high. They were not prepared either to cut themselves off from every trace of traditional values, or to renounce all further relationship with the Western civilization which Marxists dismissed as 'bourgeois'. These people were well aware of the inadequacy of tradition on its own, and also of the failure of the French colonists to give their country the full benefits of the civilization of France itself. But they preferred giving the West another chance, under circumstances in which Viet-Nam was now politically independent, rather than accept the harsh discipline of Communism. It was to men of this stamp that responsibility for the government of South Viet-Nam fell in 1954.

It has often been said that the Communist leaders in Hanoi expected the South to dissolve into chaos long before the date fixed for the holding of elections (July 1956). But there was no guarantee that what emerged from the chaos would be a pliable pro-Communist regime ready to unify the northern and southern zones on Hanoi's terms. The migration of between thirty- and eighty-thousand 'hard-core' Communist troops to the North in 1954 left the party cadres who remained behind in no position to force their way to power in the immediate future. In the five years which followed the Geneva Agreement the most important conflicts south of the seventeenth parallel were between different groups of non-Communists, and it was some time before those conflicts gave the Communists an opportunity to resume their struggle for control of the country.

The groups in the South which seemed most likely to benefit from the partition were the Caodaists and the *Hoa-Hao* Buddhists, both of which had men under arms and controlled sizeable

territories where the Communists still had no foothold. But the
sects were weak in three important respects. First, they had no
single leader capable of uniting them into an effective political
force; which is not to say that such a man might not have emerged
given time, but time indeed was short. Secondly, having depended
on French subventions to pay their troops they had no large
supplies of ready money: again, in time they would be able to
raise taxes from their respective provinces, but in the short term
they might be thrown off balance by a government in Saigon that
suddenly refused to continue French payments. Thirdly, and
perhaps most importantly, the sects did not attract the sympathy
of the Americans. Hardly any American at that time understood
the nature of the appeal of these religions to the Cochinchinese
peasantry, and they were not much impressed by the Caodaists'
veneration of such apparently minor world figures as Victor
Hugo. (The Caodaists themselves had made much more of such
veneration in their French-language literature than they did in
their own worship, in order to convince outsiders of their attachment to France.) The Americans dismissed the sects either as the
equivalent of 'feudal warlords' or else as unreliable opponents of
Communism, and the incompatibility of these two interpretations was not dwelt upon.

In the circumstances of June-July 1954 it was impossible
for any man to take office as prime minister in Saigon without
the approval of the Americans. The man chosen for the task was
not a native of Cochinchina at all, but a man from Huê, Ngô
Dinh Diêm. An ascetic Catholic, a fervent nationalist and anti-
Communist, Diêm had all the qualities that official Americans of
the McCarthy-Dulles era admired. His most important asset
however was one which the Americans did not really appreciate
until much later: the younger brother whom he made his
Counsellor, and who was undoubtedly one of the most astute
Vietnamese politicians of his generation. It was probably Ngô
Dinh Nhu who created the situation of 1954 in which his elder
brother was the most obvious candidate for the premiership, and
it was probably he who worked out the tactics by which the
Caodaists and the *Hoa-Hao* were out-manoeuvred in Cochinchina during the following year. The Americans might call the
tune as far as finance was concerned, and their announcement
that no one but Diêm would be given United States aid helped

him a great deal. But they had far too little understanding of the subtleties of Vietnamese politics to exert decisive control over day-to-day events.

Following Diêm's appointment, the sect leaders demanded in September 1954 a place in his government; this they were given, for at that stage the prime minister's first priority was to prevent a military coup.[1] But the following February the end of the French subvention out of which the sects' armies had been paid gave him his cue for a more vigorous policy towards them, and towards the *Binh-Xuyên* secret society. In March these groups responded to Diêm's challenge by forming a 'spiritual union', with the object of ousting the government. Their ultimatum to Diêm and Nhu to resign was rejected, and during the course of the following six months the brothers succeeded in outwitting and checkmating their opponents in Saigon. By October, the Diêm government was strong enough to hold a referendum and obtained overwhelming support for a Republic: Bao-Dai was deposed as Head of State, and Diêm himself became President. The new Republic was inaugurated on 26th October 1955. In February of the next year, government troops occupied Tây-Ninh, forcing Pham Công Tac to flee to Cambodia where he died in 1958. The conflict between the new regime and its Cochinchinese subjects was by no means over, as we shall see. But Diêm and Nhu had won the first round, and were free for the time being to concentrate upon running the southern zone.

Ngô Dinh Diêm has been described as 'the last Confucian' but the ideas upon which his government was based (even though he did not always live up to them) were more complex than that.[2] He was not trying to revive the Confucian monarchical tradition; where he differed from the Communists was in taking Confucian ethics for granted. The brothers were indeed heirs to a dual tradition. Born in 1901 and 1910 respectively, they were the sons of a scholar-official at Huê who for a time was minister of rites under the emperor Thanh-Thai. But the family had been Catholic since the seventeenth century, and had suffered persecution on several occasions before the coming of the French. The brothers were brought up as Catholics; at the same time they could not but be influenced by the virtues and traditions of the Confucian court. Diêm, who did not go abroad until he was nearly fifty, was educated to become a scholar-official himself. For a few months in 1933 he served as Bao-Dai's minister of the interior, but resigned when it became clear that the emperor's attempt at modernization was not to be allowed to include any measure of independence. Nhu on the other hand was sent to study in France, at the École des Chartes, and during the 1940s became a keeper of the imperial archives at Huê. By 1945 both the brothers were active in political movements against the French, but as Catholics (if for no other reason) they refused to have any truck with the Communists. Any possibility of their joining the *Viêt-Minh* was destroyed when in August 1945 a group belonging to that organization burnt down the family house at Huê and murdered their eldest brother, Ngô Dinh Khôi.

Not surprisingly, the political philosophy of the Ngô brothers in power was one which embraced elements of both Catholicism and Confucianism. Known to the West as 'Personalism' that philosophy was their alternative to the Marxism-Leninism of Hô Chi Minh. Its Catholic element, together with its name, derived from the writings of the French philosopher Emmanuel Mournier, which Nhu first discovered as a student in Paris in the 1930s. Mounier differed from many Catholic political thinkers in taking the secularization of the State for granted. His principal concern was not with legalistic debate about the relative spheres of Church and State, but was an attempt to reconcile the thought of two men who were not Catholics at all: Marx and Kierkegaard. What appealed to him about both writers was their rejection of the Hegelian 'absolute idea'. But he could not accept either the impersonal strain in Marxism or the remoteness from social realities of the Danish thinker. He wanted to combine Marx's insistence on the importance of material conditions with Kierkegaard's belief in the spirituality of the person. Towards the end of his life (he died in 1950) Mounier wrote:

> The choice is not between a blind impersonalism—an enormous cancer that proliferates until it kills—and the profound despair which prefers to be annihilated standing up. There are men who have begun to dispel these monstrous terrors by developing a richer notion of the personality of man, of his relations with his world and with his works.[3]

He counted amongst his forerunners Charles Peguy, Karl Jaspers, Martin Buber, and Nicholas Berdyaev.

It is unlikely that Nhu grasped all the nuances of the French and German existentialism which underlay Mounier's writings. But from a political standpoint he found in them two ideas which enabled him to oppose with greater assurance the Communism whose frightening aspect he and his family had first seen in 1930–1. One of them was the Frenchman's bitter antipathy towards the impersonal totalitarianism of the mass party, be it Fascist or Communist, which he saw as the Hegelian Idea institutionalized. The other was his emphasis upon the community as the protector of personal dignity, and in particular upon the family. The traditional Vietnamese family system had not afforded quite this kind of protection to its members, and Nhu cannot have been totally impervious to the new mood which—as one can see in the Hanoi novels of the 1930s—was challenging the dictatorial side of filial piety. But he believed that, whilst the clan should no longer deny its members any kind of individuality, the family should not be allowed to disintegrate completely. As well as stressing the family as an institution, Mounier called for greater equality between the sexes within it. One of the most 'Personalist' of all the actions of the Diêm-Nhu government after 1954 was Madame Nhu's unpopular family law which protected women from male exploitation by banning divorce.

This ideal view of the human person could of course be related to certain traditional ideals, and by making the connection Diêm no doubt hoped to render it more intelligible to his fellow-countrymen; perhaps also to himself. The 'New Life' movement of Chiang Kai-shek in the thirties (Chiang incidentally was also a Christian) had set an example along these lines, in its elevation of the four virtues of *li* (propriety), *yi* (justice), *lien* (integrity), and *ch'ih* (consciousness of honour). Diêm and Nhu chose as slogans for their own movement two different concepts, but ones whose meaning and spirit was very similar to those of the *Kuo-Min-Tang*: *tin*, meaning sincerity in the practice of virtue, and *thanh* meaning a true awareness of one's duty and loyalty to others. They also placed great stress on the concept of *nhân* (Chinese *jen*, meaning humanity and love), which they combined with the word *vi* (person) to translate into Vietnamese Mounier's idea of the person. Neither Diem nor Nhu it would seem had any great talent for

writing, but a number of other people published books during
the later fifties in order to explain the Personalist philosophy and
to relate it to the more familiar teachings of Confucius. But
Vietnamese Personalism was not an attempt to revive the institutions of Confucianism under a new guise, and one can describe
Ngô Dinh Diêm as 'the last Confucian' in only a very limited
sense.

Neither however was his regime the heir to the Constitutionalist
movement of the period before 1945, even though it promulgated
a Constitution in 1956. Like all others who have held power in
Saigon since independence, Diêm and Nhu were very conscious
of being revolutionaries. Personalism was their philosophy of
revolution. Unfortunately, compared with Marxism, Mounier's
thought was somewhat vague on the question of revolution.
Formulated in and for a society which had experienced its
revolution several generations earlier, French Personalism was
weakest at the points where Diêm and Nhu most needed it to be
strong. As far as Viet-Nam was concerned, it provided them with
a sense of direction but not with a detailed plan for action and
organization. They therefore had to work out their own specific
application of its ideals. They went furthest towards doing so in
the development of a land policy.

Diêm's ideas on the subject of land can be seen in some of his
speeches, for example his New Year address of 1959 in which he
enunciated the principle that every family should have at least a
garden plot as its 'basic property', regardless of whether his
primary occupation was farming. The principle was not utterly
unreasonable in a country without any serious land scarcity. The
Saigon government had in fact already begun to apply this
principle soon after the partition, by settling on uncleared land
many of the refugees who had fled from Tongking. It was one of
the most successful aspects of Diêm's policy, and showed that
given a spirit of enterprise American financial aid could be put
to good use. But when it came to taking land away from families
who already had too much, the government was less firm in its
purpose. There were some areas in the southern zone which had
been under sufficiently firm *Viêt-Minh* control for a policy of
confiscation and redistribution to have been carried out before
the partition. In those areas, the return of the landlords and their
insistence upon collecting arrears of rent made a mockery of any

official statements about 'basic property'. But in a society with an influential landowning group it was not easy for a government none too firmly entrenched in power to demand restraint in such matters. In October 1956 it passed an ordinance for the redistribution of land above the level of 100 hectares per family. But even when this measure was implemented, it was not enough to transform a landlord-tenant pattern into one in which peasant-proprietorship was the norm.

From about the middle of 1959, Diêm began a new kind of application of his idea: the creation of *agrovilles*, which would be semi-rural, semi-urban communities in which all families could enjoy the amenities of the town and yet still have their basic garden-property.[4] At the same time they would be more easily defended against Communist attack, and would therefore contribute to security. But to transform a society of villages and towns into a society of *agrovilles* was an ambitious idea at the best of times; in the situation of growing rural unrest which was already developing in Cochinchina by 1959, it was utterly impracticable. Nor was it a very popular plan in itself, for the physical creation of the new type of settlements involved something like a forced-labour system, and a naturally conservative peasantry did not appreciate the need for so much disciplined effort. In fact only twenty-three of these communities were ever brought into existence. The strategic hamlets, which were the preoccupation of Diêm's local government policy after 1961, involved some regrouping of the rural population, but for security reasons rather than in relation to ideas for social improvement.

If the Personalist philosophy provided some inspiration in the field of land policy, in that of economic planning it provided none. It was in no sense a philosophy of development, at least for an agrarian society trying to modernize itself, and in the economic field Diêm and Nhu could do more than accept American assumptions about the relationship between progress and free enterprise. A great deal of aid was in fact given, and some of it was put to good purpose, notably in the sphere of technical and educational development. But there was no overall plan for development, and the attempt to launch one in 1957 ended in failure. Even the degree of co-ordination achieved in India under the five-year plans of 1952–62 proved impossible in South Viet-Nam. The question of how much economic progress the country actually made during the Diêm years has been the subject of controversy, and it is impossible to measure it with any degree of accuracy. But it seems very probable that much of the apparently greater prosperity of the South by comparison with the Communist North was due less to long-term capital investment than to the availability of a large supply of consumer goods imported with American aid.[5]

By 1960 however economic development of any kind was beginning to suffer seriously from the growing problem of political control over rural areas. In an economy dependent to a large extent on the export of primary produce, notably rice and rubber, it was difficult to maintain the momentum of growth if the countryside which produced the export crops was not kept in a fair state of peace and security. If the government could not control the villages, then both economic and political modernization would be impossible.

The problem of control was the most important of all those facing the Saigon government after 1955. It was an analogous problem to that which the Communists faced in the North, and which the terror of land reform enabled them to solve. It was the same problem which had perpetually troubled the French, whose ultimate failure to deal with it had given the Communists their initial opportunity. The methods of a Communist land reform campaign were not open to the government in the South, pledged as it was to respect personal freedom and human dignity. But neither was it enough simply to take over—or to reconstruct —the French system of local government.

From 1956, South Viet-Nam had a Constitution whose theoretical source of authority or legality was a referendum in which 98 per cent of the electorate of the southern zone voted in favour of Diêm's proposal for a republic rather than a monarchy. Constitutionally, since the President and National Assembly were elected by the people, they represented the aspirations of the people. The very notion of 'control' is alien to democratic theory: it is the people who are supposed to control the government.

In Confucian theory too, the idea of control was condemned, for social harmony was believed to depend upon men's virtues. But there was a world of difference between the restraints of

Confucianism and those envisaged by Western democracy. The latter is founded upon two principles, both of which were foreign to the Vietnamese tradition: the rule of law, and representative government achieved through elections. The principle of law derived from the belief, traceable to the works of Aristotle and perhaps further back still, that good government depends on good laws. We saw in an earlier chapter how the Vietnamese tradition assumed the reverse, that virtue lies (if at all) in the person of the official and not in the laws or decrees he administers. The notion that laws might be so absolute that even rulers must obey them was directly opposed to such a tradition. So too was the practice of electing officials on the principle of popular representation, which originated in ancient Rome and was elaborated by the societies of medieval Western Europe. The feudal theory of government required that the monarch should consult his vassals before taking important decisions. As time went on procedures developed for the consultation not only of the feudal nobility but also of the bourgeoisie (in the literal sense of town-dwellers). Thus the foundations were laid for a Parliament in England and an Estates-General in France, out of which grew the modern conception of democracy.

Viet-Nam never had a feudal system in that sense of the word. When Marxists apply the term to traditional Viet-Nam they are using it in a more general sense, invented by Marx, to distinguish a pattern of economic relationships rather than a specific institutional system. The Confucian ruler selected his high officials for their virtue, judged by their performance in examinations; the wishes of the people did not enter into it. And although he made grants of land to them, he did not create hereditary fiefs whose future holders would have the right to become officials. He did not bestow upon anyone the right to advise merely by virtue of holding land. There was thus little scope for the development of feudal procedures of consultation in the natural course of events. In the villages perhaps, there was sometimes a genuine election of officials and a tradition of village meetings and discussion of affairs. But this never extended to levels above the district. The first Vietnamese experience of the procedure of electing local representatives to serve at the centre did not come until the French introduced the Conseil Colonial. But the colonial government did not allow this to develop into anything like true democracy, and constitutionalism was given little encouragement even after 1920.

It is hardly surprising therefore that the Constitution of 1956 did not supersede existing institutions and political habits. It was merely grafted on to the old framework of society, and inevitably for most Vietnamese it was less real than institutions with which they were more familiar. The realities of power still depended, as they had in the French period, on the ability of the government to keep the villages under control, or on that of an opposition movement to create a network of secret associations. Government forces were able to drive the Caodaists and *Hoa-Hao* Buddhists out of Saigon relatively easily, and to crush the *Binh-Xuyên* society in Cholon; they were even able to occupy Tây-Ninh and force the Caodaist Superior into exile. But these organizations still had roots in the countryside, and it was no easy matter to prevent their continued existence in the villages.

In order to cope more effectively with this problem of control, Diêm and Nhu developed their own political party into something like a mass organization. Its core, the *Cân-Lao Nhân-Vi Dang* ('Workers' Personalism Party'), was created by Nhu in or before 1954 in support of his brother. When they obtained power this party was expanded, and auxiliary movements were created. One of the most important of them was the *Liên-Doan Công-Chuc Cach-Mang Quôc-Gia* ('National League of Revolutionary Civil Servants') formed as early as 1954 and an important factor in the victory of Diêm over Bao-Dai the following year. In view of the Communist method of subversion by winning over civil servants, such an organization was probably a necessary defence for the new government. With the inauguration of the Republic a much wider organization was created, the *Phong-Trao Cach-Mang Quôc-Gia* ('Movement for National Revolution'). Then there were the more specialized associations, including a youth movement and also Madame Nhu's 'Women's Solidarity Movement' whose formal aim was to improve the lot of women in society. These various movements were active not only in Saigon but also in towns and villages throughout the country.[6] One of their functions was to rally support for the government in national elections; but also they were supposed to counter the spread of Communist and other subversive groups in rural areas. In the absence of archival evidence (which is unlikely to be forthcoming on this subject), it is impossible to measure their effectiveness except in terms of their ultimate failure to prevent the growth of the Liberation Front or even to protect Diêm against non-Communist enemies.

The *Cân-Lao* officials acquired a reputation for corruption and coercion which may or may not have been deserved. They were said to have directly imitated the methods which the Communists had applied so successfully in the North: successfully, that is, in the establishment of effective control from Hanoi. If that was true, then perhaps one should conclude that Diêm's organization was not ruthless enough. Certainly it was very much less ruthless than the Communists; perhaps where it was at fault was in departing from the ideals of Personalism somewhat haphazardly, to favour particular individuals or to harass particular opponents of the regime. However, the final verdict on what the party actually did is probably less important in the present context than the fact that its reputation was bad: it failed to win the confidence of the mass of the population, and the *sense* of injustice was allowed to grow.[7] As for the attempts of the Movement for National Revolution to educate the peasantry in Personalism, as the Communists indoctrinated the people on their side, it seems to be generally agreed that little progress was made. Perhaps Personalism was too subtle a philosophy for the people to grasp, by comparison with Marxism-Leninism; or perhaps it was badly taught.

A well-informed British observer, Mr Dennis Duncanson, has argued cogently that the problem of control could only be effectively solved, in a way compatible with Western ideals, when South Viet-Nam developed an efficient civil service. No such bureaucratic efficiency was achieved under Diêm, and corruption was therefore inevitable. There is much to be said in favour of this diagnosis of the South Vietnamese dilemma: Western democracy itself depends at least as much on fair and efficient government as on parliamentary representation. But the obstacles to its development in the conditions of Diêm's Viet-Nam were enormous. In the short term only sound political leadership could create conditions more favourable to it; and whilst Diêm often stressed his constitutional position as 'leader of the nation', the leadership he actually gave proved inadequate.

The eventual consequence of the government's failure to control the countryside of South Viet-Nam was the renewal of war. How this came about is a subject fraught with controversy. The official American explanation is that the new war stemmed from aggression on the part of the government of North Viet-Nam: that the Communists unleashed upon the South their special technique of 'revolutionary warfare' with the object of conquest.[8] The government of the United States has never been convinced, it would seem, that the Geneva Agreement was not a political settlement and that Viet-Nam has never been formally constituted as two sovereign states. However, if it is accepted that by virtue of the Franco-Vietnamese treaty of June 1954 the Saigon government has formal sovereignty, it is not necessary to invoke the fiction of dual sovereignty in order to justify United States policy towards the South. It would then become possible to admit that the renewal of the war there was due initially to internal political causes rather than to external military attack.

There were of course Communists involved. The origins of the *Viêt-Công* can be traced back to the operations of the *Viêt-Minh* in Southern Annam and Cochinchina before 1954. In the former area there was probably complete continuity between one organization and the other, for provinces like Binh-Dinh and Quang-Ngai had been strongholds of Communism since 1930 or before. But in Cochinchina Communist strength had never been so great as in those provinces. We have seen that even in 1954 they were only one amongst a number of groups with grass-roots influence in the villages and with followers in possession of arms. In order to obtain better control of Cochinchina, they began about 1958 to create the movement which came to be known as the *Mat-Trân Dân-Tôc Giai-Phong Miên-Nam Viêt-Nam* (the 'National Front for the Liberation of the South of Viet-Nam'). Interestingly the word used for 'nation' here is not *quôc-gia* which means literally 'nation-family', but *dân-tôc* whose meaning is more akin to 'race' or 'people'.

The process by which this new organization was formed and gathered strength is in the nature of the situation not well documented. But enough has been said in earlier chapters of this essay to indicate that the process has to be seen in village terms as well as in terms of South Viet-Nam as a whole. Village politics are not easily penetrated by the outsider (even a Vietnamese outsider), and in circumstances of this kind hard information is scarce indeed. Probably in many villages there were factional conflicts of long standing, such as that which we saw at Môc-Hoa in the 1890s; village politics have probably not changed fundamentally since that time. If so, it would be possible for a budding political front to gather support by playing off the 'out' faction against that in power, regardless at this stage of any ideological considerations. Many villages too had branches of the religious sects whose leadership Diêm had so deliberately antagonized at the outset of his rule. Dr Hickey, in his study of the Cochinchinese village of Khanh-Hâu (Long-An province), shows that in one particular local community there were two branches of the *Cao-Dai* religion and also a reformed Buddhist group, all of them very active in the later 1950s.[9] It would be in keeping with Communist methods for them to infiltrate such religious groups and to try to use them for their own ends. In the case of one of the Caodaist sects, the *Tiên-Thiên* ('Former Heaven') sect, that seems to have been precisely what they did, with some success.

It is very likely that the Front increased its membership by means of the 'take-over bid' method which was described earlier with reference to the period after 1925. Now, that method was supplemented by the more violent one of assassination to eliminate people standing in the way of the front, be they leaders of rival associations or over-zealous government officials. Power continued to grow out of the barrel of the gun. But not all those who joined the Front necessarily did so out of fear or terror: the Communists were able to play on many very real grievances, especially amongst the adepts of the religious sects. A considerable number of the latter were probably amongst the twenty thousand or more people imprisoned by the Diêm government in the years after 1955 who (it is now generally agreed) were certainly not all Communists.[10] In some areas too the peasants were aggrieved by the government's land-policy, and the demand that they should pay money for holdings which they had occupied freely during the war against the French. The Communists may too have exploited southern regionalism in the interests of a movement whose eventual aim was reunification with the North.

The regionalism which permeated Vietnamese politics in the

pre-French period, and which was an important factor in the frequency of revolts and unrest, is still an important factor in South Viet-Nam. The arrival on the scene of several hundred thousand Tongkingese in 1954–5 tended to reinforce it; so too did the fact that the Republic of Viet-Nam included both Saigon and Huê, neither of which was eager to recognize the superiority of the other as capital. Some Vietnamese, especially natives of Cochinchina, are inclined to the view that Ngô Dinh Diêm and his brother could never have succeeded in effectively controlling the provinces of the South (that is, Cochinchina) because he himself was a native of Huê. Not only that, but he very quickly alienated the most important potential leaders in the South by his attack on the sects. Some Cochinchinese it is true worked with Diêm, notably his vice-president Nguyên Ngoc Tho and two of his leading generals Duong Van Minh and Trân Van Dôn. But to a remarkable extent his top officials were men from the Centre, or else refugees from Tongking. The fact that so many leading officials were outsiders must surely have limited the government's ability to manipulate events in the Cochinchinese villages, quite apart from any question of political popularity.

But whatever its origins, by 1960 the Liberation Front was an effective force in the southern provinces of South Viet-Nam. Its development from that year until 1964 has been analysed in some detail by Mr. Douglas Pike in a book based largely on captured documents.[11] From the information he gives it is possible to deduce something of the original alliance of groups which formed it. Besides the Communists themselves who at this stage kept very much in the background, they included the Democratic Party, possibly a Communist Front but one with a very moderate programme; the *Tiên-Thiên* branch of the Caodaists; and a Cambodian Buddhist group. Many other less well-known associations may well have been drawn in, without having representation in the main committees of the Front, including perhaps some of the former *Binh-Xuyên* bandits. The formal leadership of both the *Hoa-Hao* Buddhists and the Tây-Ninh Caodaists appear to have held aloof from the Front and the Saigon government alike at this time. Conceivably the most potent non-Communist organization in Cochinchina, they were simply left on one side following their ouster from the capital by Diêm in 1955.

As time went on, the Communist cadres gradually emerged from the background to play an increasingly prominent part in the work of the Front they had surreptitiously created; which is what one would expect by analogy with the development of the *Viêt-Minh* Front between 1945 and 1951. But this time one must ask, which Communists? For at the centre of the controversy about the renewal of the war is the question of the relationship between the Liberation Front in the South and the government of the Democratic Republic in Hanoi. Mr. Pike seems to offer a key to the answer by showing that in fact the relationship between the southern Communists and Hanoi changed a good deal over time.[12] Within the Front as a whole, the position of the Communists became stronger during the years after 1959 or 1960. An important step in the process was the foundation, towards the end of 1961, of the *Dang Nhân-Dân Cach-Mang Viêt-Nam* (the 'Viet-Nam People's Revolutionary Party'). But that party, though firmly Communist, seems to have been still very much a party of southern-born Communists. It was not until about 1963 that the Southerners within the Communist movement began to fall under the tight discipline of the Northerners who had previously advised and supported them. The trend continued during the next two years, as more and more cadres and troops from the Democratic Republic infiltrated into the South. By the end of 1965 the independent southern origins of the Liberation Front had ceased to be a major factor in the situation, for it was by then wholly dependent on northern troops for what chance it had of ever gaining control of South Viet-Nam.

This interpretation should not be taken as a denial of the assertion that infiltration of cadres from North to South began as early as 1959. But that infiltration by comparison with what was to come in 1963 and later, was on a small scale; and many of those who infiltrated in the early phase were Southerners who had gone north in 1954, returning to join those of their comrades who had remained behind. Nor too, can one ignore the declared support of Hanoi for the Liberation Front. The Third Congress of the *Lao-Dông* Party in Hanoi in September 1960 affirmed its support for the new movement in the South, and in December of that year the Liberation Front was placed on a more formal basis. But it must be remembered that the same Congress approved the Democratic Republic's first Five Year Plan, scheduled to begin in 1961, which suggests that the majority of the Hanoi leaders were at that time more concerned with internal economic development than with external adventures. They did not at this stage envisage full-scale war in the South.

Down to 1963, indeed, Mr Pike's evidence indicates that the strategy of the Communists in South Viet-Nam was geared to the objective of a 'general uprising' (khoi-nghia, literally to 'rise in support of justice'). The events of 1945, in which the Communists seized Hanoi and other major centres, had been a 'general uprising' of this kind; what they wanted now was to repeat that success. They were of course in possession of arms long before 1963, but their strategy was not yet one of full-scale guerrilla war. It was at some stage between about April and September 1963 that the Communists (and this decision probably was taken in Hanoi) came to the conclusion that the strategy of 'general uprising' was not enough. The balance of the Front's activities was therefore changed, making 'armed revolt' the new objective. In September two generals of the North Vietnamese Army held a military conference just across the Cambodian frontier to reorganize the forces of the Liberation Front; and in the following month a series of retraining courses in military tactics was held at various places in the Communist-controlled area of the South. The number of 'incidents' between Viêt-Công and government troops increased from 500 in September to 1,200 in October of that year.[13]

It may be of some significance that this decision coincided not only with the imposition of firmer Northern discipline over the People's Revolutionary Party, but also with a shift in the foreign policy of the Democratic Republic. The Hanoi leadership had previously steered a middle course in the Sino-Soviet dispute; but during 1963 it began to veer towards China and to take a harder line on the issue of 'peaceful coexistence'. Liu Shao-ch'i was welcomed to Hanoi in May, and in September the Democratic Republic sided with China in its refusal to sign the Test-Ban Treaty. Hanoi remained firmly committed to the Chinese side until after the fall of Khrushchev in Moscow, in October 1964.[14] By that time the change-over to military revolt was a *fait accompli*. Relating together all the changes of Hanoi policy which occurred during the summer and autumn of 1963 one is drawn to the conclusion that they represent a major turning-point in the development of the current Vietnamese War, and perhaps the point at which a many-sided political conflict began to be transformed into a straight military conflict between Hanoi (with outside support) and Washington.

XII

An American Solution?

BACK in the 1870s the young official Bui Viên had urged the emperor Tu Duc to appeal to the United States for assistance against the threat of further French conquests. His hope went unfulfilled, but eighty years later the Americans eventually did begin to play a prominent role in Vietnamese affairs: not as protectors against another Western power, but in order to save Viet-Nam from Communist China. In the five years from 1951 to 1956 there was a gradual transformation of Viet-Nam's relationship with the West, as France gave way to the United States as the principal Western power in this part of South East Asia. This represented a major break in the continuity of Western influence in Indochina, and one whose importance should not be underrated.

If one looks at those parts of Asia where constitutional independence developed out of European rule—notably India, Ceylon and Malaysia—it is evident that the key role was played by a relatively small elite which drew its Western education and ideas from a single country, Britain. They were able to look to the same country both for cultural inspiration and for economic and political aid, for some considerable time after gaining independence. And when they sought aid and alliances elsewhere, they did so largely in order to avoid a situation where a single foreign power might gain too strong an influence over them while their independence was still young.

In the years after 1954 the French-educated elite of Saigon found themselves in a much more complicated position. If the Americans expected that the Vietnamese, hating their former colonial rulers, would immediately hasten to abandon everything French, they were disappointed. The long-standing cultural allegiance to France was not easily broken by the tide of political change. Many of the officials, and even cabinet ministers, of the Diêm administration were men who had served in the French

colonial bureaucracy and knew only French ideas and procedures of government.[1] The best schools in Saigon continued to be
French-controlled down to 1966, with French as the principal
language of instruction. Even the younger members of the elite did
not find it easy to accustom themselves to look towards America
for cultural and political inspiration. One might even say that
South Viet-Nam faced a whole new challenge from the West,
arising from the domination of its independence by a power
with whose culture it was unfamiliar.

It is difficult to imagine two peoples culturally further apart
than the Vietnamese (even those with a wide French education)
and the Americans. On the one hand the Vietnamese: exceedingly
polite in all their relations with their fellow-men, yet at the
same time proud of their ability to conceal their deepest feelings
and plans, and often remarkably inexplicit in making decisions
and in action. At the other extreme the Americans, who can be
equally polite but who are probably the most explicit of all
Western peoples and whose culture is founded upon respect for
efficiency and precision. In the cultural confrontation between
them, the explicit American was often no match for the more
subtle and inscrutible Vietnamese.

The Vietnamese non-Communists who sought United States
aid after 1954 did not do so out of admiration for American
culture, of which they knew little, but because they believed that
the sheer power of America was their only protection against
enemies in China and North Viet-Nam. Any discussion of the
relationship between South Viet-Nam and the United States
since 1954 must at some point be focused upon the question
why that power failed. For fail it did, in the Diêm years, to the
extent that the purpose of American policy was to avoid the war
which by 1963 had begun to materialize: and this remains true
whatever may be the outcome of the war itself.

No answer to the question can be more than tentative at
present, for the final assessment of United States policy in Viet-
Nam must depend upon source materials not likely to be made
available to researchers for some time to come. But the evidence
available suggests avenues along which an answer might be sought.
One school of thought dwells on the military and security factors,

and the failure of the Americans to develop adequate methods of coping with Maoist 'revolutionary warfare'. In the Eisenhower period the American generals responsible for training the army of the republic of Viet-Nam concentrated on preparing it to meet a frontal invasion from the North, comparable to that which had occurred in Korea. It was not until the time of President Kennedy that 'counter-insurgency' became the order of the day. In 1961 the President twice rejected advice to send ten thousand combat troops to Viet-Nam in favour of a policy of helping the Vietnamese themselves to develop measures that combined political and military techniques. It was in this context that the Diêm government inaugurated its programme of strategic hamlets in April 1962. The idea derived from British experience in Malaya, and its essential principle was the regrouping of the rural population in order to isolate the insurgent forces. But regroupment alone was not enough. Brigadier Clutterbuck, in his study of the Malayan emergency of which he had first-hand experience, emphasized the importance in British policy there of an effective police system, capable of maintaining order in the villages. Without such a network it is unlikely that the government in Malaya could have re-covered control of the situation sufficiently to be able to destroy the guerrilla army in the jungle.[2] A police network of this kind did not exist in Viet-Nam in 1954 and has not been created since. Whether it was practically possible to create one, given that the Americans were advisers and not a colonial authority, is debatable.

These organizational factors do not however explain every-thing, and it is possible that they were of no more than secondary importance. Those who have argued for the comparability of the Malayan and the South Vietnamese situations have tended too often to ignore the great complexity of Cochinchina's rural society: the ubiquity of its secret organizations and sects and the attachment of the peasantry to the land where their ancestors lie buried. The origins and growth of the Liberation Front were essentially political, and whatever one's conclusions about the degree of involvement of the Hanoi government, the Front could not have become strong without favourable political circumstances in the South. The ultimate solution to the problem of control over South Viet-Nam probably did lie in security organizations and efficient government; but to begin with it was a political problem. In the Vietnamese political tradition control of the principal city had never been enough to guarantee control over the countryside: it was necessary to curb the potentially rebellious activities of secret associations and sects, and this remained true in Cochinchina in the twentieth century. In 1954 such secret organizations were already in existence, and in a strong position in some areas: whether the South was restored to its former stability would depend on how the 'politico-religious sects' were treated by the government in Saigon. As it turned out, the conflict which developed between the Diêm regime and the Cochinchinese peasantry was the principal factor enabling the southern Communists to build up their strength.

Had the Americans truly understood this situation they would surely have done the utmost to prevent such a conflict from breaking out; their actions throughout the Diêm period suggest that their understanding was very limited indeed. It is not easy of course to assess the relative rôles of the Vietnamese and their American advisers in the internal politics of South Viet-Nam. But there are strong indications that at some point in the autumn of 1954 the Eisenhower Administration made a positive decision to support Diêm against the 'spiritual union' of the sects; and at that stage the prime minister's survival depended a great deal on the American threat to withhold aid from any other party that seized power. It may well be doubted whether in making this choice the Americans realized that they were not merely taking sides in a factional dispute, but were in effect choosing the man upon whose personality would depend the success or failure of their plans for Viet-Nam. Diêm had many good qualities, but his inability to win over the sects (and not just defeat them) suggests that he was not really the man the Americans ought to have chosen. To argue that there was no alternative is to forget that Diêm owed a great deal of his own prominence before he became premier to the Americans themselves. Lack of choice is in any case no defence where the charge is inadequate knowledge of a situation.

Sun Tzu's advice to 'know your enemy' would have been a great help to the Americans had they heeded it at this point. Equally relevant might have been the advice to 'know your friend'. For in their relationship with Diêm himself the Americans made further errors of judgment. They failed to appreciate that in Vietnamese eyes loyalty should be to the person, not to his ideas or opinions. Their support was based on the belief that Diêm shared their own ideals: but when it became increasingly apparent that he did not, a loud debate began in American circles as to whether they should continue their support or not. Relations between Siagon and Washington were strained by the knowledge that this debate was going on, and Diêm seems never to have wholly trusted his allies despite his initial dependence on them. In the end his doubts proved justified, when the Kennedy administration finally decided to abandon its former protégé to the wolves. In so doing they showed themselves surprisingly unaware of what was actually happening in the country. A good many Cochinchinese had by this time joined the Liberation Front; and a good many other Vietnamese (including those of Central Viet-Nam and some of the Tongkingese refugees) belonged to political groups opposed to both Communism and Diêm. But it was only the intervention of the Buddhist monks of Central Viet-Nam in the summer of 1963 that made any serious impact on American policy: it was their demonstrations, and their skill in playing off the journalists against the diplomats in Saigon, that turned American officialdom against Diêm. Few if any Americans at this point understood the Buddhism of the Lotus School in Viet-Nam, and consequently they over-estimated its importance in relation to the country at large. Perhaps it was no more than an unfortunate coincidence, made possible by limited intelligence about Communist planning, that their change of attitude occurred just at the moment when the Liberation Front was preparing to switch its tactics from the general up-rising to the armed revolt.

These mistakes of political judgment stemmed from ignorance, which was the bane of American policy in Viet-Nam throughout the Diêm period: ignorance not so much of current facts as of their significance in terms of an unfamiliar cultural framework. The most surprising thing is that the ignorance did not decline: it was so great that most policy-makers seem almost to have been unconscious of it. A small number of Americans became familiar with the Vietnamese ways of thought and behaviour, and with the working of their institutions; but their number was not sufficiently great to change the attitudes prevailing in the corridors of power. As for academic study of Viet-Nam, the subject was all but ignored by most American universities. As late as 1967

Professor Fairbank was lamenting that it would be another ten years before academic understanding of Vietnamese society and culture in the English-speaking world reached the same level as that already attained in the fields of China and Japan.[3] But in the difficult task of working out viable policies towards the countries of Asia, knowledge and cultural understanding are not merely luxuries in which Westerners may or may not choose to indulge. They are a necessity.

In Viet-Nam the 'organization man' went to war, expecting his statistical superiority to bring speedy victory. Characteristic of this approach was a remark of the Secretary of Defence in 1962, on his return from a visit to Saigon: 'Every quantitative measurement we have shows we are winning this war'.[4] Nowhere indeed has the occidental mania for measurement and precise calculation gone further than in North America. The United States, it is true, could never have become the dynamic nation it now is without a large-scale mechanization of its material life. But side by side with that process has gone the tendency for men's thought to become mechanized too: the invention of interchangeable parts has found its spiritual parallel in a desire to turn knowledge about societies into the concepts and statistical data of a computerized social science. The tendency is not, of course, shared by all Americans; but it is very evident both in the study of politics and in the practice of government. Such mechanistic generalization is often fatal to the deeper understanding of other men's cultures and ways of thought, which in Asia have not undergone the same process of mechanization. Unfortunately when the crucial factors in a situation are political psychology and the ability to manipulate unfamiliar institutions, quantitive measurement is not enough.

The dictum of Clausewitz (quoted, incidentally, by Truong Chinh in his pamphlet of 1947) was that 'War is the continuation of politics by other means'. One of the mistakes of the Americans in Viet-Nam was to suppose that the reverse can be true: that politics in such situations is no more than an extension of war. War is very often a matter of statistics; but politics very definitely is not. Political success depends on judgment, which in a situation of cultural confrontation involves the understanding of an alien psychology. In this the Asians very often have the advantage, for many of them are more familiar with Western ways of thought than Westerners are with their Asian cultures. This is not merely a matter of knowing languages, but one of understanding people. Communism is said to be a force which holds itself aloof from cultural differences, employing tactics that are essentially the same wherever they appear in the world. This may be so, but it remains true that in Viet-Nam or anywhere else the rest of society has its own cultural and psychological peculiarities. And how Communists fare in any society depends on their own capacity for political manoeuvre within a cultural and institutional framework already in existence. The shortest answer to the question why American power failed the Vietnamese after 1954 is that the men responsible for making policy in Washington ignored the cultural factor in the situation with which they were dealing.

What after all *is* power? Since the rise of mercantilism and the discovery of 'political arithmetick' in the seventeenth century, it has become a habit in the West to assume that power can always be measured by means of military and economic statistics. But in practice the only measure of power is success. Economic capacity and technology can add greatly to a nation's strength in certain circumstances; but they can be effectively utilized only to the extent that a situation has been correctly assessed and specific objectives properly identified. The potential for military victory cannot always be assumed to give power in and of itself. The mercantilist illusion works only so long as men are prepared to say, with Metternich *apropos* of the armies of Alexander I: 'One cannot argue with so many hundred thousand men.' The Chinese and Vietnamese Communists have rejected this equation that wealth equals power, at least as far as warfare on their own soil is concerned. The underlying supposition of 'guerrilla strategy' and 'people's war' is that no matter how powerful a Western army might be in theory, it must prove its power in practice by fighting on the ground. Against such an enemy there are no victories to be had by the mere possession of powerful weapons: either they must be actually used, or he must be defeated by some other means. It was because the Americans failed to understand this that in Viet-Nam the weapons had to be used.

When it comes to the question of what the Americans themselves were trying to achieve in Viet-Nam in this period, the answer is less easily discovered than might be supposed. Unlike the French, the Americans have not theorized a great deal about their relationships with Asians in Asia, and there is not much literature comparable to that which appeared in France in the latter part of the nineteenth century discussing the methods of imperial expansion and colonial rule. We must look instead to the statements of politicians, which tend to be in very general terms. One of the most important can be found in the letter which President Eisenhower addressed to Ngô Dinh Diêm in October 1954. It identified two objectives which between them cover most of the things the Americans actually did in South Viet-Nam during the next ten years. First, the purpose of American aid was:

> to assist the government of Viet-Nam in developing and maintaining a strong, viable state, capable of resisting attempted subversion or aggression through military means.

But secondly, the President went on to speak of the need for reforms on the part of the authorities in Saigon, and expressed his hope for a Vietnamese government:

> so enlightened in purpose and effective in performance that it will be respected both at home and abroad.[5]

The former of these objectives was undoubtedly the more important. The Americans had no primary interest in conquering any part of Viet-Nam, or in exerting permanently an indirect control over its internal affairs. Their motive for being there was to 'contain' China: the significance of Viet-Nam in this respect was simply that it was decided to draw the line of containment half way along the Vietnamese coast. Nevertheless, once the line had been drawn, the Americans were committed to ensuring that the country immediately to the south of the seventeenth parallel was not only politically stable but also a fine example of the progress that was possible within the 'Free World'. What this really meant is implicit rather than explicit in President Eisenhower's letter: the key phrases being 'enlightened in purpose' and 'effective in performance'. Effectiveness depended a great deal on economic stability, and large amounts of money were poured into Viet-Nam towards this end. (The theory underlying American economic aid was discussed briefly in Chapter IX.) But what of 'enlightenment'? The State of Viet-Nam was apparently expected to allow freedom to its subjects and a measure of participation or representation in the government. In the minds of many Americans, the extent to which that expectation was fulfilled became the yardstick by which they measured the success of Vietnamese development. The hidden assumption on which much of American policy in Viet-Nam was based was that the Vietnamese, given proper opportunity would live up to the ideals of liberty and democracy that had been born in the European enlightenment of the eighteenth century, and had been written into the American Constitution following the War of Independence.

The French failure to bring enlightenment to Viet-Nam hung over everything the Americans did in Viet-Nam in the Diêm period. The Vietnamese desire for independence seemed entirely natural to the Americans: had not they themselves once had to struggle against a colonial power? With their own anti-colonial tradition they felt they had something to offer to an Asian nation which no ex-imperialist European could give: sympathy. As for the theories of 'assimilation' or 'association' which had pre-occupied the French, they were condemned out of hand. But this benevolence was allowed to conceal (even from the Americans themselves) that they had not thought out any fundamentally new approach to the problem of cultural relationships between the white and the yellow races. Their policies proceeded not from theories but from assumptions, about the nature of human progress in general. Unfortunately those assumptions did not derive from any serious study of Asia, but from their own limited historical experience. In other words, the Americans fell into the trap of supposing that Asians, for all their apparent differences from Westerners, are at heart simply *people* who have not yet attained the same level of progress as that achieved by the Americans themselves.

The assumption is well illustrated by a speech of Secretary of State Acheson in 1950, soon after the final Communist victory in China. He denied that the sole interest of the United States in Asia was to stop Communism:

> Our real interest is in those people as people. It is because Communism is hostile to that interest that we want to stop it. But it happens that the best way of doing both things is to do just exactly what the people of Asia want to do, which is to develop a soundness

of administration of these new governments, and to develop their resources and technical skills so that they are not subject to penetration either through ignorance or because they believe these false promises (of the Communists), or because their is real distress in their areas.[6]

All too few Americans have challenged this assumption. Liberals and conservatives alike in the American political firmament have taken it for granted that their country is the new guardian of the values of the Enlightenment. Despite their rejection of formal theories about a Western 'mission civilisatrice', their view of human progress is often Americo-centric. As the most powerful nation on earth, the United States has taken upon itself the responsibility for leading mankind towards its manifest destiny. In 1961 President Kennedy found it necessary to warn his people:

> We must face the fact that the United States is neither omnipotent nor omniscient . . . that we cannot impose our will upon the other ninety-four per cent of mankind . . . and therefore that there cannot be an American solution to every world problem.[7]

But by then the United States had embarked upon a policy which supposed that there was an American solution to the problem of Viet-Nam. They did so with only a very limited appreciation of the many problems that had arisen out of Viet-Nam's complex historical relationship with the West.

Throughout the period from about 1904 to 1954, the Vietnamese had not been struggling merely for independence: they knew that they could only sustain their independence, once it was achieved, if they could also succeed in modernizing their country and strengthening its economy. Like the Chinese, they viewed the West not in terms of Europe's (or America's) own idealism, but in terms of what they themselves needed in order to develop a modern independent nation. Once they had their independence, what they borrowed from the West was for them to decide, not for any outsider.

Their attitude to the West during the decades of French rule may be said to have had three variations. (To regard them as three progressive phases would be to assume that only the third was valid, which many Vietnamese are reluctant to do.) First,

there was what one might call the *t'i-yung* variation: in their
first contacts with the nineteenth-century West, the Vietnamese
had imagined that all they needed to do was to borrow Western
techniques, whilst keeping their institutional and ethical traditions
intact. In Viet-Nam, this variation was in fact never tried; but
in China it proved a failure. Second, there was the variation
which sought to combine institutional reform (or even revolution,
in the political sphere) with the maintenance of traditional
religion and ethics so long as they did not clash with the need
for political change. This was the variation expressed in the ideas
of Liang Ch'i-ch'ao. In China itself, under Chiang K'ai-shek, it
too proved a failure; but in Japan it was extremely successful. The
third variation was that of the revolution which would destroy
tradition completely and replace it with a new social theory:
Marxism-Leninism. This revolution would not be confined to
changes in political and economic institutions, but would strike
at the root of traditional attitudes by reforming also men's minds.

This third variation, which was applied in China after 1949
and in North Viet-Nam after 1954, was abhorrent to the Americans.
Since the first variation was no longer a serious possibility, they
(and the non-Communist Vietnamese) were left with only one
possibility: the second. Whatever emerged in South Viet-Nam
would, to be successful, need to combine elements of tradition
with vigorous institutional modernization. Diêm's philosophy of
Personalism was an attempt, in some ways a very appropriate one,
to achieve this combination of ancient and modern; had the
Caodaists gained power instead of Diêm in 1954, it is possible that
they too would have produced an equally appropriate combination of their own. But whatever philosophy of change was
adopted, it was not likely to be one that would coincide exactly
with American ideas about freedom under law.

The Americans were not very well equipped by their own
historical development to understand the problems which
tradition posed for the non-Communist Vietnamese. Their own
modernization had been a gradual process, developing out of a
colonial society on the East Coast, which had itself already
escaped from many of the limitations of tradition that existed
in Europe. What survived of the traditional attitude to human
relationships, derived from feudal Europe, was swept away by
the Civil War of the 1860s. But that was a revolution only for the

States of the South: in the North, and even more in the great West, the Americans never faced the need to revolutionize their own society and throw off traditional restraints on modernization. Their own struggle for independence was thus not a struggle against tradition, and Americans have tended as a result to underestimate both the strength and the diversity of tradition in Asia. In this they are at a disadvantage by comparison with European countries, and also with Russia, all of which have had to face the problem of escape from tradition in one way or another. The disadvantage is liable to be aggravated by unconsciousness of the extent to which American institutions have themselves evolved from the European traditions they have left behind. The rule of law and the concept of representative government, for example, were not culturally neutral: they derived ultimately from tendencies in the Western feudal tradition which have been absent from the traditions of East Asia. For all these reasons, the American intrusion into Asia after 1945 was a move fraught with dangers for all concerned.

To say these things is not to deny the virtues of democracy itself. To recognize that the rule of law and representative government are ideas alien to the tradition of Viet-Nam need not imply that there was never any possibility of their developing in that country. By the time Viet-Nam became independent the traditional system was dead, and whatever replaced it (and replaced also the colonial system) would be to some extent alien and new. Communism was in many of its features every bit as alien as were the principles of democracy, and there was no inherent reason why Communism should prove more appropriate to Viet-Nam's needs than a system incorporating Western ideas about government and economic growth. But that could only happen if the Vietnamese who wanted such a system were capable of bringing it about, and if their American allies appreciated the immensity of the problems involved. The Americans failed in understanding, just as their power failed to guarantee peace and stability: the consequence was the war of escalation which became a dominant factor in the world scene during the 1960s.

What had initially been a political and financial commitment to support South Viet-Nam became, step by step, a military one involving the use of America's own forces. For the majority of those who feel most strongly about it, this conflict has become a symbol of the world-wide confrontation between Communism and the Free World. But at a deeper level it is also a symbol of the cultural confrontation between East Asia and the West, and of the tragic failure of a Western power to deal effectively with an oriental situation. As far as South Viet-Nam itself is concerned, the war may well sweep away so completely the traditional framework that whatever emerges from it will have to be modern, whether Communist or Democratic. But elsewhere the extreme violence and the scale of the war is likely to damage faith in the Western achievement throughout Asia. There is a danger that because of it the West will in future be respected only for its power and not at all for its civilization: and when that power fails, as it sometimes will, the damage may be reflected in a declining sense of purpose in the West itself.

Meanwhile, in the villages of South Viet-Nam where the ravages of war are most keenly felt, it is not to be wondered at if the peasant still clings to his belief in Fate at a time when no other set of beliefs or explanations is enough to make sense of the sufferings he has to bear.

EPILOGUE

Epilogue

In the year 1862 the inhabitants of the Cochinchinese province of Go-Cong composed a declaration against the French, warning the invaders that they would fight to the death for the return of the territory ceded the previous year. It included an eloquent summary of their attitude to the foreigners:

> Your country belongs to the Western seas, ours to the seas of the East. Just as the horse and the buffalo differ between themselves, so do we differ by our language, our writings and our customs. Man has been created in different races. Everywhere man has the same value, but his nature is not the same.[1]

As conquerers the French were very much aware of their mission to civilize the Vietnamese: to make their nature as well as their humanity conform to the ideals of the West. Yet despite several generations of French rule, the Vietnamese are still for the most part conscious of being separated from Westerners by an invisible but very real cultural barrier. Have they not changed at all under the impact of the occidental challenge?

The question is less easily answered than one might imagine. In some respects they have changed a great deal. Materially they have added considerably to their technical skills, from the ability to drive a pedicab to piloting an aeroplane. Their country was made smaller by the introduction of modern communications and transport, and their educational system was transformed by the intrusion of practical subjects like mathematics, chemistry and engineering. They even changed their writing system, so that most of them no longer read Chinese characters. On the intellectual plane, the 'opening up' of Viet-Nam forced them to adjust to a new and wider view of the world. The traditional Vietnamese conception of a world dominated by China, in which they themselves occupied perhaps the second most important place, was shattered by their discovery of the West. New lines of political and social thought led to a new sense of nationality and the idea of the nation as the proper framework for political activity. For many, not only Communists, the idea of revolution replaced that of Fate or the Mandate of Heaven as the proper basis of political power. And the Confucian-Taoist idea of a universe governed by the principles of harmony gave way to a cosmology derived from Western natural science. For all those Vietnamese who have participated in this brave new world of occidental techniques and learning, some measure of change has been inevitable.

But when it comes to that deeper and more nebulous thing usually called 'personality' or sometimes 'social character', that something which distinguished the traditional Vietnamese as a person from the modern European, the changes are more difficult to measure. Even those Vietnamese most thoroughly educated in French learning had their roots in a family life which was, and still is for the most part, very different from the family life of Europeans. Complete personal transformation was rare, if not impossible; yet some measure of change was likely, and was made more so when young people moved from the environment of the village to that of the Westernized urban centres of Hanoi or Saigon. Family discipline was often reduced, and to their own children such people often allowed greater freedom than had ever been tolerated in the past.

Some people—not usually the most educated in either Vietnamese or French learning—allowed their children to concentrate so hard upon acquiring Western techniques that they lost touch completely with their own tradition. This represented change indeed. But these young people were seldom able to arrive at a true understanding of the spirit of the West. The contemporary writer Thu Van, in a 'Vietnamese Letter to President Johnson' composed in 1967, characterized such people as 'native strangers'.[2] In their approach to the West 'they sought not a culture but a means to become wealthy and powerful as the foreigner'. She drew a contrast between them and another, much smaller group of Vietnamese students of the West whom she called 'occidentalists': men and women who were masters of their own culture and were thereby enabled to appreciate the culture and vastness of the West as well as its techniques. Such people were rare, but their role in Vietnamese society was nevertheless very great, for they were the people who could lead the way in bridging the gulf between two different civilizations, and so explain the brave new world in terms that their own people could understand. Very often they played a leading part in the religious revival. Some became Catholics (though only a minority of converts were of this kind) and their presence in the Church made it possible for Vietnamese priests to take over from missionaries long before political independence was achieved. Others made a reappraisal of traditional religions, and participated in the Buddhist revival or else in the growth of Caodaism, the one religion which tried to unite the faiths of East and West. And there were some who rejected all religion, but adopted with a comparable religious fervour the political creed of Marxism. Thu Van's examples of the occidentalists are not at all a politically oriented list: they include Hô Chi Minh, as well as Ngô Dinh Diêm, the novelist Nguyên Tuong Tam (Nhât Linh) and also the Caodaist Nguyên Ngoc Bich.

Those who tried to blend the culture of East and West were deliberately eclectic. But those whose discovery of revolutionary political philosophies led them to reject tradition entirely did not always escape traditional habits of thought. Even the Marxist philosophy as it is interpreted by the Vietnamese mind may have its links with the past. For there is a sense in which Communism might be said to strengthen rather than to undermine belief in Fate. In day-to-day policy decisions, the Marxist idea of *praxis* demands a study of concrete conditions and a determination to change the world instead of being dominated by it; but when it comes to the dialectics of history there is room for a less practical view. The historical process itself is the guarantee of eventual success: in this, History has taken on the role of Heaven. Just as the Mandate of Heaven could in the old days pass from one dynasty to another, now the Mandate of History is held to be passing from one class to another. This is hardly an aspect of Vietnamese Marxism that would find its way into documents published in Hanoi, but it seems possible that some Communist cadres see in this way the philosophy they have been taught. As for the ordinary peasant, does he make any sharp distinction in his mind between the 'sorcerer' or 'bonze' who once claimed to know the future decreed by Heaven, and the party cadre who now insists that he knows what has been decreed by History? Whenever ideas are translated from one language and culture to another it is impossible to be sure that the words have precisely the same meaning for the two peoples involved. Where the languages differ as greatly as do French and English from Vietnamese and Chinese, it seemed almost inevitable that there will arise subtle changes of meaning and usage. And if words are difficult to translate, then customs, institutions and attitudes are even more so.

Those colonists who wanted to make Vietnamese into Frenchmen were setting themselves an impossible task. The Vietnamese, with their tradition of eclecticism, might wish to borrow some things from the West; but they would always wish to remain Vietnamese. It was the misfortune of Viet-Nam that the French did not begin to appreciate the impossibility of their 'mission civilisatrice' until after 1945. For the most part indeed, they did not do so until brought up against the difficulties of reconquest during the war against the *Viêt-Minh*. Amongst the small minority of Frenchmen who did appreciate it at an earlier stage was the young art critic André Malraux, who spent some time in Indochina during the years 1923–5. Unlike most of his compatriots, he went there not to educate or govern others but to achieve a greater understanding of himself. The year before, he had written:

> We can feel only by comparison. . . . The Greek genius will be better understood through the contrast of a Greek statue with an Egyptian or Asiatic statue than by the examination of a hundred Greek statues.[3]

His whole attitude to both his own civilization and those of Asia was different from that of the colons of Saigon, and very soon he found himself at loggerheads with the French authorities. They accused him of stealing sculptures from the ancient monuments of Cambodia, which were theoretically protected by a government decree: as a result he was sentenced to three years' imprisonment by a court at Phnom Penh, though later the charges were quoshed by an appeal to Paris. In retaliation, Malraux took up journalism in Saigon, and in the pages of *Indochine* lambasted the colonial authorities for failing to live up to the ideals of the politicians at home. He consequently made a personal enemy of the Governor of Cochinchina, Maurice Cognacq, who after a couple of months brought about the closure of the paper by intimidating the printers. What distinguished Malraux's subsequent writings in the period down to 1933 was his willingness to treat Asians as culturally the equals of Westerners, and to recognize in their desire for revolution one of the fundamental themes of the modern world. Asia, he found, was more than a mere foil for the understanding of Greek art.

Nevertheless the arrogance of the colon struck him as a manifestation of his own civilization just as important as the Greek statue, and in his short book *La Tentation de l'Occident* (1926) he explored the relationship between the two. It took the form of an exchange of letters between an imaginary Chinese visitor to Europe and a (possibly less imaginary) Frenchman who knew something of China. The thing that impressed his Chinese most about Western civilization was its endless activity. Whereas the Chinese ideal was one of harmony with the world, the Westerner seemed constantly to assert himself against it. In Europe everyone seemed to be directed by a consciousness of his own individual existence, apart from the universe and apart from God; and from this arose a desire to shape the universe according to his will. In art—the Greek statue for example—the occidental tradition was dominated by representation, the desire to capture active reality in plastic form. The Chinese painter was not concerned with such an impossible task, but sought only to express in art his own sympathy for what he saw. In politics Malraux's imaginary Chinese found a symbol of Western aspiration in the ruins of ancient Rome: the vestiges of an empire founded upon self-sacrifice, but whose only claim to grandeur lay in the sacrifice itself. Vast numbers of slaves were called upon to expend themselves in the interests of sheer power: but what good is power, asks the Chinese, unless one is the emperor? Despite the violence and cruelty that have characterized Chinese and Vietnamese history, the traditional values of those countries never glorified power for its own sake. Neither their Gods nor their rulers were invested with absolute omnipotence.

It was the Westerners' quest for power that took them to the ends of the earth in the era of capitalism and colonization, and led the French to conquer Viet-Nam. In his finest novel *La Condition Humaine* (1933) Malraux epitomized this occidental approach to Asia in the character of Ferral, the French banker whose philosophy is summed up in his assertion:

> A man is the sum total of his actions, of the things he has done and of the things he may do yet. . . . I am my roads, my work.[4]

Indochina was but one more of the things the French mind sought to transform into something it was not. They did indeed transform it, but not into anything they could have foreseen or desired. Malraux was conscious of the inevitable failure of the West, of the impossibility of remaking Asia in its own image. He was conscious too of the agony of the Westerner who discovered his own limitations. He placed into the mouth of another character in the same novel words which sum up his sense of the futility of Western endeavour:

> each man suffers because he thinks. Fundamentally the mind only conceives of man as eternal, and so all consciousness of this life can be nothing but an agony. . . . Every man dreams of being God.

Malraux was not advocating that Westerners should prefer the traditional values of China to their own. The Asians were themselves rejecting those values in the course of a revolution of world-wide significance. What the twentieth century needed was some new set of values that would transcend all traditional cultures, East and West alike. Malraux himself never solved the problem which he identified in his earlier works. In *La Condition Humaine* he seemed at times to suggest that the answer lay in Marxism, and the Communist form of revolution. But he never wholly committed himself to that view, and ultimately he retreated from international idealism into a nationalism (though not a traditionalism) of his own. What he recognized very clearly was that the claim to final and ultimate cultural superiority, the claim to have a 'mission civilisatrice', was no more than a temporary escape from the problem. The West must not be afraid to look the East squarely in the face and accept its cultural challenge.

There are no easy formulae that will enable us to transcend the cultural differences between Viet-Nam (or any other Asian country) and the West. The only thing that will serve is cultural understanding, slowly and painfully arrived at through study and experience. Greater knowledge of Asia on the part of a handful of specialists is an important pre-requisite for this, and we shall need to move beyond the point where only a tiny minority of Westerners have any knowledge of an Asian language and its culture. But more important still is the need for a fundamental change of attitudes in the Western world, for only that will enable a change in the basis of political decisions. Until the present decade this need could be ignored. It was enough to make speeches about the equality of races and the desirability of mutual understanding, and to treat Asian equality as a matter for politeness rather than action. But in Viet-Nam the consequences of inadequate cultural understanding have begun to materialize. The United States has not over-reached its physical resources: but its knowledge of Asians has proved too limited to support the ambitions of its policy.

It lies beyond the scope of this short essay to determine whether future policies of the West in Asia should be directed towards maintaining power and influence, or whether it is possible to concentrate solely on the provision of material and technical aid. If the lesson of Viet-Nam has any bearing on these larger issues, it is that events there demonstrate how sadly ill-equipped the West at present is to play any part at all in the East. A century ago the Europeans forced East Asia to respond to the challenge of technological superiority. That superiority still exists and many Asians are still eager to learn the skills and techniques of the West. But politically they have found the measure of Western civilization and power. In place of the old challenge, a new one has developed: a challenge from Asia to the West, of a different and more complicated kind. Whatever our future aims may be, we can no longer rely upon our own achievements and superiority being taken for granted by Asians. The Westerner in the East must now be culturally on the defensive: if he wishes either to influence or to help, he must first be prepared to learn.

Notes

PROLOGUE

1. On traditional Vietnamese chronology see P. Huard and M. Durand: *Connaissance du Viet-Nam* (Hanoi, 1954), pp. 75–77.
2. Trân Van Giap: 'Le Bouddhisme en Annam des Origines au XIIIe Siecle', *Bull. de l'Ecole Française d'Extrême-Orient*, vol. xxxii (Hanoi, 1932), p. 259; R. Lingat: 'Les Suicides Religieux au Siam' in *Felicitation Volumes of South East Asian Studies presented to His Highness Prince Dhaninivat*, vol. i (Bangkok, 1955), pp. 71–5; and *Echo Annamite* (Saigon newspaper), 31st March 1930.

   On Buddhist scriptures relating to this practice, see J. Filliozat: 'La Mort Volontaire par le Feu at la Tradition Bouddhique Indienne', *Journal Asiatique*, vol. ccli (Paris, 1963), fasc. i, pp. 21–51.
3. Contrast, for example, the interpretation in Marguerite Higgins: *Our Viet-Nam Nightmare* (New York, 1965), with that of David Halberstam: *The Making of a Quagmire* (New York, 1964). Both these correspondents were in Saigon in the summer of 1963.
4. The best available introduction to Vietnamese history in the pre-French periods, in a Western language, is Lê Thanh Khôi: *Le Viet-Nam: Histoire et Civilisation* (Paris, 1955). See also Joseph Buttinger: *The Smaller Dragon* (New York, 1958).
5. For a survey of the traditional Vietnamese system of government see R. Petit: *La Monarchie Annamite* (Paris, 1931).

PART ONE

Chapter I

1. Accounts of the traditional Chinese background are innumerable and too well known to cite here. Comparable works on Viet-Nam are less numerous. See P. Huard and M. Durand: *Connaissance du Viet-Nam* (Hanoi, 1954), and also M.Durand: 'Quelques eléménts de l'Univers moral des Vietnamiens', *Bulletin de la Société des Études Indochinoises*, new series, vol. xxvii (Saigon, 1952).

2. Quoted from the translation by D. C. Lau (Penguin Books, Harmondsworth, 1963), p. 105. On Nguyên Binh Kiêm, see Duong Dinh Khuê: *Les Chefs d'Oeuvre de la Litterature Vietnamienne* (Saigon, 1966), pp. 67–8.

3. Quoted from the translation by Lin Yu-tang, *The Wisdom of Confucius* (London, 1958), p. 123.

4. For a long discussion of the importance of this idea of God as law-maker in the development of Western thought see Joseph Needham: *Science and Civilisation in China*, ii (Cambridge, 1956), ch. 18.

5. Cf. H. J. R. Murray: *A History of Chess* (Oxford, 1913), pp. 121 ff.

6. The by now classic example of this comparison is that of K. A. Wittfogel: *Oriental Despotism, a Comparative Study of Total Power* (Yale, 1957).

7. This absence of an orthodox *sangha*, rather than any specific difference of belief, is probably the most important distinction between the (Mahayana) Buddhism of Viet-Nam and the Theravada Buddhism of Cambodia, Siam and Burma. The nature of Vietnamese Buddhism in the twentieth century will be discussed in Chapter V below.

8. The story is recounted in Nguyên Dang Thuc: *Asian Culture and Vietnamese Humanism* (Saigon, 1965), pp. 126–38.

9. Cf. J. Chesneaux: *Les Sociétés Secrètes en Chine* (Paris, 1965); Georges Coulet: *Les Sociétés Secrètes en Terre d'Annam* (Saigon, 1926); and also Leon F. Comber: *Chinese Secret Societies in Malaya* (New York, 1959).

10. On persecution in China see J. J. M. De Groot: *Sectarianism and Religious Persecution in China* (Leiden, 1901); but de Groot's implication that the Confucian motive for persecution was a desire for religious as well as political orthodoxy is not now accepted. On Vietnamese persecutions of Christianity, see G. Taboulet, *La Geste Française en Indo-chine*, vol. i (Paris, 1955).

11. The poem was composed by Nguyên Du about 1813, but was based on an earlier Chinese novel. The Vietnamese poem has been translated into French more than once, most recently by Xuân Phuc and Xuân Viêt in the series 'Connaissance de l'Orient' (UNESCO, Paris, 1961). The quotation below is rendered into English from the latter French edition.
    Cf. Duong Dinh Khuê, *op. cit.*, pp.

12. G. Coulet, *op. cit.*, contains a general discussion of the *thây-phap*, as well as documentary evidence of the activities of such men in the secret society movements of 1913–16.

14. On Phan Dinh Phung, see Nguyên Phut Tân: *A Modern History of Viet-Nam* (Saigon, 1964), pp. 241–79.

Chapter II

1. Some of these poems are translated in Duong Dinh Khuê: *Les Chefs d'Oeuvre de la Litterature Vietnamienne* (Saigon, 1966), pp. 320–328.

2. It has been translated into French: Ngô Dinh Diêm, Nguyên Dinh Hoe and Trân Xuân Toan: 'L'Ambassade de Phan Thanh Gian, 1863–4', *Bull. des Amis du Vieux Huê*, 1919 and 1921 (Huê).

3. A list of his writings together with a biographical note will be found in A. Brébion and A. Cabaton: *Dictionnaire de Bio-bibliographie de l'Indochine Française* (Paris, 1935).

4. No adequate account of Tô's career or memorials exists in a Western language. The brief summary here is based on Pham Van Son: *Viêt-Su Tân-Biên*, vol. v, pt. i (Saigon, 1962), pp. 263–72. There had been an embassy to Paris earlier, but the French government refused to receive it. See also Pierre Daudin and Lê Van Phuc: 'Phan Thanh Gian et sa Famille', *Bull. de la Société des Études Indochinoises*, n.s. xvi (Saigon, 1941).

5. Thai Van Kiêm: 'Les Premières Relations entre le Viêt-Nam et les États-Unis d'Amérique', *Bull. de la Soc. des Études Indochinoises*, n.s., xxxvii (1962), pp. 302ff.

6. J. R. Levenson: *Confucian China and its Modern Fate*, 3 vols. (London, 1958–65).

7. Duong Dinh Khuê, *op. cit.*, pp. 266–75.

8. See J. R. Levenson: *Liang Ch'i-ch'ao and the Mind of Modern China* (Harvard, 1954), for a thorough analysis of Liang's ideas.

9. See Pham Van Son: *Viêt-Su Tân-Biên*, v, pt. ii (*Viêt-Nam Cach-Mang Cân-Su*) (Saigon, 1963), pp. 362–7, for a full account of Phan Bôi Châu's life; cf. below, Chapter VII.

10. Benjamin Schwarz: *In Search of Wealth and Power: Yen Fu and the West* (Harvard, 1964).

11. The best available biography of Sun Yat-sen is M. L. Sharman: *Sun Yat-sen, a Critical Biography* (New York, 1934). I have not been able to discover the date of the first translation of Sun's writings into Vietnamese; but there was a French translation published in 1929, which would be available at least to Vietnamese students at that time studying in Paris.

12. This and other Vietnamese political movements of the 1920s will be discussed in Chapter VII below.

13. J. Needham: *Science and Civilisation in China*, vol. ii, ch. 10, pp. 89–98. On the problem of Chinese and Vietnamese methods of logic see, for example, P. Huard: 'Les Chemins du Raisonnement et de la Logique en Extrême-Orient', *Bull. de la Société des Études Indochinoises*, n.s., vol. xxiv, pt. 3 (1949).

Chapter III

1. The Chinese tribute system from the seventeenth to the nineteenth centuries has been analysed in detail by J. K. Fairbank and S. Y. Teng: 'On the Ch'ing Tributary System', *Harvard Journal of Asiatic Studies*, vol. vi (Harvard, 1941). On the history of Viet-Nam's relationship with China see Lê Thanh Khôi: *Le Viet-Nam: Histoire et Civilisation* (Paris, 1955).

2. *The Dynastic Chronicles of the Bangkok Era: The Fourth Reign*. Translated by Chadin Flood, vol. ii (Tokyo, 1966), pp. 300–4.

3. There is a detailed study of this division of Dai-Viet between the Trinh and the Nguyên, and of the subsequent wars between the two families, in L. Cadière: 'Le Mur de Dông-Hoi, Étude sur l'Établissement des Nguyên en Cochinchine'. *Bull. de l'École Française d'Extrême-Orient*, vi (Hanoi, 1906).

4. M. Gaultier: *Minh Mang* (Paris, 1935).

5. For a good, detailed account of this period, and of French activity in Viet-Nam generally down to about 1885, see A. Schreiner: *Abrégé de l'Histoire d'Annam* (Saigon, 1906).

6. Cf. L. Finot: 'L'Archéologie Indochinoise, 1917–30', *Bull. de la Commission Archéologique de l'Indochine* (Paris, 1931); there is of course a large quantity of academic literature on the subject.

7. O. Mandelshtam: *Collected Works*, edited by G. P. Strune and B. A. Filipoff (New York, 1966).

   I owe this reference to Mr Robin Milner-Gulland of the University of Sussex.

8. Alexandre de Rhodes: *Dictionarium Annamaticum, Lusitanum et Latinum* (Rome, 1651). De Rhodes had been in Viet-Nam for long periods between 1615 and 1645; but the long-accepted version that he was the first to create a Romanized script for Vietnamese has been challenged by Father Thanh Lang. For a good account of the development of *quôc-ngu* writing see Dinh Xuân Nguyên (Thanh Lang): *Apport Français dans la Littérature Vietnamienne* (Saigon, 1962), pp. 26–30.

9. On the development of Vietnamese literature in the 1920s and 1930s, see Dinh Xuân Nguyên, *op. cit.*; Pham Thê Ngu: *Viêt-Nam Van-Hoc Su Gian-Uoc Tân-Biên*, vol. iii (Saigon, 1965); and also S. D. O'Harrow: *The Growth of Modern Vietnamese Prose Fiction* (unpublished thesis, M.A., University of London, 1965).

10. In the sixty years before the French annexed Saigon, the capital had been at Huê; before that the Saigon area had been within the virtually independent kingdom of the Nguyên princes (also ruled from Huê) ever since its first settlement by Vietnamese in the mid-seventeenth century. Earlier than that, Cochinchina had

been part of Cambodia. Under French rule, although Hanoi was the capital of the whole Union Indochinoise from 1887 Cochinchina still had considerable autonomy thanks to the fact that it was a colony with a direct relationship to Paris, whereas the rest of the Union consisted of protectorates.

PART TWO

Chapter IV

1. The literature of French colonial theory is immense; for an introduction to it see R. F. Betts: *Assimilation and Association in French Colonial Theory, 1890–1914* (New York, 1961).

2. Cf. Nguyên Huu Khang: *La Commune Annamite, Étude historique, juridique et economique* (Paris, 1946), pp. 51–7.

3. The best introduction to the Vietnamese village is G. C. Hickey: *Village in Viet-Nam* (Yale, 1964), but it must be remembered that it relates specifically to a village in Cochinchina. Another useful study, giving the picture for Tongking in a more generalized way, is P. Ory: *La Commune Annamite au Tonkin* (Paris, 1894). On the Chinese background, and especially the importance of the clan in South China, see M. Freedman: *Lineage Organsation in Southeastern China* (London, 1958).

4. Phan Huy Chu: *Lich-Triêu Hiên-Chuong Loai-Chi*, compiled about 1820 and surviving in several copies (in Chinese); it was extensively used by Nguyên Huu Khang, *op. cit.* For a summary of traditional village legislation over the centuries, cf. Nghiêm Dang: *Viet-Nam, Politics and Public Administration* (Honolulu, 1966), pp. 146–50.

5. Môc-Hoa is now in Kiên-Tuong province; many of the South Vietnamese provinces were renamed, with new boundaries, by Ngô Dinh Diêm.

6. 'Rapport du Gouverneur de la Cochinchine sur la Situation Politique du Pays, 1922.' (National Archives, Saigon.)

7. Cf. Chapter I, note 9, above. Coulet's work gives the only detailed account of the secret society revolt of 1916 in Cochinchina.

8. 'Rapport du Gouverneur de la Cochinchine, etc., 1917.' (National Archives, Saigon.)

9. The statistics for 1930 were published in Yves Henri: *Economie Agricole de l'Indochine* (Hanoi, 1932).

Chapter V

1. J. R. Levenson: *Confucian China and its Modern Fate*, vol. ii, pp. 14 ff., cf. Review of Trân Trong Kim's volumes by E. Gaspardone, *Bull. de l'École Française d'Extrême-Orient*, 1930 and 1933.

2. Figures from *The Religions of Viet-Nam in Faith and Fact* (San Francisco, 1966; published for U.S. Navy). This is a minimum figure for the Caodaists; other sources give one million or more adepts.

3. G. Coulet: *Cultes et Religions de l'Indochine Annamite* (Saigon, 1929), pp. 179–86. I am indebted to Mrs Marjorie Topley for information about the *Tao-Yuan*, which is also known as the 'Red Swastika Society'.

There is no satisfactory account of the development of Caodaism in any Western language, but see: Gouvernement-Général de l'Indochine: *Contribution à l'Histoire des Mouvements Politiques de l'Indochine Française*, vol. vii, *Le Caodaisme* (Hanoi, 1937); also G. Gobron: *Histoire du Caodaisme* (Paris, 1948); and G. C. Hickey, *Village in Vietnam* (Yale, 1964), Appendix B. The account here is based on these works and also conversations with Caodaists in Saigon.

4. On the role of the medium (*đồng*) in some North Vietnamese sects, see M. Durand: *Technique et Panthéon des Médiums Vietnamienne* (Paris, 1959).

5. There is an account of *Hoa-Hao* Buddhism in B. B. Fall: 'The Political-Religious Sects of Viet-Nam', *Pacific Affairs*, September 1955, later reprinted in his *Viet-Nam Witness, 1953–66* (New York, 1966), pp. 148–54. *Hoa-Hao* (like the Chinese *Tai-Ping*) means literally 'Great Peace'.

6. Donald Lancaster: *The Emancipation of French Indochina* (London, 1961), pp. 89–90. The best account of Japanese policy towards Vietnamese nationalist and religious groups is in P. Devillers: *Histoire du Viet-Nam de 1940 à 1952* (Paris, 1952), pp. 88 ff.

7. Phan Xuân Hoa: *Tam-Muoi-Bây Nam Cach-Mênh Viêt-Nam* (Hanoi, 1949), p. 100.

8. Cf. Donald E. Smith: *Religion and Politics in Burma* (Princeton, 1965).

9. For an introduction to Japanese Buddhism, see M. Anesaki: *Religious Life of the Japanese People* (Tokyo, 1938).

10. Cf. Wing-tsit Chan: *Religious Trends in Modern China* (New York, 1953).

11. The best introduction to Vietnamese Buddhism is in Mai Tho Truyên: *Le Bouddhisme au Viet-Nam* (Saigon, 1962), originally published in 'Présence du Bouddhisme', *France-Asie*, xvi (Saigon, 1959).

The attempt here to compare Vietnamese and Japanese Buddhism is based on the author's own observations in Saigon and Huê in 1966; the Vietnamese Buddhists do not openly admit that there are two separate sects amongst them, but the differences between Lotus Buddhism and Amidism are evident to the informed observer.

11. Trân Van Giap: 'Le Bouddhisme en Annam', *Bull. de l'École Française d'Extrême-Orient*, xxxii, 1932.

13. On the early history of Christianity in Viet-Nam see G. Taboulet, *La Geste Française en Indochine*, vol. i (Paris, 1955); and also G. Coulet, *Cultes et Religions* (cited above). The figures for 1966 are from the source cited in note 1 (Chapter V), above.

Chapter VI

1. The principal Western account of the Constitutionalist Party after 1917 is that of I. Milton Sacks: 'Marxism in Viet-Nam' in F. N. Trager: *Marxism in South East Asia* (Stanford, 1959), but it is very brief (not being an integral part of Professor Sacks' subject in that article). All accounts of the party give its date of foundation as 1923, and therefore ignore completely its early development between 1917 and that year.

2. On the ideas of Chailley-Bert and Harmand see, to begin with, R. F. Betts: *Assimilation and Association, etc.* (cited in note 1, Chapter IV, above).

3. Quoted from T. F. Power: *Jules Ferry and the Renaissance of French Imperialism* (New York, 1944).

4. On this movement see Nguyên Phut Tan: *A Modern History of Viet-Nam* (Saigon, 1964), chapters on Phan Châu Trinh and Phan Bôi Châu; cf. also note 9, Chapter II, above.

5. Most of the information given here about the Constitutionalist Party is derived from this newspaper, published in Saigon between 1917 and 1925; and from its successor *La Tribune Indochinoise* (Saigon, 1926–42). See also Georges Garros: *Forceries Humaines: L'Indochine litigieuse, Esquisse d'une Entente Franco-Annamite* (Paris, 1926).

6. Nghiêm Dang: *Viet-Nam, Politics and Public Administration* (cited above), pp. 59, 133; and 'Rapport du Gouverneur de la Cochinchine sur la Situation Politique du Pays, 1922' (National Archives, Saigon).

7. Quotation translated from *La Tribune Indochinoise*, 29th June 1929; cf. Nguyên Dang Thuc: *Asian Culture and Vietnamese Humanism* (Saigon, 1965), pp. 54 ff.

Chapter VII

1. Nguyên An Ninh: *La France en Indochine* (Paris, 1925).
   No Western source has a full account of the career of Nguyên

An Ninh: see *Dân-Quyên* (Saigon newspaper, in Vietnamese), 16th August 1964; *L'Avenir du Tonkin*, 5th May 1926; and *La Lutte*, 1936–7 *passim*, for the Congress movement of those years.

2. Nguyên Phut Tan: *A Modern History of Viet-Nam* (cited above, note 4, Chapter VI).

3. The only full-length biography of Hô is Jean Lacouture: *Hô Chi Minh* (Paris, 1967); it includes references to other available sources.

4. The Governor-General was Klobukowski; the speech from which the quotation is translated was printed in *Le Courrier Saigonnais*, 27th November 1909.

5. Gouvernement-Général de l'Indochine: *Contribution à l'Histoire des Movements Politiques de l'Indochine*, vol. i: *Le 'Parti Revolutionnaire du Jeune Annam'* (Hanoi, 1933).

6. Same series, vol. ii: *Le 'Parti National Annamite' au Tonkin* (Hanoi, 1933).

7. Same series, vol. iv: *Le Parti Communiste Indochinois* (Hanoi, 1934), pp.　　.

8. On the Trotskyists in this period, see I. M. Sacks, 'Marxism in Viet-Nam' in F. N. Trager: *Marxism in South-East Asia* (Stanford, 1959).

9. For the composition of this government see P. Devillers: *Histoire du Viet-Nam de 1940 à 1952* (Paris, 1952), pp. 125–7. No detailed account of its short history has been written.

10. On the development of the *Viet-Minh* front see B. B. Fall: *Le Viet-Minh* (Paris, 1960); also J. Lacouture, *op. cit.*

Chapter VIII

1. Quoted by Jerome Ch'en: *Mao and the Chinese Revolution* (London, 1965), p. 223.

2. Truong Chinh: *The Resistance will Win* (Hanoi, 1960), reprinted in *Primer for Revolt* (New York, 1963); originally published in a Vietnamese Communist journal, 1946–7.

   Vo Nguyên Giap: *People's War, People's Army* (Hanoi, 1961), also reprinted in an American edition with an introduction by B. B. Fall (New York, 1962).

3. A number of books and articles in Vietnamese dealing with such heroes appeared in the early 1940s. They included a new translation by Mac Bao Tiên of Nguyên Trai: *Lam-Son Thuc-Luc* (1944), which was a contemporary account of Lê Loi's struggles against the Chinese; and Hoa Bang: *Quang-Trung Anh-Hung Dân-Tôc* (Hanoi, 1944), dealing with the career and victories of Quang-

Trung, 'hero of the people'; the latter author also published essays on Lê Loi and Trân Hung Dao about this time.

4. Cf. L. Cadière: 'Le Mur de Dông-Hoi, Étude sur l'Établissement des Nguyên en Cochinchine', *Bull. de l'École Française d'Extrême Orient*, vi (Hanoi, 1906).

5. Bernard B. Fall: *Street without Joy* (Harrisburg, 1961).

6. The text of the Geneva Agreement and Declaration is reprinted in Marvin E. Gettleman: *Viet-Nam, History, Documents and Opinion on a major World Crisis* (Penguin Books, Harmondsworth, 1965), pp. 144–68.

7. This too is reproduced in Gettleman, *op. cit.*, pp. 64–7.

8. D. Lancaster: *The Emancipation of French Indochina* (London, 1961), citing for the full text of the 4th June treaty, *L'Année Politique, 1954*, pp. 572–3.

PART THREE

Chapter IX

1. The text of this speech, from which the quotation at the beginning of Part Three is taken, is also reproduced by Gettleman, *op. cit.*, pp. 341–7.

2. Cf. W. J. Buch: 'La Compagnie des Indes Néerlandaises et l'Indochine', *Bull. de l'École Française d'Extrême-Orient* (Hanoi, 1936).

3. Samuel Baron: *A Description of the Kingdom of Tonqueen* (original edition 1686; reprinted in John Churchill: *Collection of Voyages and Travels*, vol. iv, London, 1732).

4. Charles Robequain: *L'Evolution Economique de l'Indochine Française* (Paris, 1939; English translation, 1944) gives the best account of French economic achievement in Indochina.

5. Cf. Donald Lancaster, *op. cit.*, pp. 98–101.

6. P. Gourou: *Les Paysans du Delta Tonkinois* (Paris, 1936).

7. In his contribution to P. J. Honey: *North Viet-Nam To-Day* (New York, 1962), originally published in *China Quarterly*, no. ix, January–March 1962, p. 109. Dr Bich argued that the Diem government, at that time still in power, should trade with North Viet-Nam.

8. W. W. Rostow: *The Stages of Economic Growth* (Cambridge, 1960), pp. 19, 26.

9. Trân Quôc Vuong, Ha Van Tan, *et al.*: *Lich-Su Chê-Dô Phong-Kiên Viêt-Nam* (Hanoi, 1960): introduction by Trân Van Giau, in vol. i, p. 4.

10. Lê Duân: 'Socialist Industrialisation', a speech at the seventh

session of the Central Committee of the Lao-Dông Party, 1963, in *On the Socialist Revolution in Viet-Nam*, vol. ii (Hanoi, 1965), p. 14.

Chapter X

1. Mao Tse-tung: *On Contradiction* (English translation, Peking, 1960), p. 1. The original was written in 1937.
2. Appendix to F. Engels: *Ludwig Feuerbach and the End of Classical German Philosophy* (English edition, Moscow, 1950).
3. R. Deloustal: 'Ressources financières et economiques de l'État dans l'Ancien Annam', *Revue Indochinoise*, n.s. xlii–xliii (Hanoi, 1924–25).
4. Hoang Van Chi: *From Colonialism to Communism, a Case History of North Viet-Nam* (London, 1954).
5. *The Quynh-Luu Uprisings* (Saigon, 1958).
6. These figures are given in the Resolution of the Fifth Plenum of the Central Committee of the *Lao-Dông* Party, July 1961, translated in *Vietnamese Studies*, no. 2; *Agricultural Problems* (Hanoi, 1964); see also V. P. Karamyshev: *Agriculture in the Democratic Republic of Viet-Nam* (Russian edition, Moscow, 1959; English translation by U.S. Joint Publications Research Service, Washington, 1961).
7. Cf. Chapter III, note 10, above. The study by S. D. O'Harrow is particularly concerned with the work of Nhât Linh. It should be compared with the translations of early socialist and Marxist writing in Viet-Nam, such as that of Ngô Tât Tô, in 'Littérature du Viet-Nam', *Europe*, nos. 387–8 (Paris, 1961).
8. Huu Mai: *The Last Stronghold* (English translation, Hanoi, 1963); the novel itself is dated April 1961.
9. Hoang Van Chi: *op. cit.*, Part iv.
10. Quoted by Nguyên Dang Thuc: *Asian Culture and Vietnamese Humanism* (Saigon, 1965), p. 96; in an article on the *Nhân-Van* affair.

Chapter XI

1. One of the clearest accounts of Diem's struggle for power in the years 1954–5 is that of Donald Lancaster: *The Emancipation of French Indochina* (London, 1961), chapters xviii and xx. See also Joseph Buttinger: *Viet-Nam, a Dragon Embattled* (New York, 1967), vol. ii, chapter xi.
2. Denis Warner: *The Last Confucian* (London, 1963), which gives a useful insight into the Diêm period despite its evident bias against the government. A less hostile general survey is Robert Scigliano:

South Viet-Nam, Nation under Stress (Boston, 1963). The fullest biographical details on Diem and Nhu are to be found in Bernard B. Fall: *The Two Viet-Nams, a Political and Military Analysis* (New York, 1963), ch. xii. To these studies of the Diêm administration may now be added Dennis J. Duncanson: *Government and Revolution in Viet-Nam* (London, 1968).

3. Emanuel Mounier: *Personalism* (English translation, London, 1952), p. xix. The best account of Vietnamese Personalism is that by John C. Donnell: 'Personalism in Viet-Nam' in Wesley R. Fishel: *Problems of Freedom: South Viet-Nam since Independence* (Michigan S.U., East Lansing, 1961).

4. Cf. Nghiêm Dang: *Viet-Nam, Politics and Public Administration* (Honolulu, 1966), pp. 157-9.

5. For a critical assessment of the South Vietnamese economy in the first half of the Diêm period see B. B. Fall: 'South Viet-Nam's Internal Problems', *Pacific Affairs*, September 1958, summarized in the same author's *Viet-Nam Witness* (New York, 1966), pp. 169-189.

6. The activities of these movements in one particular village are indicated by G. C. Hickey: *Village in Viet-Nam* (Yale, 1964), pp. 10, 202, etc.; see also Nghiêm Dang, *op. cit.*, pp. 198-9.

7. For a damming account of the *Cân-Lao* party, see D. Warner, *op. cit.*, pp. 116 ff.

8. The official version is given most fully in the 'White Paper', U.S. Department of State: *Aggression from the North* (Washington, 1965).

9. G. C. Hickey, *op. cit.*, pp. 58-73.

10. Cf. G. M. Kahin and J. Lewis: *The United States in Vietnam* (New York, 1967), p. 100.

11. Douglas Pike: *Viet-Cong: the Organisation and Techniques of the National Liberation Front of South Vietnam* (M.I.T. Press, Cambridge, Mass., 1966).

12. Ibid., pp. 154-65, etc. This interpretation of Mr Pike's data, which he himself does not pursue vigorously, should not be taken to imply that Hanoi had *no* influence in the South before 1963; it is a question of the tightness of the control.

13. Ibid., p. 162; and *Sunday Times*, 23rd February 1964.

14. The policy of the Democratic Republic of Viet-Nam towards the Sino-Soviet dispute down to 1963 has been studied in detail by P. J. Honey: *Communism in North Viet-Nam* (M.I.T. Press, 1963). Indications of a hardening of the line by Hanoi towards the struggle in the South about the middle of 1963 are contained in Nguyên Chi Thanh: 'Who will win in South Viet-Nam?', *Hoc-Tâp*, July 1963; English translation in *Vietnamese Studies*, no. 1 (Hanoi,

1964). General Thanh was later in command of North Vietnamese troops in the South, until his death (apparently in action) in the summer of 1967.

Chapter XII

1. Cf. R. Scigliano: *South Viet-Nam, Nation under Stress* (Boston, 1963), p. 49.
2. Richard Clutterbuck: *The Long, Long War: the Emergency in Malaya* (London, 1967), especially ch. viii.
3. In a speech at the International Congress of Orientalists, Ann Arbor (Michigan), August 1967.
4. A. M. Schlesinger, jr.: *The Bitter Heritage* (Boston, 1966), p. 31.
5. *Public Papers of the Presidents: Dwight D. Eisenhower 1954* (Washington, 1960), no. 306 (p. 949).
6. Dean Acheson: 'Crisis in Asia, an Examination of United States Policy', *Department of State Bulletin*, xxii (Washington, 1950), pp. 111–18.
7. Speech to the University of Washington, quoted in Theodore C. Sorenson: *Kennedy* (London, 1965), p. 511.

EPILOGUE

1. Admiral Reveillère: 'Patriotisme Annamite', *Revue Indochinoise*, 6th year, no. 190, 9th June 1902, pp. 515–17. I am indebted to Dr Milton Osborne of the University of Monash for this quotation.
2. Thu Van: 'A Vietnamese Letter to President Johnson', *Michigan Quarterly Review*, vol. vi, April 1967.
3. Quoted from Malraux's preface to the catalogue for the 'Exposition D. Galanis' (Paris, 1922), by W. G. Langlois: *André Malraux, the Indochina Adventure* (London, 1966). The latter is a detailed account of Malraux's experiences in Saigon and Cambodia; it also throws valuable light on the political atmosphere of Cochinchina in 1923–5.
4. Quoted from the English translation: André Malraux: *Man's Estate* (Penguin Books, Harmondsworth, 1961), p. 215; the second quotation is ibid., p. 316.

Index

203

THE INITIAL INSULT

Also by Mindy McGinnis

Be Not Far from Me

Heroine

The Female of the Species

This Darkness Mine

A Madness So Discreet

In a Handful of Dust

Not a Drop to Drink

Given to the Sea

Given to the Earth

THE INDIAN INSULT

MINDY McGINNIS

 KATHERINE TEGEN BOOKS
An Imprint of HarperCollins Publishers

Katherine Tegen Books is an imprint of HarperCollins Publishers.

The Initial Insult
Copyright © 2021 by Mindy McGinnis
All rights reserved. Printed in the United States of America.
No part of this book may be used or reproduced in any manner
whatsoever without written permission except in the case of brief
quotations embodied in critical articles and reviews. For information
address HarperCollins Children's Books, a division of HarperCollins
Publishers, 195 Broadway, New York, NY 10007.
www.epicreads.com

Library of Congress Control Number: 2020938948
ISBN 978-0-06-298242-1

Typography by Erin Fitzsimmons
21 22 23 24 25   PC/LSCH   10 9 8 7 6 5 4 3 2 1
❖
First Edition

For Amanda.
We've been in the dark together.

THE INITIAL INSULT

Chapter 1

Tress

Out here, something can turn to nothing real fast.

The buildings fade out as you drive from town, paved roads turn to gravel, and then to dirt. Cell phone towers start to disappear, electric lines begin to sag, and soon, you're nowhere. Grandpa Cecil says that's a good thing, says the animals like it that way. But the animals he's talking about are in cages, and I don't think they like much about life at all.

Most of them were bred in captivity, but those that weren't—like the panther—they've got a different feel about them. Something in the eyes. Something they lost. They watch me and Cecil, waiting for us to make the mistake that will give it back to them. I'm always aware when I'm near the cages, but Cecil's awareness drifts a little with the drink, and he's got a bad eye on account of it, damaged and filmed-over gray.

The cat got it, and Cecil swears he wants the other.

The sign out by the road reads "Amontillado Animal Attractions," but last week somebody spray-painted "White Trash Zoo" over it. I'm scraping away with the end of a screwdriver, tiny curls of red paint falling around my feet, the tips of the poison ivy vine that climbs the sign post brushing against my arms. I'm not worried; I don't get poison ivy. Cecil says that's on account of my mom, but she's gone, so I can't ask her if she got the rash or not. I push deeper, accidentally digging into the planks and sending a chip flying off into the overgrown ditch, a new scar bright against the old wood.

An autumn sun is burning into my back, giving the last of the summer warmth to my skin as I work. School started two months ago, but it's still hot down in the valley, and the school board spent their whole last meeting debating with parents over the cost of air-conditioning. That and the flu that's burning through Prospero, the next town over. It turned into an argument about taxes and the last levy failing, then the school nurse getting shouted down by someone with a WebMD printout. My cousin, Ribbit, told us all about it, said pretty soon the parents were fighting with each other, about what was more important—health or air-conditioning.

Me, I don't have parents. Just Grandpa Cecil. That's
something of mine that turned to nothing overnight
back in fifth grade, my house and my allowance and
my toys and clothes all following about a month after.
Friends took more time to disappear. But they did.

"Air-conditioning," Cecil huffed when Ribbit stopped
by, his rusted-out truck idling in the driveway because
he's never been quite at ease with the animals.

"Walk outside," Cecil said. "There's air."

Air-conditioning was for pussies, Cecil went on, and
he didn't raise none of them. I didn't argue against that,
since the person he did raise is gone now, and what he
does for me can't exactly be called parenting. More like
just making sure I don't die, and if I do, that it's not
because one of the animals killed me. Then his business
would be shot.

"Nice sign," Ribbit had said when he put the truck in
reverse, ready to head back to the Usher house, down the
road. I hadn't noticed it until he pointed it out, our sign
being something I looked at every day but never really
saw, like Cecil's milky eye rolling in its socket. The spray
paint was new enough to still be shiny but old enough
to have soaked in. Days, then. For days people down in
town had likely been laughing, and me driving right past
it in Cecil's old truck, coming home from school to feed
the animals their bloody, raw-meat dinners, not seeing

it. Not seeing the insult, painted in bright red right at my own doorstep.

Cecil had raised his ball cap and scratched his head, honestly stumped. "Who would go and do a thing like that?"

I know. I know exactly who.

It's got to be someone who doesn't mind driving the switchback over the ridge in the dark, the turns so tight you pray you don't meet someone, because these roads weren't meant for more than one car at a time.

Someone who knew Goldie-Dog, my ancient mutt who I named back before I had much of a vocabulary, and would still follow me to the cages at feeding time, even though I'd be done and headed back to the house by the time she got to the first pen. The gator got Goldie last week, little tufts of gold-white hair floating in her pond as she eyed me, silent in the morning light.

Someone who thinks they're better than us, someone with—I'm sure—things like air-conditioning and a flu shot and a car with a muffler on it because Cecil and I never heard a damn thing, and the dog never made a peep. Maybe because Goldie was as good as dead already, the deadly V trail of the gator dancing on the surface as she made her move.

Someone who wanted to make sure we know what we are and bothered to drive out of town, past the buildings and the cell towers, past the paved roads and up into the hills, coming back down on the other side out here to our little place. Coming out here to lead Goldie to the water and leave their mark on our doorstep. They left something for nothing and came to take a little bit more from us.

I can see it. I can hear it. I can smell it. She's in her shiny blue car, music blaring until they're close to the house, windows open to air out the sickly sweet smell of weed. She probably shushed the others—the new friends she brought along to torment an old one—probably closed her car door real quiet and slipped Goldie-Dog a treat when she came to greet her, still familiar with her scent after all these years. A kind one. A comforting one. A scent she would've trusted, right up until the gator's jaws snapped down on her spine.

I imagine my old friend even did the sign herself, maybe worrying a bit when the spray can was louder than she thought it would be or shaking her hand when her finger got stiff from pushing down. She was smart enough to take the cans with her, and I bet she even threw them in the dumpster behind the gas station on the way back home after dropping off her friends, probably screwing Hugh Broward in the back seat before she went on home.

I've borne it all with patience, the years of small cuts

that heal over, my heart a pulpy mass of scars. But it was still beating, at least I could say that, right up until she took Goldie from me. Now it's a dead thing, still in my chest. And if I can't feel the good things anymore, then doing a few bad ones shouldn't hurt a bit.

And they are long overdue.

I dig viciously at the last bit of paint, and my screwdriver slips, flying out from under my fingers and sending my hand into a hard scrape against the wood. The pain is sharp and bright, and a shock pulses to the tips of my fingers. There's a splinter in my palm, running from the top of my wrist up into my fate line, close enough to the surface of the skin that I can see the grain in the wood, but deep enough that it's going to hurt like a bitch coming out. I grip it with my teeth and pull, the sun baking my back and a trickle of blood snaking down my arm as I do. In his cage, the panther huffs, tail twitching, suddenly bright-eyed. He can smell it.

I spit the splinter into the ditch, where it pings off one of Cecil's beer bottles.

I'm not like Cecil, wondering who would go and do a thing like that.

I know who.

It was Felicity Turnado.

Chapter 2

Felicity

I'm being carried again, but this time at least I know by who.

Hugh's calf tattoo flashes in front of my eyes as he walks, our school mascot—a raven—flicking with every other step. He's got me hauled over his shoulder, my hip to his ear, my long hair almost reaching the grass as he carries me out past Gretchen Astor's barn, into the woods behind. Plenty of hoots and hollers follow us: the guys urging Hugh to get some, the girls adding their own thoughts, none of them out of concern. My friends—at least, that's what we call each other—watching me half-comatose and being carried off into the dark.

Hugh's tat crosses my vision a few more times, and then he settles me gently onto a rock, the one we always use when the party is at Gretchen's. I slip like water through his arms, sagging into him as he settles in beside me, his body as steady and sure as the boulder underneath me. No wonder everybody calls him "Huge," although the girls are always asking me if there's another reason, eager to know.

"You okay?" he asks.

I don't have words, am past that point, but I do manage to nod. From the house comes another yell, someone emptying a beer over somebody else's head, a splash as yet another person is pushed into the pool—a joke that never gets old . . . to them, anyway. They think he's out here pounding me into the ground, taking advantage of the pretty drunk girl, dragging her into the dark. They think he's the danger. The truth is, I'm safer with Hugh Broward than anyone else on earth.

I've always loved to be carried, and begged my father often when I was little. Arms up and open, trusting. Nobody ever tells me no. Not Dad. Not Huge. Not whoever carried me away from Tress Montor's parents so many years ago. I don't know who that was, just that my arms were too weak to wrap around them, my vision blurry, the blood running down the side of my head hot and sticky in the last of the late-fall heat, drawing mosquitoes.

One buzzes around me now, its call high and whiny. I smack at it, missing completely and hitting myself in the mouth, where there's still a small, silver scar in the corner from my own teeth biting down when . . . when something. No one knows what happened the night the Montors disappeared, not even me—and I was the only one there. Me and whoever carried me.

"Your aim sucks," Huge says, easily swatting the mosquito out of the air.

Everything sucks right now. My motor coordination. My limb control. My life. I start to slide again, slipping down past Hugh's knees to the ground. He grabs my wrist, lowering me gently.

"Close?" he asks, and I nod.

He unbuttons my shorts, easing them down to my ankles, followed by my underwear. Then he walks away, far enough that I can't see his silhouette, hear his steps crunching the dead leaves, or smell the faded scent of his cologne.

The whirling in my head slows, centers, focuses, like a cat that's been circling prey, ready to pounce. It does, and the seizure comes, my hands clenching and unclenching in the dirt on either side of me, my feet grinding into the ground, pressing dirt into the silk underwear tangled around my sandals. Mom always details the seizures to me, after, even though I've told her that I am aware right before I have them, that I can see and feel and hear and taste every damn thing. Better than normal, even.

It's during them that I can't recall. A light turned off. A clipped reel from a film.

There are branches overhead, darkly black against the stars, the dead leaves rustling against my hair. I hear and see and feel everything tremendously right now, the world in high def until the focus fades to a pinprick and I'm going, I'm going, I'm going . . .

I'm gone.

The leaves will be in my hair when Hugh and I come back from the woods, that and the dirt on my back causing snide smiles. I usually come around with a burning taste in my mouth, the memory of my last sounds— guttural, helpless—sending a spike of embarrassment to chase all the misfiring in my brain. Sometimes the worst happens; this was one of those times. There's warm urine between my legs, harsh and acidic, soaking into the forest floor.

I sit up, easing myself, shakily, onto the rock, pulling my underwear back into place, followed by my shorts. The first time Hugh was too mortified to take them down all the way, but he's learned over the years. He comes when I call, settling beside me. I lean into him.

"You know . . . ," he says slowly, a conversation we've had more than once starting all over again.

"There are medications," I finish for him. "Yes, I know. I take them."

"But they don't mix well with drinking." It's his turn

to finish my sentence. "Or with that other shit you do," he adds.

"I do lots of shit," I say. And it's true. I'm a shitty person.

"So maybe cut it out," Hugh says, an edge in his tone he's not used with me before. One that cuts, sharp, like the smell of my urine, only just beginning to fade as a few cold, fat drops of rain start to fall.

"I don't want to," I tell him, taking him by the hand and leading him back toward Gretchen's and the sounds of the party; shrill screeches as the rain starts to fall in earnest and the occasional yap of William Wilson, her seriously stressed-out poodle.

And Felicity Turnado doesn't have to stop, doesn't have to do anything she doesn't want to do. That's the truth. There's a deeper truth, though. The *why* of it. A truth that I keep to myself, bound deep and dark, surfacing out of my mind in the still moments before sleep, crawling up, climbing out, finding light, whispering to me in the night.

Because if I stop drinking and drop the pills, if I take better care of myself and let good people love me and give my own love to those who deserve it, I'll have everything that Tress Montor doesn't. And I don't deserve that.

Because I'm the reason she has nothing.

Chapter 3

Cat

My cousins come in the night,
Feline paws pattering
in the cool.
Piling onto my back, we give,
each to the other,
Warmth and memories—
both carried in blood.
They settle on me, curl against my belly,
our soft clicks
And rough tongues, filling the night.
They wish for what I have,
Food—roof—clean coat—fresh water.
I want what they are.
Achingly thin. Slip under the fence
A young one rolls, sleep making her reckless.

Slides down my pelt,

Pooling near my mouth.

Another feline's bones in my teeth would be bitter.

So instead I lick, a mat

Separates under my will, like the rabbits who crack open

when they wander too close.

She is young, and warm,

blood close to the skin with sleep.

It doesn't have to be spilled. For me

To smell the memories, best and last.

If I took her she would be

mother / rain

I huff, her pelt billowing under my breath.

Deeper is her last meal

still in her blood,

death mixing with her life, quiet as it fades.

warm / poison

A possum passes the cage, coat dripping from the wet grass.

Quiet and cold, blood not talking.

He is not my kin.

Or my meal.

Today the girl, in the sun, blood brought by wood,

a strong scent on the breeze,

Felicity / hate

Chapter 4

Tress

"The Allan house, really?"

"Yep." Ribbit nods, his toes flicking in the pond water as bluegills nibble on them. "They're tearing it down."

"Huh," I say, rolling up my jeans and joining him on the tailgate of his truck, backed up to the pond so we can dangle our legs in.

The Usher house looms behind us, built by Ribbit's ancestor to show the world what he could do. What the world did in return was eat his fortune, and now the rocks he took from the ground are working their way back to it, tumbling down in a stiff wind. When we were kids Ribbit's dad wouldn't let us play near the foundation, said a stone could come down on our heads and we'd be done for. And now the old Allan place is going the same way. Something to nothing.

It bothers me, for reasons I can't say.

"Why, though?" I ask, instinctively pulling back from the first fish that comes in to investigate my feet. "Why tear it down now?"

"Stay still," Ribbit instructs. "It's like a free pedicure. People in the city pay money for this."

"That's why you spend so much time at the pond?" I ask. "Pedicures?"

"I don't know *why now*, with the Allan house," he says, ignoring my jibe. "But it came up at the last township meeting that it's an 'attraction for the youth.'"

There's always got to be an Usher on the township council, same with the school board. Nothing is official until the oldest family in Amontillado weighs in. Right now Lenore—Ribbit's mother—fills the chair, her maiden name a strong enough pull to count. Nobody had blinked when she gave Ribbit her name, his dad— an easily swayable Troyer—bending to her will. Ribbit likes to go with her to all the meetings, a little Usher apprentice on her heels from the moment he could walk. His devotion to her has never faded, his presence in local politics now an assumed. It makes him feel needed and necessary, which doesn't happen much.

Plus, the adults are the only ones who call him by

his real name, Kermit. The kids renamed him Ribbit the first day of kindergarten, and he never argued. He's not a fighter, my cousin. He likes to say he's a lover, but he's a little too skinny and a lot too awkward to be that, either.

He pulls his legs up out of the water, the zigzag scar on the back of his calf still raised and red even though it happened a long time ago. Ribbit and I had been adventuring in some of the old Usher outbuildings, where a kid could find all kinds of great stuff—old bottles, scraps of metal; once, we even tripped over a tombstone out on the back acre, collapsed into the ground and wiped smooth from a century of rain and wind, a long-dead Usher underneath us as we ran, laughing above them.

The Usher property was our playground, until Ribbit and I went over an old fence that wasn't ready for our weight. It gave out underneath him, the rusty barbed wire still sharp, digging in deep and tearing his leg open as he went down. My mom said I couldn't play at my cousin's anymore, said her older sister didn't do a good job keeping the property safe for kids. But Mom was gone not long after that, and Cecil couldn't have cared less if I was safe or not, as long as I came home in time to do the chores.

"Attraction for the youth," I repeat with a snort,

thinking of the old Allan house, as dilapidated as the Usher property, if not more. "That's not news, not to anybody. Half our parents partied out there."

"And it's where half of us were conceived," Ribbit adds, for which I give him a shove. He takes my blow easily, swaying with the push and ending back where he was, upright, beside me, our shoulders touching.

The Allan house. We've all spent time there, frightened our feet will punch through rotting floors, or a beam come down on our heads. I've put my hands on the walls, plaster coming loose, even at the lightest touch, and wondered if I might feel something. A deeper call, or a beating heart. Cecil is an Allan, which means I am, too, twice diluted, but still . . . it's there.

My mom would've been an Allan, if Grandma hadn't been the last of the Ushers. She'd refused to marry, saying she'd rather see the Usher blood die than have it walk around in a body that didn't carry the name. Cecil, the youngest of the Allan brothers, had taken her up on the offer, his own ancestral home already a crumbled ruin. When both his brothers died in Vietnam their name went the same way as the house is about to: something to nothing.

"They talked about the animals again," Ribbit says.

I sigh, the exhalation going all the way down to my feet and scattering the fish that had gathered there.

"Cecil's got permits for all of them."

Ribbit stretches, his long arms curling back behind his red hair, shaggy and in need of a cut. "I don't think it's the permits that are the problem. People just don't like knowing there's a crocodile nearby."

"It's an alligator," I tell him.

"Whatever. Next time a kid gets bit, you know Cecil's going down."

I pull my feet out of the water, toes dripping, one finger in Ribbit's face. "First of all, he didn't get bit— he was scratched by the orangutan, and second, he was inside the line."

I repaint the lines every Sunday, a yellow stripe in the ground to mark what's safe and what's not. Some mom wanted a better shot of her kid with Rue, and our waiver is worded the way it is for a reason.

"People are stupid," I say, putting my feet back in the water, letting the coolness slip up my legs as I sink into the pond, wishing it could touch the heat in my chest.

"People are," he agrees. "Dill Riley coughed at the township meeting, and everybody about lost their shit."

"Old Dill or Young Dill?" I ask, even though Young Dill probably has a least thirty years on both of us.

"Old Dill."

"Flu?" I ask, but Ribbit only shrugs. There's been a nasty strain running through the county, tearing up

guts and leaving people wilted and pale in its wake. They
gave out flu shots for free at the clinic last week, urging
the very young and very old to get vaccinated. I guess
that's how death works, clipping us off at both ends.

"Doesn't matter if Dill had it or not," Ribbit says.
"We all treated him like he did. He could've swung a
dead cat with a long tail and not hit anybody. People got
far away, fast."

"Hmm . . . ," I say, trying to remember if any of our
zoo visitors have been coughing, and wondering if they
could pass it to the animals. Last thing we need to be is
the Amontillado *Dead* Animal Attractions. I slip farther
out into the water to where it grows colder, near the
drop-off.

"Hey, don't . . ." Ribbit scoots closer to the edge of
the tailgate, one hand on my shoulder. He hates it when
I go in the water.

"I can swim," I remind him.

"I can't," he tells me for the millionth time. "So stop
making me nervous."

"It's the panther the township should be worried
about, not the alligator," I say, ignoring him as the mud
I stirred up settles, the fish coming back in to see what
changed in their world.

"They are."

I sigh again and pull myself back up onto the tailgate,

the ends of my jeans wet where I didn't roll them up far enough. "You have anything good to tell me?"

"There's gonna be a party," he offers. "Last one, before the Allan house is torn down."

"Yeah?" I say, unrolling my pant legs.

"Everybody'll be there," Ribbit pushes. "I figured you could, you know, maybe make some money."

I stop struggling with the wet denim. He's got a point. Where there's a party there's plenty of wants, and I'm able to fill them, taking care of my own needs in return. I've been looking out for myself long enough to smell opportunity, but I know the scent of danger, too. If the township council finally gets it into their head to come after Amontillado Animal Attractions, Lenore Usher's vote won't be enough to save us, and I can't say for sure that she'd back us. She and my mom might have had the same last name and shared the same blood, but it takes more than that to make someone family.

Grandma died before I knew her, slow and awful, by all accounts. The slow part she was thankful for, calling a lawyer to her bedside to take the house right out from under Cecil's feet and give it to Lenore. The awful part I don't like to think on much. Lenore told me once she died screaming, clutching her belly and refusing to leave her land. Lenore put her mom in the ground the next day, her father out of the house within the week.

My mom landed on her feet, marrying a Montor. Cecil landed in the trailer and has been rolling downhill ever since.

I don't love Cecil's trailer, but it's got a roof and four walls. And a mortgage. One that gets paid more by what we grow on the back acre than the animals that live up front. But at least the animals let us pretend to be respectable.

What bothers me, though, is that I know Ribbit isn't talking about the party because he's worried about my financial situation. He brought it up because he can't go alone. One drink and he'll do anything that's asked of him, strip down, bark like a dog, or funnel a quart of vinegar straight to his gut . . . or somewhere else. I've seen him do all these things, and smile doing them, because it makes people laugh. He doesn't understand that it's not because he's funny but because he's the joke.

I hate when they do that to him.

I hate that he lets them.

But I know why, and I kind of get it. Lenore's had him jumping to her beck and call since he had his feet under him, and the only time she had a smile for Ribbit is when he did as he was asked. If Cecil had trained up our animals half as well as Lenore did her son, I wouldn't have to go to the Allan house tomorrow night just to keep our electricity on.

A minnow comes in close to investigate where my feet have been, the last swirls of mud finally settling. A larger bluegill follows behind, curious. I wonder for a second if the bluegill is the minnow's mom or dad. I've been doing that ever since my own parents disappeared, coupling up smaller animals with larger ones, not wanting even a fish to feel the pain of being an orphan. I can't even claim the title of orphan, not yet. Next month will mark seven years since anyone has seen my mom or dad. Until then, I'm just a ward and Cecil my guardian, because we don't use words like *grandpa* or *granddaughter* to refer to each other. That would imply an emotional connection that isn't there.

But the blood connection is there, one I can't deny because you can see it in the way we both hold our heads high, or square our shoulders when someone walks up to us too quick for comfort. Maybe I learned it from watching him, but I don't think so. I think there's a steel streak in me that comes from Cecil, and I think that same bit of steel is partly what's held up the Allan house for all these years, not the brick and mortar. I've felt it every time I've walked into a party, something calling to me, something saying I belong there.

I know that house, and not just because I've scouted out the best places to do my business dealings at parties. I know that house because it knows me, and we've both been abandoned. There are dark corners inside of it, as there are in me. And if it's going to be destroyed, I've got someone in mind to go down with it.

I shake off my feet, pull my sandals back on. "Everybody's going?"

Ribbit nods quickly, sensing that I'm about to cave.

"All right," I agree. "I'll come."

The fish flash away as I move, my shadow crossing the water, their world changing again, light to dark, in a moment. Like mine. At least theirs changes back quick, the sun returning to warm them.

My world can't be fixed. But maybe it can be put right.

Chapter 5

Felicity

In Amontillado, calling someone *rich* is an insult. Everybody knows who has money and who doesn't, so you don't need to go around showing it off, especially if you're new blood, like we are. Of course, *new blood* means your family hasn't been around for at least five generations. Time carries more weight than money in Amontillado, something Gretchen Astor enjoys reminding me of every time we pass the stone pillar in the center of town with the founding fathers' names inscribed: *Allan. Astor. Montor. Usher.*

I'd like to think she's not doing it on purpose, that maybe running her fingers over her last name as we walk by is an unconscious movement, something she's learned from watching her parents, who worship at the altar of their surname and expect the rest of us to as well. But everything I know of Gretchen is careful and calculated, and despite my money—and we do have it—this is her silently reminding me that *Turnado* isn't up there and never will be.

That little snub isn't the only thing that bothers me about that pillar, though. The Allans are gone. The Ushers are still here, struggling along, clinging to the power embedded in the history of their last name. It's sad enough, knowing how the Allan and Usher lines of Amontillado ended up. It's the other name—Montor— that gives me goose bumps, and for the opposite reason. Nobody knows what happened to Lee Montor, the last male survivor of his name.

And Tress . . . She turned her back on the town— literally—when she went to live in the hills with her grandfather, and metaphorically by refusing help from everyone who tried to give it. And people did try—I know, because I was one of them—to do what they could for the last Montor. But Tress is Tress, and Mom says that pride always was a Montor trait. That and thinking they're better than everyone else, she had told me once, with a sniff. That's how I know Mom wishes *Turnado* was up on that pillar, too.

But it's not.

New money might spend the same as old, but it still

isn't worth as much to the people of Amontillado. So Mom and Dad were careful, putting a deck on the back of the house first, waiting a few years to add the porch on the front. Mom says nobody's better than anybody else, and we don't want people thinking the Turnados got too big for their britches all the sudden. The gas pocket the company hit on our land wasn't exactly a secret—you can't hide a long line of white company trucks. But Dad says every landowner in Amontillado has some money from gas, it's just that nobody needs to know exactly how much.

I don't even know how much, just that they stopped talking about community college a few years back, then told me if I wanted my own car I could pick something out . . . just nothing flashy. They didn't have to clarify. Gretchen Astor's dad had bought himself a BMW when we were in junior high. Somebody spray-painted *ASStor* across the hood two days later. He took the hit and traded it in for a Civic. That car had all the bells and whistles: heated seats, satellite radio, entertainment centers for the kids in the back. Gretchen's mom had worried that it was still too much, but the Civic had passed. Like her dad said—as long as you keep the money out of sight, you're allowed to have it.

Brynn Whitaker is sprawled on my bed, a separator between her toes, her tongue half pushed out between her teeth as she concentrates on painting them. "You're sticking with the clown thing?" she asks.

"Yes," I say.

The package described my Halloween costume as a "sexy clown." Brynn said there was no such thing, but she's going as a taco, so her opinion doesn't weigh very heavily with me.

"I like the bells," I tell her, and I do feel a little validated as I slip the jester's cap on.

It's cute, the purple and pink ends each tipped with a silver bell. They ring when I toss my hair over one shoulder, the curls tickling the bare skin between my shoulder blades. There was not a lot of fabric in that package, for it costing thirty bucks. What there is of it is thin as hell, and it sticks to me like water. I can even see the dimple of my belly button, which is only a few inches above where the skirt fans out into slashes, each of those carrying their own bell.

Brynn glances up from her toes, her skeptical expression falling away. "Fuck. You are a sexy clown."

"Yep," I agree. I know I am. People will be looking at me, which is nothing new. But they'll be able to hear me, too. The bells will signal my entrance and exit, everybody's eyes and ears full of Felicity Turnado. And maybe I can even feel good about myself, for one fucking second.

"Help me out?" Brynn asks, lifting her taco costume from where it's propped in the corner. She's wearing one of my leotards under it—a bright green one from when the dance studio did *Peter Pan*—and when her arms pop out the side and her head comes out the top, she's the most awkward thing I've ever seen. And she's thrilled.

"Ridiculous," I tell her as she spins, apparently happy as she floats in bulky foam. "How am I going to get you into the car?"

"I'll ride in the back," she says. "Unless you're too sexy to drive."

Both our phones go off at the same time, the ringer we set for the school announcement system—"Fuck School," by the Replacements—filling my bedroom.

"What the hell?" Brynn asks, echoing my thoughts.

It's a Friday night. Everybody's big plans are to head to the football game, then out to the Allan house. There's no reason for the school to be calling.

"Oh my God, you don't think they know about the party, do you?" Brynn asks, eyes wide above her tulle lettuce.

"Right," I say, picking up my phone. "And they're using the all-call system to warn us off. You're a genius."

I accept the call, as does Brynn, so Principal Anho's voice is in stereo when she says: "Due to reports of a sharp increase in the flu within the district, the health department in coordination with the superintendent and myself have decided it is in the best interest of the public's health to cancel this evening's football game."

"Awww . . ." Brynn's face falls. I can't imagine her disappointment at not being able to show her taco outfit to the whole town.

"We've still got the party," I remind her. "And now we've got it sooner."

I cut off Anho as she goes on about a possible mandatory curfew if the outbreak worsens, but Brynn leaves her phone on long enough for us to hear her cough, a wet throaty sound that definitely brought something up with it.

"Ew," Brynn says, upper lip raised in distaste. She's holding her phone farther away from herself now, like she's afraid she can catch something through the speaker.

But I'm still stuck on the last thing Anho had mentioned—the possibility of a curfew. Cops in Amontillado tend to leave us alone. They know we're drinking, but they don't make a big deal out of it as long as we stay in the same place long enough to sober up. If the town council institutes a curfew, though, turning a blind eye won't be something we can count on anymore.

A blind eye. I shudder, thinking of Tress's grandpa and his dead white eye.

"Gross," I say, without thinking.

"Yeah," Brynn agrees, still holding her phone at arm's length. "I think Anho choked up a lung."

But I'm not thinking about Anho, or Brynn, or even Tress's grandpa anymore. I'm thinking about me and what I need in order to feel good. Other people around me, their noise filling up my headspace. Eyes on me, letting me know I'm worth looking at. A drink in my hand and a pill in my fist, making everything fade out, edges fuzzy, nothing sharp anywhere. Not my memories. Not my conscience.

Everything needs to be soft and dull, the world a pillow for me to fall into.

And in order for it to happen, I need to make a phone call.

It used to be we would text, when we were younger. Lots of emojis. Hearts and smiley faces. Poop, of course. She still giggled back then, I remember the sound. Now her voice has a permanent hard edge on it, like the one time she cornered me at school after I texted at three in the morning, telling me *calls only*.

"Texts are evidence," she said. "And I don't trust you to be smart enough to send ones that aren't incriminating. Phone calls can't prove shit. We could be talking about anything."

She gave me a once-over then, eyes sweeping the latest outfit that had come in the mail. There's only one good place to shop around here, and if you go there you're guaranteed to end up wearing the same thing as three other girls. So Mom got me a Stitch Fix account a couple of years ago. The third time I asked her to do the checkout process for me she just saved her credit card info on the site and told me to *be responsible.*

I'm not. I just buy everything. Sometimes I don't even open the boxes. Mom has never said anything. We don't check credit card statements anymore.

That day in the hall Tress was wearing a shirt of mine that I'd taken to Goodwill, something I'd never even worn. I could see the two little holes at the neckline where she'd torn the tags out, and it closed my throat a little. If we were still friends, I would've just given her that shirt, maybe loaned it to her after she went through my overflowing closet. She wouldn't have found it picking through outdated shit at Goodwill, a folded twenty in her back pocket, one that probably came from me filling my need.

I glance at Brynn, but she's adjusting her lettuce in the mirror. I quietly pull open my desk drawer, lift my birth control pills to grab a few twenties off the stack of bills underneath. I've got a couple hundred just sitting there. Mom always hands me some cash as I'm going out the door, if I need money for pizza or gas, or if I'm going out with Hugh. Especially if I'm going out with Hugh. The Browards don't have land with a gas pocket on it.

Sometimes Mom hands me money as I'm leaving, and then Dad stops me in the garage and hands me more. I don't tell either of them about the other, which is how I've got a nice stash sitting here, waiting for me to pass it on to someone else.

Someone who will use my money to buy my clothes at the poor store, not knowing. She'd be pissed, I think as I slide the cash into my bra, since sexy clowns don't get pockets.

She'd be so pissed.

Calls only, she'd said that day in the hall. *We could be talking about anything.* Except Tress Montor and I don't talk about just anything. Only illegal stuff. In short, transactional sentences. But it's something, I guess. Something I found to keep her from floating away from me entirely. Something that makes the world a soft place for me and keeps cash flowing into hers.

I can't give Tress anything. She won't accept my clothes, my texts, or my friendship. But I can give her money, folded into a tight square, our skin barely touching as we hand off. The one time I slipped an extra bill in my payment I found it the next morning under my windshield wiper. I know she didn't drive over, because that truck of Cecil's doesn't have a muffler and the whole neighborhood would've called the cops on her in the middle of the night for breaking the noise ordinance.

She probably walked down out of the hills in the black of night to return twenty dollars, rejecting my charity and keeping her conscience clean.

Twenty bucks for a clean conscience. Sounds nice.

I've handed a lot more than that to Tress over the past couple of years. It doesn't help. But I keep trying. I slip past Brynn into my bathroom, my sexy clown reflection staring me down as I dial. She picks up, blunt and monosyllabic.

"Yeah?"

"You coming to the Allan house?" I ask, realizing my mistake when there's no immediate response. A friend would ask her that, someone who was going to meet up with her at the party. I'm not a friend; I'm a customer.

"I need a couple forties," I say quickly. "Maybe some weed?"

Tress's weed is shit, but I'll pass it off to Hugh.

There's a rustling on the other end, like Tress is checking her supply. Then a short answer, quick and concise. "'Kay."

"See you there," I say.

But there's just a click as she hangs up.

Chapter 6

Tress

I need manacles.

Everything else came together pretty quickly and is already tucked into the back of Cecil's truck. The drill and bit, some masonry tools and Quikrete from back when Cecil tried to make a little patio to put the grill on. We found that grill in the ditch, and the concrete he poured has the imprint of the alligator's tail in it, because she got out before it dried. She ate a few of our chickens, and we might have never known the electric on her fence had gone out if not for the racket and the flying feathers. I had to lure her back to her little swamp with a side of beef, then spray her off with the garden hose so the concrete didn't dry in her tail.

And now I'm searching through the lean-to, looking for manacles.

"What a fucking life," I say, then bite my tongue. For all I know my mom and dad don't even have that. I've asked the questions and done the searching, didn't get answers or make any discoveries. Hitting brick walls doesn't feel good physically or metaphorically; I've got scars on my knuckles to prove the first, and memories of being sent on my way by well-meaning adults when I asked hard questions about my parents' disappearance to back up the second. Tonight, I'm going to ask the one person who knows something, the one person that pure human decency has kept me from talking to. I'm done with that. What I've got in mind isn't decent, not by a long shot.

And I need those manacles.

"Cecil!" I call, hoping my voice carries over our acreage. He always says his land is rocky, good-for-nothing shit . . . but there's a lot of it. And it's the truth. Usually we just yell if we need something, hollering until the other answers because if we walked around trying to find each other, we'd spend half the day wandering. Cecil's drinking problem combined with being hard of hearing means that there's an unfair amount of yelling on my end. Once or twice I've found him passed out in the weeds, and sometimes I think he pretends his hearing is worse than it is, especially when what needs to be done is anything resembling work.

"*Cecil!*" I yell again, in the direction of the back

twenty acres. It rolls down to where our summer crop is growing, but there's also a stream, and he could be fishing. It's not Cecil that answers me but the low whine of a Weedwacker. I follow the sound past the enclosures, keeping an eye on the cat while I do—he flicks his tail at me, cool and calm—as I make my way toward the front of the trailer. Cecil is out by the road, whacking weeds down around the mailbox.

Figures. That's the one thing he'll do with consistency—get the mail.

I gesture for him to turn off the Weedwacker, but he finishes what he started first and I've got to duck around the pieces of shredded poison ivy flying through the air. He finally sets the Weedwacker down, and I see that he didn't load it with a string; Cecil put a circular saw blade on the end. It spins as it slows, individual teeth finally showing themselves as it comes to rest.

"Jesus, Cecil," I say. "You'll take your leg off with that."

He nods, agreeing. "Or the cat's, she gets it in her head to come after me again."

"He," I correct. "The panther is a male."

"Acts like a woman," he says, looking over his shoulder at the cages as he spits. "Holds little things against you. Doesn't forget. Bides her time."

I've been hearing this shit long enough that I figure Grandma might've been smiling when she signed her will, despite the cancer eating her alive. I'm willing to bet the *little things* she held against him were probably larger and more general, like him being a dick and the occasional insufferable—yet mercifully concise— diatribes. I will give him that. Cecil doesn't have a lot to say, it's just that all of it is spiteful.

"I need the manacles," I tell him.

"What'd Rue do?" he asks.

"Nothing," I say quickly, jumping to the orangutan's defense. "I just need the manacles."

Cecil's eyes tighten. The network of lines around the blue eye deepen; the muscles around the ruined one remain slack from where the cat's claws went in deep, slashing everything to tatters. "You being weird?"

I've been living with Cecil since the fifth grade, and the closest we ever get to *the talk* is when he asks me if I'm "being weird."

"No, I just need them." I give him a hard stare then, one that I remember Mom using on Dad when she was done with words and had moved on to something more powerful. They didn't fight a lot, but when they did and Mom pulled out that look, I knew it was over. So I studied her, mimicked the set jaw, narrowed eyes, cock of the hips, slightly raised eyebrows. The whole posture says, *Come at me.* But it also says whatever I want it to say, or whatever the person I'm arguing with is scared of.

I imagine when I give this look to Cecil right now

it says, *There are at least fifteen animal rights violations in our backyard and I can make that very clear, very quickly to very many people, if you don't tell me where the manacles are. You don't need to know why I want them.*

He grunts and picks up the Weedwacker, the circular blade spinning lazily. "West shed," is all he says, before jerking it back to life, a cloud of smoke erupting between us, followed by the high whine of the blade slicing through live vines. Poison ivy sprays across my back as I walk away, and I know he did it on purpose.

It's a pansy-ass, passive-aggressive, cheap move. One that he would deny if I turned around and called him out on it. But I don't. Instead, I clench my fists and head toward the shed, passing Rue's cage as I do. She follows along beside me for a second, grabbing the bars and showing me her teeth.

It's a smile. If you don't know orangutans, you can't tell if they want to hug you or kill you. And they can, but this one won't. At least, she won't kill *me*. I stop, reaching through the bars to touch Rue's face, and she cups my hand, pushing it tighter against her cheek.

"Hey, Rue," I say, keeping my voice low and calm. Yesterday I told Ribbit that the town council should be less concerned about the alligator and more about the cat. But the truth is that the scariest thing in here is probably this sweet girl, mostly because you wouldn't see it coming when she decided it was time to snap your neck.

So I'm careful when I reach through the bars, combing out some tangles in her hair. She turns, aware of what I'm doing, showing me a spot she's been working on. I finish the job for her, pulling out a clump of mud and touching the sore skin underneath.

"I'll get some salve for that," I tell her, and she grunts at me like she understands.

I tried to teach her sign language once and was starting to see indications of progress, until all she wanted to do was flip me off. Every time I approached the cage she'd give me a huge grin and a double bird. I couldn't figure out where she learned it until one day I turned around and saw Cecil behind me, giving me the finger and laughing his ass off.

"Fucker," I say, and Rue nods along with me.

I sign *goodbye* at her, but she turns her back, either refusing to show me that she remembers the sign or irritated that I'm leaving her already.

But I've got things to do, which is why I'm not going to give Cecil shit about the poison ivy sticking between my shoulder blades or tell Rue that I don't have time to talk right now. I've got things to do, like find out what happened to my parents seven years ago.

And for that, I need manacles.

Chapter 7

Cat

The girl moves—sometimes—
as I do. Sleek. Purposeful.
I know the walk.
Something dies tonight.
She moves between us, watching me,
watching her.
The man, flashes silver, smells of machine.
A breeze brings her to me, meat and green things.
Death and life. She carries both.
Green sap, on her skin.
Drying earth blood.
A gust rattles the bones,
inside my cage. A collection of meals
Long eaten. Their memories, faded, gone.

She goes, with chains, heavy thoughts.

The man carries silver-flash-danger,

Closer.

Eyes me.

He'll feed us tonight, bleary and slow-smelling,

throwing old meat.

He makes smoke, fills the air with bees,

light sparks. Small shakes. High hums.

I hunker, teeth out, ears down. Muscles tight under, nothing

to leap at,

only silver-flash-danger, biting bars, metal singing.

He stops, sees me down. Makes noises, low now.

His lips curling,

mine too.

He goes, leaving hot metal in the air, curled hind legs beneath

me.

The Almost Human in the dusk, hands behind bars,

like butterflies.

Motion again, same. And same. And again.

What Almost Human says, I see—

silver-flash-danger danced wide,

severed the lock-cage-door-shut-trapped.

I flex my feet, claws extended.

And wait for the smell

of old meat.

Chapter 8

Felicity

I started early.

Brynn didn't say much when I cracked a beer open at my house, but she took her taco costume off so she could drive. Her mouth is tight as we head out to the Allan house, my bells jingling as I nod along with the music. Hugh and David Evans pass us on the way out of town, honking like they've accomplished something when they swerve in front of my car. I raise my beer at them in response, like I agree. Brynn silently reaches out, touches my elbow, pushes my arm down out of sight.

"What?" I say, a little bit shitty. "I'm not driving."

"No," she says. "The only Black girl in town is. We get pulled over, who do you think the shit's going to land on? The pretty white girl, or me?"

I take another slug of beer, knowing she's right. But still, it's not like we're going to get caught. "There's nobody out here," I say. "And besides, your dad is white."

Brynn sighs heavily. "That doesn't outweigh my mom being Black. Might even make it worse."

I'm quiet after that, the beer can slick in my hand. I don't know what to say. Except my brain doesn't get that message to my mouth in time, and I hear myself mutter, "Well, there's nobody out here, anyway."

It's true, which is why the Allan house is such a great spot. It's an old brick house, three stories, surrounded by acres of woods that have crept right up to the house in the years it's been abandoned. Gretchen's mom says nobody has lived here since she can remember, and her grandma says the same. The Allans built this place, had the money to fill it with expensive shit, too. Sometimes I wonder if they roll in their graves every time Cecil Allan comes into town, drunk and depositing a wad of cash at the bank, staring down the teller with one eye and daring her to ask where it came from.

Gretchen's mom told us the Allan name was tainted before him, though. Something about a drunk in the family, embarrassing stories, glory won and lost, slipping between their fingers. She claims they just split one night, owing everybody money and a few people more than that. Cecil's line were the poor relations without the money to even skip town. Which is why he jumped at the chance to marry an Usher, eyeing the house and the land that came with it, even if his family name dropped by the wayside as part of the agreement. She says Cecil may be the last person with the Allan name left in Amontillado, but the Allan boys had fun in their day, so there's still plenty of their blood walking around, claiming to be something else.

Bastards aren't exactly news around here. We all know each other well enough to spot a family trait on a face without the name it belongs to. But like my dad says, when you point at someone, there's three fingers pointing back at you. Regardless, most of the Allans split, leaving behind a few babies without their name and a mansion full of furniture, the people in town picking and choosing what they wanted, less and less leaving the house over the years as it rotted where it stood.

There's not much left now, just the stuff that was too heavy for anyone to move, like a grand piano and a big old grandfather clock that stands at the foot of the staircase. It's freaked me out more than once, when I'm high as hell and come up those stairs to see my own reflection staring back at me in the glass front, lost, confused, a mess. There's more than a little bit of my spit dried on the front of that clock, when I told that girl what I thought of her, not using words.

Brynn pulls into the drive, branches scraping the top of my car as she winds her way back to the house. It's already a rager. Somebody hauled a generator out here, and there are naked light bulbs strung around what's left of the sagging porch, the glow of electricity coming from inside as well.

"Sweet," Brynn says, but I'm not thrilled about it. I've got to meet up with Tress, and that requires darkness. She won't do business anywhere people can see. We could go out to the yard, or the woods, but the lights also mean that couples who rely on the dark corners of the Allan house will probably be going outdoors for their privacy tonight.

Something hits the car. Something big, and we both jump; Brynn lets out a little yelp, hands tightening around the wheel.

"Ladies," Hugh says, face pressed against the windshield as he sprawls across the hood.

I smack the glass where his face is. "Get off my car, shithead."

He smiles but moves, and Brynn puts a hand on her chest.

"Scared me," she says.

I act like it didn't, like my heart isn't racing. My bells jingle as I get out, and Hugh flicks at one of them. It spins around and hits me in the eye.

"Sorry," he says, but it's a half-assed apology; he's beelining for Brynn. He passes me and catches up to her, as she hauls her taco outfit under one arm.

"Tacos! Awesome!" he says, and she gives him a side-eye before she realizes he's serious, and then she starts to show him how she made it. His interest is more on where her leotard gapes at the chest than the properties of foam. I laugh a little to myself, the second beer I'm already chugging starting to flow in my veins. She catches his gaze and chucks him under the chin.

"My face is up here, and you're a monument to testosterone," Brynn says.

And one big-ass monument. When we clear the rise he's backlit by the house, hulking over Brynn, even counting all her taco parts.

"Huge! Wait up!" Dave comes streaking past me, leaving a trail of pot smoke behind him. It's skunky and cheap. He must've got it from Tress.

I help Brynn pull her taco costume over her head, adjusting her lettuce and arranging her hair down the back so that it hangs nicely. I've got to admit, she looks good.

"Sexy taco," I tell her, and she laughs. I forgive her for being such a mom back on the road when she made me hide my beer.

We get past the hangers-on at the porch: underclass-men and people not confident enough to walk right in. A few of the younger football players latch on to Hugh, trying to get him to bitch with them about the canceled game. He talks to them for a second, but it just takes Brynn's hand resting on his arm, urging him on into the house, and he caves. I hand off my empty can to a kid who's leaning against one of the pillars, taking the full one off his hands. He treats it like the compliment it is.

Felicity Turnado just acknowledged his existence.

Once we're inside, I definitely decide I prefer the Allan house without lights. There are holes in the walls, little piles of plaster on the floor and mouse prints running through where it's been ground to a fine dust. There's wallpaper still attached in places, sloughing down and sagging from the walls, a few studs visible. The nails that stick out of them are pure rust, with square heads, something Dad says is how you know something is *really* old. I head for the stairs, which still have a bit of gran-deur about them, like the mom at the pool who still has great legs and knows it.

People are crowded on the staircase, and I've got to pick my way through them. Somebody sneaks a squeeze of my ass, and I give them a little kick for it. Whoever he is, he yells and drops his drink, earning a shove from whoever he splattered. I don't turn around to see who it was. I've got a goal. I need to find Tress, and sooner rather than later, while I've still got a little bit of liquid courage to talk to her. I thread the crowd, slipping past a couple of geek sophomores who are—I think—trying to fix the clock at the head of the staircase.

"Are you serious?" I ask them, and one of them turns to look at me, unfazed by my naked legs so close to his face.

"It's got a pendulum," he explains. "Which means it's a harmonic oscillator. If we clean it up, put the parts in working order, and introduce some kinetic energy, it's completely feasible that we could get it running."

"Neat," I say, which is a nice word that when you say it just right, becomes something else. Years of listening to Mom and Dad have taught me how to wield tone like a weapon.

I brush past the geeks, but they aren't interested, already lost in a pile of cogs on the floor, heads together. I go to the railing on the second floor, scanning the crowd below for Tress's hair, black and shining. I don't see it, and I give a little kick to the railing in frustration, sending a spindle falling into the people below me. Somebody yells, and I give them a little wave.

Because I'm Felicity Turnado, which means I can take a freshman's beer and kick a guy who grabs me and accidentally rain splintered wood on people, but the one thing I can't do is ask anybody if they know where Tress Montor is.

She runs a decent but discreet business, setting up somewhere secluded at a party and dealing until her stash is depleted and her pockets full, declaring the store closed and leaving before anyone offers her a beer, or tries to make small talk past ounces or milligrams.

I scout out rooms on the second floor, toeing a few early hard partiers out of the way, freshmen who hit it too fast on their first—and only—night at the Allan house. I'm considering that I might have to wander up to the third floor when I spot her, or rather, I spot her cousin.

Ribbit Usher is the most awkward thing I've ever seen, and I'm counting Brynn's taco in that. But while Brynn can take the taco off, revealing her hard-as-nails volleyball body underneath, Ribbit can't strip off his freckled skin or take any of the rough angles off his arms and legs. I slam what's left of the beer I lifted, reconsidering my opinion as Ribbit stretches his arms in the air, illustrating something for Tress's benefit.

He's got broad shoulders, and I bet he could fill out with some muscle. Maybe if someone like Hugh pulled him aside and showed him how to bench he could be salvageable. Gretchen and I could lighten his hair, take the red down a touch. But that would never happen, I think,

crushing my can. Hugh can't stand Ribbit, something
he's tried to explain to me before, when we were out on
our own, after one of my seizures.

"That kid's just not right," Hugh had said, even
though Ribbit's the same age we are. "Something about
him . . . I don't know." Hugh had shrugged, not able to
put words to it. "Remember when Gretchen's dog bit
him?"

"William Wilson?" I'd asked.

"Huh? No, when it bit Usher."

"William Wilson is the dog, dumbo," I'd said, swatting at his arm.

"Jesus, what a stuck-up name for a dog. Figures. Anyway, that dog has been at parties with people yelling and
screaming, getting shoved into pools, and once, somebody spray-painted him yellow, remember that?"

"Yeah, maybe," I'd said, not sure what Hugh had
been driving at.

"But the one time—the only time—that dog ever
bites anybody, it's Ribbit Usher, and for no reason."

"So?"

"So, dogs know things, Felicity. You've got to listen
to their instincts. Dogs and babies."

"Yeah, well." My eyes had wandered to a corner, where
Gretchen was pressed up between the wall and a junior.
"Give Gretchen another few minutes and maybe you can

get the opinion of a baby in about nine months."

Instincts or not, I think Hugh just doesn't understand a boy who doesn't know what *offside* means. Personally, I can't say I mind Ribbit one bit, especially not when he lights up like one of the strung bulbs the second he sees me.

"Felicity!" he calls, waving frantically as I come down the stairs. Tress pulls his arm down, whispering something into his ear, probably telling him not to be such a puppy.

I don't mind. I like puppies.

"Ribbit," I say, making my way over to them. "You made it."

I say that like he isn't at every party, isn't always trying to do anything he can to please everyone else. He'll grab drinks and find lost earrings. He even made a tampon run one time. Last month he spent most of the night in the woods because Gretchen's dog ran out there in a panic after Hugh tried to crowd-surf and there wasn't enough crowd for his bulk. The resulting crash had made William Wilson bolt for the door, and while everyone else made a joke out of running through the woods and calling for him, Ribbit had wandered, borrowing phones when his battery died, until he found the dog, wet and muddy, but not exactly grateful. He'd scratched the crap out of Ribbit when he tried to pick

him up—more evidence to log into Hugh's instinct file,
I guess.

Although Ribbit did score one successful pickup that
night—Gretchen's thanks had come in the form of more
than just words. And good for him; Gretchen hands it
out like candy at Halloween and there's no reason he
shouldn't be in on it with the other trick-or-treaters.

"Like my lights?" Ribbit asks, motioning overhead.

"You did this?" I ask.

"Yeah." He nods, a blush spreading. "I thought everyone might like it. Last night, and all."

I think everyone does, but I'm not quite able to fake
enthusiasm, and Ribbit's face falls.

"You don't like it?"

"I . . ." How do I explain the way the exposed studs
make me feel? The little mouse prints and the faded,
falling wallpaper? "I guess it just makes me sad," I say.
"This used to be a really nice place, once."

Tress nods in agreement, surprising me. "Something
to nothing," she says.

Then I remember that Ribbit himself lives in a place
just as crumbly as this one—stone, not brick—but still.
And he actually *lives* there, whereas we only hit this place
every few weeks.

"But it's cool," I say quickly, putting my hand on his
arm. Somebody bumps into me, and I'm pushed forward,

fully into him, my chest and belly flat against his.

"Whoops," he says, grabbing both my elbows, and I'm suddenly, weirdly, flustered.

"Sorry," we both say at the same time, then laugh at each other.

"I got some beer on you," I say, brushing at the front of his shirt where the foam landed.

"Oh, it's . . . fine . . ." Ribbit's voice trails off, strangled when I touch him.

"You didn't wear a costume," I say, flicking the beer off my fingers.

Ribbit looks down at his T-shirt and jeans, almost apologetically. "No, I . . . it took longer than I thought to get all the lights strung. I was going to go back and change. I still can? I mean . . ."

He's offering to leave the party and change his clothes because I sounded slightly disappointed. That's Ribbit Usher for you. Kinda cute. Very pathetic.

"You look perfect," he blusters on.

"Yep," Tress agrees. "Perfect."

But the way she says it isn't a compliment. It comes out the same way I said *neat* to the sophomores with the clock. She'd been tacitly ignoring whatever weird flirtation was going on between me and her cousin, but now I've got her attention.

"You look . . ." I don't know what she looks like, or

if it's even supposed to be a costume. She's got on all black, and her hoodie is pulled up loosely around her face, shadowing her eyes.

"Like death," Ribbit says. "I mean, I don't know if it's on purpose or not, but Tress looks like death."

Tress sighs then, eyes going back to the crowd. "You need anything?" she asks quietly.

"Yeah," I say, dropping my voice, too.

"Okay." She swigs from a red Solo cup, still not looking at me. "Through the kitchen, there's a door down to the cellar. Five minutes. I'll meet you."

I nod, then look back at Ribbit. He smiles immediately, like he's a character in a video game that is programmed for one thing only. "Get me a drink?" I ask.

I only have to ask once.

Chapter 9

Tress

Ribbit comes back with two beers and hands one off to Felicity, who takes it with a smile and then disappears—obviously not the reaction he was hoping for.

"What did you expect?" I ask him, as he stares into his own cup. "You really thought she was going to hang out with you?"

He shrugs and takes a swig, seeming to forget that he's not going to drink tonight . . . and that it's my job to keep him from doing it.

"I don't know," he says. "Maybe? It's not impossible, right? I mean, she was totally talking to me for a second there."

"Yep, one second." I scan the crowd again, looking to see if anyone noticed Felicity slipping out to the kitchen. I'm checking for Hugh, especially. He keeps an eye on her most of the time, and I need him distracted.

Beside me, Ribbit tilts his beer back all the way, drowning his sorrows. There's a small gathering at the front door, a lot of cleavage and sequins clustered around Gretchen as her voice rises, a high panicked noise above the general party talk.

"He should be right there, I mean right there," she's saying, tears ruining her Cleopatra makeup. "I told him to stay in the car because of last time, and William Wilson *always* stays. He would stay if he was on fire. But I left my window down, and I . . ."

Ribbit is on his way over to help as soon as he sees the tears, and I shake my head. Not so much at him being a total pushover, but because a missing dog—again—is not quite the distraction I'm looking for. I need more.

Suddenly, midsentence, Gretchen pukes.

Everyone around her spreads outward, along with the spatters of Gretchen's dinner. Except for, of course, Ribbit, who only crosses the distance between them more quickly and immediately begins cleaning up Gretchen.

"Lightweight." David Evans is half laughing, half trying to control his own gag reflex when he says it. Next to him, Hugh is shaking his head.

"Gretchen wasn't drinking," he says. And that's when David loses his own battle, pushing Hugh aside as he dashes for the door. He's not quick enough, and everyone tries to make a path as David comes charging, puke spraying through his fingers.

And *that* is a distraction.

Everyone in the kitchen is spilling out, curious about the yelling. I go against the traffic, forcing my way through with elbows until I find Felicity, pink and purple and jingly and gorgeous, waiting for me by the door to the cellar.

"What's going on?" she asks.

"Gretchen just puked. And David," I add, opening the door and motioning for her to go ahead of me.

"Are they okay?" she asks, but she's not worried enough to go check for herself, or actually offer any assistance. It's more important that she get high. She pauses for a second, hands in front of her as she feels for the banister. "Tress? I can't see."

"Sorry," I tell her, flicking my phone on. We go forward by its pale light, Felicity carefully picking her way. I wait for her to get a few steps below me, then turn, and flick the hook-and-eye lock on the basement door. It's shiny against everything else. Bright and new. Because I put it there an hour ago.

"Tress?" she calls again, her voice higher and a little panicked since I turned my back and took the light with me.

"Sorry," I say again, and follow behind her, holding the light above her head so she can see.

It's dank in the basement, two hundred years of mildew gathering together like a blanket in the air. Tress coughs, and it almost turns into a gag as she gets to the bottom of the steps, the bells on her little slippers jangling merrily as she wanders out onto the dirt floor.

"Tress?" she says again, her voice small and lost, trusting, like it had been when we were kids. "I don't feel so good."

She's got her arms crossed in front of her, goose bumps rising even though I can see bright spots on her cheeks. She hasn't seen what's behind her yet; the hole in the wall and the pile of bricks beside it, the chair facing it, or the pail of mortar.

Felicity hasn't seen any of that because she's looking right at me, eyes wide. "Did you say Gretchen puked? Was she . . . like from drinking, or was she sick?"

I shrug.

"Because there were some people upstairs, just kind of lying there. I thought it was a little early for them to be passed out but . . . oh my God, Tress. What if everyone has the flu?"

Then more importantly, she adds, "What if *I've* got the flu?"

"It won't be what kills you," I tell her.

Then I hit her with a brick.

Chapter 10

Felicity

I wait for the boy's voice.

It's always there, after. A nice low, soothing thread that I follow up to consciousness. He'll talk about his grandma, who he lives with, and how he does this with her, waiting patiently for her to come back around after a seizure. I sometimes can't remember his name, and he'll tell me, pinging my memory until I say his name back to him, and he'll help me up, brush my clothes off, and smooth down my hair.

He is a nice boy, that boy . . . Hugh.

Memory is slippery for a few minutes after, and I'll wander, confused inside my own head, not knowing where I am or how I got there, who I am with or if I am safe. But when I hear Hugh's voice I know that I am okay. But this time, something is different. I don't hear Hugh, and there's something wet running down my neck. I move to brush it away, but I can't. My arms won't move. There's a jangling noise, the sound of tiny bells but also something lower, more sinister.

"Hugh?" I ask.

He doesn't answer, and something is very wrong. My head hurts terribly. My hands, too. There is a heavy smell in the air, and I'm slumped forward, hung by my arms, wrists straining against . . . chains.

I open my eyes.

I did not have a seizure.

Hugh is not here.

And I am not safe.

Chapter 11

Tress

"Hey," I say when Felicity opens her eyes.

I'm glad she came around. Not because I was worried that I hit her too hard, or that there was more blood than I expected; I've seen plenty of blood in my life and know that head wounds always look worse than they actually are. The McCaffrey Ranch gives us any cows that die unexpectedly, with the caveat that they come to Amontillado Animal Attractions as they left there—in one piece. I've been cutting up dead cows with chain saws since I was thirteen, so, no, blood doesn't bother me one bit. Especially not Felicity Turnado's. But I'm glad to see her come around, anyway. I'm glad she's conscious because I need her talking.

She shifts in her chains, her wrists already chafed as

she comes to her feet, dazed and a little woozy. A ribbon of blood winds around her neck from where I hit her with the brick, bright red against the gray pallor of her skin. Felicity does not look good, even for a girl with a concussion who is chained to a wall.

"Tress?" she asks, but that note of trust is gone. Now she's scared. As she should be.

Felicity rattles her chains again. Her first instinct is to tug at them, but I anchored the manacles into the stone foundation of the Allan house. She's not getting out of those unless I let her out.

"What the fuck?" Fear turns into anger quickly, her eyes bright under her jester's cap, which was knocked sideways when I wrestled her body into the badly lit corner. There's a naked light bulb above me now. While she was out I ran a wire along the beams up the stairs, connecting to Ribbit's electrical contribution to the party. A little illumination for our long night.

I haven't answered her yet, and Felicity moves to the next logical emotion—panic. I planned on this, turning the volume up on the music in the kitchen before I followed Felicity down the stairs. She'll scream herself hoarse long before the party winds down.

She yells for Hugh first, which I expected. Then Brynn and Gretchen and David. At least two of them are actively vomiting on themselves, and Felicity knows that. This is true panic; complete loss of logical function. She pulls on her chains, gouging her own wrists in the process, small drops of blood splattering onto the floor at her feet. She's kicking, too, lunging at me as she screams. One of her jester slippers flies off and hits a ceiling beam, fluttering back down, light and useless as the bell chimes.

It takes a few minutes for her to burn down, but when she does Felicity Turnado is a goddamn mess. Tears have streaked her makeup and she's worked herself into a sweat, her flimsy costume sticking to her skin and showing every goose bump that ripples to the surface once she's done throwing her fit. She's kicked up a fair amount of coal dust, too, blackening both of her legs up to the knee.

"Done?" I ask.

"Tress," she rasps at me, cap now hanging down over one eye. "What the fuck are you doing?"

"Let me tell you," I say, pulling my chair up. It's an old one, something I salvaged from a third-floor bedroom. It's decorative, small and spindly, a chair for a lady to sit on in front of her mirror while doing her makeup. That mirror was broken when I found it, the drawers of the vanity swollen with rot and sticking forever shut.

"I'm going to make you talk to me," I say.

"You don't have to chain me up to get me to talk to you," Felicity shouts, voice breaking on *talk*.

"But I do if I want you to be *honest*."

She settles in her chains, eyes bright and boring into mine. "What do you want?"

"I want to know what happened the night my parents disappeared."

Chapter 12

Felicity

It's the worst thing she could say to me.

If she wanted money, I could make sure she got it. Needed a car to drive out of her shitty life, I'd buy her one. But I can't give her what I don't have.

"I don't—" She holds her hand up, and I obediently fall silent.

"Let me tell you what's going on here before you finish that sentence." She gets out of the chair and comes closer to me, hands on either side of the crevice I'm chained inside of.

"You're in a coal chute. Those manacles are anchored into limestone with masonry screws. I've learned a lot about containment in my life, and trust me, you're not getting out."

"This is insane," I spit at her, not sparing my words. "Hugh will be looking for me."

"Hugh is currently distracted," she says, and she sounds so confident that I feel a ripple of unease, something different from the panic that hit earlier. Before I was an animal, reacting with venom. Now I'm a human . . . a scared one who hears a voice inside her head say, *This is really happening.* Then, underneath that, the little voice that whispers in my ear at night . . . *You deserve it.*

Fuck that, is usually how I respond to the voice before falling asleep. And I do the same now. I'm Felicity Turnado, and I can't just disappear from a party without anybody noticing.

"My friends will know I'm gone," I say. "Remember what those are? Friends?"

That last bit is shitty, but so is hitting someone with a brick. Tress only shakes her head, not bothered in the least.

"You really need to know the consequences before you talk." I go still, my voice a dead thing in my throat, gaze following Tress as she walks back to the chair, the bulb above her head making her eyes dark pools.

"I want to know what happened that night," she says again. "But I've got a lot of other things to say to you, too. So we're going to take our time, and we're going to talk everything out."

I nod enthusiastically. This is something I've actually wanted to do forever.

"But," Tress says, holding one finger in the air. "If I don't like what you say . . ."

She walks over to a pile of bricks, one that looks like it's been sitting there since the beginning of time, left over from what they didn't use on the house. Tress picks one up, comes closer to my little nook. My pulse jumps, tight and hot where the metal bites into my wrist.

"If I don't like what you say . . ." She fades off, shrugging her chin over her shoulder. Behind her there's a smooth brick wall, the face uninterrupted, each brick notched into the next in a tightly constructed pattern. One section is slightly brighter than the rest, out of place.

"There were two coal chutes," Tress says. "I practiced."

Chapter 13

Tress

Felicity totally loses her shit.

I can't blame her, but I also don't have to watch it. I go back upstairs, partially to double-check that the noise level of her freak-out isn't penetrating to the partiers. Her screeches are fading when I'm halfway up the stairs, drowned out by the music in the kitchen. I can still pick out a few words—ones that I doubt her mother knows she uses—when I put my ear to the wooden door, trying to ascertain if there's anyone in there before I open it. I can't hear any movement, so I flick the hook off and take the plunge.

A couple of juniors are going at each other in the corner, but they're really into what they're doing and their eyes are closed. I let the door click shut, then edge past them, out into the main room. More people have shown up, and the staircase is packed, the geeks who are working on the clock giving everyone orders about tiptoeing around the pieces and parts they've got laid out everywhere.

"Hello! There's a system at work here!" One of the boys shouts at a football player who trounces right past him. But the jock isn't interested; he's got one hand on his stomach, the other covering his mouth, his skin a sickly green.

Huh . . . Maybe Felicity wasn't totally wrong about the flu.

I pause for a second, anxious to know if her screams are coming up through the floorboards. They're not. All I can hear is the low hum of party talk, and crying from somewhere outside, high-pitched and desperate. Curious, I follow the sound out onto the porch, where Hugh, David, and Brynn have shifted the underclassmen out onto the lawn and are gathered around Gretchen in a protective circle.

"He probably had to take a piss," David says, his skin still sallow, one hand on Gretchen's shoulder. She shakes her head.

"William Wilson wouldn't get out of the car unless I told him he could," she hiccups, wiping her face with the edge of David's shirt. "He's a very good boy."

She gets to her feet, swaying a little, her own color not good. "William!" she calls out into the dark. "William Wilson Astor, you get back here right now!"

"Wow, whipping out the full name, huh?" Brynn says.

Hugh pats Gretchen's hair, carefully avoiding a splatter of puke from earlier. "I'm sure he'll come back."

"What if he doesn't," Gretchen wails. "What if it's like last time? He got so scared and nobody knew where he was, and the only person who actually *helped* me was"—she hiccups again—"Ribbit."

Hugh's jaw tenses, and my cousin appears out of the darkness, the light on his phone flicking off. I go to his side, grabbing his arm as he's about to step up onto the porch.

"You might want to split," I tell him.

"Huh, why?" His breath has beer on it, his eyes bleary. It only takes one, with Ribbit.

"Because Hugh doesn't exactly like you, and—"

"Hey!" As if I'd conjured him, Hugh elbows his way through the crowd on the porch, his fist tight around the neck of Ribbit's T-shirt before he can even get his hands up in surrender.

"You sick little shit," he seethes into Ribbit's face. "You hide that little dog away so you can save the day again, get a little off Gretchen?"

"Whoa, hey." I put my hand on Hugh's arm, but it's like metal.

"I know he's your cousin, Tress, but this is between us," he says to me.

So I hit him.

Hitting Hugh Broward with my bare hand is like pitting a mosquito against a car going eighty miles an hour. Nothing happens except I get hurt. I cradle my hand to my chest, and Hugh's eyes bounce off Ribbit for one second to meet mine, then settle back on his prey. We know each other well enough to be aware he's not going to let go of my cousin, and I'm not going to stand down and let Ribbit get hurt.

"He didn't do anything," I say. "Leave him alone."

"You don't know shit," Hugh says. "I've told you before; he's a squirrelly little bastard."

"I'm not . . . ," Ribbit argues, his voice shaky. "I'm a good guy."

"Dude." David comes over, puts his hand on Hugh's shoulder. "I don't think it was him. He's been with us the whole time."

"Of course he has," Huge says, giving Ribbit a little shake. "Parasite."

"No, man," David goes on, his skin still green, wobbly on his feet. "He didn't do anything to the dog."

"That's your area, right?" I snipe at David, thinking of Goldie's hair floating on the surface of the gator pond, the wet paint on our sign, someone putting a name to us that isn't Allan or Usher. Just white trash.

David blinks slowly, his gaze dull. "What the fuck are you talking about?"

"Forget it," I say, as I watch Hugh's grip loosen on Ribbit's shirt. I'm settling that score with someone else, down in the basement. "Let him go, Hugh."

Hugh gives me a long look, a fire behind his eyes I've never seen there before. I've known Hugh awhile, but it's always been the teddy bear side of him I see. I've never had to stand my ground against him, because until tonight, Hugh and I have always been on the same page. Now I'm seeing something new, something I'd always heard was there but never witnessed. And if there's something in Hugh Broward I've never seen, maybe there's something in my cousin, too. But Ribbit is just hanging from his fist like a piece of meat, actually smiling, showing all his teeth and inviting Huge to knock them down his throat.

"Your dude-bro vouched for him," I say, and Hugh lowers Ribbit until his feet are on the ground. "Happy?"

"No, I'm pretty fucking far from happy. I don't trust you, douchebag." He pushes Ribbit in the chest with one finger, and my cousin almost goes off the edge of the porch. "You're sticking with me for the rest of the night, got it? I'm keeping an eye on you so that you can't *miraculously* find the dog."

Ribbit nods, understanding. Pitifully, he seems almost

happy. He gets to make time with Hugh now, even if he is a prisoner.

I need to get back downstairs.

That's when my phone rings.

Chapter 14

Cat

Something small, made smaller
inside my mouth.
A new best / last.
Gretchen / shadow

Chapter 15

Felicity

I'm shaking.

I don't know if it's anger, or if it's because I'm cold, or because I'm sick. I ranted at Tress's retreating back as she went up the stairs, and now I'm exhausted. My throat feels like it's in bloody tatters. My whole body is quivering, nerves on high alert . . . or maybe it's because I've got a fever, and my body is trying to shed heat.

Everything is wrong, and I've got small trails of blood running down both arms. The stream from my head seems to have stopped, but there's a drying red trickle going down into my cleavage. I hear the basement door, and my head jerks up, the ridiculous jester cap swinging to the side, hanging by a hair pin.

"Hugh?" I call, my voice raspy and useless.

"Calm down . . . listen . . . *listen* . . ." It's Tress, and she's on the phone, clearly irritated. She comes back to her chair, and it creaks under her weight.

"It was definitely locked," she says, crossing her legs. "No, I did not let the panther loose just to fuck with you."

A long stream of profanity to match the one I'd been screaming at her earlier comes out of the phone, and she holds it away from her ear. "Cecil . . . ," she sighs. "And did it kill you?"

Another extended answer comes—an angry one—but Tress only shakes her head. "What do you want me to do? Wander around calling, *Here, kitty, kitty?*"

Apparently her grandpa doesn't have a better suggestion, because Tress hangs up on him, another incensed response cut off with the swipe of her thumb. Tress blows her hair out of her eyes and glances up at me.

"Panther's loose," she says by way of explanation. Like it's not incredibly alarming. Like she's not saying it to someone she's chained to a wall and threatened to bury alive. My heart kicks up a beat just thinking about it.

Tress is still in her chair, her eyebrows drawn together, looking at her phone. She's distracted, not thinking about me, or her parents. Maybe I can keep it that way.

"What do you even do when a panther is loose?" I ask. "That seems . . . hard."

It's a really stupid thing to say, but Tress nods in agreement.

"Yeah, well, we can hope he comes home, where there's shelter and food but . . ." She glances at me, and we're having a conversation. A totally fucked-up one, but we're talking.

"Cecil hasn't exactly been nice to that cat," she says. "If it comes home, it won't be for anything good."

"Uh-huh," I say, encouraging her. "So what do you do?"

She shrugs. "Not much you can do. Hope it doesn't kill anybody, first off. And pray nobody spots it. People find out it got loose, and we're done."

"Right . . . ," I say, trying to think of how I can spin this, turn the topic away from Cecil Allan losing his income and a wild animal killing people. But there's really no way for me to keep this conversation positive.

"So yeah." Tress stands, stuffing her phone into her jeans pocket. "Hope and pray, that's pretty much it. Not much we *can* do, so I'm not going to worry about it."

She picks out a brick, turning it in her hands. My pulse thrums; my belly turns to liquid.

"Tress . . ." I shake, my bells jingling. "Could you . . ." I'm wild, searching for something to say. Anything. "Could you get this hat out of my face?"

It's ridiculous. And it works.

"Sure." She comes over, gently disentangling pins

from my hair. Her face is inches from mine, and I could headbutt her or bite her, but it wouldn't buy me anything. She'd just be pissed, and I'd still be chained to a wall. I need to take a different route, try instead to remind her that we used to be friends. That once, we really loved each other.

"There you go," she says, putting my cap back into place, pinning it neatly. The bobby pins slide across my scalp, tickling and bringing back a hundred memories of Tress braiding my hair or combing it out, me showing her how to put on mascara, and the one time we got into her mom's dye and ruined their new bathroom tiling.

I've got tears in my eyes as she steps back, and Tress is upset, too, her brows drawn tightly together, her mouth a thin line as she inspects a few of my loose hairs that stuck to her fingers.

"Shit," she says. "I forgot to put salve on Rue."

"Rue?" I ask. "Who's Rue?"

"Doesn't matter." Tress shakes the strands loose, then turns her back to me. She's shaking. Not as much as I am, but it's there, a small tremor running under her skin.

"Tress," I whisper. "I don't know what happened to your parents."

She sighs, shoulders falling . . . and reaches for a brick.

"You're going to want to be more careful about what you say, Felicity."

I take a kick at her as she picks up the first brick, but she only backs out of the way, my second slipper flying off and over her shoulder.

"Quit," she says, as calmly as she informed me about the loose panther.

"Or what?" I snap at her, all hints of a whisper gone from my voice. "You'll hold me against my will? Brick me up in a wall because you're a fucking insane person?"

"I can always knock you out again," she tells me. "You'll wake up in total darkness."

Tress lets that sit a second, then continues. "At least if you're awake you've got a chance in hell of talking me out of this."

I'm quiet while she lays the first brick but can't help it when she reaches for another. "Two?" I ask, dropping my voice low, using the tone that I used on Ribbit earlier, when he literally ran to get me a beer. But Tress is not her cousin, and she sees right through my shit.

"That's for kicking at the first one," she says.

I'm dying to take a shot at Tress while she kneels in front of me. I could do some damage, too; maybe knock some of her teeth out, or at least break her nose. But I won't, and she knows it. I won't because I need to keep her happy. She lays an entire first row; four bricks across, like she's testing me. I don't say anything, as instructed.

"All right," she finally says, rocking back on her heels and dropping the spade into the mortar bucket. "We need to talk about freshman year."

Upstairs, a clock chimes.

Chapter 16

Tress

Freshman Year

Shit. That's what I wake up to—actual shit.

There's a raccoon at the foot of my bed, pawing through the clothes I had carefully laid out to wear to school today. I yelp when I see it, and it reactively shits, erasing any chance I had of maybe spot-cleaning its grubby little pawprints from the shirt I'd managed to snag from Goodwill, tags still on.

"Cecil!" I yell as the raccoon scurries out of my room, down the hallway, and out the trailer door . . . which is standing open.

"Huh?" Cecil stirs from his spot on the couch, bumping the rickety coffee table and sending a cascade of beer bottles onto the floor, not all of them empty. A flood of beer follows the raccoon toward the door, because this place isn't exactly level.

"You left the front door open," I tell him, to which he gives a laugh, waves his hand at it, and goes back to sleep, rolling over to show me his back. You work with animals long enough, you learn body language thoroughly. I'm dismissed.

I rifle through my laundry basket, hoping there's something salvageable I can wear. But we haven't had the cash for the laundromat this week, which is why I'd lifted a few things from Goodwill. It wasn't the first time, and I never feel great about it, but Cecil says the Goodwill is a nonprofit anyway so I shouldn't worry too much about it.

Truth is, I can't. I've got bigger concerns.

Like I literally have nothing to wear to school. I've been washing bras and underwear in the sink and hanging them out to dry, but that's the only clean stuff I've got. Everything else is . . . a touch south of smelly. I find a pair of jeans that have Rue's hair all over them but otherwise look okay. I shake them out, sending orangutan hair across my room.

I can hear the bus coming up the ridge, gears grinding as it makes the climb. In their pens, Zee and Dee, our resident zebra and ostrich, sniff the wind, finding the diesel fumes. I grab the least-rumpled T-shirt I can find and dash into Cecil's room, snagging an old bowling jersey from the back of his closet. I slip it on and douse myself with body spray so that I don't smell too much like mildew. I just catch the bus, find a seat by myself in the back, and jam my earbuds in. My hair is in a dirty ponytail because the well went dry last night, but combined with this weird-ass bowling jersey and my wrinkled shirt I might be able to pull off some kind of grunge vibe. Make this look like it's all on purpose.

I definitely get a whiff of Rue when I walk into the school, so I go to the bathroom and try to dab hand sanitizer in a few different places. There's a bunch of upperclassmen in there I don't know, so I just get a handful from the dispenser and duck into a stall. There's some whispering, a muttered "What the hell?," followed by giggles.

Great. I wander into the atrium, hoping to spot somebody—anybody—I can stand with . . . or at least, near. I scan the crowd but don't see any friendly faces—Gretchen Astor actually looks at me and starts laughing. The only thing she doesn't do is point. Except, I'm sure she does, once I walk away. I stick my chin out and try to find a corner, preferably somewhere dark, before the bell rings.

There's another whisper behind me as I pass, then a snort. I turn around, headed back to the bathroom to see if I'm bleeding through my jeans or something. I mean, I know I'm not making the cover of *Vogue* anytime soon, but I didn't think my clothes were *that* bad.

"Hey," a guy's voice calls out. I don't think it's for me. It can't be for me. I speed up.

"Hey!" he yells again, and there's a tap on my shoulder. I turn around, and there's a football player smiling at me. "Your shirt is ballin'."

I search his face, scrutinizing it for any sign that he's fucking with me. Weirdly, I don't see any.

"Thanks," I say cautiously.

"No, I mean, like, it's *ballin'*."

"Right, thanks," I say again, backing away.

I duck back into the bathroom, against the crowd that's headed into the halls. There are shouts as people reconnect after the summer break, a lot of hugging. But I'm in the bathroom, inspecting my underwear. Most girls just ask their friends to check their asses when they get up to dump their lunch tray. Me, I don't have friends like that.

I'm not bleeding, so I don't really know what the giggling was about. I'm taking off my pants to check the butt anyway, when the loudspeaker comes on, cutting through the chatter of the halls, right into the bathroom.

"Tress Montor, please report to the guidance office."

"Seriously?" I ask my pants.

There's already a line there, people wanting schedule changes or complaining about not having a study hall. Mrs. Febrezio spots me and takes my elbow, ushering me past them and into her office.

"Tress," she says. "It's seven fifty on the first day of school, and I've already had complaints from teachers about your shirt."

"My . . . what?"

I must look baffled, because she drops the strict look. "Your shirt," she repeats, searching my face.

"I . . ."

"Tress." Her face softens a little a more. "Do you even know what's on the back?"

I take off Cecil's bowling jersey, and flip it around.

It's got two bowling balls and one pin embroidered on it, arranged so that it looks like a cock and balls. Above that, where a last name should be, it just reads DICK.

"Ballin'," I whisper to myself.

"Excuse me?" Febrezio's sympathy disappears.

"Sorry, I . . ." I'm trying not to laugh. I bite the inside of my cheek hard enough to taste metal. "No, I didn't know. Swear."

She nods, but I can tell I lost points by being amused.

"I've got some shirts from lost and found you can choose from," she says. "Unless you want to just wear . . ." Her voice fades off, taking in the tee I had on under the jersey. It's a rumpled mess, but she's had too much training to say so.

"I'm fine," I say, stuffing Cecil's jersey into my book-bag. "Sorry about the . . ." I almost say *cock and balls* but stop myself. I've been living with Cecil so long my filter isn't always in place.

"Have a good day, Tress," Febrezio calls behind me, but I'm already slipping past the row of kids who want study hall, don't want study hall, or just want to align their schedules more closely with their friends'.

I'm cruising through the halls, scanning lockers for my number when someone grabs my elbow. "Dude, what happened to your shirt?"

It's the football player again, all smiles and teeth, and I think of Rue. She's either going to hug you or kill you. I give him the benefit of the doubt, something I don't do often.

"I've been castrated," I say, shrugging.

He laughs, and a few people turn to look. I'm struggling to find words, to think of what to say next. I almost unzip my backpack and offer him the jersey, since he likes it so much, but then he clamps a hand onto my shoulder, and I reassess. It would never fit him. This guy is huge.

"Huge," I say, the word filling the gap between us. "Hugh Broward."

"Yeah," he says. "See you around, Tress Montor."

I nod like he didn't just give me a gift, then turn to my locker. The staff put signs on all the freshman lockers, little welcome banners with our names. My eyes slide to the one next to mine, curious, and my heart goes up into my throat just as I hear a gasp behind me.

I turn to see Felicity Turnado, clean and beautiful and perfect. I still feel good about making Hugh Broward laugh; I can still feel the weight of his hand on my shoulder. So there's a lightness in my chest that lifts a little more when I see her, a buoyancy that rises to my face and pulls the corners of my mouth up.

I'm smiling at Felicity Turnado when she turns her back on me and walks away.

Chapter 17

Felicity

Freshman Year

I don't have anything to wear.

Correction—I have too many choices. I'm staring at my closet, wondering how best to usher in high school, overwhelmed by the fact that I have an unnatural amount of clothing. It's the first day of freshman year, and while being Felicity Turnado mattered in junior high, it doesn't mean shit to the upperclassmen. What I wear today will announce to everyone where I see myself fitting in, so I've got to make it count. I'm not an athlete, and it's not like I own a ton of sweatpants and hoodies anyway, so that look is easily shot down. I'm smart, but not sure how much I want to push that. I've been playing down the cute smart girl thing since I ditched my glasses for LASIK in seventh grade.

I'm in the choir and was tapped to sing the national anthem at junior high graduation, but I'm not sure the arts crowd is quite where I click. I've got the boho clothes for it, and if I wear my hair down and loose I can rock the free-spirit hippie thing. But there's a lot of confidence required for that, and the little part I landed in the junior high musical last year got me a backstage pass. Even behind the curtain the stage kids were always on, being funny, dramatic, or just all out *themselves*—like they had nothing to be ashamed of. Maybe they don't. That's probably why I never felt comfortable.

I didn't mind the attention, though . . . not at all.

With that thought, I grab a pair of ripped jean shorts and a cute little tank. Enough to show off what I've got while still playing it safe with dress code. The labels are from brands that will set me apart but not *above*. That's important. Really important, in Amontillado.

I look in the mirror, adjusting a fold there, applying a little more mascara here. Dabbing my lipstick off when I realize the color is too much, too confident. I've got to attract boys but not alienate girls. Especially as a freshman. I want upperclassmen to notice me, but I can't be pegged as fresh meat by the boys, or as a threat by the girls. It's a fine line, a delicate balance, and I can't make a misstep.

I'm still the girl who was with the Montors when

they disappeared, the one who doesn't know what happened—or won't say. I'm a mystery to most, a pity case to some, and complicit to a few holdouts. Amontillado still hasn't decided what I am, five years later.

I straighten my shoulders and put on the smile I've been practicing in the mirror.

I've got to show them that I'm Felicity Turnado, and I am just fine.

Mom drops me off at school without making too much of a fuss. She hasn't let me ride the bus since second grade, when I had my first seizure moments after walking in the door at home. She's convinced I'm going to seize during the ride, with no one noticing until they open the doors in front of our house and I don't get up. She's a worst-case scenario type of person. I can't say I blame her there, though, given that the Montors—and their car—disappeared into thin air, leaving me wet, gasping, and forgetful on the riverbank. I don't have the best track record with moving vehicles.

"Bye, Mom," I call over my shoulder as I leave, ducking out from under her arm as she reaches for me.

I sail into the atrium like I don't care, like I'm not noticing every single person who notices me, not weighing the glances and determining where I land on their judgment scale. There are a few junior girls giving my tanned legs the stink-eye, but Brynn spots me and comes over, gives me a hug. Their attitude changes immediately, which tells me they must be athletes. Brynn's been burning a hole in volleyball records since sixth grade; if she accepts me, they will, too.

"You look good," she tells me, and I pay the compliment back, meaning it. She's got dark skin and knows how to set it off . . . not that she needs to. Everything looks good on that build.

"What's your first period?" she asks, taking me by the hand and leading me over to where the juniors are gathered.

"Um . . ." I glance at my phone. "English."

"Cool," Brynn says. "Me too. Walk together?"

"Yes." I jump at her offer. Brynn introduces me to the other girls, and they warm up immediately when she tells them that I kept book for the eighth-grade volleyball team.

"We need a new book," one of the girls says, obviously eyeing me. "You know the sport?"

"I don't play, but I know it," I tell her.

In and out, the closest I'll ever get to being an athlete, myself. Brynn has played in school and travel leagues her whole life, and if you wanted to spend any time with her, you ended up watching a few games. Maybe a few hundred. I tend to run from projectiles—or just cover my face and scream—but that doesn't mean I'm not into sports. I showed enough interest that the coach invited me to come to some scrimmages and taught me how to keep book. She said having a parent keep book was just inviting an unwanted coach to the bench. I'm practically a pro now; my book is tight. No smudges, no pencil strikes that are unsure, substitutions recorded like clockwork. You could look at my record of a game and relive it, accurately, play for play.

In junior high tournaments last year I noticed that Prospero was serving out of rotation. I'd glanced around, hoping an adult would say something, but both our coaches were consulting with the players, and they hadn't spotted it. I checked my book again, stunned that something so obvious could slide. But my book didn't lie, and I cleared my throat.

I didn't miss the sneer on the Prospero coach's face when I handed my book over to the officials, expecting a child's unsure notes, a vague perception of reality. Instead, they'd consulted, nodding, and we ended up getting a point out of the mess. When the table official handed the book back to me, he said, "Good work, kid," and gave me a high five.

It felt good, like something I'd done had actually mattered. But I can't be too enthusiastic, or these juniors will automatically peg me as a social climber.

"You should come to a practice, introduce yourself to coach before scrimmages start," one of them says. She's tall, broad, probably a middle hitter.

"Cool." I nod. "I mean, I'd do it. If you need me."

"She's the best," Brynn says. "Felicity's mind is like a steel trap." She snaps her hands together to illustrate, and I jump.

"Nice," another girl says, and I give her the smile I tried on at home.

She smiles back. Good. My smile works on upper-classmen.

There's a little more bounce in my step as I search for my locker. I'm scanning numbers, looking for mine as mini reunions occur every five steps. I've gotten about twenty hugs and twice as many once-overs from guys by the time I find it.

Right next to Tress Montor.

Shit. *Shit shit shit.*

The panic grabs me, instantaneous and crushing. My pulse quickens, my breath stops in my chest, and my brain goes to slush. I don't even have language anymore, just the need to run. It's been like this since that night; I can't even look at Tress without having an all-out anxiety attack. Guilt rushes in, filling my whole body like it's a helium tank and I'm a balloon . . . one that's about to burst.

Black spots fill my vision, and I know I have to breathe, so I inhale, gulping like a drowning person. A little bit of control comes back, enough that words can be strung together again. It's not a relief. They come in a tidal wave, like always, an attack on myself inside my own mind.

You're the reason they left the house in the middle of the night.
You're the one who can't remember what happened.
You're the last person to see Tress's parents alive.
It's your fault.

I'm going to lose it. Break open right here in the middle of the hallway, leaving a puddle of insecurities and guilt for everyone to slip in.

Tress turns and sees me.

She hasn't mastered her face the way I have, hasn't learned that emotions shouldn't be shown. We were so close for so long that this still happens sometimes—we'll catch each other's eye unexpectedly, and she'll light up, just a little bit. Tress Montor is still happy to see me.

I can't take it. I spin on my heel and walk away.

I tell them in the office that I need a locker reassignment. The secretary gives my little jean shorts a glance and tells me that locker placements aren't negotiable. I tell her there's a used condom in mine, and that I'm going to call my dad—who is on the school board—if they don't change it. Right now.

That gets her moving. She points me to a chair and goes to the inner office door, says something muffled to Mrs. Anho, the principal. I text Hugh, thumbs flashing, giving him my locker number and combo and asking him if he can put a used condom in it.

He doesn't even ask why, just sends me a thumbs-up. He's been protecting me from mean girls, older boys, and the occasional creepy adult ever since a senior snapped my bikini top at the pool in seventh grade. Hugh "accidentally" did a cannonball right on top of his head, which resulted in the squad being called and Hugh getting kicked out of the pool for the rest of the summer.

But Hugh can't fix everything. He can't save me from the past, or what I did. The secretary gives my shorts another glance, and I nervously tug on the hems. When I'm sitting down, they are way shorter than I thought. Great. I told myself what I wore today was going to announce to everyone who Felicity Turnado is. Apparently, she's a little tramp who needs a boy to bail her out when she has panic attacks.

I lean forward, putting my head in my hands, letting my hair fall in sheets on either side of me, shutting out the world.

Shutting out Tress Montor.

Chapter 18

Felicity

"No, it wasn't like that," I say as Tress balances a brick in her palm. She looks at me over the edge, dubious.

"Wasn't like what?" she repeats. "Wasn't like you had your locker moved so that you didn't have to be near me?"

"No, Tress . . ."

I clear my throat, thinking hard. It's difficult when it feels like my head is spinning one direction, my gut another.

"It's so hard," I tell her. "I . . ."

Words are slipping, sliding away from me as my focus fades, my vision going in and out. I can't weigh everything carefully, can't evaluate each syllable and second like I usually would. As Tress wanted: I'm stuck with being honest.

"I can't even look at you," I say, and that flicker of interest that was in her face goes still and hard.

"This wall gets high enough, pretty soon you won't have to," she says.

She lays a brick, the wet smell of the mortar rising into my nose.

"No, wait," I say. "I didn't mean—"

Tress reaches for another, and I'm utterly quiet.

But she lays it anyway.

Chapter 19

Tress

Felicity is not catching on quickly.

She needs a minute after I put down the second row of bricks, so I go upstairs, listening again at the door for noises in the kitchen. There aren't any, and when I open it even the couple from the corner is gone. The music is still on, the single speaker belting out a tune for no one and nothing. The running hum of the party is gone, too. I'm tense, listening, poised like I've seen the cat do when he doesn't like something he hears.

Or doesn't hear.

Then it comes, a wall of sound—laughter, actually—rolling from the entrance hall. I relax, square my shoulders, flick some wet mortar off my hands, and pull my hood back up before following the sound. The party isn't over;

it's just relocated. Hugh is holding court at the top of the staircase, admirers fanned out across the steps below him as he holds a phone up to capture . . . Ribbit?

"What the fuck?" I whisper to myself, slipping behind a group of freshmen who weren't lucky enough to score a spot on the steps. They've got their phones out, too, and Ribbit is neatly squared in their sights.

"Now," Hugh says loudly, positioning his chair— a ridiculously overstuffed thing someone must have pulled from in front of the fireplace—so that he's at an angle to Ribbit, whose chair is smaller. He sways in it, the legs wobbling with his attempts to sit straight.

"Let's get a volunteer from the audience," Hugh says.

"What's going on?" I ask, tugging on a girl's elbow.

She half shrugs, eyes red-rimmed and fever spots on her cheeks. "Dunno. They're doing, like, a talk show kind of thing, I guess? This guy, I swear, it doesn't even matter what you ask him, he answers it. It's *hilarious*."

Oh, shit. I've seen this before. Get one drink in Ribbit and he'll do anything for you. Get two and he'll answer anything you ask him with total, absolute, 100 percent honesty. No filter. No holds barred.

"A volunteer?" Hugh says again, and a girl stands, her arms pinwheeling wildly around her when she almost loses her balance on the stairs. It's Maddie Anho, the principal's daughter. Hugh gets up and comes down to her, reaching out for her fingertips and leading her the rest of the way like they're on the Oscars or something.

Maddie faces Ribbit at the top of the stairs, her body outlined by the massive clock. The pendulum is swinging, flashing on either side of her as it does, playing peekaboo with the crowd. Those guys must have managed to fix it. It chimes quietly, an abbreviated song for the quarter hour. I rise on tiptoes, squinting to get a good look.

"Well, they kind of fixed it," I say to myself.

"Go ahead, ask him anything," Hugh encourages Maddie.

"Huh?" the girl next to me asks, her jaws chewing away on a wad of gum. Underneath the peppermint, I can smell the faint stench of puke.

"The clock," I tell her, my eyes following the smaller hand as it slides upward from the large, embossed number three. "It's running backward." It goes on like that for a full minute, then seems to change its mind and run forward again.

"Scale of one to five, how hot am I?" Maddie asks Ribbit, posing with her hands on her hips for optimum illustration of her curves and the princess costume she's wearing.

More phones come out.

Ribbit doesn't seem impressed. He holds his hand out

flat, then wiggles it. Maddie's face falls, and everyone bursts out laughing. I relax a little; at least it's directed at her and not him.

"I mean, I'd bang you," Ribbit says quickly. "But you're not really my type. Your mom, however . . . I would *totally* do your mom."

Everyone dies. Almost literally. A kid sitting next to my feet is laughing so hard that he chokes, a spurt of vomit coming out one side of his mouth as he collapses, still giggling as he passes out, warm and heavy against my shins.

"Oh my God." The girl next to me turns to her friend. "Did you get that? He just said he wants to bang the principal."

The other freshman nods, her focus still tight on her phone, her arm high above the crowd as she zooms in on Ribbit's face. She pulls up Instagram and starts a new story, using hashtags #HonestUsher and #TrueLoser. I'm about to stop her, my hand frozen in midair, when Ribbit adds:

"I'd bang the history teacher, too."

The noise rises again, loud with fresh laughter. Everyone is here. Everyone is invested. No one is looking for Felicity Turnado.

I turn, and go back down to the basement.

Chapter 20

Cat

The smell of sick, strong,
humans made weak.
I circle after I eat, small hairs on my tongue.
A cousin comes, prowling. I show her my teeth,
spots of blood.
She cleans my whiskers, pushes under my chin, searching
for warmth.
Heat from the house, bricks on my back.
She curls, between my paws, a small hum rising.
Her contentment flows, touching my own.
She pulls a story from me, our blood speaking.
Another time. Another place.
Before the bars and the man. Before the old meat
and the Almost Human.

I tell her of baking sun, faraway plains.
She shows me a blade, the stub of her tail.
I rest, my skull sheltering her body.
Humans, *we say.*
And together, shudder.

Chapter 21

Felicity

Twenty-two rows. That's the number I came up with when Tress walked away from me. Twenty-two rows, four bricks in each row, eighty-eight bricks until I'm not Felicity Turnado anymore but just a part of the foundation of the Allan house. A house that's about to be torn down. I shiver, my bells creating a joyful soundtrack for my fear.

I hear the cellar door, but I don't bother crying out. I know it's Tress. I can tell by her footsteps, a tread I memorized as a child from all the overnights at our houses—before I began having seizures. Tress was always the brave one, the one who would sneak downstairs for snacks in the middle of the night, come back up to my room with Skittles and Twizzlers swiped from the cupboard, our mouths multicolored and sticky as the night wore on and we talked and talked and talked.

Words came easily then. We'd chat about parents and pets, whatever show we were watching. We'd reenact the latest memes and take pictures of each other, laughing as Tress tried to do the splits, one foot balanced on my bed, the other on my dresser.

"When did it change?"

I say it aloud, and Tress glances up from her phone, where she's thumbing through Instagram.

"Seriously? You're asking me?"

"No . . ." I shake my head, searching for the words. "I mean, I know—okay? I know when it changed. I'm not . . . I'm not stupid."

I'm defending myself with the last statement a little bit. Enough so that she knows I'm not going to just be a piece of meat hanging here but not enough to piss her off.

"I know you're not," Tress says. "You never were."

I remember leaning over a math book, working out a problem while Tress looked on, brow furrowed in concentration.

"You told me not to pretend I was," I say quietly. "Remember that?"

"Yep." She nods. "Story problems."

"Story problems," I agree, rolling my eyes, and we both laugh.

It's a sound I know well, and have missed. My higher giggle mixing with her low tones, the music of my child-hood, now accentuated by the rattle of chains.

Tress shakes her head. "I don't care how many apples Lucy bought at the store and how many people she needs to feed with them, and how much money she has and how much they cost, and how much change she'll get. The stories were always so stupid, you know?"

She sits on the chair, and I hear her phone buzz in her back pocket.

The average brick is two inches tall. Felicity is five foot five. How many bricks will it take for her former best friend to seal her into a wall?

I shake my head, dispelling the thought. I already know the answer, anyway. "You said I shouldn't pretend to be stupid, because I never wanted to raise my hand in class."

"You didn't want the boys to think you were *too smart*," Tress says, making air quotes around the last words.

"You said I can be smart and pretty," I go on. "I can be both."

"You are both," Tress says.

"Right," I agree. "So . . . if I'm not stupid, Tress, why would I stand here and insist that I don't know what happened that night, if I really did? Why would I let this continue if I could stop it just by being honest?"

Tress is nodding along with me, like she knew I would say this, and a pit of fear opens in my stomach, my heart falling into it. I thought I was being clever, reconnecting with her and leading her through a logical chain that would undo the ones she's got me in. But instead she's just agreeing, like I'm following a script she already had laid out. Like she knew exactly what I was doing.

Tress stands up, selects a brick. "You wouldn't tell me, because you're not scared enough yet," she says, reaching for the mortar pail. "You wouldn't tell me because fear is a powerful motivator. But you know what's stronger?"

She comes closer, toes touching the bricks she's already laid, face close to mine. "Shame," she says.

And she's got me there. She's got me dead to rights.

Chapter 22

Tress

Felicity's face falls, and her knees go out, her wrists alone supporting her as she sags. Her head drops, the jester cap sliding to the front again, but I saw her expression when I hit her with *shame*, and it told me everything I need to know. She went from pretty to ugly with just one word, the spark behind her eyes when we laughed suddenly stomped out. I know what defeat looks like. I know shame, thoroughly and completely.

Felicity Turnado knows something. And I'm going to find out what.

But I need her full attention in order to do that, and right now it looks like she needs to stew for a minute. My phone goes off in my pocket—again—and I pull it out for a glance. Cecil is actually attempting to text for the first time in his life, since I'm not answering any of his calls.

> Cat 🐱 dance. Kill some odyssey were ✔

I stare at it for a second, completely lost. I end up having to retype everything into my phone and take some suggestions from autocorrect to try to translate it. What I finally work out is: "Cat dangerous. Kills somebody and we're done."

"No shit," I say to my phone. What Cecil didn't do is send any suggestions about how a person is supposed to go about capturing a panther and leading it docilely back to its cage in the middle of the night. I know there's a dart gun back at home, but stalking a cat is a dangerous business that becomes impossible when it's a black cat in utter darkness.

Nope. Cecil will have to wait. Or sober up and do it himself—there's a thought.

My phone vibrates in my hand, drawing my attention to a string of tweets and Instagram posts featuring the hashtags I'd set on notifications—#HonestUsher and #TrueLoser. There are hundreds of alerts, and they're picking up steam. People I know are using it, but it's being retweeted and reposted at an alarming rate, strangers getting in on the game. Someone even has a livestream going on Facebook . . . and it has over three hundred viewers at the moment.

I hop on to see Ribbit leaning dangerously to one side of his chair; the only thing apparently balancing him is a beer in the other hand. Somebody is keeping him refreshed, making sure the show doesn't end before they're done watching.

"Next question," Hugh says, and the camera goes over to him, large and kingly in his stuffed chair.

"What are you doing?" I ask the screen. Hugh's a good guy; we've got a friendship that's rooted in my cock-and-balls shirt from freshman year. I know that if I send him a text right now and ask him to stop, he will.

But I don't.

"This one is from . . ." Hugh glances at his phone, seems confused, then starts again. "This person wants to know if you've ever shit your pants."

The camera swings back to Ribbit, who seems to be thinking very hard. "Yes," he says, his face dead serious. "You know the pizza they sell at the pool?"

The whole crowd groans, and the camera pans them, some people nodding enthusiastically, wanting to know the rest, others covering their mouths in horror.

"It runs right through you," Ribbit says, enjoying the reaction. "You know . . . *runs*?"

The camera swings back to Hugh for a reaction, but his eyes are on his phone as he scrolls through it.

"I tried to make it to the bathroom," Ribbit goes

on, turning to the crowd. "But even though I was *running* . . ." He leans into the pun, enjoying the shocked reactions. He pauses for effect. "I didn't quite make it. I'm pretty sure I left a little something in the pool."

Everybody goes nuts, some people overjoyed, others disgusted. Brynn Whitaker goes up to Hugh, clearly unhappy. She grabs his arm, whispers something in his ear. Ribbit spots her and points with his beer hand, froth splashing over the front-row viewers.

"You were there," he says, speech slurring. "You had on a pink bikini."

The crowd whoops, and Brynn gets a few catcalls, the concerned look on her face quickly switching over to anger.

"Your boob popped out," Ribbit continues. "I held on to that image for months. Like, really *held on to it*," he says, and mimes jerking off.

The Facebook stream goes nuts along with the crowd upstairs. Hearts and laughing faces and thumbs-ups are flying across my screen when I switch over to text. My fingers hover for a minute, debating. The hashtags are gaining momentum and the livestream has a thousand people now. Me texting Hugh isn't going to stop this. Brynn shakes off Hugh's hand when he tries to grab her, and she storms off. I watch her exit the screen accompanied by the hard strikes of her footsteps above my head as she stomps away.

Bells jingle, and I glance up. Felicity has raised her head, fresh tears streaking down her face. "Tress," she says, my name barely a whisper. "I don't know anything. You've got to believe me."

"Yeah." I shove my phone into my back pocket and stand up, the chair creaking under me. "See, the thing is . . . I don't."

Another roll of laughter comes from upstairs, loud enough to reach us in our solitude.

"What's going on?" Felicity asks, eyes going to the floor above us.

"Ribbit got drunk," I tell her. "He's answering anything anybody asks him, and it's going viral."

Felicity shakes her head. "They'll eat him alive."

I shrug. "They're your friends."

"It's your cousin," she snaps back. "Aren't you going to do something?"

"I am doing something," I tell her, and I pick up a brick.

She goes quiet and watchful, eyes following me.

"Eighty-eight bricks," Felicity says, the fever spots in her cheeks brighter now. "Eighty-eight bricks and Lucy should just buy all the apples; that way everyone can have as many as they want."

"Or maybe," I say, weighing the brick in my hand

before I lay the third row. "Maybe she has to steal them, because she's fucking poor."

There's a lull upstairs, and I hear the clock, running backward to chime the hour.

Chapter 23

Felicity

Sixth Grade

My phone lights up with a text, and my heart goes up into my throat when I see the name. I play it cool as I go downstairs, stepping over the pile of shoes Mom set aside to go to the yard sale fundraiser to benefit the PTO. She became the president right after I started having seizures, and now she's at the school all the time. Mom always manages to find something to do in my classroom, one eye on me. Last week David Evans told me my mom was hot, and I stomped on his foot. I got in trouble and had to apologize to him in front of the class.

"Do we hit boys?" Mom asked in the car on the way home, the school buses I'm not allowed to ride anymore blocking traffic.

"No," I muttered, and she nodded, meeting my eyes in the rearview mirror.

"What do we do when a boy says something nice to us?"

"Say thank you." I repeated the lesson she's been drilling into me since I started to get boobs, but David didn't say something nice to me. He said it about my mom. And his face didn't look nice when he said it.

"Moooom," I call out, scanning the empty first floor from the open staircase.

I spot both Mom and Dad hanging out on the new deck. Even with the sliding door shut, I know they're fighting. I can tell because Mom keeps her face blank, neither accepting or denying anything Dad says. He's told her before—one time when they forgot to shut the door—that it makes him *fucking insane*. I'm not supposed to know he says that word, or that the word even exists. I know a lot of things I'm not supposed to, mostly because Mom and Dad get angry with each other, and when they're angry they're loud, too.

But Mom keeps making the face Dad hates. She's good at it. I've started practicing it in the mirror. Apparently making boys *fucking insane* is something that works; Mom always gets what she wants.

If I can catch them at a bad moment my own news might slip past, as they both try really, really hard to act like everything is okay. That's something that we're *all* good at. I flip back the lock and am about to jerk open the door, when I stop in my tracks, catching the last few words out of Dad's mouth.

"—goddamn birthday party! There's no reason why they can't spend the night!"

"Really? *Really?*" Mom asks, dragging out the second one, like maybe Dad made a mistake by saying what he did. By the look on his face, he might be thinking the same thing. "Because we all know what happened last time our daughter had a sleepover."

Yeah, we do. Us and the whole town. In my hand, my phone buzzes again. My fingers are sweaty, smearing the name on the screen: *Tress Montor.*

The last time our daughter had a sleepover. I touch my fingers to the side of my lip, where the scar still lingers, even though Mom has told me twice there's a doctor who can make it like it never happened.

I already feel like a lot of things never happened, like the big chunk of time I can't remember from that night at Tress's. But I remember what came before, super well. Mom and Dad had been fighting out on the back deck, just like this. Outside, where they thought I couldn't hear. But I am small and quiet, and I'd sat halfway up the steps, listening.

"If she wants to go to the Montors' there's no reason why not," Dad said.

"No reason?" Mom shot back, her voice angrier than his, and louder. "It only has to happen once, Brandon, just once. One seizure and everybody knows that the Turnados have something in their blood, and who will marry her then?"

I squirmed on the stairs then, thinking about the fact that my dad had a real name, more than the idea of getting married.

"*Married?*" Dad's voice rose to match Mom's then, cracking. "Jesus Christ, she's in sixth grade, April! And this isn't the seventeenth century."

"No," Mom said. "But it's Amontillado. You didn't grow up here. You don't know. People still talk about the Evans boy marrying that Troyer girl out of the kindness of his heart, knowing full well insanity runs in their family."

"You sure it's not the only one?" Dad bellowed, and then there was a smacking sound that made me jump, the hem of my nightgown fluttering with the move-ment. Mom had come around the corner, shaking her hand, freezing when she spotted me on the steps.

"What did you hear?" she asked, but all I could do was shake my head.

Like I did when I came home from school to find her on the floor, a froth around her lips. Like I did when I caught her taking my seizure medication, her mouth a tight line around the pill. Like I did when she told me, for the thousandth time, "Never let anyone know there is something wrong with you."

I have become very good at pretending there is nothing wrong. So good that now, as I slide open the screen door, I put on the face I've been practicing. Mom's face. Blankness, waiting for the other person's reaction.

"Tress RSVP'd," I say. "She'll be here tomorrow for the party."

"Okay," Mom says in her fake, cheery voice, the one she practices as much I do the face. The door is almost latched again when Mom stops it with her foot. "Wait. Who?"

"Tress," I say, keeping my voice light and airy, like hers. You can get away with a lot if you keep a polite tone. I've learned that from watching Mom. She bartered down the salesman at the car lot last week to a price that had actually made Dad hug her. We drove off the lot together, Mom looking in the rearview mirror at the salesman with a smile.

"He has no idea what hit him," she said, then told me to set the air however I wanted it because we had dual climate control now. And heated seats. The clothes I was wearing still smell like a new car, leather and plastic and steel, shiny and bright. Clean. New. A lot of my stuff is new these days.

"Tress," I repeat. "Remember her?"

Mom's blank face folds a bit, into a scowl, and I know I messed up. I messed up because I sounded like Dad. And—like Mom said that night before I ran to Tress's house—nobody likes a smart-ass.

But I hear Jackson Troyer really likes yours.

That's what Dad had said, right before there was another sound that wasn't a slap but something harder, something I didn't want to know more about, so I ran. Went down the road and across the bridge and out into the night, like Tress and I used to sing—

Over the river and through the woods to my best friend's house I go . . .

"Yes," Mom says calmly now, eyeing me. "Of course I remember Tress. I didn't realize that you'd invited her. I'm just wondering if it's a good idea for you to see her. Won't that be . . ."

"Difficult?" I fill in for her, using the word my therapist applies to just about everything.

Is it difficult for you to move past that night?

Do you have difficulties remembering because of the trauma?

How difficult is it to manage your panic attacks recently?

Would you say that your relationship with Tress is difficult now?

No. I'd say it's gone, over, done with. And that's not okay with me. I don't know what happened to the Montors that night, but I know that my mom wants to pretend that it was nothing. That nothing happened and Tress never existed. But she did, and she still does, and she's my friend, and I want her at my birthday party. Even if my mom doesn't.

I stick my chin out. That's Dad's move and I know Mom doesn't like it, but we're past the part where we pretend to be polite.

"Yes, *difficult* is a good word," Mom says, reaching to take my hand. I let her have it, but I don't squeeze back. I just let my hand lie in hers, because *difficult* is not a good word.

"It won't be," I say. "Tress is my friend. Why shouldn't she be at my party?"

It's a dumb question. I know why. Because I was with her parents in their car the night they disappeared, and I haven't hung out with Tress since then, even though it's been months. Mom and Dad said we couldn't really talk to each other because there was an open investigation, and we were both witnesses. Everybody wanted to make sure our stories were kept straight, that we didn't end up "muddying the waters" by conferring with each other.

But, like the investigator who talked to Mom explained, I'm a witness, but only *kind of*. Technically I was there when something happened to the Montors, but whatever it was, I seized right before it happened. I was there . . . but not there. I was in the car, and then I was on the bank by the river, my nightgown covered in mud and pee, crying because someone carried me there but then they left. I was alone, and I was cold, and I was scared.

But I wasn't a witness. I had hoped that meant I could talk to Tress, but really it just meant that I go to therapy more often. And that the officer who I told about the seizures gets a big box of doughnuts delivered to his desk every Monday morning.

"Honey." Mom is being careful with me now, using the voice that she uses when I'm coming up from a seizure, when she thinks I'm having trouble understanding English. I don't. Not then, and not now.

"I just thought it might be uncomfortable for you, to be reminded of . . . everything."

I pull my hand back, out of hers. "I can't be reminded of something I can't remember."

"Okay." The blank face is back on. I'm starting to understand why it makes Dad *fucking insane.* "But what about the other girls? Won't it be awkward for them?"

"No," I say, even though I know it probably will. Mom knows it, too, and she can hear it in my voice.

"Well." Mom reaches out, rubs my arm since I won't give her my hand back. "It's your birthday party, Felicity. If you want Tress to come, then she comes. I just want it to be fun. It's a party. *Everyone* should be able to have fun."

She slides past me through the door, clicking it shut behind her and leaving me on the deck with Dad. He shakes his head, raises his beer to me in a salute, and downs the rest of it. Just like the car salesman . . . sometimes we don't know what just hit us.

"So then Jackie said that she heard David Evans was going out with a seventh grader, and I said there's no way that's true." Gretchen scratches her head as she sucks on her Popsicle, the red color sticking to the edges of her lips. Somehow she manages to get it all just on her lips, dying them a permanent bloodred. The rest of us have it smeared around our mouths. Like kids.

We are kids, I remind myself. But like my therapist says, sometimes kids don't get to stay kids for very long.

Brynn bites into her Popsicle, the sight making me wince. My teeth are super sensitive, and I always have to roll anything cold around in my mouth, warming it up before I take the leap of actually biting down. Brynn goes in like the Popsicle is her enemy, chomping off half of it with one bite.

She catches me looking at her and rolls her eyes. We're going to have to hear about David Evans and who he may or may not be going out with until someone interrupts Gretchen. Maddie is too invested in painting her toenails to be much help. Her Popsicle is about to drip onto my new bedspread, but I don't care.

I am waiting on something much more important to happen.

"Felicity!" Mom's voice sings out. "Your guest is here!"

Everyone else, Mom announced as *your friend*.

Gretchen breaks off, and all the girls look at me with questions on their faces. This is the group. Our group, the one that formed at the beginning of this school year with pinkie promises and matching hoodies and a group-text conversation that has been going on for months. We're all here. No one is missing.

Then Tress is in the doorway, a sleeping bag tucked under her arm, unlaced boots flopping on her feet. She's got a smudge of dirt in the hollow under her neck, a fading bruise across her upper arm. There's a scab covering most of one knee, a chunk of dead skin that almost falls off when I give her the biggest hug ever.

"I'm glad you're here," I say in her ear, quiet, just for us.

"Hey," she says back. She's stiff in my arms, but the stiffness eases out when I don't relent in my squeezing. Tress melts a little, just like a Popsicle, once I've warmed it up a bit.

"Oops," Maddie says from behind us. "I think I made a mess."

"You can't *think* you made a mess," Brynn says. "You either did or you didn't."

"I made a mess, then," Maddie says agreeably.

"I've got it," Brynn says, hopping up. She slips past us, reaching out one hand to awkwardly clap Tress on the shoulder. "Hey, Tress," she says casually.

"Hey," Tress says back, stiffening again.

Still on the floor, Gretchen's eyes narrow at Tress's sleeping bag, still tucked under her arm. "Is this a sleepover? The invitation didn't say it was a sleepover."

Under my arm, Tress goes still as stone.

"I need somewhere to stay," Tress says, at the same time that I say, "Of course it's a sleepover!"

It's definitely not a sleepover. Mom wouldn't even consider it, in case I had a seizure. In case Maddie and Gretchen and Brynn see me pee my pants and twitch and roll on the floor like an insane person. A person who has something wrong with them. A person who no one will want to marry, because then their kids might have it, too.

Gretchen eyes me, sucking hard on her Popsicle. "If she's staying over, then I'm staying over," she finally says.

"Well, yeah!" I say, because like Mom said, we want to make sure *everybody* is having a good time. I'll be sure to bring that up when I break the news to her.

"'Kay," Gretchen says, reaching up to scratch her head again. "I'll text my dad."

Brynn comes back with wet paper towels and wipes down Maddie's arm—which is dripping with red Popsicle water.

"Hey, we're staying the night now," she tells Brynn, who shakes her head.

"Can't," Brynn says. "I've got volleyball camp in the morning."

"Oh," Maddie says quietly, and I know she's thinking the same thing I am. Without Brynn here to rein her in, Gretchen will go after Tress any chance she gets. And Maddie—I know—will follow the leader.

That just leaves me. I tighten my arm around Tress, pulling her against my side.

"I'm glad you're here," I say again.

Chapter 24

Tress

Sixth Grade

I stomp down hard on the shovel, accidentally cracking carrots as I do. But Zee won't care. Zebras aren't all that picky about their food. Not like how Gretchen Astor always asks the cafeteria lady to cut the crust off her sandwiches. The first time Cecil showed me how to dig carrots for the animals I asked if he was going to wash them first. He'd thumped me on the head with the bunch, dirt raining down on my hair.

"Probably do you a little good to eat some dirt, too," he said.

In the paddock, Zee brays at me. He saw me come into the garden with the shovel, and he's no dummy. It's snack time. Goldie-Dog leaves my heels, trots over to Zee's paddock, and slips between the slats, craning her neck so they can touch noses.

Goldie's rear end is a mess of mats, mud, and probably some poop, too. Cecil won't let her in the house, so my dog has had to settle for finding a spot in the barn. She made friends with Zee real quick, but Dee—the ostrich—didn't like Goldie at all. Cecil wasn't too happy about that; Zee and Dee came as a pair, and they share the same paddock. Having Goldie zip in and out was causing "hostilities," according to Cecil, and if I wanted to keep my dog, she'd better learn her place.

Two months ago, I still had the nerve to plant my feet and stick my chin out. I'd told Cecil that I'd run away before I let him take my dog to the pound.

"Who said anything about the pound?" Cecil said, and pointed at the shotgun propped in the corner.

So Goldie had to learn her place, which meant I had to teach Dee that she wasn't a threat. I guess that's how I learned my place, too, out there with the animals. Just a week in the paddock and Zee was nudging my back, checking my pockets for treats. And while Dee and I weren't exactly friends, the ostrich stopped flapping her wings at me and making herself big every time I climbed the fence. She'd only charged me the once, when my back was turned.

That's how I learned not to turn my back. On anything.

Cecil kept the pens cleaner than the house, on account of the ASPCA people doing unannounced drop-ins. It didn't take long for me to figure out the animals were better company anyway; I'd learned not to turn my back on Cecil, either.

And how to haul manure and clean hooves. How to brush a coat and trim a mane. How much to feed each animal and where to catch the biggest fish out of the creek for the alligator. I shudder, remembering the flash of silver scales as a tail disappeared down her throat. I lean against Zee to absorb some of her warmth. She grunts deep in her throat and crunches on her carrots, the orange ends disappearing into her mouth, the green tops following behind.

Dee spots us and comes over, her bulk shifting from side to side. She stretches her neck out and pecks me, like a reminder that she's here, and hungry, too.

"You're ugly," I tell her.

It's hard to like an ostrich.

You can't like or dislike an alligator; you just have to be careful around it. She keeps to herself in her little pond, and we turn off the electric fence to pop in and check that it's decently stocked with fish . . . but only after being sure she's well-fed with a few big ones from the stream first.

"Can't trust her," Cecil told me gruffly, the first time

we walked into the alligator's pen. It seems to be the basic rule around here.

But mostly Rue, Cecil warned me. It took me the longest to warm up to the orangutan. He called her the *o-rang-o-tangy* and said she'd tear my face off if I gave her the chance. I wasn't allowed to go in her pen—a large, fenced-in open-air area with a single tree growing in it for her to swing in. There was a closed-in building attached, where she could go if it rained, or when the vet came for medical attention. But for the most part Rue stayed in her tree, eyes following me when I moved around the paddocks and cages.

I hadn't liked it. Hadn't liked the way she was almost human . . . but not quite. How sometimes she walked along beside me when I came near the cage. I'd felt stalked, hunted, until the one day she stretched an arm through the fencing and handed me something. I'd reached out automatically, palm up.

And Rue had put a piece of shit in my hand.

"What?" I'd looked down at it, shocked, then back up to see Rue giving me . . . well, giving me a shit-eating grin.

"You asshole!" I'd said—a word that Cecil dropped a lot around the cages—and done the only thing that seemed like the right reaction. I threw it at her.

She'd been thrilled, ducking her head and jumping

into the tree to grab an apple from the stash she kept up there, throwing it at me the second I turned my back. It sailed through the square holes of the fence and I understood; we were playing a game.

I'd gathered a few things, some apples from the orchard, a tennis ball I usually tossed with Goldie, and a balled-up sock from the box of mismatches. Rue and I spent most of the afternoon throwing things at each other, which I guess is how you make friends with an orangutan.

She's watching me now from her tree; I can see her eyeing me through the leaves. She'll probably wait until I'm in throwing distance and peg me from afar. She's gotten pretty good at judging what will fit through the fence holes and what won't, and her aim is improving.

"All right, Zee," I tell the zebra, giving her a last rub on the neck. "You're good."

Goldie slips through the paddock slats as I climb over, her dirty haunches bouncing as she runs in front of me. I really need to trim her up, give her a bath. Not that long ago she had monthly appointments with the groomer and would come home with a bow on top of her head, Mom and Dad telling her she was a good girl, a pretty girl. Dad would roll around on the ground with Goldie, then grab my leg and pull me into the pile, telling me I was a good girl, too, while I shrieked and reached for Mom, who would pretend I was invisible.

"What is that?" she'd say, cocking her head. "I think I hear my daughter . . . but I can't see her. Weird."

I squash the thought as soon as I have it, painful because it came true. Mom can't see me now, neither can Dad, and I bet they can't hear me, either. Felicity Turnado showed up at my house in her nightgown, crying, asking if she could spend the night, and after that everything changed. Goldie isn't an indoor dog anymore, and she isn't a clean dog anymore. Cecil doesn't tell me that I'm a good girl, either, no matter how clean the pens are or how hard I work. That's just the way it is.

The tennis ball hits me square in the forehead, and Goldie grabs it on the third bounce, running off with her head in the air. I rub the spot.

"Nice, Rue," I tell her. I hold my hands up, empty. Goldie ran off with my only ammo. "You win." She gives me a chirp and comes down, graceful and effortless, swinging easily through the power of her own strength. She drops in front of me, cocking her head when my phone goes off in my back pocket. There's a question on her face—what is this new thing?

I'm as surprised as she is. Right after Mom and Dad disappeared there had been a lot of messages, kids from school asking if I was all right (I wasn't) and if there was anything they could do (they couldn't). But the messages had dwindled as time passed, and my new situation became old. I wasn't news anymore. I was just poor now. I couldn't do the movies or the mall without that awkward moment when someone else's mom handed me a folded twenty, or spend the night without being encouraged to take a shower *and scrub real good* before bedtime.

I stopped taking the twenties, started refusing to scrub real good, and the pity invitations didn't come anymore. The only person I hadn't heard from in months was the person I wanted to talk to the most: Felicity. So when I pull the phone out of my back pocket and see that I've got a text from her, and that she wants me to come to her birthday party, I say the first thing that comes to mind, some more words that Cecil taught me.

"Holy shit."

In her cage, Rue grins at me.

I am not glad I came to the party.

Cecil was not happy when I told him I wasn't doing chores tonight, because it means he can't get blackout drunk for another extra hour. I didn't even think about asking him to drive me into town, and I would've walked the whole way if Ribbit's mom hadn't spotted me hiking down the road with my backpack and sleeping bag. I'd grabbed the bag after Cecil yelled at me that a girl who doesn't pull her weight doesn't need a bed to sleep in at night. I've been locked out for less, and slept in the stable more than once when Cecil was in a mood. If I can stay at Felicity's, at least I won't smell like an ostrich in the morning.

Aunt Lenore gave me a ride to Felicity's house, a little line in between her eyebrows. She told me to have a good time when I got out of the car, Cecil's old boots slapping against the Turnados' paved walkway. Cecil took most of my stuff to Goodwill when I moved in with him, said he didn't have the kind of room that Mom and Dad did and that I didn't need most of that stuff anyway. What I needed was to learn not to be spoiled.

I guess one of the things that spoiled me was having my own shoes, because Cecil traded all of them to some guy at the bar who forgot to get his kid a birthday present in exchange for a bottle of whiskey. So now I have on his old boots, the dried mud and probably more than a little animal shit tracking all over Felicity's bedroom carpet. Which, I notice, is new.

April—Felicity's mom—was weird with me, one hand on my shoulder as she guided me to Felicity's room, like I didn't know the way. Then Gretchen had mentioned invitations. I didn't get one of those. I got a text last night, last minute.

I'm standing here, wearing an old man's shoes,

holding a sleeping bag I'm not supposed to have, staring down a bunch of girls I don't really like. And despite the weight of Felicity's arm across my shoulders, something is being made very clear to me.

I don't belong here.

Chapter 25

Felicity

Sixth Grade

We're friends again.

It happened slowly, starting with the fact that no one had brought any sleeping bags—breaking the news to Mom that this was now a sleepover had *not* been awesome—and so we ended up making a pile of blankets on the floor of my room. We're cuddled in, a bag of Doritos passing between us, wiping cheesy fingers on whatever we can find.

Mom had carried Tress's boots outside with a wrinkled nose, and I had given her a pair of my pajamas. She's almost like us, now, with the right clothes on and that scab on her knee covered. Almost. There's still something about her eyes, and how she's being too careful, watching Gretchen like she's waiting for her to attack.

Which she hasn't done . . . so far.

Brynn's mom picked her up about an hour ago and me, Gretchen, Maddie, and Tress had torn through a package of cookies and a case of soda that Dad had slipped into my room, with a wink and a thumbs-up. I'm guessing Mom is lying on the couch downstairs, her mouth a thin, flat line as she crosses her fingers and prays I don't have a seizure in front of everyone. Either that or worrying about the soda rotting my teeth out of my head. She always says my smile is my best feature. I guess if I didn't have seizures maybe that would be my best feature instead.

It might rot my teeth, but the sugar is helping us all get along. We've got the giggles, and Tress has even loosened up a little bit.

"Hey," she says, bumping me with her elbow. "Do your impression of Mr. Stephens."

"Oh . . ," I say, my stomach bottoming out a little bit.

"Do her what?" Gretchen asks.

"She can do Mr. Stephens," Tress says. "She's, like, really good at impressions."

It's true, I am. But it's not something I do for just anybody. Last time Mom caught me mimicking our mailman, Dad in a laughing fit on the couch, she told me it wasn't nice to make fun of people.

"I'm not making fun," I insisted. "I'm just—"

"Pretending to be a sixty-year-old man?" Mom asked, raising an eyebrow. "That's weird, Felicity."

Maybe it is weird, I don't know. I'd kept my impressions just for Tress since then, but now Maddie and Gretchen are looking at me expectantly.

"All right," I say, standing up. A cascade of cookie crumbs rolls off my front as I get into position, throwing my shoulders back and making myself big, barrel-chested like Mr. Stephens, our science teacher.

"Volcanoes," I say, dropping my voice really low and rounding out my vowels. "Are truly a miracle of geology."

Maddie erupts in a fit of giggles, and Tress claps. Gretchen just looks at me, wide-eyed.

"That was . . . bizarre," she finally says.

Weird, my mom's voice echoes in the back of my head, and I falter on my feet, wondering how Gretchen would react if I dropped to the floor right now, foaming at the mouth. *Bizarre* would just be the beginning.

"Do another one, do another one," Maddie says. "Do Captain Choir!"

I roll into an impression of Mrs. Adams, our music teacher, smacking the undersides of my arms to make my skin wobble, which totally is making fun of someone. But even Gretchen is laughing now, so I keep going.

"Oh, do Ms. Frampton!" Gretchen says.

That one's harder. Ms. Frampton is a complete

airhead of a substitute that we get sometimes. She's really young and nice and just seems to want everyone to be happy. Last time we had her she brought homemade cookies, and then lost control of the classroom when Jessica Stanhope had an allergic reaction to the nuts in them. We haven't seen Ms. Frampton since then.

I screw my eyes shut, trying to remember her. Trying to recall the set of her face, small repeated movements, the lilt of her voice. All the things that make a person unique.

"Hello, class," I singsong as I breeze through the doorway, pretending like I've just arrived. "How are we today? I've got cookies for everyone . . . except Jessica."

"Like Jessica needs any more cookies," Gretchen says, holding her hands out from her waist. Maddie erupts into giggles, but Tress is frozen in place, her face a tight mask.

I don't know what happened. It's not like she's friends with Jessica or anything, and my impression wasn't that bad. I hit the high notes of Ms. Frampton's voice, the cadence of her speech with a little downturn at the end. No . . . wait. That's not right. I wasn't doing Ms. Frampton at all; I fell back on mimicking a voice that I've heard a million times.

I was doing Annabelle Montor.

And by the look on Tress's face, I nailed it.

Chapter 26

Tress

Sixth Grade

"I have to go to the bathroom."

It's true, but not because I have to pee. I'm going to puke. I'm going to lose Coke and Doritos and Oreos all over these girls who have parents. I push past Felicity, and she reaches for me, her fingers glancing over my arm. It's just like my mom said when I rolled around on the ground with Dad and Goldie . . . *I can hear you, but I can't see you.* I might never see my mom again for as long as I live, but I just heard her voice. And it came out of Felicity Turnado's mouth.

"Don't touch me," I growl, ducking out from under her reach.

I can't be near her right now. I slam the bathroom door so hard it bounces off the frame, and I know that

April might be coming to investigate—loud noises at the Turnado household aren't a thing—but then I'm over the toilet and losing everything, and I couldn't care less what April thinks about slamming doors.

I flush it all down and roll over onto my back for a second while I get myself under control. I don't think Felicity meant to do that, don't think she had any intention of bringing the image of my mother back to me, full force, right when I was beginning to think I might be the kind of girl who still went to birthday parties. Who still laughed with other girls. Who might even still have friends.

The leg of Felicity's pajama bottoms is bunched up above my knee, the sliding dive I made to get to the toilet in time giving me a fresh burn right across the kneecap. There will be a scab to match the other leg in a couple days. A tear slips out, and I reach above me, roll out some toilet paper to dab my eyes and the sweat from my forehead. I've got to get cleaned up, get myself under control—*get my shit together*, Cecil would say. I give my nose a good blow and then open the cupboard to throw the wad of paper away. April has all the trash cans in the house tucked away in corners, behind doors, out of sight. I toss the tissue, miss, and have to dig around to find it, knocking over a box of tampons in the process.

Felicity must have started, I realize . . . then think

about the fact that I didn't know. I didn't know because she didn't tell me. And she didn't tell me because—

"Because we're not friends anymore," I say aloud.

We're not. I knew that. I knew it when I got a text from her and had to double-check that she actually meant to invite me to her party, that she didn't accidentally text the wrong person. I knew it when April carried my boots outside. I knew it when Felicity hugged me—so tight, too tight—with a desperation to deny what she already knew, too.

We're not friends anymore.

And, while that may be true, something else is as well. There's a box of tampons in this house, and there aren't any where I live now. When I asked Cecil to add them to the shopping list he told me it'd be a cold day in hell before someone caught him in that aisle, and that I should just *hold it* until I got to school.

"It doesn't work that way," I'd told him, but he said he'd gotten this far in life without learning women's business, and that was just fine. Which for him, I suppose it was.

Me, I need tampons.

And here are some, right in front of me.

I grab the box and stuff it down the front of Felicity's pajamas. If I get back into the bedroom and get under the pile of blankets I can slip it out of my pants and into my backpack once everybody else is asleep. I straighten up, close the cupboard and give my reflection one last check before turning toward the door, where a shadow slides away.

Gretchen's quick, but I'm faster. You don't live around wild animals for months without developing reflexes. I grab her wrist as she tries to spin away from me.

"Let me go," she says, pulling away. But I've got her in a good grip; I can feel the tiny bones of her wrist grinding together as I clamp down.

"Guys?"

Felicity and Maddie are standing in the bedroom doorway, confused. I let go of Gretchen's wrist and she holds it against her chest.

"What's going on?" Felicity asks, eyes moving between the two of us.

"Tress stole your tampons," Gretchen says, shooting me a nasty look as she rubs her wrist.

"Did not!" I say, lying reflexively. Everyone looks at the obvious outline of a box in the waistline of my pajamas. Felicity's pajamas. Felicity's tampons.

"Hey! Let's . . . let's watch a movie!" Felicity says brightly, voice high and fake, like her mom's. "You can pick, Gretchen. Doesn't that one cute guy you like have something new out? Or like a special on HBO? There's that new horror show, I heard it's super scary!"

She's trying, but it's not enough. We're going to pretend that everything is fine, that I belong here, that we can all just watch a movie together and go back to having a sleepover at a birthday party after one girl puked her guts out and then stole someone else's tampons. The girl who can't buy her own. The girl who doesn't belong.

I duck back into the bathroom and toss the box under the sink, not caring that I knock over a dozen bottles in the process. They're all lined up, matching sets of shampoo and conditioner in bright colors. I push over the last two for good measure, go back to the bedroom and curl up under some of the blankets without a word, my back to the others, snuggled into a nest of my own making.

I can't be here, but I can't go home, either.

I don't have one of those anymore.

I lie still, listening to the others drop off, one by one. Maddie goes first, her little comments about the movie falling away into light snores. Gretchen sticks it out longer, but eventually she asks Felicity if she can sleep in the bed because sleeping on the floor is just not comfortable enough. Felicity tells her that yes, of course she can, and soon Gretchen is out, too, her breathing deep and regular.

I hear Felicity get up, tiptoeing around the others. I hear the bathroom door swing open, the higher creak of the cupboard door following that, and the sound of her straightening her shampoo bottles. She comes back to the bedroom, steps over me lightly, unzips my backpack, and puts the tampons inside.

I lay there, stiff and sweating, until there's a glimmer of light outside. I sneak out and walk home, stopping to throw the tampons into the river. The box comes open as it falls, and they float downstream, refusing to sink, bobbing brightly against the dark brown of the water. They're packaged in different colors, the foil flashing pink and neon green, the sun reflecting off them as they go with the current, for everyone to see.

Something that doesn't belong.

Tossed away.

Trash.

Just like me.

Chapter 27

Felicity

"I was trying to help you," I say, bristling. "You needed tampons; I gave them to you. I was trying to be your friend!"

Tress is shaking her head. Slowly. Calmly. But I wouldn't say patiently. No, I wouldn't call it that.

"My friend?" she asks, crossing her arms. "Giving me things doesn't make you my friend, Felicity. It's . . ." Her face contorts, and I know she's trying to find a way to say what she wants to say without using the word *charity*.

She clears her throat, trying again. "It doesn't make you my friend. Giving me stuff makes me . . . less than."

Tress Montor < Felicity Turnado

"I never looked at it like that," I say.

"No." Tress comes to her feet, mortar trowel in

hand. "Of course you didn't. You were just thinking of yourself, how it made *you* feel to give me stuff. And how did it make you feel, Felicity?" she asks, stepping closer.

I grind my teeth, shredding the new layer of enamel that was recently applied in an attempt to undo years of damage . . . years of me doing exactly this—grinding my teeth and thinking about Tress Montor.

Because yeah, it did make me feel better to give her things—clothes, pairs of shoes when there was a BOGO, books that my ever-hopeful librarian aunt bought me for Christmas that I was never going to read. Over the years it went way beyond tampons, every box that I dropped on her doorstep late at night lightening the load on my heart.

They came back sometimes—but not always.

"Don't act all insulted," I say, though I am keeping an eye on the trowel. "You didn't return everything. So don't stand there all high and mighty and act like you're above a handout."

"No," Tress says. "Only what I could balance on my bike, or carry, once I outgrew my bike. The rest ended up in the river."

"That's . . ." I imagine designer-label clothes, tags still on, hardcover bestsellers floating down the river along with bottles of body spray. "That's ridiculous, Tress. Jesus, swallow your pride."

"*Pride?*" Her grip on the trowel tightens, knuckles going white. "You actually think I have some of that?"

Tears pool in her eyes, and she turns away from me, shoulders hunched, back tense with an urge to strike out at something. When she speaks, her voice is an empty echo, bouncing back to me off the stone walls.

"When you gave me things, it made you feel better—and that's all you thought about, how it made you feel. You never thought maybe it made me feel even worse. I wasn't your friend, Felicity. I was your pity project."

"What was I supposed to do?" I ask, anger pushing the words past my enamel-capped teeth. "How was I supposed to make everything better?"

She turns back to me, eyes wet.

"You were supposed to tell the truth."

The truth . . . a slippery element stuck somewhere between what I witnessed but wasn't there for, something I saw but can't remember. "Tress." I lick my lips, gloss coming off on my tongue.

It's gone, along with my makeup, which has mixed with tears and blood and has dried on my cleavage. All my armor is melting away, but my tits are still high, almost to my chin because of the push-up bra I'm wearing under my costume. I came to this party prepared . . . but not for this. Not for Tress Montor.

I remember what I looked like before I left, the last

glance at the mirror that showed me Felicity Turnado—bold, confident, sexy. A girl who takes beers from boys and they're thankful for it, because maybe our fingers brushed. A girl who other girls mimic, dress like, act like, follow around. I've cut more than one of them with my tongue, knocked them down a few pegs when they climbed too close, putting them back where they belong. Beneath me.

Fuck Tress Montor, and fuck her pride.

I toss my head and straighten my shoulders. "Those jeans you're wearing are mine," I say. "Seven for All Mankind, boot cut, size 6. The pullover you had on at school Monday was mine, too, Collina Strada, crew neck, medium. So don't stand there and talk to me about not taking my charity. You are, even if you don't know it."

I said something similar to a girl from Prospero at the football game last week. She wanted to knock me back by telling me she screwed Hugh. It's more than likely the truth, but I covered the drop in my gut by saying it was my shirt he ripped off her, and that's probably what turned him on in the first place, that she was almost me . . . but not quite. She ran away from me crying, the sequins on the Parker Isaac top that used to hang in my closet flashing as she went.

But Tress doesn't even blink. She comes closer, leaning in to give me a hard look. I'm the first one to flinch. Content, she pulls back.

"These may be your jeans," she says. "But it's also your blood on them. So don't get too cocky."

I can't argue with that. I want to, I want to kick and scream and call her names. But when she motions at me to be silent, I stop talking. Because while I might have made my point, Tress follows it up by making one of her own. Not with words, but brick and mortar. She lays the fourth row, calmly, steadily, with no outward sign that I upset her at all.

That's the fourth of twenty-two rows, I think. *Fourth of twenty-two.* It sounds kind of like football, but we're not playing a game down here. I've got eighteen rows left to convince Tress not to bury me alive. Eighteen rows to convince her that I deserve to live. Problem is, I don't know if I can. Another problem is, I'm not entirely sure that I do.

"Okay," she says, pushing her hair out of her face. "Now we need to talk about junior year."

Chapter 28

Tress

Junior Year

I'm staring at a college application, wondering if *wrestling alligators* is something I should put under special skills or not. There certainly is a trick to it, and I've got it down . . . plus some nasty scars on my legs to show for it. There's a general rustle behind me in the library. Brynn and Gretchen are whispering about something; David Evans comes in and informs the librarian his summer reading report is due tomorrow so she should give him the shortest thing on the required reading list. She hands him T. S. Eliot's *The Waste Land* with a small smile.

"Good luck," she says, keeping her face professional. But inside, I'm sure she's laughing like Rue did the one time Cecil tripped and fell into her septic drainage.

I turn back to my computer screen, angling it so that

nobody can see what I'm doing. I don't need everybody talking about the fact that Tress Montor was looking at colleges, trying to translate the language on the FAFSA website. I can't just walk up to a college admissions office and tell them I've got both Allan and Usher blood in me but no money. That might matter in Amontillado, but once I leave here, I'm just a poor kid with a crappy résumé, all my money in dirty, wadded bills that I slip off the pile before handing it over to Cecil, who is sometimes sober enough to double-check the count, sometimes not.

"Jesus Christ," I say, leaning back in my chair and looking at the tuition prices. Even the cheaper ones feel astronomical. It doesn't help that I have no idea what to claim for our income. Whenever I ask Cecil about it all he does is shake his head, or say, "Not good and not getting any better."

"What's up?"

Hugh flops into the seat next to me, his knees scraping against mine. They're darkly tanned from the summer, and even hairier than Rue's. I quickly minimize my window but not before he catches the movement.

"Looking at porn?" he asks too loudly.

"No," I harsh whisper at him. "And we're in a library."

"Huh." He looks around him like he's surprised. "Weird."

"For you," I agree. "Why are you even here?"

Then I see Brynn looking at him over a book, glancing down quickly when he notices her.

"Ohhhhh," I say. Hugh blushes a little bit, and I smack his leg. "You could try talking to her, not just following her around, creep."

He moves in closer to me, lowering his voice as well. "Okay, so I tried that, but here's the thing—she's like . . . nice."

"Oh, that's new and different for you, huh?"

"No, I mean . . ." He glances around, drops his voice to a whisper. "So, like, everybody thinks I'm with Felicity, you know?"

"If by *with* you mean hooking up at parties, then yes, people think that."

"Right!" Hugh says, apparently thrilled I understand. "But it's not like that."

I'm pulled in despite myself, still hungry after all these years for any inside information about my former best friend. "Not like that how?"

"We're not, like, a thing. We're not together. It's . . ." He leans back in his chair, and sighs. "It's complicated."

"Genitals make life hard," I say, and it's his turn to smack me.

"Seriously?" he asks. "Genitals?"

"That's what they're called."

"Whatever." Hugh shakes his head. "Point is— Brynn's a nice girl, and she's friends with Felicity."

"And if she thinks Felicity is into you, she's not going to cross her friend," I finish for him. "So just tell Brynn that you're not doing genital stuff with Felicity."

"It's not that simple," he says, suddenly choosing his words more carefully. "Felicity needs me for . . . things."

I'm quiet, searching his face. I know Hugh pretty well—well enough to know that he doesn't do drugs. And I know my market well enough to know that he's not selling, either, because I haven't seen my sales go down—I don't have a competitor. So Felicity doesn't need him for the same thing she needs me for.

"Whatever it is," I tell him. "She's using you."

"It's not like that, Tress," Hugh says. "Felicity's got problems you know nothing about."

"Right," I agree, turning away from him. "Not like mine; the whole town knows my issues."

Hugh lets it slide; there's nothing he can say to that. David has joined Brynn and Gretchen at their table, brow furrowed in intense concentration as he tries to plow through *The Waste Land*.

"Whoa, dude, you've got to beef up this résumé."

I turn back to my computer to see that Hugh's looking at my application. "Dick," I say. "That's private."

"No, for real," he says, reaching out for the keyboard. "Check this out."

I grudgingly push the keyboard toward him, and he starts typing away with a surprisingly fast hunt-and-peck method.

"So you don't want to outright lie," he says. "Because they might follow up. I'm guessing you don't have any job references?"

I nod, silently thanking him. Hugh knows that I can't name the Amontillado Animal Attractions as my employer, much less put Cecil down as a reference. Our Facebook page itself would bar me from most campuses in twenty seconds, not to mention probably bring the ASPCA down on our heads. And I can imagine Cecil fielding a phone call from an admissions office, telling them he didn't raise no pussy that needs air-conditioning—or a higher education.

Self-starter, highly motivated, and adaptable to changing situations, Hugh types.

"Nice," I say grudgingly. It's certainly all true, especially being adaptable. Last week I had to relocate my entire store when somebody let the cops know there were drug deals going down in the old barn out on 26. I think learning the patterns of a grumpy ostrich's mood swings counts as adaptable, too.

"But the extracurriculars need some fluffing." Hugh

eyes the screen, resting his chin on his hand. "I know you don't play any sports—"

"You mean, you know I can't afford to play any sports," I correct him, but he just waves his hand. Amontillado went to pay-to-play a few years ago, taking with it any chance I had of stepping foot onto a court or field. Not that it mattered. Even if I had the cash, I don't have a car, and there's no way Cecil would drive my ass back and forth to practices.

"Sports look good on paper," Hugh says. "But that's not the only thing people put on their résumés."

"Right, but all of them require some sort of actual participation," I tell him, ticking off the clubs on my fingers. "Student council, FFA, even book club. All those kids are constantly doing shit I can't."

Basically, anything that requires time and a pair of wheels.

"What about class officer?" Hugh asks. "It's kind of a bullshit title. You don't really do much of anything—What?" He breaks off when he sees me rolling my eyes.

"You really think there's a chance in hell? Class officers are pure popularity contests, and you know it."

"President and VP, maybe," he admits.

"And nobody is going to let me handle money," I tell him. "No way I get treasurer."

"So run for secretary."

My mouth is already open for a comeback, but none comes out. I end up settling for, "Yeah right."

"Why not? Now you're just being a pain in the ass, and you know it," Hugh says. "Last year they couldn't even get anybody to put their name up for it at the class meeting."

This is true, but the *they* in question were Gretchen and Brynn—already elected president and VP—and half the reason nobody wanted to fill the other roles was because they didn't want to put up with Gretchen's shit. Finally some flunkies had raised their hands and automatically got the positions simply because nobody else offered themselves up as tribute.

I glance over at their table. Brynn I can take; she actually seems kind of cool. Gretchen I can *take*; as in, take her out at the knees if she starts anything with me. And it would be good to have something on my extracurriculars, since I can't claim my job without self-incrimination.

"All right," I say to Hugh. "I'll give it a shot."

"Nice," he says. "Now, let me show you what the internet is actually for."

Chapter 29

Felicity

Junior Year

"So then David said there was some freshman at two-a-days who passed out, and when they lifted his legs to get the blood to run to his head he wasn't wearing his jock strap and his balls popped out of his shorts . . . or should I say *ball*?"

"He only had one?" Brynn asks.

"One," Gretchen says, holding a finger in the air, in case we don't get it.

"I'm surprised he had any, the way he hits," Hugh says, and Brynn winces.

I look down at my lunch, shaking my head. Hugh can never see that she's not impressed when he says shitty things. Gretchen sure is, though. She stops eating to run both her hands over the expanse of his chest.

"Everything bounces off this brick wall," she says, practically purring.

Brynn becomes completely entranced by her pizza at that point, and I have to stop myself from clarifying that the only thing that hasn't bounced off Hugh's chest is Gretchen. He won't have anything to do with her, despite her multiple attempts.

I'm stirring my soup—something called "cheesy hamburger" that consists of gelatinous cheese and hunks of meat—when the freshman in question walks by, his face turning a bright red when Hugh shouts, "Uno!"

Hugh jumps up and gives him a high five, which the kid returns half-heartedly, balancing his lunch tray in the other hand and trying not to tip over when Hugh hits him harder than strictly necessary.

"Did you have to do that?" Brynn asks when Hugh comes back to our table.

"What?" Hugh says. "He loved it."

Brynn gathers up her stuff and walks away, leaving a stricken Hugh behind.

"What'd I do?" he asks, looking at me for clarification.

I could tell him. Explain that Brynn has an ex-boyfriend she could never quite please, how even the affection he showed her always had an edge on it, or a taunt, just like what Hugh did when he called that poor kid Uno. Or . . .

I could just shrug, because David is coming over to join us, and he always brings out the worst in Hugh, and I don't think my voice will carry over his.

"What's up with you?" Gretchen asks, giving me an elbow right when my spoon is halfway to my mouth. Cheesy hamburger sprays across my lap, the grease soaking in, the cheese leaving a residue.

"Sorry," she says, handing me a napkin.

"Nothing's up with me," I tell her, dabbing at the mess.

"Really? 'Cause those are the first words you've said all lunch."

They might actually be the first words I've said all day, but Gretchen doesn't need to know that. I didn't have a good night. Something was trying to break through, old memories rising like they'd been filled with helium, fighting their way to the surface. I can feel them, sometimes—floating dread. My therapist says it would be best if I let them into the light, deal with whatever it is trying to come out.

But I can't. So instead I popped an Oxy and had dreams with red lights and water, the feeling of floating not being limited to the drugs in my bloodstream. I was being carried, not smoothly and efficiently the way Hugh does, the raven tattoo flashing in and out of my vision, but sloppily, awkwardly, my rescuer—or attacker?— running through the woods, branches slashing my legs, long and exposed under my nightgown.

Gretchen snaps her fingers in front of my face, rousing me. I jump, knocking my soup bowl, this time the mess slopping onto the table—not anyone's clothes.

"Jesus—get with the program, Turnado," David says.

"Fuck off," Hugh snaps at him, and the mood at our table is most definitely altered—because of me. I'm not being the bright, smiling blonde today. Not being the person they know.

"Sorry," I say. "Didn't sleep much last night."

"That's my boy," David says, slapping Hugh on the back.

Brynn is gone, so Hugh lets it hang, like maybe we were having insane sex for hours and that's why I'm not at the top of my game today. When really it's the opposite; I slept too much. I'm slow and foggy, the Oxy still doing its job even when I'm done needing it to.

Brynn has moved over to the table with the volleyball team, and Hugh wanders in their direction, knowing one of them will call for him to join them. A sophomore does, and he plops down next to her. Brynn looks away when he tugs at the girl's fishtail braid.

He's hopeless. Always on for the boys, always *onto* the girls. Except for the few of us he recognizes as human beings. The ones he'd have to actually form a relationship with, not just fuck and toss. He'll come to our rescue every time, a white knight who rides away before he has to take more responsibility than just saving you. Or maybe I've just been seriously friend-zoned and am bitter.

"We need to talk about prom."

I assume Gretchen directed that to David, getting a top-tier date locked in early. But a few seconds later she's snapping her fingers in front of my face again.

"Hello? Prom?"

"Yeah, prom," I say, desperate to make myself agreeable.

"Right," she says, watching me closely. "Junior class officers are in charge of it, and I'm not letting ours come off like last year's."

I have to agree with her. Last year they tried to do a *Little Mermaid*–themed dance and rented out an aquarium. Which would've been cool, but nobody bothered to clarify with the aquarium staff that it was for a prom, not just a class trip, so a bunch of decked-out teens ended up sitting through lessons about endangered species and forced to participate in a scavenger hunt identifying types of fish. Although, I did have two proposals of marriage and there was at least one fist fight over me, so not a total loss.

"Obviously me and Brynn have got prez and vice in the bag, but we can't have those diseases from last year."

"Meg and Lisa?" I ask. "I thought they were fine."

"No, I mean like *actual diseases*, Turnado. Don't you remember?"

I do remember. Meg Cofflero and Lisa Johnson had done a fundraiser for multiple sclerosis, asking that we all pay whatever we felt was appropriate for our prom tickets, while anything over the price of admission was donated to medical research. Mom and Dad had donated a ridiculous amount, asking that they be put down as anonymous. There were a lot of those on the program at dinner, a trifold that had the five- through fifty-dollar donors listed, the word *anonymous* becoming more prevalent as the numbers got higher.

"We are not having prom at the hospital," Gretchen says, putting down her fork with a clang.

"Who said we were?" I shoot back.

"Felicity," she says patiently, "that's what will happen. Trust me. Everybody was so happy with Meg and Lisa and all their community-minded *thoughtfulness*." She puts the last in air quotes.

"Did you know Meg's sister has MS?" she goes on. "That's the whole reason they did it. It's not like they're actually raising money for sick people. I bet everything went right into her family's checking account."

I seriously doubt that, but I don't have the energy to fight with Gretchen. Besides, even if it did all go to pay the Coffleros' medical bills, I don't even care.

"MS sucks," I say, turning over a spoonful of now cold and lumpy soup.

"Uh, so does prom in a cancer ward."

"Way not cool," David chimes in, a bite of mac and cheese falling out of his mouth.

"I already talked to Maddie Anho, and she said she'd run for treasurer, so you'll be secretary," Gretchen says, like it's all decided.

"Wait? What?" I ask.

"Sec-re-tary," Gretchen says, breaking down the syllables for me. "Even if Meg or Lisa try to run, you know they won't win against you."

"Oh my God," David says. "You're cockblocking class elections."

I flip my spoon over again, watching fat and cheese roll off it in an oily stream. I don't want to be secretary. I don't want to plan prom. And I don't want to be sitting here with David and Gretchen. I don't want to think anymore.

I want to go home. I want to go to bed.

"Meeting's at one, auditorium." Gretchen pats my arm. "It's mandatory."

Class meetings are mandatory for the whole school; I know that.

But I don't think that's what Gretchen means.

* * *

Everyone files into the auditorium, eyes sliding across each other as we assess after the summer break. We've been in school a week, but there are still some surprises: the cute girl who suddenly became hot; the hot guy who doesn't have the same shine to him anymore; the pasty person who apparently went outside for the first time and looks better for it.

I feel eyes on me, too—a lot. I know my exterior looks amazing. No one needs to know about the rest.

Mrs. Febrezio is our class adviser, and when she goes up to the podium everybody gets quiet more quickly than they would for anyone else. She writes more reference letters for colleges than anyone in the district, and nobody wants to burn bridges.

"All right." She clears her throat. "You all know the drill. I'll open nominations for the offices, and we'll vote by show of hands. President?"

She surveys the crowd, and Maddie stands up. "I nominate Gretchen Astor."

"I second," Brynn pipes up. Nobody even attempts to run against her, and the inevitable wave of hands go into the air, sealing the deal.

"Vice?" Febrezio calls, but Gretchen is on her feet before she's finished with even that one syllable.

"I nominate Brynn Whitaker."

"Second," Hugh yells, loudly enough that there are giggles. The pattern repeats itself, with no one wanting to face off against the volleyball star . . . or maybe they just don't want to be the person who challenges the only Black girl and look like an asshole. Or . . . wait. Brynn would win anyway. Am I being racist? While my Oxy-riddled brain tries to puzzle that out, Brynn wins and we move on to treasurer.

"I nominate Maddie Anho," Brynn says, but Lisa John-son is right behind her, and nominates Meg Cofflero. Beside me, Gretchen tenses. Meg then nominates Lisa, and it becomes clear that they are trying to split the vote just enough that Maddie won't slide into the spot so easily. People are looking up from their phones now, aware that the room just got tense.

Febrezio calls for a vote, and it's actually close. Mad-die wins, but it's not the landslide Gretchen was looking for. Beside me, she's texting furiously, promising people free prom tickets and open-campus lunch for upper-classmen if they vote for her candidate for secretary.

"Secretary?" Febrezio calls, and Gretchen jumps up. I reach out to grab her arm at the last second and manage to snag her, pulling her back down.

"Ouch! The fuck?" she says to me, too angry to notice the people around us covering their smiles.

Lisa stands and nominates Meg.

"I don't want to," I tell Gretchen.

"What do you mean you don't want to?" she repeats back to me, like I spoke another language or something.

Meg stands and nominates Lisa.

"I . . . just don't want to," I say, my tongue heavy in my mouth, my brain too slow to process words as the Oxy keeps its promise.

Gretchen's eyes narrow at me, and suddenly Hugh is standing, taking everyone by surprise when he says, "I nominate Tress Montor."

It gets super quiet then, and all eyes go to Tress. She's sitting by herself in the back, her gaze bouncing off everyone else's. She won't hang her head, but she doesn't know what to do with all that attention, either.

"What the fuck is he doing?" Gretchen asks me, like I'm supposed to know. "Great. Now we're going to have a safari-themed prom, and that crocodile is going to eat somebody."

"It's an alligator," I say, but Gretchen slips my grasp and jumps up right before Febrezio closes the nominations.

"I nominate Felicity Turnado," she shouts, and some of the tension leaves the room. Everybody knows what Gretchen wants now. They know who they're supposed to vote for.

I win.

Of course I do.

I always win.

Chapter 30

Tress

"I needed that," I tell her, tapping the edge of the mortar knife against the pail.

"I didn't want it," Felicity says.

"That's not the point."

I get up as another wave of laughter comes from above us, a few shocked gasps for punctuation. Dear Lord, what did Ribbit say this time?

"I didn't want it," Felicity says again, more force behind her words. "Gretchen—"

"But you *got* it," I say, cutting her off. "Something I would have had to fight for, barely had the guts to *want* . . . and you just walk into it."

We're quiet, watching each other for a minute; the silence stretches upstairs, and I fight the urge to check my phone, follow the hashtags, see what Hugh has Ribbit doing now.

Felicity takes a deep breath, and I notice that her skin is a chalky gray under her makeup, the smeared foundation and bright fever spots the only color to her face.

"Would it have mattered?" she says quietly.

"What?" I refocus, back on her eyes, sharp and glittery.

"You wanted honesty, right? That's the whole goal? So, let's be honest, *Tress*," she practically hisses, coming alive.

"Let's pretend for one second that you got class secretary—what then? How does this scenario play out, in your mind? One extracurricular and colleges are falling all over you? Maybe you give a good interview and borrow Brynn's clothes—because you're besties now, right? And the admissions committee looks at your application and says, wait, everyone! Kick out the valedictorians and varsity athletes—make room for this girl! She's the junior-class secretary!

"Hoooooooooraaaaaaaaaaaayyyyyy!" Felicity does a bizarre shimmy inside her chains, costume bells jingling in a frenzy.

"Fuck you," I say, the words tight and flat, barely inching out past my teeth.

"No, *fuck you*," Felicity says, swaying from her wrists

as her knees give out underneath her. "That is not on me, Tress Montor. High school sucks, and life is unfair, but you're not pinning the fact that you're not going to college on me. That one is not my fault."

My anger is a steel bar inside me, supporting my spine. We were always like this, even when we were little, burning hot and cold. You should worry when Felicity Turnado starts screaming . . . and you should be scared when I stop talking.

Heat can't sustain itself. A hot day will build into a summer storm, washing out the air and bringing relief. But breaking a cold snap requires an entire shift in the atmosphere, a change in the environment. Felicity is fire and I am ice, and she burns out before I'm halfway through the fifth row of bricks, adding some extra mortar every time she mutters *fuck you* under her breath. I slap the side of her ankle with the trowel when she kicks out at me. It hits right on the bone, and I feel the reverberation down in the handle. Her ankle blackens immediately, a dark bruise spreading as I set another brick.

Chapter 31

Felicity

Fuck you is all I can hear in my head, and it's coming out of my mouth. That is not smart, but I can't stop it. My therapist said a lot about accepting the things I can't change, and one of those is that Tress's parents are gone. She also said I should stop beating myself up for everything—the things I did do, but also things I didn't do. There are a thousand reasons Tress isn't going to college, and she can't hang any of them on me.

So I did what my therapist told me to do. I stood up for myself.

Now I'm so exhausted I can't even do that. Instead, I'm hanging from manacles after screaming obscenities at the person who has me entirely at her disposal and just added three more inches to my rapidly closing tomb.

I need to fire my therapist.

Tress has got the look on her face that I know means trouble. My explosion is over. Maybe forty-five seconds of anger—righteous anger, I will give myself that—is gone now. And for my troubles I've put Tress into a mood that will take me hours to talk her out of . . . if I can stay conscious for that long.

It's become a question.

She didn't exactly give me a love tap with that brick, and the few beers I'd downed with no food aren't doing me any favors, either. Whatever is going on with my gut is not improving, and my arms are beginning to cramp from being over my head for . . . how long? An hour? Three? I raise my head, spots of light exploding in my vision as I search for her among them, my head swimming.

I find her, focus hard on her face, pale and tight under the bare bulb. Her jaw is set and the little muscles along her jawline are flickering. Why am I trying to soften her up? It's useless. Better to take a route she'll respect, at least. Let's get this over with. I spit. The glob, which tastes of blood, lands somewhere near my feet.

"Okay, so let's just do this," I say. "What do you want to talk about now? Somebody you had a crush on never noticed you, is that on me? How about that broken arm you had in eighth grade? Totally my fault, right?

Obviously, anything that ever went wrong in your life comes back to me so what's the next topic?"

Tress tosses the trowel into her mortar bucket, drops of liquid concrete flying out around her. "Walking in the rain," she says.

And it's not some poetic allusion. I know exactly what she's talking about.

And it's not good.

Upstairs, the clock chimes.

Chapter 32

Tress

Seventh Grade

There's a big red *D* on the top of my science test. Next to it, in beautiful, flowing cursive, Mrs. Trevor wrote, *Try harder! You know the answers!*

Except I don't.

Not to the science, and not to a lot bigger questions, either. Specifically, what happened to my mom and dad. It's been three years, and at first I tried to do what Cecil told me to—just forget about it. I learned very quickly that when Cecil tells you to do something, you do it. So when he told me to forget about it, I tried. I tried very hard.

I tried when I was feeding the animals and when I was cleaning out pens. I tried when I was supposed to be listening in class or when I was supposed to be asleep. I tried constantly, but they kept surfacing—faces and voices, thoughts and smells, little reminders that jumped up to grab me when I was baling straw or wading in Ribbit's pond.

I look at Mrs. Trevor's advice and think maybe it's better than Cecil's. Maybe I should try harder to find out what happened, instead of just forgetting about it.

I crumple up the test and toss it in the trash can after the bell rings, walking past the bus riders lining up at the back door, slipping behind Mrs. Anho's back as Maddie rushes up to her with a problem. Something new she can't handle.

Good Lord, what would that girl do if something really bad happened to her?

Curl up and die, that's what.

And maybe that's what my parents did, and maybe not. I just don't know. All I know is that I went from living in a nice house with my family to living in a trailer with my grandpa and whatever wild animal comes in the door because he doesn't always remember to shut it.

Also, because raccoons are wily bastards. That's what Cecil would say.

A lot of the things Cecil would say have been slipping into my vocabulary the past few years, which has landed me in detention more than once. I saw Felicity Turnado glancing in the window of detention one time, spotting me, and looking away. She has no idea what the inside of that room looks like. Never will, either.

Felicity Turnado doesn't say things like *wily bastard*, because she probably hasn't heard that kind of language in her nice house with her family. In her nice life that my life used to be like, until . . . something happened.

What? I don't know. But maybe I need to try harder.

I haven't been to the public library since my parents disappeared. I'm pretty sure there were some library books at my house that got packed up with all my other stuff. Everything ended up at Goodwill because Cecil said my bedroom was about to get a lot smaller.

The air-conditioning *whooshes* in my face when I walk in, the gust puffing some of my own smell back up into my nose. I'm carrying around the faint scent of zebra with me, having brushed out Zee earlier this morning while I waited on the bus. A bus I didn't get back onto to go home. Instead, I came here, to the library. To try harder.

The librarian glances up, her *Nice to see you* smile slipping when she spots me. It's not nice to see me, it's awkward to see me. That's what the smile tightens into; that's what I see on all the faces of Amontillado now. Pity.

I go right to a bank of computers, but there's a sign-in screen, and I don't have my library card with me, so I go back up to the front desk, to the *Nice to pity you* smile.

"Hi, I don't have my library card with me and I need to use a computer, so can you sign in for me, or something? My name is Tress."

It's a lot. You forget how to talk to people when you're mostly only talking to animals.

"Hello, Tress," the librarian says. "I know you. Do you remember me?"

Of course she knows me. It's Amontillado. And yes, I remember her. Her name is Cindy. She's got some gray hair now and a few wrinkles. Must've gotten married, that's what Cecil would say.

"We can get you a new card," Cindy says, typing away at her computer.

"I don't need a new card," I tell her. "I have a card. I used to come here, before."

Before something happened.

"Yes." Cindy taps away, not looking up at me. "But your card would have expired. They expire if they haven't been used in a year, and I haven't seen you here since . . ."

Since something happened.

"Well, it's been more than a year," Cindy finishes.

I don't say anything. We stand there in silence until she must find something super interesting on her computer because she says, "There it is!" much too loudly.

Heads turn. They turn and see me and pity me.

"Yes." Cindy clears her throat. "It looks like your card has expired and . . ." Her eyes are moving over the screen, which I can see reflected in her glasses, some red type standing out. It probably says I have library books that are years overdue. It probably says that I don't have parents. It probably says, *Be really, really polite to this girl because we all feel sorry for her.* Cindy punches some buttons and the red writing disappears, my lost books and overdue fines and damaged materials washed away in a wave of pity.

There's a new card in my hand, hard and shiny. I log on to a computer in the corner, one tucked away where no one can see what I'm doing. Where no one can see that I'm googling my parents. The first thing that pops up is a story from the *Amontillado Alerter.*

That's a dumbass thing to call a paper. That's what Cecil says.

No clues in missing couple case
Police are asking for the public's help in their continued search for Lee and Annabelle Montor, who went missing from their home this past Saturday night. Anyone with information regarding their whereabouts is asked to call the hotline printed below. There are no more details to share at this time.

Not on the *Amontillado Alerter* site . . . I can just
imagine the editor chewing her lip and deciding what
she could print and what she couldn't. The facts were
scarce—my mom and dad left home with Felicity in
the car, and they never came back. Felicity was found in
her nightgown by the riverbank, soaking wet, concussed
and bleeding. But she was a minor, and I'm sure the
Turnados fought like hell to keep her identity out of the
limelight. The editor wouldn't have been able to print
much without wandering into the realm of pure gossip.
But it's a small town and I don't need the newspaper to
get details. There are plenty of those on social media.
The Amontillado Block Watch page is particularly
helpful.

I heard they found the girl down by the river.

She was still at home. Their daughter is the one that
called the cops when they didn't come back. Dumbass.
Don't spread rumors.

Other girl . . . dumbass.

Page Admin here, reminding everyone to keep it friendly.

He was plenty friendly, if you know what I mean. Came
back to bite him in the ass, if you ask me.

Nobody did.

Why the woman? Why kill his wife? You better stop running your mouth before somebody shuts it for you.

Page Admin here, there is no proof the couple in question is dead, and no proof of foul play. Please can we keep to the facts?

What facts? Nobody knows shit. Poof. They gone.

And it's Lee and Annabelle Montor, Jesus. We all know it. Why bother saying "the couple in question?"

Lee and Annabelle AND Jesus? Things are getting rough around here. ROTFL

You're making jokes? People are dead. It's not funny.

WE DON'T KNOW ANYBODY DIED

WE DON'T KNOW THEY DIDN'T

Srsly? Come on, people. They're gone. Their car is gone. Their kid was left at home alone. The other kid was found on the riverbank, assaulted. They're effing dead.

Assaulted?!!? Someone touched that little girl???? Why don't we know about this??? I have kids. I need to know what's going on!!!!! I have a RIGHT to know what's going on.

She wasn't assaulted. My cousin is an EMT. She had injuries consistent with being in a mild collision, and some head trauma.

—You shouldn't be repeating what first responders say.

—First responders shouldn't be talking!!!!!

Hey you sicko thought she got touched you're the one with head trauma

Page Admin here, I'm locking down this thread to prevent further discussion. This is an ongoing police investigation and nothing being posted here is relevant or helpful.

No, it's not relevant, or helpful. I already knew all these things—and also that Facebook is a shit show. But one phrase does stand out: *This is an ongoing police investigation.*

It still is, three years later. Nobody knows if my parents are alive or dead, and if I follow both options to their logical conclusions, the answer is ugly. Either they abandoned me, or they're dead. My throat closes up. These aren't new thoughts; they're the same ones that have been bubbling up for years, repeating themselves as I lay curled in my bed—or the stable, if Cecil decided I hadn't earned the right to come inside for the night.

But there are other thoughts, too, like the fact that Mom would have known I'd end up living with either

Cecil or Aunt Lenore, raised alongside wild animals in cages, or growing up in a house that was falling down.

Or they're dead. Their bodies rotting somewhere, all bone by now, like the ones scattered around the panther's pen. Something to nothing.

I've turned over both options, plenty of times.

I don't know which one I prefer.

I log off the computer, copying down the hotline that was set up for the public to call with information on the Montor disappearance, although I doubt it's still active.

The light is fading by the time I leave the library, clouds rolling in to cover up the sun. Dead leaves skitter across the pavement while I watch a few kids from school unlock their bikes from the rack and take off for home, hoping to beat the rain.

I've got no chance of that. I'm on foot, with a ways to go. This is something I didn't think about when I dodged Mrs. Anho at school. The bus is my ride home. Well, it's my ride back to where I live. Now, I'm stuck walking.

I zip up my coat—an old Carhartt jacket I'd found at a church yard sale, with the price tag of ten dollars on it. I'd showed it to Cecil, telling him it was a steal.

"Steal, damn right," he'd said, and tossed it into the truck without paying for it.

I keep my head down as I walk out of town, the

sidewalks stopping once I'm outside the village limits. I'm on the berm then, boots kicking up gravel when it starts to rain. The drops are cold and wet, heavy and starting to pelt me, starting to sting, when the first car goes by.

They slow down, and when I glance up the driver—a man—inspects me, seems to consider stopping, then decides not to. Can't say I blame him. He's watching his own ass. Something I've learned plenty about living at Amontillado Animal Attractions. The next driver, though, is a woman, and she goes so far as to roll her window down until someone leans over the back seat and whispers in her ear. Gretchen Astor.

The car moves on.

I'm soaked to my skin, my hair hanging in dark streams by the time I'm headed uphill. I figure I've got about five miles to go, and only three if I decide to stop at Ribbit's house and get dried off. There's a car coming at me now, headlights on, slicing through the rain. I move over, giving them plenty of room. The last thing I need is to get clipped. This one doesn't even slow down, doesn't even consider it. It hits a pothole right in front of me, sending a wave of cold, gritty water into my teeth.

"Fuck you," I scream, spinning with it as it passes me, both fingers out in a double bird. "Fuck you all over the place!"

I know that car. I've ridden in it. Been in the back seat with my best friend, sharing Skittles and handing a Coke back and forth—but only when it was just her dad with us, because her mom is funny about sugar. *Makes you fat*, she says.

April Turnado is not fat. Far from it. Her too-skinny face had given me a glance as they swept past, her eyes big and round. Felicity was in the passenger seat, her head swiveling to follow me, her mouth moving as she told her mom something. I could see words coming out, her lipstick outlining her bright teeth, but couldn't hear them. I guess I didn't need to. I know what she said. *Keep going.*

Three years ago, I was dry and warm and safe, dialing the police when I woke up to an empty house. Felicity woke up wet and cold and confused, lying on a riverbank. Now Felicity is the one who is dry and warm and safe and I'm the one soaking wet, wondering what the hell just happened.

What did happen, Felicity?

Exactly what the hell happened?

Chapter 33

Felicity

Seventh Grade

We're driving home from Dr. Gabriella's, the rain a white sheet outside the windshield.

"So . . ." Mom turns on the defrost, hoping I'll fill in before she has to ask.

I don't.

"How did it go?"

"Fine," I say. This is my go-to answer. School is fine. My friends are fine. My therapist appointment was fine.

"Honey, if you don't think Dr. Gabriella is helping you—"

"She is," I say quickly, realizing my misstep. "I . . . she is."

Mom's eyebrows draw together, but she doesn't push me further. I know I need to go on, share more about what happens during my sessions, but the truth is I talk a hell of a lot more about my mom than I do Tress Montor.

"I . . . Gretchen's dog has an infected toe pad," I say. Because it's something I heard about all day. Big news. World-ending stuff.

"Oh," Mom says. "That's too bad." But she's not really listening. She's squinting at something in the distance, a shape on the side of the road. "Is that someone walking?"

We get closer, the wipers clearing the windshield for a single moment when Tress looks up and makes eye contact with me.

"Holy shit!" I say, and Mom gasps.

"Felicity Turnado! Language!"

"That was Tress, Mom! We've got to turn around and pick her up, give her a ride."

Mom doesn't stop. She doesn't even slow down.

"Mom?"

She glances over at me, her mouth a thin line. "You say Dr. Gabriella is helping you; I believe it. And I'm not undoing any of that by picking up Tress Montor."

"But . . ." I spin in my seat, watching Tress disappear into the storm. "It's raining."

"Yes," Mom says, speeding the wipers up a notch. "It is."

Chapter 34

Tress

Seventh Grade

It's Lenore Usher who finally picks me up.

"Tress?" My aunt calls, rolling down the passenger-side window.

I climb in, dripping all over. "Sorry," I say, pulling my wet clothes away from my skin.

"Sorry," I say again when I notice a huge clod of mud I dragged into the car. Lenore has that effect on people; you just start apologizing to her, even if you don't know what you did wrong. Because she makes you feel like you definitely did something.

I glance at her, but she's not looking at me, or the mess I'm making in her car. She's focused on the road, staring over the wheel as we climb into the hills.

"I missed the bus," I say, even though she didn't ask.

"Cecil didn't notice?"

I shake my head. She doesn't call him *Dad* or *your grandpa*. He's just Cecil. Feels about right. "No, ma'am, Cecil didn't notice."

I don't call anybody *ma'am*. Not Mrs. Anho, not my science teacher, not Cindy the pity librarian. But it pops out around Lenore Usher, probably because that's what Ribbit calls her. Not *Mom*. Which, if I really think about it, kind of makes sense. He's been following her around since he could walk, going to council meetings and committee gatherings, where everybody else made damn sure to call her *ma'am*.

It was probably Ribbit's first word.

Mine was *mama*. I know that. It's written in my baby book, the one I hide under my mattress because I don't want Cecil to know that I kept it. He calls sentimental things *senti-shit-all*.

We drive past the Usher house, looming out of the storm, a fresh wound in the side where a rock fell away. Lenore pulls into our driveway, some gravel spinning out from under her tires. She puts the car in park, lets the engine idle. Zee brays his welcome, his upper half sticking out from his barn door. Goldie-Dog runs up to the car, despite the rain, jumping onto the passenger side and leaving a muddy paw smear across the window when she slides off.

"Sorry," I say to Lenore, but she only nods, and suddenly I'm tired of apologizing to her. I'm tired of pity smiles and being told to try harder. I'm tired of not knowing what the hell happened.

"What happened to my parents?" I ask Lenore.

Goldie jumps again, not understanding why I haven't gotten out yet, leaving a second smear. I don't apologize for that one. I sit in my aunt's car, rain streaming off me.

"What happened to them?" I ask again.

She flexes her jaw, small muscles jumping as she turns to me. Her eyes are bright, little pinpricks of light dancing off the tears that rest there, refusing to fall.

"I'm sorry, Tress," she says, another apology filling the air. "I'm sorry, but nobody knows."

I don't thank her, for the ride, or the condolences. I slam the door when I get out, Goldie on my heels as I tromp to the trailer, shutting the door in her face because Cecil won't let her in, even though he lets raccoons and possums and once a muskrat, wander on in. I kick off my boots at the door and mud flies, sticking to the wall above the couch, where Cecil lies, unconscious.

Turns out my effort of trying harder has revealed that nobody knows any more than I do. Which is approximately nothing. I flop onto my bed, the stale smell of the bare mattress rising around me as I stare at my palm, where I etched the hotline from the *Amontillado Alerter* to

call if I have information about the disappearance of
Lee and Annabelle Montor.

I don't have information. I don't know shit. But it's
the only thing my afternoon of research dug up, so I
dial it, broken-off fingernails tapping against my cell
screen. There's a series of clicks, and then an automated
voice informs me that the number I have dialed is no
longer in service. I'm instructed to hang up, confirm the
number I'm attempting to reach, and try again.

Try harder.

I can't. I'm thirteen years old, and I don't have parents, and I don't know what to ask or who to talk to and
maybe they left me or maybe they died but either way
I'm alone and listening to a dial tone, when suddenly
there's a voice.

"Amontillado Police Department, Officer Riley."

That's it. A succession of two facts—something that
was so hard to come by before that I don't know what
to do. My throat closes, and all the words reverse, back
down into my belly, like a hard little ball.

"Officer Riley," he says again, and I've lived with a
drunk long enough to recognize the slight slur on *officer*,
the intense concentration that has gone into pronounc-
ing it correctly. Almost correctly. For some reason, it's
comforting. I don't know what I would have done if a
crisp, clean, succinct voice had answered. Probably hung

up in the face of someone who has their shit together. Officer Riley doesn't.

And I get that.

"I was calling the hotline about the Montor disappearance," I say.

"Yeah that gets forwarded here now," he says. I imagine *here* as a tiny office, badly lit, Officer Riley riding out the last few years before retirement behind a desk with a drawer that has a bottle in it.

Riley . . . I do what everyone in Amontillado does—run his last name through a checklist. I've heard it before, and there are plenty of tombstones with that name on it in the cemetery. But they aren't big stones, and they aren't capped off with weeping angels or other signs of wealth or power following the deceased Riley into the afterlife.

The Montors don't have stones at all—we've got a big-ass mausoleum that one of our ancestors built by hand, dragging the stones in from the fields. There is some comfort in knowing that when I die, my body will go to a better place than the one I live in now.

I draw myself up, straightening my shoulders, and inject some pride into my voice.

"I'm calling about the disappearance," I say.

"Yeah, you know something?"

"No," I say. "But I'm Tress Montor, and I want to

know what happened to my parents."

There's a moment of silence, followed by a guttural laugh. I imagine Officer Riley's belly giggling behind his desk, and picture the bottle coming out of the drawer. Sure enough, I hear a soft gurgle in the background, Riley pouring himself some confidence.

"Yeah, you're a Montor all right," he says. "Got some stones, calling in. You're what . . . eleven, twelve?"

"Thirteen," I say tightly.

"Oh, thirteen," he says. "Pardon me. Well, listen, kid—"

"Tress," I say, and I hear him take a drink, the swallow wet in my ear.

"Tress," he repeats, this time without the edge. "All right, Tress Montor. Listen—and I mean it—you listen to me, now. Your mom and dad fell off the grid. Do you know what I'm saying?"

"Like nobody has heard from them?"

"Heard from them or seen them, sure. But it's more than that, kid—sorry, Tress. They made no calls, made no purchases, after that night. The last cell signal from either of their phones came from near that bridge—you know which one I mean?"

Of course I do. It's the one around the corner from our old house, at the bottom of the hill. The one Felicity and I sang about going over the river and through the woods to our best friend's house. It's where the police—maybe even Officer Riley—found Felicity. It's at the edge of town . . . right where something starts turning into nothing.

"Yeah, I know it," I say.

"You know what I'm looking at right now?" Riley asks me.

"Nope," I say.

"My desk calendar. You know what one of those is?" *Those is* comes out in a slurry that I've got to pick apart and translate before I can answer.

"I know what a desk calendar is," I say.

"Well, you kids with your phones these days—" Riley begins, then cuts himself off, like enunciating *these days* wore him out. "I'm looking at tomorrow," he goes on. "I boxed it off in red and drew a big happy face in the middle of it. You know why?"

"No," I say.

"Because it's my retirement day, and if it wasn't, I would've hung up on you the second you said who you was."

Were, I think quietly.

"But you didn't," I remind him, and he sighs.

"No, I didn't." He's quiet for a second, and I think maybe he's got a hard little ball of words in his stomach, too, one that he's been waiting to unload on someone.

"No trace of your parents has ever been found; we

have no leads on this case. And by that I mean forensic, and otherwise. You're the only person who's ever called the tip line—you know that?"

Of course I didn't know that. But I stay quiet, let him cough out the thing he's been choking on for years.

"Lee and Annabelle Montor are the only missing-persons case we've ever had, and it's locked up tight. Not solved; I mean locked up. Nobody's talking. You know what it means when nobody's talking in Amontillado?"

"It means somebody important wants it kept quiet," I say. It's an old lesson, one I knew even before I came to live with Cecil. It might not be taught like the alphabet in school, but it's learned around the dinner table, inferred with down-turned mouths and quick subject changes.

"Uh-huh," Riley agrees. "And what makes you an important person in Amontillado?"

"Your name," I tell him.

"Or your money," he says back.

I let that sit, collecting it with the other words forming the hard ball in my gut.

"And, kid, one more thing—"

"Yeah?"

"What do you see when you turn over a rock?"

"Bugs," I say automatically, having watched Rue search for a snack more times than I can count.

"Bugs and worms and all kinds of shit—sorry. All

kinds of gross stuff you didn't know was there and maybe didn't *need* to know," Riley says. "You turn over this rock, you're going to see those things. Things that people want left under there, in the dark."

"I do need to know," I tell him.

"Then be careful," he says. "And only believe about half of what you hear."

"Okay," I say. "Thank you. Thank you for talking to me."

"And, kid?"

"Yeah?"

"If half of what you hear doesn't make your parents sound like great people . . . well, that's probably the half that's true."

I clench the phone in my hand, the hard ball of words turning into something else, hot anger, surging, ready to come up and blister Riley's ear, giving him something to take with him into retirement. But I don't have time to turn the emotion into words before he hangs up.

I think of the Turnado car, splashing past me. I think of Lenore Usher, her lips a thin line when she tells me nobody knows what happened to my parents.

"Somebody knows," I say into my phone, even though no one is listening.

"Felicity Turnado knows."

Chapter 35

Felicity

"I don't know!" I spit back at her. I'm pissed, but it's lacking the sharp edges of earlier, and not just because before when I got rowdy I think she might have broken my ankle. No, I'm not kicking and screaming because this time . . . I think she might have me.

That day that we drove past Tress in the rain is something that never stuck well with me, watching my former best friend flipping us off in the rearview mirror, dirty water running down her face. It's a moment that might have come up in truth or dare, if someone asked me what I'm most ashamed of in my life. Or, at least, in seventh grade. But we stopped playing truth or dare a long time ago, moved on to spin the bottle and strip poker.

I never was very good at cards.

Driving past Tress that day was a shitty thing to do, and I know it, deep down. I told Brynn about it once, when I'd had too much to drink and we were both taking a time-out at one of Gretchen's parties, just kind of chilling in lawn chairs and staring up at the stars.

"Well," Brynn had said, brow furrowed and thinking hard. "If it was a dog, would you have stopped and picked it up?"

The truth is that yes, I would have. The truth is, that I would treat a dog better than I treated Tress Montor that day.

But it's also true that I wasn't the one driving. I remember my mom flicking on the windshield wipers, Tress's figure disappearing in the rain. Mom left her there on purpose, leaving a not-so-subtle message in her wake. Did she do the same with the cops? Let them know that if the Montor disappearance was not-so-thoroughly investigated, the Turnados would appreciate that . . . possibly in the form of a donation that made it possible for them to buy a new fleet of police cruisers that year?

Whatever is left in my stomach rolls at the thought, and my mind revolts along with it. If that happened, it wasn't my fault.

"I couldn't just force my mom to pull over, you know,"

I say, adding a brick to my defense, just as Tress reaches
for one of her own. A more solid one to trump my meta-
phor, because another truth is that I can construct quite
the wall of self-righteous, blustering excuses to defend
myself, but the one Tress is building is very real, and
growing rapidly.

22 rows of bricks / 3 = 7.333

I'm nearly a third of the way toward being dead. I
don't like math anymore.

It's like the boa constrictor song we sang as kids, with
the snake slowly swallowing us up, except I'm not sliding down a snake's throat. The bricks are rising like the
tide, and once they close over my head—

"Tress," I say madly, hoping to distract her as she
lays some mortar, sliding the first brick of the sixth row
into place. "Have you really thought about this? Like
actually, truly, really sat down and thought about this?"

"Yep," she says, tapping the brick into place.

"And you thought about the fact that you could go
to jail?"

She's on her knees, fitting the last one with precision,
when she leans back and gives me a long, cold stare.

"Have you thought about it? *Actually, truly, really*
thought about it? Yeah, I could go to jail, Felicity. But
there are spaces between the bars of my cell. Things like
light and oxygen can get in. You"—she taps her trowel

against the brick—"you won't have that."

"Light," she says, tapping the brick again.

"Oxygen." She adds one last tap. "So have *you* thought about it? *Jail* is another word for *punishment*. I'll take it, because I'll deserve it."

She comes to her feet, leans in. I pull back, my skull grating against stone.

"What do you deserve, Felicity Turnado? And have you been punished?"

"Yes," I tell her, and it's the most honest thing I've said yet. "Yes, I have."

Tress thinks about that for a second, her eyes boring into mine and finding some truth there. "Maybe you have," she half agrees. "But not by me."

That part I can't argue with her about. The problem with Tress is that a lot of what she says also doesn't make me look very good. The other problem is a lot of what she says is true. I shift in my manacles, and my jester cap flops forward again, a shank of my hair, matted with blood, coming with it. I blow at it half-heartedly to get it out of my face, but it's too heavy with gore to move much.

"I've got it," Tress says, once more tucking my hair back, pinning it down. This time the bobby pins scrape across the swelling where she hit me with the brick, and I wince. She holds a shock of my hair for second, one perfect curl that has somehow managed to hold its shape in the damp, and avoid any blood splatter.

She raises her eyes to mine and says, "Let's talk about lice."

Shit.

Chapter 36

Tress

Sixth Grade

Rue is peeling a banana when a truck pulls into our drive. She yells to get my attention, but she doesn't need to; I was trying to pull some of the larger mats out of Goldie's tail, and she bolted out from underneath my hands at the sight of the truck to happily greet it, like maybe whoever is here might be coming to take her away, take her somewhere better.

I do what I've been told—run and get Cecil. Cecil told me early on that he didn't much care what kind of grades I got in school, or if I acted up there, either. His only rules were (1) help him take care of the animals, (2) stay out of his way when I'm not, (3) come get him if anybody shows up at the house, (4) don't come down to the lower acre, and (5) don't be weird, which I figured out meant sex by the way his eyebrows came together when he said it.

I prefer the animals to him, so rules one and two are not a problem. Rule five I'm not worried about, either, for lots of reasons. Rule three I messed up the first couple times because, if I'm being honest, I'm a little bit proud of the animals—especially Zee, once I got her cleaned up nice. The first time a car pulled in, slowing down after spotting the "Amontillado Animal Attractions" sign, I'd run out to greet them, waving like a kid with a lemonade stand.

Cecil had laid into me for that, said he needed to be the first one to see any visitors because he was the one who had to size them up. Amontillado Animal Attractions doesn't have any prices posted—that's because Cecil makes them up on the spot, after evaluating what they're driving and wearing, their last name, how many kids they've got, and—in his words—*the cut of their jib.*

What that actually means is that he charges more to people he doesn't like.

I've seen him let a minivan full of kids with no shoes come in for five bucks and charge fifty to a curious lady on her own, driving a shiny car. I told him after the family left that it was nice of him to let them in for so little, to which he'd told me that nice didn't come into it.

"They only had five bucks, kid," he said, rubbing

the top of my head—the only sign of affection he ever allows. "And I wanted it."

I can say a lot about Cecil, but I can't say he never taught me anything.

Today, though, there's something different about the vehicle that pulls in. It's not a minivan with no hubcaps full of screaming kids, and it's not a bored soccer mom with an afternoon on her hands. It's a small truck with a big cage in the back, axles doing their best to keep up with the payload.

I light out for the back acre. There's a point past where I'm not supposed to go. I've been told to just stand and give a yell for Cecil. I've caught a whiff of skunk down there once or twice, so I've always assumed he's got some critters down there that he doesn't want me around. But today the standing and shouting doesn't work, and there's an impatient honk from whoever's behind the wheel of that truck.

So now I've got to decide which rule I break—the one about coming to get him when someone's in the driveway, or the one about not going down to the lower acre? I hear the truck's engine cut out and the man say something. Whatever is in that cage lets out a shriek, getting one in return from the driver. Goldie comes running in my direction, her tail between her legs and pure fear in her eyes. Which makes my decision for me. I'd rather deal with Cecil and skunks than whatever is in the back of that truck.

I jog down the path, Goldie on my heels, keeping the stream on my left, a field full of ragweed higher than my head on the right. Cecil says there's no point tilling the back acre, that the soil is shit and that the ragweed keeps pussies with allergies away. I climb a little fence that goes across the path, getting a decent shock at the top that makes me fall to the ground.

"Shit!" I yell, and Goldie goes nuts on the other side of the fence. She's pacing, panicked, trying to reach me and barking her head off.

"Tress?" Cecil's voice comes from the field, and he rises from the green rows, pruning shears in his hand. "What the hell you doing back here?"

"There's someone up at the house," I tell him, inspecting the burn across my ankle from the electrified wire. I glance up at the fence I fell from to see yellow clips running across the top wire, attached to an electrical box, a trail camera strung up in the tree beside it.

Nice. I'm sure Cecil got a great shot of my face as I fell.

He grabs me by my upper arm, pulling me to my feet. "I told you—"

"You weren't coming," I say. "And the guy's got a cage and . . ." I think of the shriek I heard, unable to place it.

"And there's something in it."

Cecil lets go of my arm. "All right, hang on." He goes over to the electrical box, unplugs the wiring and climbs over the fence. My gaze slides off him and over to the green rows. These are shorter. It's not ragweed, and the skunk smell is stronger down here. Way stronger.

"C'mon, girl," Cecil yells at me. "Get moving."

I scale the fence, following in Cecil's footsteps as we head back to the house, Goldie constantly shoving her nose into my hand, looking for reassurance that I'm okay . . . or maybe that she'll be okay, that I'll protect her.

"What is it?" I ask, breathless. "What's in the truck?"

"Surprise," Cecil says. "Little something some guy needed to get rid of."

More like it wants rid of him, I think as we come up into the yard, and the truck shakes on its wheels as whatever's in the cage makes a lunge at the guy, standing off to the side.

The men shake hands, and Cecil slips him a sandwich bag full of something, then they're backing up to the new enclosure, the one opposite Rue's. She starts yelling at them, and throwing some of her stored fruit. An overripe peach bounces off the passenger-side window, splatting all over.

"Shut her up!" Cecil yells at me, but there's not much

I can do. Rue's got a whiff of what's in the cage, and she doesn't like it. She's all the way at the top of her tree, yelling and letting everyone know she's not happy about the new development. In the paddock, Zee and Dee have already fled to the far corner, nuzzling together for comfort.

Cecil pulls the gate to the new enclosure open, and the guy backs the truck up as close as he can, the edge of the cage just inside. He cuts the engine, gets into the back of the truck—bringing a high yowl of complaint from inside the cage. Then he climbs on top of it, reaching through the fence of the enclosure to open the cage's latch.

There's a clang of metal on metal, a dark streak, and then a puff of dirt as the animal—a panther—slides to a halt, changing directions fast when he sees the man's hand is still inside the cage. The cat lunges, but he pulls back just in time, laughing a little to cover his fear.

"Bastard almost got me," he tells Cecil, sweat rolling off his forehead.

The cat retreats to a corner, growling low in its chest as the truck pulls away. Cecil swings the door shut quickly, snapping a lock down on it. I didn't realize I was backed up all the way against Rue's cage until her arm snakes out. In a second, I'm smashed against the fence, wire cutting into my cheek, Rue's iron grip not letting me pull away. The men don't notice. They're headed toward the house, Cecil cracking open a beer.

Shit, shit, shit. Cecil was right, she's going to tear my face off. Her smell is strong, like body odor and a wet dog, all in one. Goldie is going nuts, barking and yelping. She jumps, biting at Rue's arms, but the orangutan grabs her with one hand and gives her a toss. Goldie yelps and rolls, a spray of dirt rising up behind her. The cat follows the movement, lunging against his own bars to get a swipe in as Goldie skids to a halt, inches away from his claws.

"Rue," I say, swallowing hard. "Please . . ."

One of her hands lets go, but the other is still holding me firmly against the cage. Her free hand flips through my hair, searching, scurrying. She pinches down, pulls her hand back, inspects something between her fingers and pops it in her mouth. I've seen her do this before—Cecil said Goldie's flea medication was too damn expensive and the *o-rang-o-tangy* could clean her up just fine. It had taken a leash and a lot of calm words on my part, but I'd talked Goldie into sitting still while Rue groomed her, taking advantage of the free snacks at the same time.

Just like she's doing to me right now.

"Oh my God," I say, my words as squished as my face, jammed against the fence. "Do I have lice, Rue?"

The only answer I get is the shit-eating grin, as she pops another one into her mouth. Goldie gets her feet back under her and scampers away from the cat's cage, calmer now that she sees that Rue doesn't mean me any harm. She cowers next to me, pushing against my leg as I bend my head, letting Rue inspect me. The orangutan reaches out, gives my dog an apologetic pat as her other hand works through my hair, picking me clean.

I slide down to the ground, resting against the cage, Rue's fingers moving through my hair, mesmerizing. I repeat the action, ruffling Goldie's fur. She tucks her head into my armpit, pushing forward into me for comfort. I burrow my face into her neck, parting her hair, trying to get down past the smell of the pens and the shit, past the present. Because if I breathe deep enough, I can still pick up the faint traces of shampoo from her last visit to the groomer. And underneath that, if I concentrate, I can smell my mother.

Chapter 37

Felicity

Sixth Grade

"Mom?" I call down the stairs, fingernails digging into my scalp. "Mom? Do we have any dandruff shampoo?"

"What? No," Mom says hurriedly, as she comes around the corner. "Have you seen my keys?"

"They're on the table," I say, pointing toward the groceries she just brought home—everything organic and gluten- and cruelty- and antibiotic-free. Dad says they're also taste- and fun-free, to which Mom said last night that at least they can eat their dinner without guilt. I can't. But that's got nothing to do with what's on my plate.

"Okay," Mom says, grabbing her keys. "You ready?"

"Ready?" I ask, still scratching. "For what?"

"You've got an appointment with Dr. Gabriella today,

remember? I made the appointment after . . . after your birthday party."

She slips a little, not wanting to say the real reason for scheduling an extra session with my therapist. Her smile is practiced and pasted on, like her lips forgot to slide back over her teeth and now are resting in perma-smile. I know it very well. It's stuck not just on her face but on every wall of the house, our annual family pictures announcing that *yes* we are happy—look at our faces. I've been practicing a little myself lately, figuring out what it takes to knock Mom's smile off. I take a swipe now, knowing the one word that always hits home.

"You can just say it, you know," I tell her, as I follow Mom out to the car. "You can just say we're going to see Dr. Gabriella because of Tress."

We all freaked out when we woke up to find Tress gone Sunday morning. Gretchen had sat in my bed, clutching one of my pillows and trying to look like she wasn't upset. But I knew Gretchen—whether I liked her or not. Her lips, still stained candy red, but now dry and flaking, had been crushed in a straight line, her teeth shut tight against any guilt she might have about what she'd said to Tress the night before.

Maddie had immediately broken into tears, saying now the whole family was missing—which had sent my stomach spiraling. I was in a panic by the time I woke up Mom, a sobbing, hysterical mess. Dad had brought everyone downstairs, asking if anyone had seen her leave or heard anything strange, while Mom made phone calls, what few there were to make.

Lenore—Ribbit's mom—was zero help, and Tress's grandpa wasn't picking up the phone. I tried texting Tress, but she wasn't answering my texts. Or my calls. Or responding to voice mails.

"Okay," Mom said, yanking a sweatshirt on over her pajamas. "I'm driving out there."

Gretchen gasped, her hand clenched tight around the orange juice Dad had poured for her. "You're going to the white trash zoo?"

"Gretchen!" Dad admonished, but she didn't even blush.

"I mean, like, you've had your tetanus shot, right?" she'd asked.

"I'm coming with you," I'd announced. Mom had been too worried to argue, and I'd left Maddie and Gretchen to Dad's pancakes while we drove up the ridge silently, a light rain falling. We pulled into the Amontillado Animal Attractions, and my mom let out a long breath, her rush of relief filling the whole car.

There was Tress, standing out by the animal pens, brushing the zebra.

"Don't—" Mom had begun to say, but I was already

out of the car, rushing toward Tress. I'd wrapped my arms around her, squeezing tight.

"I thought you were gone," I'd said.

And Tress, stiff and unresponsive in my arms, simply said, "I am."

"So, your friend"—behind me, Dr. Gabriella turns a page of her notes—"Gretchen."

"Gretchen's not my friend," I say. It just pops out, like how sometimes I accidentally belch and Mom makes me leave the table. But this is worse. These are words I didn't know were in me. There's a pause.

Dr. Gabriella put me on the couch after our second appointment. "You're always looking at me for a reaction," she'd said. "You worry so much about saying the wrong thing that I can hardly get you to say anything."

So she put me on the couch, facing the wall, with her sitting behind me. It had felt weird, at first, but once I got used to it, I found out she was right. It was a lot easier to just say what I thought if I wasn't checking for someone else's reaction before continuing.

When I admitted as much she told me I should try it in real life sometime.

Now Dr. Gabriella asks, "If Gretchen isn't your friend why was she at your birthday party?"

I look at my hands, pick at a hangnail there. "I don't

know . . . can you have friends you don't actually like sometimes?"

"Yes," she says. "Friendship is complicated. So Gretchen said something that upset Tress?"

"Yeah." I reach up, scratch my itching scalp. "She said she stole my tamp—"

"I'm sorry, I'm going to have to stop you." Behind me, Dr. Gabriella gets up, her high heels clicking across the wooden floor of her office. She calls my mom in from the waiting room, and I sit up, worried.

What did I do? Did I say something wrong?

"April," Dr. Gabriella says. "Did you know that Felicity has lice?"

"Well, I wouldn't have her in my house again, that's all I'm saying," Jill Astor says as she makes a face, primly pinching two fingers together as she slides a nit off a strand of Gretchen's hair.

We're having a post-birthday-party party.

Mom had driven home from my appointment with red cheeks, her voice cracking as she yelled at Dad over the phone. "Dr. Gabriella has to fumigate her couch. And I have to call all the other moms. I have to tell them their children got lice at *my daughter's* birthday party."

She ordered in food and invited the girls and their moms for what she called a "nit-picking" party. The other moms brought bottles of wine with them, making a joke out of it. Brynn, Gretchen, Maddie, and I had lined up as our moms poured stinky stuff on our heads, told us to keep ourselves busy on our phones, and started drinking.

They're blaming Tress. And they're not being quiet about it.

"First she runs off, scaring everyone half to death," Jill goes on. "And now this!" She waves one gloved hand at the four of us, heads bowed, wet hair hanging in curtains over our faces as we lean forward around the card table Mom had set up.

"Where is Tress?" Brynn's mom, Angela, asks. On my head, I feel my mom's hands stiffen.

"You didn't really expect April to invite her here, did you?" Jill asks, refilling her wineglass.

"How else is the poor girl supposed to get clean?" Angela says, keeping her eyes on the back of Brynn's head. "Do you really think that old man is going to look after her?"

"Well, he obviously doesn't," Jill says. "Gretchen's head was just *crawling*—"

"Felicity isn't too bad," my mom pipes up.

"Neither is Maddie," adds Kira Anho, who had been quiet until now and has hardly taken a drink. Mom had to push her to take a glass at all, saying that she wasn't our principal yet.

"Brynn hardly has any," her mom says.

"Well, Black kids don't really get lice, though, do they?" Jill says, quaffing the rest of her wine.

"Jill!" my mom says. "Maybe you should lay off the wine."

Everyone laughs, like they're supposed to. Everyone except Brynn and Angela. Brynn is next to me, her arm pressed against mine. It's stiff, all the muscles tightened up, waiting for the moment to pass, or wanting to strike out, slap the laughter out of the air. I don't know which.

"What?" Gretchen's mom says. "That's what I heard. I mean, maybe it's different since she's mixed race—"

"Did you hear that the dollar store is closing?" Mrs. Anho pipes up, shutting down Gretchen's mom.

"No, that's too bad," my mom says, happy for the subject change. "I mean, we don't shop there, of course, but it will be a loss for a lot of families."

I can't see Brynn's face, our hair hanging between us. I can't see Angela, either, but I can feel a wall of tension behind me, her quiet rage something that my friend has inherited, something she puts on like a coat for a cold day at recess. Except I guess in Amontillado it's always a cold day at recess for Brynn and Angela. My thumbs fly across my phone as I text her.

> I don't think Tress had lice.
>
> I think it was Gretchen.

Next to me, her phone vibrates. Seconds later, a bubble appears on my screen.

> Yep.

> And her mom's a bitch.

I stifle a giggle, not wanting anyone to know we're texting, or that Brynn just called Jill Astor a bitch. I look down at my phone, at the texts I sent.

> I don't think Tress had lice.

> I think it was Gretchen.

I know it's true. Gretchen had been itching the night of my party, not Tress. Mom had burned all the bedding, the little red mess from Maddie's melting Popsicle going up in flames along with Gretchen's lice, still clinging to my pillow—the one she'd used.

I think about Dr. Gabriella, and how she'd turned my back to her, how looking at a painting of trees instead of her face had made it easier to tell the truth. I think about her telling me to try that in real life sometime.

I don't have a painting of trees, but I do have my hair falling around me in a curtain right now, blocking off everyone else so I can't see them. There's a script right in front of me, the words written out so that all I have to do is read them. Say them aloud.

My mom tilts my head a different direction and I minimize my texts.

I don't say the words. I'm learning.

Girls who live in a trailer with their grandfather at an animal zoo have lice.

Girls who have private therapists do not.

Hours later my scalp is pink and tingling, and Mom is putting fresh sheets on my bed. They're brand-new, with the little lines from being folded in the package still pressed firmly into them, even when she snaps them in the air above my mattress. A year ago I would've been under them, yelping as Mom tucked in the corners, made fake cries about the weird lump in the center, and tried to push it back down while I giggled, pressing back.

Now I'm squashed into a corner of the room, holding tight to a brand-new stuffed animal that had taken the place of all my burned ones, and trying to put together the perfect sentence to call my mom a liar.

"Mom . . . I think Gretchen was the one with lice. And I think you know it, too."

She doesn't stop moving, only gives the pillow she's sliding into its new case an unnecessarily hard thumping. "It doesn't really matter, does it? You all ended up with it."

"It matters when you're blaming Tress," I say.

"I'm not blaming Tress," Mom says tightly, stretching out over the bed to smooth the corners. "Jill Astor is."

"But you didn't tell her she was wrong!" I yell, my

fingers digging deep into the teddy bear. "You didn't tell her it was Gretchen! And you didn't defend Tress!"

A little voice in my head adds something much worse: *Neither did you.*

"Honey . . . ," Mom sighs, resting her head on my pillow. She looks at me, my back flattened into the corner, a death grip on my teddy bear.

"C'mere," she says, wiggling her fingers at me.

I go, sliding under the fresh new sheets and letting Mom's arms come around me in a hug, nice and loose, comforting. It's not like the hug I gave Tress; not a hug that you're worried someone is going to break free of.

"I know things are really difficult for Tress right now," Mom says, her breath in my ear. "But arguing with Jill Astor isn't going to make anything better for her. It would only cause hard feelings and arguments and more problems than we've already got. Do you understand?"

I nod. I do understand. But I wasn't talking about our problems. I was talking about Tress's. Mom presses her face into my hair, her voice warm and soft in my ear.

"I've only got one little girl in the whole world. You're the most important thing to me, and I'm not going to let anything happen to you."

"Nothing happened to me, Mom," I say, shrinking a little. "I didn't get hurt."

"There are different ways of getting hurt," Mom says.

"You're still here in your bed, warm and safe. But . . ."

She doesn't finish, at least not immediately. I know she's being careful with me, trying to find a nice way to tell me I'm not the same girl who ran to Tress Montor's house that night. She's right. I'm here, all in one piece. But only on the outside.

On the inside, all my pieces are a jumble. A puzzle that's been dropped.

"I know, Mom," I say, rolling over to face her, snuggling my head under her chin. "I know I'm not . . . okay."

Her grip tightens. Too much.

"You are fine," she says, her voice rising. "There is nothing wrong with you."

Mentally, I take notes: *There is nothing wrong with Felicity Turnado. Gretchen Astor did not bring lice to a birthday party.*

"If there's nothing wrong with me, why do I have to see Dr. Gabriella?"

Mom pushes some of my hair out of my eyes. "Things changed that night, Felicity. For Tress, definitely, but for you, too. You can't remember what it was, but something horrible happened, and you were there. That's a hard thing for a kid to deal with. It's a hard thing for anyone to deal with. There's nothing wrong with going to therapy, and there's nothing wrong with you," she says again, emphatically. "But something happened to you. It's like . . ." She scans my room, thinking hard.

"It's like your porcelain doll," she says, pointing to the dresser. "If she had a tiny crack would you say she was broken?"

"No," I say.

"And she wouldn't be." Mom nods. "But a crack makes her just a little bit weaker, and the next time she falls . . ."

"She'll break," I say.

"Right. But you're not made of porcelain, are you? You can heal. And we're taking you to see Dr. Gabriella so that the little crack you've got can close up, nice and tight."

"So I'm ready for the next time I fall," I add.

"Well . . ." Mom stares at the ceiling now, her voice floating up to my rotating fan, her eyes following the shadows there. "I guess so, yeah. But I'm a mommy, and mommies don't like to think their little girls are ever going to fall, and we do everything we can to stop it."

"So who stops Tress from falling now?" I ask. "What about her cracks? Is she seeing a doctor to make her better, too?"

"I kind of doubt it, honey," Mom says, rolling over to face me. "But she's not my little girl—you are. You're the one I've got to think about, worry about, and protect."

Suddenly, I understand.

"You think being around Tress is going to make me crack more."

She nods. "I think it might."

I fall back on the one argument I've got, the one that should be the strongest, knock down anything else. "But she's my friend."

Mom's mouth goes tight, words she's not saying pulling her lips down.

"What?" I ask.

"Jill said that Tress hurt Gretchen the other night," Mom says, eyes boring into mine. "Is that true?"

I feel heat in my stomach, the need to defend Tress hot and strong. "Gretchen was being nasty."

"But did Tress hurt her?" Mom asks again. I think about the marks on Gretchen's wrist, red and bright, matching her lips. I shrug.

"Felicity, I know that you and Tress were close—"

"We were best friends," I say, then correct myself. "We *are* best friends."

"—but you have to think about the fact that Tress's life is different now. And that means Tress probably will be, too."

I want to tell Mom she's wrong, but I remember how Tress reacted to my hug, like she was expecting to be hit instead. I remember how she watched Gretchen, warily, always on guard.

"Okay," I say, tears pooling in my eyes as I stare upward at the ceiling, begging them not to fall, not to overflow and run down into my ears, where the voice lives, feeding it.

Mom gives me a hug and a kiss good night, turns on the night-light I had to start using again after the— well . . . after. She leaves the door open a few inches, in case I need to sneak into bed with them in the middle of the night—something else I've started doing again.

I let the tears go eventually, sliding down the sides of my cheeks. I tilt my head so they won't go into my ears, creating hot, salty pools on my new pillowcase.

I think of Tress, how she's a wild animal now.

I think of the creased-new sheets underneath me and the matching bottles of shampoo and conditioner lined up, ready for me to use them to smell good, be pretty, take care.

I think Tress isn't the only one changing.

Chapter 38

Tress

Sixth Grade

The cat is waiting for me when I wake up in the morning. It paces inside the cage, watching me as I wait for the bus. I fed it last night, hauling the head of a steer over my shoulders into the cage, the cat locked inside the enclosed section. The corrugated metal had rippled and rolled as the cat lunged against it, smelling meat, smelling blood. The head was freshly cut, the jagged end of the spinal column poking my shoulder where Cecil had decapitated it, tossing aside different sections for the animals. The blood had run down my arms and legs in rivers, the cat, wild to get at it, howling at the scent. After I was out and Cecil loosed him, the cat sniffed the head, then looked at me through the cage—the other bloody thing.

He'd bitten into the carcass, but kept his eyes on me while he did.

It's the same now, the cat's eyes following my movements as I climb onto the bus, the other kids pressing against the windows, checking out the new addition. Their heads swivel as the bus pulls away, the blue smoke of diesel fumes finally obscuring their vision. I imagine the cat doing the same in his cage, gaze following me until I am out of sight. Whether he views me as the person who brings his food, or actual food, I don't know.

At school I keep my head down, funnel through the other kids to get to my locker, where someone has stuck maxi pads on it. There are three, the wings opened like the frogs we'd dissected in science, skin pinned back to show their vulnerable insides. I blush furiously and tear them off. I try to throw them on the ground but one sticks to my hand, and I have to shake it, hard, the pad flapping like a terrified bird before it falls off. Someone giggles. A phone comes out.

I spin the combination on my locker, not looking up. I'm about to pull it open when a hand slams it shut, large and wide, with hairy knuckles. The janitor nods at me, apologetic. "Sorry, kid, I've got to fumigate it."

"You what?" I ask, trying hard to focus on him and not my classmates, who are staring.

"Fumigate," he repeats, holding up a canister that

shows a bug lying on its back, a green cloud over its head, legs folded, eyes the comic book *x*'s of death. I'm still staring at it, confused when he adds, "For lice."

A few more giggles roll through the crowd, gathering steam until they reach the back where people are standing on tiptoe, asking what's going on. I turn, shouldering my way through everyone. A girl yelps when I step on her foot by accident, but when she yells, "Yuck! Cooties!" I decide to grind down, twisting hard. Her cry of annoyance turns into true pain as I break out into the open, right into our principal, Mrs. Prellis.

"Tress," she says. "Why don't you come with me?"

She's smiling, but it's an order, her hand pinched tight on my elbow as we make our way down the hall, the last late arrivals hurrying to get to class before the bell. Mrs. Prellis escorts me into her office, closing the door behind her.

"Have a seat," she says, and her voice is warm, but she's taking note of which chair I sit in, marking it to be wiped down after I leave. "So," she says as she leans forward on her desk, elbows creating a temple that leads up to her bright smile. One that's trying really hard to make me comfortable.

"I don't have lice," I say. And it's true. I don't. Not anymore, thanks to Rue.

"I'm aware that there was a sleepover this weekend

and that the invited girls likely were all exposed to head lice." She pauses, but I let the silence continue, not giving her anything. "I was glad to hear you were at the party, Tress."

Nobody else was glad about it, including me. But I don't say that. I just stare her down, waiting. Like the cat. She clears her throat. "I talked to the mothers, and we've established that all the girls—"

"Have mothers," I finish for her.

She stops, stunned. "Excuse me?"

"They all have mothers," I say. "And they made sure their daughters are clean."

"Yes." Mrs. Prellis nods, but her voice is wary. "So if you would allow the school nurse to—"

"No."

"I . . ." Mrs. Prellis shakes her head. "I don't understand. Tress, if you don't have lice—"

"I don't."

"Then you'll let us determine that, and we can all go about our day—"

"Like normal," I interrupt again, and this time Mrs. Prellis bites down on her bottom lip, a little blood rising in her cheeks.

"Like normal kids that go home and their normal moms feed them a normal dinner and they sleep in a normal bed," I go on. "They don't have lice and TV dinners and a mattress on the floor and wild animals outside."

"Tress, do you feel safe at home?"

Mrs. Prellis is recentered again, back in the place she knows, where she takes care of kids and looks out for everybody. Especially the ones with the right last names.

"Safe?" I repeat the principal's question, remembering the streams of still-warm steer blood running down my back, the weight of its massive head balanced on my shoulder, the cat's screams through the thin sheets of metal. Metal like my locker, the janitor's hairy hand swinging it shut, the crowd, pushing in, also scenting blood.

"It's the only place I feel safe," I tell her.

Chapter 39

Felicity

"I tried," I say. "I told Mom it wasn't you who had—"

"Maybe," Tress interrupts me, deadly cold. "But you didn't tell Gretchen or Maddie. You didn't tell them not to stick pads to my locker or let Principal Prellis know it didn't need to be fumigated. My only good coat was in there. It smelled like bug spray all winter. *I* smelled like it."

Her voice cuts off, checked by emotion. "You have no idea what that's like."

No, I don't. And the truth is I probably never will. A tear slips out, and Tress flicks it away, angrily. Her phone has been going off nonstop, vibrating ever closer to the edge of the chair, like a lemming ready to take the leap. She snags it at the last second, and as she glances at it her whole body goes rigid, the trowel dropping from her hand, splattering mortar on the hem of her jeans. Her eyes rise to mine, and if we're not friends anymore, we're not exactly enemies in this moment, either.

Faces don't change, and I can still read her like a book. Tress Montor is scared . . . and that terrifies me.

"Tress," I say, my heart beating pathetically against my rib cage, anxious for release from the rising panic. "What is it?"

She doesn't speak, only turns the phone to me. I can see the party above us, Hugh facing Ribbit, the clock between them, a sea of faces below, phones held aloft. Above them on the second-floor landing, black padded feet circle, tail flicking.

Chapter 40

Cat

A strange girl
smells of salt as she walks
darkness eating her sounds
—one sound—over and over,
Deep gasps between.
The cousin bolts, her escape draws attention
and the girl's sound goes light and high
With hope.
A light she makes follows the path
where a tail should be
stubbed out, by human hands.
I yawn-stretch, hackles rising.
Make myself bigger
follow sounds and smells

more promising than her as she
searches for something lost.

Chapter 41

Tress

"Shit."

Felicity's voice is light and breathless when she spots the cat on the livestream. "What do we do?" she asks.

I flick the video away, thinking. The jolt of panic I felt at the sight of the velvety paws has settled into a line of reasoning, each fact easing out the high peaks of adrenaline in my bloodstream.

"The cat isn't hungry," I say, "or he already would've grabbed someone."

I pull the video back up, analyzing the few frames where he can be spotted.

"He's not hunting, either," I say, thinking aloud. "He's too loose, just strolling. He's . . ."

Felicity leans forward, chains jangling as she watches

the video with me. "He's prowling," she says. It's a good word for it. He's moving cautious and slow, investigating while avoiding attention.

"Right," I tell her. "But he's curious, and cats don't just hunt when they're hungry. They'll kill for sport."

I make a decision, grab my backpack from the corner, and slip it over my shoulders.

"What are you doing?" Felicity asks, her voice high and tight again, no longer low and commiserating with mine.

"I've got to . . ." What? What have I got to do? Catch a wild animal with my bare hands?

"Don't you leave me down here, Tress Montor," Felicity orders, somehow maintaining an edge of authority even though she's helpless.

"It's okay. It'll be okay," I tell her. "I'll lock the door."

It's a dumbass thing to say, and not only because I put the lock on the *inside* of the door. I don't know why I'm comforting the person I'm specifically trying to keep on edge. But I am, and I keep doing it. "I'll be back," I call over my shoulder as I walk away, Felicity's pleas following me.

I emerge into the kitchen to find Brynn crying and mixing water and beer into a Solo cup. I freeze, more alarmed at the sight of her than I would have been if the cat was waiting patiently for me, tail curled around its front paws.

"What the fuck?" Brynn says when she spots me, eyes going to the basement door as it clicks shut behind me.

"I mean, what the actual fuck?"

"I—"

I'm trying to formulate an answer when I realize it's a rhetorical question. Brynn isn't asking me why I was in the basement. I don't think she even cares. She cracks another beer and foam sprays onto the bright green leotard she's wearing. I recognize it from the livestream; she's the person feeding Ribbit his drinks.

"You're watering it down," I say, surveying the mess of empty cans and water bottles strewn across the counter.

"Yeah," she says, wiping tears off her face. "He'll die of alcohol poisoning if I don't. And they're just . . . they're just . . . they're letting it happen." She starts crying again, full sobs wracking her body as she hangs over the porcelain sink, tears falling against mold that has crept up the sides.

"Not even just letting it happen," she goes on. "They're *encouraging* it. Did you see this?"

She pulls out her phone, showing me the comments under the livestream.

Ask him if he's ever killed someone

Tell him to whip it out

Is he a virgin?

Fake news

Ask him if he's ever killed someone

That last one from the same poster, insistent.

"Hugh sent me this screen cap from his phone." She flips through some pics, smiling photos of her and Felicity; a group shot near a bonfire; Gretchen's dog, posing in a Halloween costume as a skeleton.

"Look," she says, pulling up a shot of a messages app with over two thousand unread notifications. "Somebody posted Hugh's account info, and he's getting questions from all over the world. It's . . . it's . . ."

She's shaking, and I take her phone from her. Not all the comments are enthusiastic.

Somebody stop this

If you're there please, someone help him. This is wrong.

Does anyone recognize where they are? Somebody needs to get out there.

Everybody chill. This is obviously all staged.

Those kids are not okay! Do you see the ones that are passed out?

They aren't passed out—look at the puke, look at their skin. They're sick.

Jesus Christ somebody call the cops

There's concern but it's all the same. Somebody—
somebody else—should do something. Comments are
coming fast and hard. I can't keep up, and Brynn's
phone shakes in my hand when a screenshot pops up,
the upper-right-hand corner circled in red with an arrow
pointing to four dark paws, leaving the shot.

What the fuck is THAT? Did anybody else see that????

Yawn . . . Staged

I hand Brynn her phone back. "I've got to go."

"Go where?" she snaps. "No, you've got to help me."

"Help you?" I ask, truly flummoxed. She's currently
double-fisting watered-down beers to take to Ribbit. I
don't see how I'm needed. But Brynn's back in control of
herself and giving me orders like I'm a freshman on the
volleyball team.

"Everybody's puking their guts out," she says. "We
need to get water into them, keep them hydrated. If you
see anybody lying down, turn them onto their side so
they don't asphyxiate on their own puke. I'll be back,"
she says, pointing one red cup at me, her eyes narrowed,
"and if I find out you went downstairs to sell drugs
instead of helping me, I swear to God, I'll call the cops
myself and we'll all be fucked."

I'll be way more fucked than anybody else, but Brynn
doesn't need to know that. "Okay," I tell her, hands in the

air in surrender. "Okay, I'll start . . . watering people."

I wait for her to disappear into the front hall, the kitchen door swinging into place behind her, then take the servants' stairs up the back—the same path the cat must have taken to avoid being seen. I stop, unzip my backpack, and pull out a flashlight. Ribbit didn't run bulbs up the back staircase, and I can't see anything once I'm more than a few steps high. The walls are close and tight here; the servants not rating the open, expansive staircase from the front room.

Sure enough, muddy prints precede me. I wave my light, following as they lead me to a kid wearing a ragged Red Hot Chili Peppers shirt. He's on his back, one shoe loose and dangling. I prop him up, feeling the heat of his skin, and lean him against the wall.

"Mom?" he asks.

I flash my light upward, following the prints, then back at him. There are bright spots on his cheeks, and his eyes are glittery, unfocused. I debate for a second, then remembering Brynn's threat, hoist him over one shoulder. I'm almost to the bottom when he loses his beers. Warm now, his vomit splatters over the back of my legs and into my shoes.

So much for karma.

I prop him in a chair at the table and put a bottle of water in front him, uncapping another one to rinse myself.

My shoes and socks are a lost cause, so I take them off and roll up the ends of my jeans before I go after the cat again, now barefoot, like him. I reclaim my bag and flashlight on the stairs, stalling when I reach the top.

Once I walk out there, I'm on camera for the whole world. So far, I've avoided being on-screen and can plausibly deny it if anyone says they saw me at the Allan house tonight. But there are enough phones out there with enough angles that as soon as I walk out into the light, my presence can be confirmed.

I slide down, back against the wall as I crouch, and check my phone. The livestream is still going, and I can hear Ribbit's voice from my hiding spot, seconds before what I see on-screen as the delay catches up.

"Six inches, I mean that's pretty average, right?"

There's some nervous male laughter, but it's suddenly interrupted by the double front doors swinging open. I hear the bang of one connecting with the wall, followed by the light trickle of plaster falling to the ground from the impact. The person livestreaming swivels to the disturbance and there's Gretchen Astor, her Cleopatra costume torn and wet, her face a dark smear of ruined mascara.

"Guys." She hiccups and holds up a dismembered tail. "Something ate my dog."

Chapter 42

Felicity

Something runs across my foot, and I jump, the involuntary movement sending a spike of pain up my leg. Tress gave my ankle a decent tap right around the twenty-fifth time I said *fuck you*, and I'm paying for it now. Pain is a constant in this new version of my life, one that, technically speaking, only just began but has superseded everything that came before it.

I feel like I've always been here, aching arms overhead, burning circles around my wrists, a starburst of pain in my ankle, a dull thudding in the back of my head, and a constant churn in my stomach. There are other concerns, too, more mundane but no less critical.

I have to pee. Like, bad.

The pressure started building right around the time

Tress was laying the second row of bricks, a small tickle, the first indication that yes, I had to pee. Now, my bladder is a bomb and my feet are going to be the target if I don't get out of here. My feet, and whatever just ran across them. I shudder, but the movement doesn't stop when I tell it to, and pretty soon I'm shaking all over.

"Not now," I say, like if I give my body verbal commands rather than just think them, it might actually listen. But this isn't a seizure; I realize that after the initial spasm passes and a new sensation starts . . . a hot jet deep inside my belly, working its way upward.

"Oh, wait . . . no."

I'm saying things to nothing and no one, alone in a dark corner, trapped and desperate as I vomit all over myself. Once I start it's hard to stop, and the tight clench of my stomach muscles is too much for my bladder. It lets go, and in a very short time, I am completely empty.

I hang, useless, a stinking sack of skin. I can feel my heart beating, small, tired, scared, moving timidly, as if asking the question *Should I keep doing this?*

At my feet, my companion stirs, running back and forth in the small space, frightened. It leaves tiny pinpoints of wet spots on my skin as it goes, which cool in seconds. A tail whips across my shins, and I know it's a rat, one that's covered in my own mess and tracking it back and forth across my feet. But I can't feel disgust.

All I feel is complete and utter solidarity.

"You better get out of here," I tell it. "She's not going to back down."

There's a moment, like it's considering my words, and then the rat is gone, shuffling over the knee-high wall Tress has built and disappearing with the flick of a tail.

I thought I was empty; I thought I had nothing left inside me.

But I do. More tears.

Chapter 43

Tress

Gretchen's announcement that something ate her dog is followed by a panic.

Everyone reacts differently, some with screams, a few mutters of disbelief, and more than a little nervous laughter, gasping noises meant to convey hilarity, but really they're saying, *I don't know what to do.*

It's been that way for a while now, the truly amused laughter at Ribbit's admission of wanting to screw the principal devolving into something more primitive, a confused sound that admits the person making it thinks they are supposed to be laughing but doesn't know if something funny is happening or not. Like maybe what used to be funny is now something else. Something darker.

Regardless, the discovery of William Wilson's demise presents the perfect opportunity. Anyone streaming has swiveled to Gretchen, all phones capturing the moment when the queen bee is surrounded by her drones, all of them soothing, touching, hugging, although I do spot a few not-so-hidden smiles. Someone tries to take the dog's tail out of Gretchen's hand, but she resists at the last moment, clutching tight to the vertebrae.

I make my move, following the cat's prints toward a bedroom on the second floor. I glance over the banister. Below me, Hugh still faces off with Ribbit, both bemused now that the attention has moved from them to Gretchen. I back away, toward the wall, but Hugh has caught the movement, and our eyes lock for a second before I duck into the bedroom.

The door clicks shut behind me, and I slide to the ground, flicking on the flashlight.

There, sitting on the bed, tail curled around front paws, the cat waits for me.

Chapter 44

Felicity

My mother was thrilled when I came home from kindergarten and announced that I had a friend.

It had been something of a concern, apparently. Mom and Dad had done everything they could for me up to that point. I'd had playdates with their friends' kids, gone to preschool, taken dance lessons, and spent summer afternoons at the pool. I realize now they were doing their best to get me entrenched with the right people. The right people with the right last names, but I wasn't doing my part. Maddie Anho got mad at me when I won a coloring contest, and she felt she stayed in the lines better than I did and that my "creativity" of color use was really just a mess. I was more interested in picking at my toes during dance class than learning how to stand on them, like Gretchen Astor.

So my social outlook was somewhat sketchy when I got on the bus with my new backpack full of freshly sharpened pencils. I remember Mom waving at me from the front porch, a smile that didn't match the rest of her face stamped securely in place, like if she let it slip I might remain perfectly unaware that everything wasn't, in fact, perfect.

I knew it wasn't.

And so did Tress Montor.

Tress had walked into kindergarten, glanced around, sat down next to me, and pulled a magnifying glass out of her backpack, along with a dead roach, encased in plastic.

"Check this out," she said. "You can see its butthole."

I was entranced.

So were Hugh and David, as well as Brynn and a couple of other girls. I remember Ribbit standing on the edge of the circle that surrounded us, not quite a part, more like a satellite, proudly announcing to anyone who would listen, "That's my cousin. Tress is my cousin."

In all the first-day-of-school splash, clothes still stiff from the hangers they'd been torn from, new sneakers getting their first bits of gravel stuck in the treads, sharp-tipped packs of crayons spilling across freshly cleaned tabletops, Tress Montor had me looking at a cockroach's ass.

When I came home and made my announcement of a new friend, there was the inevitable question to follow, Mom's smile still in the same place—hopeful, but expecting to fall.

"Who is it?"

I was five, but I knew the drill. I took an actual beach towel to the pool—long enough to stretch out on—and so did every one of the girls I was supposed to be hanging out with. Other kids skipped the towel entirely or brought something from home, meant for the shower, usually threadbare or with outright holes. I was five, but I knew that my towel was better and that the better towels and the people attached to them belonged together, our monogrammed initials on them setting us apart from the others.

I knew this because Mom patiently led me away every time I sat with Jessica Stanhope on her towel, a spread of melting Skittles between us. Mom would draw me back to the right group of people with a promise of ten minutes of screen time with the game I'd downloaded to her phone. Mom was careful; Mom was cautious. Mom was not going to let me have a new friend if that new friend didn't fit certain criteria.

And back then, Tress did.

The backpack that she produced the cockroach from was brand-new, and the magnifying glass wasn't some hokey toy for kids. It was heavy, the real deal, and the cockroach was part of an entire set. Tress had a dozen bugs of all kinds sealed in these plastic cubes, clear as glass. I knew because of the bugs that Tress was different from me; I knew by the quality of them that she was the same. So when Mom asked who my new friend was, the smile ready to fall from her face at a moment's notice, I said with confidence, "Tress Montor."

There was a careful calculation behind Mom's eyes as she considered, the smile stiffly in place as options were weighed. I knew what it was then; now I even know what the formula was.

Lee Montor + Annabelle Usher = Tress Montor.

Montor > Usher [therefore] Tress = [unknown]

In other words, Annabelle Usher married up. Her last name might be worth something, but the Usher bank account certainly wasn't. Lee Montor was a great guy from a good family who scored a beautiful wife. And they loved each other.

I close my eyes, not having to remember to know that it was true. Tress's parents had loved each other, something that had taken me some time to sort out once I started doing overnights at their place. Her house was a lot like mine in so many ways—modern and clean, with a shiny kitchen and a well-groomed dog. But Tress's house had added touches: Annabelle's garden in the back, where my yard had only a shorn lawn. A piano that wasn't there just to hold family pictures. Lee would play; I hummed the song he would rattle off for us whenever Tress asked, no music required.

"The cold song," I'd say, then an echo, Lee's voice correcting me. "Cold*play*."

It took me a while to figure out it wasn't just things that made her house different but the actual family. I bounced into their kitchen one afternoon to refill our water bottles, Tress waiting outside on the trampoline, only to surprise Lee and Annabelle. They had jumped away from each other, guiltily, Annabelle pushing black hair from her eyes.

"Hey, kiddo, what do you need?"

I'd gone back out to the trampoline, ice cubes clinking inside the bottles, and handed one to Tress. "I think your parents were kissing," I said.

"Ugh." She rolled her eyes. "Yeah, they do that a lot. Hey, want to see me flip in midair?"

I watched Tress, her hair fanning out behind her, sweaty and loose as I sucked on my water, wondering what it was like to have parents who kissed.

And it was like that for a long time, right up until it wasn't anymore.

Right up until that night.

I've shied away from it ever since, not wanting to

remember, not wanting to know what I saw. But Tress wants to know, and Tress is someone who looks right at the cockroaches.

"Right up their assholes," I agree with myself.

Tress wants to know, and Tress can take it. Remembering is the only way I'm getting out of this. And if Tress Montor wants me to remember, that's what I have to do.

Chapter 45

Cat

If I am still and quiet
I can see
other lifetimes, slipping past us,
in a place, where they ended.
The girl does not know
there is a boy above her
swinging
from the rafters,
his toes brushing her forehead.
She does not see the woman,
sobbing
at the dresser.
Does not hear the baby
screaming

in the corner.
She sees and hears and feels and knows
only now,
in this place.
And I marvel at the limits
of humans.

Chapter 46

Tress

The cat sits and stares.

His eyes go from mine, to above me, to the corner, ears turning different directions as he picks up sounds I can't even imagine. But I'd be a fool to think he isn't highly aware of me, every movement, every breath. I rest my back against the closed door, exhaustion getting the better of me.

I have that luxury, the luxury of sitting.

In the basement, Felicity does not.

"Shit," I say to myself, quietly, and gain the cat's full attention again, eyes on my lips, ears pricked forward.

"I don't know what to do," I tell him, and one ear swivels away from me, as if I have said something only worth half his attention.

"I'm holding someone captive in the basement," I tell him, and the ear comes back, cocked. "I hit her in the head with a brick and I chained her to the wall, and I've got her halfway sealed into a tomb, and I probably gave her a concussion, and I think she's got the flu, and I might have fractured her ankle."

It's a lot, when you string it all together like that. A lot of bad things that I did, all of them translatable into a different language, that of legalese and criminal charges. Kidnapping, assault, false imprisonment, menacing. My hands shake, and I rest my head against the door. There's a small thump, and the cat shifts, curious.

"The thing is," I tell him. "There's something that fixes it all. The big gamble."

His eyes latch on to mine, and I read there what is always stamped on his features, a constant feeling, one that moves through his mind, is embedded in his muscles.

"Murder," I say, and the cat yawns.

His tongue lolls out, long and pink, teeth clicking back together sharply. It's a show, put on for me. *I can kill you.*

"I can do it, too, you know," I say, and he cocks his head, almost goading.

"If I have to," I add. "I don't want to. I didn't think . . ."

I didn't think, that's the real admission here. I didn't think Felicity could last this long. Didn't think she would continue to defy me. Didn't think she would insist she doesn't remember.

"What if she doesn't?"

I'm asking questions to the cat, who has ceased listening, eyes roaming the room. My phone vibrates in my hand, and he jumps down from the bed, velvety paws dulling the thud of two hundred pounds of organic killing machine hitting the floorboards. Standing, he's the same height as I am sitting. He faces me, lifts a paw, and begins to bathe.

I risk a glance at my phone. There's a text from Hugh.

Where did you go?

I don't even consider answering him, either honestly or with a lie. Instead, I call.

"Hey." He picks up on the first ring, voice blurred from drink. "You still up there? What are you doing?"

Facing down a panther is the correct response. *Balancing the threat of going to prison for what I've already done versus the idea of outright killing Felicity and getting away with it* is another correct answer. *Realizing that my entire plan of learning about my parents' fate is worthless if Felicity truly doesn't remember* is a correct answer.

"Chilling out," I say. "Needed some space. Too much going on."

"Tell me about it," Hugh says, and I hear Ribbit in the background.

"Who is it? What do they want? Are they calling about me?" Ribbit asks. That last question is desperate, high-pitched, hopeful.

"Let me talk to my cousin," I say, and there's the sound of the phone being handed over. "Ribbit?"

"Tress?" There, always, under my name I still hear the slightest hint of worship. "Tress, are you watching? Did you see? I've got like four thousand new Twitter followers, and a shit ton of friend requests."

"They're not your friends," I say. My words are sharp and distinct, biting down on the ends of his blurry, wandering syllables. "Do you hear me? Nothing that's going on right now is okay."

"Brynn Whitaker is bringing me beers. That's more than okay."

I think of Brynn, crying in the kitchen, empty water bottles and beer cans littering the counter. "Brynn might be the only friend you have right now."

"I'll take it," Ribbit says. "Listen, I gotta go."

Downstairs I hear shuffling, the crowd moving back into their places.

"People are coming back for round two of Ribbit. Oh, and something, like, ate Gretchen's dog," Ribbit says, followed by a hiccup.

"Yeah, I know," I say. "I'm upstairs sitting across from a loose panther."

"Cool," Ribbit says, and I know he isn't listening. "Maddie got her calmed down, took her outside." There's a pause, some muttering. "Look, my man Hugh needs his phone."

Hugh's voice comes on, loose and shaky, but not as blurred with drink as Ribbit's. "Don't hate me."

"Give me a reason not to," I say.

"Look . . ." His voice drops, low and whispering. "The guys are just waiting to kick his ass, and I mean, like, in a brutal way. He said something about David's mom earlier—I mean, what's with him and moms, anyway?"

"I have no idea," I say. "And I don't hate you because . . . ?"

"Because as long as the show is going, there are cameras on him," Hugh says.

"And he's safe," I finish for him. I think of thousands of people on a livestream, friend requests, new followers, hundreds of unread messages pouring in from around the world. David and the other guys won't attack him with that many eyeballs on them. An assault conviction would certainly put a dent in their high school football careers, and an assault conviction against an Usher would land their asses in jail, minors or not. You don't get to spill old blood in Amontillado.

"Okay," I say reluctantly.

"Hey, do you know where Felicity is?" Hugh asks, his

voice back to normal. "I haven't seen her since . . . I don't know. I just haven't seen her."

"Yeah, I know where she is," I say.

"Okay, cool. Just checking on her. I look out for her, you know."

He does. The same way I look out for Ribbit. "Yeah, I get it," I tell him.

I think of the basement, the naked bulb above my chair, the mortar pail, the pile of bricks, and Felicity, a trail of blood leaking from behind her ear. Tonight, we switched responsibilities, and it is not turning out so well.

I hang up. In the corner of my phone the livestream continues. My messages app is nothing like Hugh's. I have only one notification. One I sent to myself from Brynn's phone. I exhale, my breath foul from a long night, still far from over.

Despite the cat, only inches from me, I hang my head, and I cry.

Chapter 47

Cat

There is pain in the girl,
but no injury.
I lean forwad, sniffing
for the scent of
blood and hurt and skin split and hair torn and teeth broken
and bones splintered and tendons severed and muscles
snapping
all the things that can happen.
And the girl lifts her head,
the salt smell of pain in her eyes,
and reaches for me
——like a cousin——
to touch.
But her hand is not a paw

her blood, not like mine.
And I
am not tame.
I smack, to remind.
A touch that would roll a cousin, expose their belly, tell
them,
I am alpha.
But the girl is not a cousin
only a human.
And easily opened.

Chapter 48

Felicity

Annabelle, that's the first thing, easy to remember.

Tress looks like her, so it's not hard to conjure my friend's face, then smooth out some of the sharper edges—the permanent worry line above her nose, the way she holds her body like she's always ready to fight. It didn't use to be that way. Her face used to be open, ready to laugh, her body more likely to erupt into dance than a defensive posture.

Taking away Tress's harder touches gives me Annabelle, tall and dark, graceful. There's a smile, I know that face. She's offering me a Popsicle, pressing the cool wrapper against the scrape on my knee before unwrapping it.

"There you go," she says. "Edible Band-Aid."

I laugh in the memory, and I realize Tress isn't the only one who's changed. It comes out light and airy. I'm not checking to make sure I'm *supposed* to be laughing. Not doing a quick assessment of Gretchen's or David's or Hugh's faces to make sure it's okay.

But then Annabelle's face does change, becomes more like the Tress I know today, that line of worry between her eyebrows, the edges of her mouth down-turned. There's a light touch on my forehead, and I lean into it, the fingers cool and deft. At my side, Goldie-Dog whines, her cold nose going into my palm. Something is wrong. She knows. She knows something is not right with me, and soon I'll pee my pants and Annabelle and Tress will know and everyone will know that Felicity Turnado pees her pants sometimes and froths at the mouth and rolls on the floor and no one will ever want to marry me.

"You don't have a fever," Annabelle says. "Could it be something you ate?"

I shake my head in the memory, but also here in the basement of the Allan house.

"I don't feel good," I say, and my eyes flick to Tress, standing at the top of the stairs, a teddy bear clutched against her side, looking down at us with a frown to match her mother's.

"Okay." Annabelle runs her hands down my arms, and

I shiver, goose bumps popping under my nightgown.

"I want to go home." My voice cracks as I say it, a pathetic whimper that Annabelle Montor can't ignore. It was the one place I didn't want to be, earlier. The place I ran from after I heard the sound—louder than a smack—while my parents were fighting. I ran from home and came to the Montors', and Annabelle had called my mom, said I was staying here tonight. Said it in a way that my mom couldn't argue with, and wouldn't anyway because

Montor > Turnado.

But that tone is gone from Annabelle's voice now, and I wish she hadn't used it then. Wish she hadn't agreed that I could stay. Wish that I hadn't run in the first place.

"I need to go home," I say again, insistent.

"Honey, it's . . ." She glances at her phone. "It's past midnight."

I shake my head, real tears coming now. Tears of frustration. I don't only want to go home, but I *need* to. It started up in Tress's room, a halo of light around her lamp, a pressure in the back of my head. Her voice got loud and her teeth terribly bright, and I know, without a doubt, that I'm going to seize, and soon. And that means I'll fall down and roll around, go stiff like a board and maybe even pee myself right in front of Tress.

Girls with monogrammed towels don't pee them-selves.

I gulp a deep breath, bunch my nightgown into my fists, and focus hard on Annabelle. "I want to go home."

In the basement, my cracked lips barely moving, I say it again. "I want to go home."

Chapter 49

Tress

My first reaction when the cat smacks me is to feel hurt—not actually pain, just hurt. Rule number one of wild animals: don't forget they're wild animals. I forgot. I sat here and I cried and I told a panther all my problems and then, like an idiot, I tried to pet him, because I made the mistake of thinking that he understood me, that he was my friend.

Apparently I am very bad at picking friends.

Either I try to kill them, or they try to kill me.

Deep wounds take a second to start bleeding. I know this, having suffered more than a few. The cat was only warning me, but it was enough. There are three slashes on my arm, dark and black, like three mouths opening into a part of me not meant to see light. Subcutaneous fat rolls from the edges, a yellow layer peeking out above the deeper pink of skin. Past that there's a glimpse of bone, securely fastened to gray tendon and fleshy muscle, which I see flickering for a moment before the blood flows.

Then everything is just red.

Chapter 50

Cat

There are lives outside me
present and past that I
can see
when I am still and quiet.
Go beyond that, past
still
and
quiet
To
stone
and
silence
and there are lives, inside.
I have always been cat

but not always this
Sizecolorshapesex.
Once I was smaller, like a cousin,
and died, freezing, with a girl
in our bed, held tightly together for warmth,
though we had only cold left to give
bone pressed to bone.
I remember that girl, her mouth sounds,
different from this girl's.
But in all my lives,
humans cry the same.
She leaves, arm curled to her,
metal / salt / sad / smell stays behind.
The door closes, but it is a light thing.
And I am dark and heavy.

Chapter 51

Felicity

There's a roar above me, a party I was invited to and haven't quite been able to attend. A swell of laughter spins, loops, goes different directions until it's not laughter anymore, but the sound of wind, a breeze that plays with my nightgown as I stand on the steps of the Montors' house, my hand in Annabelle's, as she stares stupidly at the empty driveway.

"Where's your car?" I ask, scratching the back of one leg with the other foot. We'd roasted marshmallows earlier in the backyard, and the last of the mosquitoes had some bites off me while I devoured my own snack.

Annabelle doesn't answer, only jangles her keys in one hand, eyes roaming up and down the street. It's late. Dark. No one is out. The only light is a rectangle on the lawn, thrown from Tress's room. I walk out into it, look up. Tress stands there, staring down, still holding the teddy bear.

I wave, half-heartedly.

She does not wave back.

She doesn't understand, doesn't know why I'm leaving, can't figure out what she did wrong to drive me away. And I'm sorry and I feel bad but I have to go and I need to go *right now* but we can't go because Annabelle can't find her car and she's not worried about me anymore. Her face does not have the worried-about-children look. It has something else. Something I am very familiar with.

The upset-with-your-father look.

And when the car lights turn onto the street and move closer to the driveway I am so happy to see that it's their car, and Lee is behind the wheel, and now I can go home. But Annabelle is not happy, and Lee is not happy when he sees her.

No one is happy. And Tress turns her lights out, leaving me to stand in the dark.

Chapter 52

Tress

I had a plan. I was going to scare the ever-living shit out of Felicity Turnado and find out what happened the night my parents disappeared, settling a few scores in the process. How I ended up being attacked by a panther and bleeding out while my cousin, Ribbit, became internet famous, I don't know. But that's where I'm at.

I'm holding my arm over my head as I go down the back staircase, but it's not making much of a difference; I'm bleeding so heavily that I actually slip in my own mess on the second step, crashing into the kitchen and knocking the wind out of me. There are black spots in my vision and a metallic taste in my mouth, the sounds of laughter from the staircase are fading in and out, going a little tinny, like when Dad used to insist on trying to find local radio stations when we were on a road trip. I curl up into a ball, willing myself to keep my shit together.

And keeping my shit together starts with keeping my arm together.

I sit up, leaning back against the wall to get a better idea of how bad the wounds are. I kick at a half-full bottle of water, rolling it near enough to me that I can grab it and pour some over my arm. All I get is a quick glance at what I already knew—it's bad—and then the blood is flowing thickly again, dripping down my arm and soaking the front of my pants.

"Okay, Montor," I say to myself. "What's the situation?"

My mom used to say that, whenever I came running to her. No matter what it was, from a bee sting to a broken nose, she always set me down and calmly asked, *What's the situation?* I asked her once why wasn't she like other moms, the ones who said, *What's wrong?*

"Because they assume something is," Mom said, rolling back the hem of my jeans.

"There is," I argued, wiping my nose. "A bee stung me."

"That's what bees do." Mom pinched the stinger between her fingernails and pulled it out. "So really, everything is perfectly *right*."

A cat had mauled me. That's what cats do. Nothing

was wrong. I just had a situation. And situations have solutions.

"I need stitches," I say, talking myself through it.

But I can't go get stitches because (1) I'm in no condition to drive, (2) no one else here is, either, (3) I'll surely be questioned about my wounds, which will lead to the cat's escape being discovered, followed by the loss of the family business, and, of course, there's (4) I've committed a handful of felonies this evening and will surely be found out if I seek medical attention.

"Okay." I nod, agreeing with my train of thought. "I can't get stitches at a hospital. What else can I do?"

Stitching myself up might be an option. I'd closed a few of Cecil's wounds when he didn't want animal services getting too interested in us. But I'm not at home. I'm at the Allan house, and the chances of finding a needle and thread are pretty slim, the availability of boiling water or a disinfectant even slimmer. So stitches are out of the question. But I need to close the wounds, and I need to do it fast.

"Okay," I agree with myself. "But how?"

The room starts to go sideways, so I lean my head back, watching the lights above me fade in and out as my focus shifts, my eyes wandering from the naked glass bulbs to the live wire above them, held in place with staples. I'd helped Ribbit hang the lights this afternoon, following his instructions and grabbing anything he needed out of my backpack.

Pliers. Hammer. Duct tape.

Duct tape.

I scramble, wriggling around to get my pack off with one good arm while trying to keep the other one elevated. I pull back the zipper with my teeth and spot the roll—the edge curled under so that it won't stick down, like Dad taught me. I grab it and just start wrapping, rolling it around and around my arm, watching the mess of my skin—the open wounds, the dripping blood—covered with length after length of neat, orderly silver tape.

It doesn't last, of course. Blood starts to seep out of the edges immediately, so I keep rolling, faster now, enough that I can actually smell the tape starting to get warm, see tiny fibers floating through the air as I spin and spin, patching myself up with the only thing I've got.

I'm sweating when I finish, patting down the end with my nose. My left arm is pure tape from elbow to wrist, and I wound it too tight; I can feel my pulse in my hand. My fingers will be blue sooner rather than later. But I'm not bleeding anymore, and that was my main concern. The situation was that I was going to bleed to death; now I'm not.

"Problem solved," I say, trying to put more confidence in my voice than I actually feel. I toss the empty tape roll in the direction of the sink but miss by a long shot. It hits the wall, leaving behind an indentation in the plaster, and falls down behind an ancient fridge.

It'll be here forever now, after the bulldozers leave and the walls have come down. Once the bricks collapse and the studs bust and the nails fly and the concrete crumbles, that little something that I put here will be a permanent part of the Allan house ruins.

I've got the chance to bury everything I've done wrong, right along with it. Leave Felicity Turnado to die, and move on with my life like nothing ever happened, same as she did to me. But I can't get the sound of her voice out of my head. Not when she screams *fuck you*, or tells me that I'm living off her charity whether I like it or not. Not when her words come out nasty because her mouth is twisted the way her mother's always has been. No, it's how she sounds when she says my name.

She says *Tress Montor* like it's a name that still matters. She says it like we're still friends.

I told the cat I could do it, could kill someone. And I don't think that's a lie. I just don't know if I can kill Felicity Turnado.

I set my jaw, grab a chair, and pull myself to my feet.

Chapter 53

Felicity

I'm not good at staying still, and Tress knows that. This has not always been true, and Tress knows that, as well.

I roll my head to the side, trying to find a spot on the rock behind me that doesn't grind against my skull. That place doesn't exist.

"Shit," I mutter, letting my head fall forward again. It's like a sunflower that's grown too heavy for its stalk, and my neck screams against the weight.

I can't move, and while I know Tress thinks the steadily growing brick wall in front of me is what's going to make me come clean, the true power in her plan is that she's forcing me to be still. To be quiet.

Tress Montor is forcing me to think about shit.

We camped out in our backyards a lot, lying on our

sleeping bags and looking at the stars, Goldie-Dog tucked between us. We talked, pointing out shapes we saw, trying to differentiate stars from satellites, planets from planes. But mostly . . . we were still.

Still and quiet, and together.

I'm not still anymore. I haven't been for a long time. My life is a rush and a whirl, running from one thing to the next, frantically planning the future and making sure—absolutely sure—that I will never be bored. That I will never be alone. That I will never have time to think.

Now, it's all I've got.

I exhale, my breath sick and rotting in this increasingly small space. I can feel my lips, dehydrated and pocked, sticking to my teeth. I bite down, peeling off a strip of thin skin. I roll it around, get some saliva going, and spit, trying to clean my mouth.

My left foot slips in the mess at my feet, and I go down, my arm jerking hard at the wrist, scraping back skin. I cry out, my voice hoarse and lost as my throat swells, choked tight with tears.

"I can't do this right now," I say, like it's a reasonable statement, like maybe we can reschedule my torture for another time. But it's also true—I can't do this. I'm going to lose my mind. I can't be here.

But I don't have to be, do I?

I went away for a little bit, earlier. Away to Tress's yard and that night in fifth grade and an empty driveway and Annabelle Montor's confused face and Lee coming back late, behind the wheel looking . . .

How did he look? I didn't know then. All I could think of was getting home before I seized, the entire world shrunk down to the electrical currents in my brain and how they might undermine me at any minute.

But I'm older now, and I know some things. I know how men look when they're caught.

"Uh-oh, Lee," I say to myself, holding back a giggle. "What were you up to?"

I close my eyes and think of Patrick Vance. I thought I'd loved him. He went to college last year and *on to better things*. That had been his wording, but what he meant was, *There's a lot of pussy here and yours isn't*. I could still see his face when I surprised him, knocking on his dorm door only to have him answer it in his boxers, a brunette with sex-bump hair in his bed.

Yep. That face. Patrick's face. Lee's face.

The manacle pulls on my wrist, but it's actually Annabelle's fingers, tight, gripping, grinding my bones together because she doesn't know where else to put her anger right now. Lee doesn't even get the car in park before Annabelle throws open the back door, helping me inside even though I try to squirm away, try to escape the pinch of her hands. She tears open the passenger door, falls into her seat, her mouth a grim line.

"Drive," she says.

"What's going on?" Lee asks, voice wary, frightened.

Annabelle's mouth moves, and I know there are words back there, words she wants to say right now, can hardly keep in. They're going to roll out like boulders and crush her husband. She glances back, looks at me, considers her options.

"Felicity doesn't feel good; she needs to go home," Annabelle says. They're tight words, harsh, bouncing off her teeth as she bites them clean, not wanting to let more out while I'm here. I shrink into the back seat, balling up my nightgown in my fists as the tension in the car elevates, along with a smell that's almost overpowering me.

It's like this when I'm about to seize—everything brighter, stronger, harder, faster, louder. It's a cloying scent, heavy like flowers, maybe fruit, right on the verge of rotting. I take a deep gasp, searching for fresher air, a pocket somewhere in this car that the perfume hasn't permeated.

Because that's what it is. Perfume.

Annabelle Montor always smells like grass clippings and earth, woodsmoke and green things growing. Annabelle Montor does not wear perfume.

I know this. She knows this. Lee knows this.

Lee's phone rests in the cupholder. Annabelle reaches for it as we back out of the driveway. He tenses up, every line in his body drawn with a straight edge.

In the back seat, I make myself very small.

Chapter 54

Tress

Ribbit is naked when I glance into the atrium.

I'm surprised it took this long.

The audience is getting more difficult to impress, and Hugh has begun taking the questions and suggestions that he skipped over in the comments before—the ones that he must have decided were too intense at the time. But times have changed, and the livestream is slipping. The views aren't quite up to where they were before Gretchen charged in and broke the momentum with her announcement about something eating her dog.

I spot her on the stairs, collapsed against the banister, red-faced and crying, nursing a beer in one hand, still holding William Wilson's tail in the other. Her friends are around her, but not as many as before. Maddie Anho has slowly been threading her way back toward the top of the stairs—more than likely trying to get into the livestream shot. Brynn is still running Ribbit's beers, but also moving through the crowd, feeling foreheads, propping people up, and handing out more water than alcohol.

Brynn is a good person.

Ribbit stands in front of the grandfather clock, fully naked, swinging his junk in time with the pendulum at the suggestion of a freshman, who finds it so thrilling that he blows beer out his nose. Hugh leads the crowd in a chant, counting off the seconds that Ribbit can keep himself synchronized with the clock. On the livestream, laughing emojis, balloons, thumbs-ups, and fireworks explode across the screen. Viewers are happy.

Hugh locks eyes with me from across the room, and shoots me a thumbs-up, unconsciously echoing his online audience. I scroll through comments, then shoot a text to Hugh.

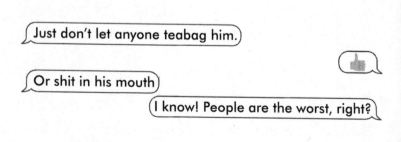

I minimize my messages app, and pull up the photo from Brynn's phone.

"Yes," I agree. "They are."

Back in the kitchen I kick beer cans and water bottles out of the way. There's a puddle of blood where I collapsed at the foot of the servants' stairs, drying already. My bare feet stick in it as I pad through the mess, making my way to the basement door. It's open about an inch, the pale glow from the single bulb downstairs outlining the edges.

I flip the hook behind me and take each step as an individual challenge. My legs are shaky, and my left hand is going numb. I can't feel the wall underneath my hand, even though I'm leaning against it for support. The dirt floor is cool under my feet when I get to the bottom. It sticks to the coagulated blood and pushes up between my toes, a gritty red-brown mess.

I flop into the chair, exhausted by the walk, my arm cradled against me. I'm hit with the mixed scents of vomit and urine, and glance up to see a chalk-white Felicity hanging in her chains, eyes vacant.

Until they meet mine.

Chapter 55

Tress and Felicity

"What the hell happened to you?"

Chapter 56

Felicity

"I was attacked by a wild animal," Tress says, and holds up her arm. It's entirely silver from elbow to wrist, layer after layer of duct tape not quite managing to stop a trickle of blood that drips from her fingers.

"Me too," I tell her, and rattle my chains.

She laughs. It's a weak sound, which is nothing I would ever associate with Tress Montor, but I'm glad to even get that out of her. She looks bad. Pale as death, and her eyes are sunken deep into her skull. Her lips are drawn against the pain, and she's so weak she can hardly keep it together, her arms and legs splayed out to either side of the chair at odd angles. As I'm watching, her eyes go dim and her head slips to the side.

"Hey!" I shout—or at least, raise my voice as much as

I can. "Don't you fucking pass out on me!"

A jolt of panic rushes up my spine. Tress is the only person who knows I'm down here. If she goes out like a light my one connection to the outside world is extinguished, too. I wish that was the only reason I'm freaked out. I wish that I hated her and could relish the idea of watching her drip-dry to death in that chair, knowing that at least she's going down with me. But that's not it. That's not it at all.

The first thing I felt when I saw Tress's sunken eyes and waxy skin wasn't joy or satisfaction or victory. All I felt was worry, a deep yank in my gut at the sight of my friend's blood.

Yeah. My friend.

I still care about Tress Montor.

Chapter 57

Tress

"If you fucking pass out on me, I swear to God, I'll . . . I'll . . ."

Felicity Turnado has nothing to threaten me with, and that's hilarious. I laugh, or at least I try to. My body isn't responding the way it's supposed to, and everything is fuzzy: the demarcations between where my body stops and other physical objects start. The passage of time. Morality.

That's kind of funny, too.

A giggle escapes, high and tinny, not quite right.

"You scared the shit out of me," Felicity says, and when I look up she's crying.

"Smells like you mean that literally," I answer, and her mouth goes tight, like she wants to get mad at me, but half a second later the edges are twitching, and she's laughing.

"Things have not been going so well down here," she says, then seems to consider things for a second. "But they've definitely been going."

I splutter, a mix of spit and giggles slipping past my lips. I'd forgotten that Felicity can be funny. Really funny. Maybe she'd forgotten that, too, because she looks half shocked at her own words, even though she's laughing along.

Or maybe it's the fact that she's laughing with *me* that's so shocking. It shouldn't be. We used to laugh a lot, get slaphappy like this at three in the morning and completely lose it over the dumbest things. But a lot has changed . . . and I can't let myself forget that.

The cat really did a number on me.

I don't know how much of my blood is upstairs in that bedroom, how much is puddled in the kitchen, how much is mixed with dirt and jammed between my toes, and how much is still in my veins. But I think the last answer is the smallest number.

I'm losing my edge, letting our laughter rekindle something that's dead. I need to remember why I'm here, and the best way to remind myself of that is to lay some damn bricks. I stumble to the rubble pile, find one I like. Felicity is still smiling when I begin working on the new row, like she thought everything was going to be okay now. Like it was fixed. Like nothing ever happened.

Something did happen—it happened to my parents. And I don't know what.

I lay one row and look up to see that Felicity has a half smile on her face, like maybe those last four bricks were supposed to be ironic, a final jab before I let her go. I start another row, my blood mixing with the mortar, the light in her eyes falling away as the wall rises. Good. Felicity Turnado needs to know what it's like to lose hope.

I sit back in the chair, a burst of black circles in my vision. The layer of bricks I just added is sloppy as hell, the mortar uneven and pitted with air holes. I did a shit job, and it's something that would earn me a clap upside the head from Cecil if I were at home.

But I'm not at home. I'm in the basement of the Allan house. And if anyone were to hit me on the side of the head right now, I'd probably just go on over and lay in the dirt until . . . until what? Until I die? Until someone finds us down here and I go to jail for the rest of my life? It's that thought—jail—not death, that gets me talking again. I don't want to live like Cecil's animals do, and I've seen the look in Rue's eyes. She'd rather be dead.

But if I'm asking Felicity to be honest, I guess I

probably should be, too. What I'm doing here tonight isn't the only thing in my life that could land me in jail, not by a long shot.

"Tress," Felicity asks, her voice weak and shaky. "What are you thinking about?"

"Patrick Vance," I tell her.

Chapter 58

Felicity

Sophomore Year

I am a fucking mess. And I like it.

I stare down into my Solo cup. I have no idea what's in it. I just know that Patrick Vance handed it to me, and I've had a crush on him since seventh grade. He handed me a little white pill to pop along with it, and I didn't even think twice, because right after that he asked for my number. Brynn had given me a sidelong look, and now she's been by my side all night, not letting me out of her sight, even though we both know Gretchen's house like the back of our hands. I mean, we practically live here on the weekends.

"I'm not going to get lost," I say, giving her an elbow. A little too hard, I guess. Her cup slops over the top, and I notice she's only drinking water.

"I'm not worried about you getting lost," she says, flicking her hand dry. "I'm worried about somebody else finding you."

"Ha," I say, because I can't come up with anything better. My mind is slow, catching up to thoughts, picking them up, examining them, then putting them back down, moving on to something else without remembering what it was holding a second before.

It's nice. It's like forgetting.

"Get your head on straight, Turnado," Brynn says. "You're wasted, and everybody knows it. You can't go wandering off on your own. I don't know half these people, and neither do you. Don't be an idiot."

"Like that guy?" I ask, pointing at Ribbit Usher.

Gretchen made the mistake of asking him if she needed to get permission from the school board for the cheerleaders to paint spirit signs in the athletic hallway. He's answering her . . . has been, for about an hour. It's turned into a lecture on parliamentary process, and Gretchen is politely trying to back out. Politely, because she can't risk losing an Usher vote from the school board. She picks up William Wilson and tucks him under her arm; he's shivering and upset at the crush of people.

"Oh! Is that your dog? I love your dog!" Ribbit says, and shoves his face into William Wilson's. The dog gives a warning growl but not much of one, before lunging at Ribbit.

He's bleeding in a second, blood spouting through his fingers from his torn lip. Gretchen grabs a towel, pressing it to his face while looking for someone to help her out. Brynn and I swivel, turning our backs immediately.

"Yeah, like that guy," Brynn says as they brush past us, Ribbit insisting that everything is fine. He doesn't need stitches. Dogs love him, he doesn't know why that one would . . . His voice fades out as they disappear into the crowd, Gretchen discreetly leading him outside so he won't bleed all over her mom's carpet.

"I will try very hard not to get bit in the face by William Wilson," I promise Brynn.

As for the rest . . . it's hard not to swear I won't be an idiot tonight. I'm wasted. But Brynn's not wrong. Word about Gretchen's party had spread a little too fast and a lot further than intended. The upperclassmen are more than welcome. Gretchen had practically rolled out the red carpet for Patrick Vance when he showed up with his entourage, but I've spotted a few varsity jackets from Prospero—the next town over—too.

So yeah, Brynn's right. We don't know everyone, and the smart move would be staying next to her. But I'm definitely getting a vibe from Patrick that he wouldn't mind being alone with me . . . and I don't have any objections. I also don't have any illusions—I know what he's interested in. I am, too. But I'd also like to ask him what that pill was.

Because I feel pretty damn good.

My eyes follow Patrick through the crowd; he's broken away from a junior girl who had a death grip on his elbow. She's staring after him, about to cry as he heads for the stairs.

"Gotta go to the bathroom," I say to Brynn, shoving my cup into her hand.

She follows my gaze, her face darkening. "Patrick? Are you for real?"

"I gotta go to the bathroom," I repeat, squeezing my legs together for emphasis. "Seriously. You can time me."

"'Kay" is all Brynn says, setting my cup aside. "But—"

I don't know what the *but* is because I'm already gone, following the huge raven on the back of Patrick's jersey. But the stairs are crowded, and apparently plenty of people actually do need to use the bathroom, because there's a line. It extends down the hall, and some of the rooms that Gretchen usually keeps shut on purpose have been opened.

She's not going to be happy about that. I stand on my tiptoes, scanning the crowd to see if I can catch a glimpse of Patrick and his Ravens jersey. But there are too many people, too many faces and colors. They're all a little fuzzy, and I think I might be about to pass out . . . except that's not right because the sounds aren't fading, they're getting louder and—shit. Whatever Patrick gave me is interfering with my anti-seizure meds.

Panic grips me. I don't want to seize. Not here. Not in front of everyone.

Who will marry you then? Mom's voice insistent, worried, cuts right through whatever that pill was. I hear her loud and clear, distinct from the rumble of the crowd.

I push through a group of people to find a wall, the banister, anything that will support me. My hands find something solid and clench on to it. It turns out that something is Hugh Broward.

"Ouch, damn." He turns around and looks down at me. His face changes from annoyance to concern.

"Felicity?" he asks.

But I can't talk, can't remember this boy's name or where I am. His arms go around me, and suddenly he's thrown me over his shoulder and I'm being carried through the hall, the flash of his calf tattoo the only thing I can see. He's barreling his way through the crowd, forcing his way to the front of the bathroom line. People argue but fall silent when they turn and see this boy, his size quieting their objections.

The bathroom door opens, and there's a girl in the

mirror, light hair a tousled mess, blue eyes wide and questioning, the pupils tiny black dots in the center.

She's scared.

She's scared.

She's gone.

"You with me?"

It's a boy's voice. Quiet. Calm.

"Felicity? You had a seizure."

Shit. Yes, I did. And that's . . . that's Hugh Broward's voice.

I sit up, and he's at my side in a second, hands on my shoulders.

"Slow," he says, and I nod in agreement, my face grimacing when I see the puke down my front.

"Oh God . . ."

"It's okay, it's okay," Hugh says.

"It's not okay," I say, choking back a sob. "I puked all over myself."

"Here." He whips off his jersey, pulling it over his head. The white T-shirt underneath is glaringly bright under the bathroom lights, and I close my eyes against it.

"You all right?"

"Yeah," I say, pushing my palms into my eyelids. Color bursts. Pinwheels spin. "Just . . ."

"Recovering, I get it," Hugh says, hands me his jersey.

"Grandma says the first few minutes after are pretty rough."

That's right, I remember now. Hugh lives with his grandmother. His parents got divorced in fifth grade. It was . . . messy—that's how Mom had put it. Must have been, for both his parents to leave Amontillado behind and him to decide he'd rather live with an old lady who has seizures.

I wet a towel, wipe off the front of my shirt as best I can. There's an angry banging on the door, three raps in a row, insistent.

"Get off already, Broward," somebody shouts.

I scrub more furiously, only driving the stain deeper into my shirt and ruining Gretchen's towel. Dismissing it as futile, I pull Hugh's jersey on over it, yanking my hair free from the back.

"How'd you know?" I ask, leaning forward to check my teeth. "How'd you know I was going to seize?"

He shrugs, his massive shoulders moving up and down in the T-shirt, like a white cloud. "You just had that look about you, the way Grandma gets. I figured you wouldn't want to go down in front of everybody."

"No," I say, rinsing and spitting. "No, I didn't."

The banging comes again, harder.

"You ready to go back into it?" Hugh asks, hand on the doorknob.

I check my reflection, adjust my hair. "Yeah," I say. "Yeah, I think so."

He twists the knob, but I stop him.

"Hey, Hugh? Why are you being so nice to me?"

He smiles, his teeth bright as his shirt. "Maybe I'm not *being* nice, Felicity," he says. "Maybe I actually *am* nice."

I watch carefully, weighing what I know of him against what I've heard. "I thought you were just some big, dumb bruiser."

He nods, like he's heard that, too. "Football, beer, and pussy."

"Yeah," I say. "So why do you let people think that?"

His hand falls from the doorknob, his eyes boring into mine. "What's your last name, Felicity?" he asks.

"Turnado," I say.

"And what's that mean in Amontillado?"

"Money," I say automatically. It's one half of the power equation, the secret everyone knows about you but doesn't resent as long as you keep it quiet, too.

"And what's my last name?" he asks.

"Broward," I answer.

"And what's that mean?"

"I . . ." I search, all the other answers came easily, but this one eludes me.

"Nothing," he says. "Not a name that matters, no

money behind it. What's my first name?"

"Hugh," I say, and he cocks his head at me. "But peo-ple call you Huge."

"Yep, and there might be a football scholarship at OSU with my name on it, if I play my cards right," he says. "Get the fuck out of here."

I think of the jewel tones of shampoo and condi-tioner lined up under my sink, one of them for colored hair. I recently went with the silver look because that's what Gretchen did and everyone else followed suit.

"So you're just doing what you're expected to do," I say. "Being the thing you're supposed to be."

He shrugs. "It's easier than proving I'm any different."

I nod, because I get it. He opens the door, and we go back out into it, together. He's pulled away from me in a second, guys asking for the details about my . . . Oh, that's nice. Assholes. Brynn's at my elbow immediately.

"Twenty-three minutes," she says, her mouth a firm line.

"What?"

"You told me to time you. It took twenty-three minutes for you to take a piss, and"—she spins me around—"apparently swap clothes with—" The humor in her voice falls flat when she sees the name on the back of the jersey I'm wearing.

"Hugh Broward, huh?" She spins me back around,

the smile on her face a little forced. "Didn't know he was on the buffet."

"He's not," I say. "I mean, we were just—"

"Taking each other's clothes off, yeah," Brynn says. But her eyes aren't on mine anymore. She's scanning the crowd. "Oh God, seriously?"

I follow her gaze to where Ribbit is letting a freshman superglue the cut on his lip. She's cute, but I know that guy pretty well—it wouldn't matter if she were a two. He's had a couple of beers, and she's in front of him. He wants her to be happy. So he's letting her superglue his face.

Twenty minutes later the tube has been passed around the room and Ribbit's eyelids are glued open, constant watering tears running down his face as he smiles at everyone who asks for a selfie. Or at least . . . he tries to smile.

A guy from Prospero glued his lips shut.

I'm at the park. I'm a beautiful girl, and it's a beautiful fall day, and I'm with a beautiful boy, and beautiful families are walking past us, smiling at the beautiful couple.

All I can think about is how I felt last night—beautiful. Inside and out.

"Oxy," Patrick had explained over the phone. "You like?"

I do like. And if Patrick is the package it comes with, that's okay, too. He hadn't seemed surprised at all when I texted him, even if he was a little taken aback that I insisted we meet today. He'd come over and felt me up within the first ten minutes of us lying on the couch, supposedly watching Netflix. I let him, then asked if he had another pill.

"Not on me," he'd said, pulling at the crotch of his jeans. "But I can get more."

"Yes," I'd said, pressing against him. "You can."

Because I wouldn't care if this guy was ugly as sin or skinny as Ribbit Usher or mean as that guy from Prospero who glued Ribbit's lips shut. That pill made me not think about things, and not thinking about things has been the goal for a very long time.

So we ended up here, after straightening our clothes. Patrick says the park is one of the places where things go down, but that he has to wait. Apparently, his dealer sets up shop on one of the lesser-used trails, one that's a loop, that way the people coming in don't see the people going out. They also send out texts to whoever is buying today, letting them know when it's their turn, further lessening the chances of users knowing who else is using.

"Smart dealer," I say. I'm not exactly proud to be here, myself.

"So . . ." Patrick reaches out, his hand encircling my knee. It's a nice hand, masculine, a scar across the back. But it's not as big as Hugh's, and he doesn't have as light of a touch.

"You and Broward?" Patrick asks.

"Huh?" I look up, blushing, aware that I'd gone into a reverie about one boy while another one had his hand on my leg.

"You and Huge," Patrick repeats. "That a thing? You came out of the bathroom with his jersey on, so I figured, you know . . ."

I think of Hugh, how kind he is, how nobody knows that—and how I doubt he'd be willing to buy Oxy for me. "Not a thing," I say.

"Cool. I wouldn't want to cross him." Patrick's hand tightens on my knee, and his phone goes off. "We're up."

I follow him to the trailhead, swatting at mosquitoes. He takes my hand as we walk and reaches back to steady me when we cross a stream, my sandals slipping off a wet rock. "Those aren't quite trail shoes," he tells me, and I swat at another mosquito.

"You didn't exactly tell me we would be hiking," I shoot back, and his eyebrows come together. Patrick doesn't like girls who talk back. I make a note, filing it away. He's still got ahold of my hand when we come around the corner, and there's Tress Montor. I drop it, backing away like we've crossed paths with a bear.

Funny thing, I reflexively put him in between me and her.

"Tress, what's up? You got my girl covered?" Patrick says, and I close my eyes. Despite all of Brynn's warnings, I did end up acting like a fucking idiot. Maybe not last night, but definitely today. Tress isn't a wild animal about to kill me on the trail, and she's not here by accident, either. Tress is Patrick's dealer.

"Your girl, huh?" she asks, eyes on me. I try to shake my head, try to show her I'd never be with a guy like that. Try to be the Felicity I used to be.

Instead, I just stand there.

Tress has no use for me; her attention is entirely on Patrick as she produces a baggie of weed, and he opens his wallet for cash. My head is spinning as I watch Tress count it off—twice—before trading him.

This is how Tress makes money.

I didn't know.

I mean, I'd overheard plenty, Mom and Dad wondering aloud how Cecil kept the lights on and the water running up at the zoo, because everyone around here who wants to see it has already gone, and nobody outside of Amontillado comes here. My parents had their own ideas about the Montor income and hadn't had too much compunction about telling me it's an open secret that Cecil grows weed out there. But they never said he was using Tress to sell, and I truly am a huge fucking idiot because it never occurred to me that she was.

Because that kind of thing would never happen in my world.

I step forward. "Tress, I . . ."

Her eyes come to mine, green and hard. Unblinking. "What do you need?"

I need to tell her to stop this. I need to tell her to come with me. I need to tell her to ditch the drugs and I'll ditch Patrick and we'll walk out of the woods together, and everything will be the same again.

But it won't. I may be an idiot, but I'm not completely stupid. It can't be the same again. Her parents are still gone, and I still don't know what happened, and I can't do anything to help her except . . .

I'm digging in my jeans, pulling out a wad of cash that Mom handed me when I went out the door with Patrick.

"Oxy," I say, handing her the whole roll. "Whatever you've got."

Chapter 59

Tress

Sophomore Year

Felicity cleaned me out. I've got customers coming and nothing to give them, but I can't pass up ready cash. Not with Cecil's medical bills piling up.

The cat took his eye about a week ago. He'd been due for worming, and I'd shot the cat in the upper shoulder with the tranq, just like usual. The cat had screamed at me for it, tore the dart out with his teeth and climbed his tree, only to fall out seconds later. I'd winced when he hit the ground, a puff of dirt landing on his glossy coat.

I don't trust that animal, but it doesn't mean I don't respect him.

Cecil had approached him with the wormer vial, cautious, ready to bolt if he needed to. The cat had twitched when he shoved the tube down his throat, gagged when he pushed the depressor. But the job was done, and the cat was still down when Cecil turned his back. And then it had changed.

The cat was up. Not as fast as normal, no, but not exactly slow, either. Maybe I shouldn't have yelled. Maybe it would've been better if the cat just got a swipe across his back, but I did. I yelled Cecil's name, reloading my tranq gun at the same time. Cecil had turned—catching a slash right across the face. Luckily, the cat had been too wonked to calculate his leap correctly, and that's all Cecil got . . . if *lucky* is the word for it.

Now he's laid up in the trailer, a swath of bandages covering half his face. He's drinking against the pain, half-thrilled some days because with that injury our Oxy supply just went through the roof, half-pissed the rest of the time because I won't let him have as much as he wants.

I can't. We need the money.

Insurance doesn't cover wild-animal attacks when you actively make the choice to live with one. So, we're kind of fucked. The one thing Cecil is real serious about is paying bills on time, because the last thing we need is people poking around the property, looking to see what we've got of value.

The answer is—just the one thing.

That one thing is half an acre of marijuana, and that's not exactly something a collection agency is interested in. But the sheriff sure would be.

The Oxy has been a nice sideline, a decent enough trickle coming in through what Cecil calls his *guys*. Cecil has always *got a guy*. It's how we procured Dee and Zee, and of course, the cat. Now the little pickup brings bottles, and the cage in the back has been replaced with a shotgun rack.

But not enough bottles.

Because now I'm the one who's *got a guy*. He's coming down the trail with some buddies, and I've got nothing to sell him because I wasn't planning on Felicity Turnado needing to get high and handing over money to make it happen.

Shit. That's the other thing. I slip off my backpack and tuck the wad of cash inside. These guys aren't going to be happy. Neither will Cecil, if they decide to jump me and take the day's earnings instead of the pills they came for.

If that's all they do to me.

I straighten my shoulders and stick out my chin, ready for the response when my usual customer shows up, two guys I don't know alongside him.

"Tress," he says, giving me an up-nod, and I give it back.

"Bad news," I tell him. "Store's closed, unless you want weed."

"Weed?" He gives half a laugh, looking at his friends,

who follow suit. "We're not after weed, you know that."

"I do," I say, keeping it as agreeable as I can. "But I can't sell you what I don't have."

"Well, that's some bullshit," one of his friends says, and I nod, still trying to keep it on the up-and-up.

"I know it," I tell them. "But I got cleaned out. Would you turn somebody away who wants to hand over their cash?"

I hold up my hands, like *What're you gonna do?* It makes me look like I'm with them, that I totally get where they're coming from, and maybe we were all in the same place to begin with—just a bunch of people scrambling for money. It also lifts my jacket enough to display the butt of the tranq gun jammed into my jeans.

One of his buddies sees it, and his eyes flick off it, nervously.

It looks enough like a real gun to do the trick. And acts enough like one, too, in a pinch. But it can only hold one dart at a time, and there's three of them.

"So you want some weed, or what?" I ask, trying to push them toward a decision. If I don't give them enough time to get angry, they might forget that they are, and settle for something less than what they came for.

"Let's talk a sec, over here," my customer says to his buddies. I nod, like that's perfectly fine, and they go off a few paces, heads together. I tighten my backpack straps, ready to run if I need to, and rest my hand on the butt of the gun.

Their voices rise, low and muttering, but then there's something else, footsteps—heavy ones—and I realize someone is coming down the path, running, by the sounds of it. I usually duck into the trees when this happens, but I don't want to be off-trail if I suddenly have to make a bolt for it. I tuck my jacket back down to cover the gun, and try to look like I'm just enjoying the view, when Hugh Broward comes tearing around the bend.

He's in jogging shorts, a soaked shirt sticking to his torso. He sees me, nods, and keeps going, his gaze gliding over the guys as he passes them. His footsteps die off, and they turn back to me, my customer in front, his friends clearly flanking him.

I don't think I'm going to like what they decided.

"Thing is, we came out here to buy Oxy," he says.

"And I don't have any," I repeat, no longer trying to keep my voice polite, this meeting civil. I know nasty and have been around when plenty of things started heading that way. Like right now.

"Right . . . but you said you did, is the thing," he says.

"And I *did*, but now it is *gone*," I repeat. "So if you—"

"Hey, Tress."

The four of us jump, all of us caught. Except, I'm glad to see Hugh, who apparently turned around and came back. He's standing there taking up the whole path, sweat pouring down his face. His gaze sweeps the three guys, assessing, and coming out in his favor.

"You all right?" he asks me.

"Yep," I say, nodding. "On my way out."

"Me too," he says. "Walk with me?"

"Sure thing," I say, giving him a bright smile. The other three back off, and Hugh motions for me to go in front of him, so that it's his back turned to them, not mine.

"Thanks," I say, once we've put some distance between them and us.

He only grunts in response, and my phone goes off in my pocket. I pull it out to see a text from the customer we left on the path behind us.

> Next time, have what I want.

I text back:

> Next time, make your mind up faster and at least you won't leave empty-handed.

Because there will be a next time. The guy spends too much money for me to send him elsewhere, even if he is kind of a creep.

"Things like that happen a lot?" Hugh asks.

I shrug. "Girl's gotta do what a girl's gotta do."

Which is true, and also reminds me. I shoot a text to Felicity Turnado, taking a stab in the dark that her number might still be the same but wording it carefully in case it's not.

> My number hasn't changed. Call me if you need anything. Anytime.

I can't turn away white trash cash, and I can't turn away Turnado cash, either.

"Well," Hugh says, picking our conversation back up. "A girl's gotta do what she's gotta do, but maybe she doesn't have to do it alone. Like, for her own safety."

"Uh-huh," I say, ducking under a branch. "And what's your cut?"

"Nothing." Hugh's footsteps fall dead behind me, and I turn to see that he's genuinely shocked. "I just don't want you getting hurt, is all. If I didn't run the trails on the weekends, that could've gone bad, back there."

"It could've," I agree, and turn back to the path. We're quiet until we break out into the light, sunshine falling on my face. "All right," I say. "I try to keep it to once a month, different spots. I'll let you know. We'll meet up and you . . ."

And he protects me, I think. For nothing. For no reason.

"Cool," he says.

We trade numbers, and I wait for the text that says what he wants in return.

It doesn't come.

Chapter 60

Felicity

Sophomore Year

"Tress and Hugh?" Maddie's voice is high, unbelieving, soaked in vodka.

"That's what I heard," Brynn says, shrugging. "I guess they've been, like, hanging out."

I think of Hugh in Gretchen's bathroom, yanking his shirt off, helping me clean up. He's a nice guy. "Good for her," I say, but I say it into my drink, the words echoing back at me from the sides of a red Solo cup.

And I mean it, kind of. I ignore the little drop in my stomach and the ideas that had taken root that day when I looked at Patrick's hand and wished it were Hugh's. It's the least I can do for Tress. Well, that and funnel her constant cash for pills.

"Whatever," Gretchen says. "There's no way Hugh is smashing trash."

I take another drink. If there's something in my mouth it'll stop the words from coming out.

"Hey, speaking of trash," Brynn says, her eyes going to the corner where I spot Patrick talking to Jessica Stanhope. She's shed something like fifty pounds in the past year, and apparently guys who wouldn't look twice at her before are now honing in. But I'm all out of *good for her*s. I make my way toward them in time to see him punch her number into his phone, then give her ass a pinch as she walks away.

"Hey," I say, coming up beside him.

"Hey," he says, slipping his arm around my waist, smooth as hell. It's been here a lot lately—with clothes both on and off.

"What was that about?" I ask, nodding toward Jessica.

"Nothing, just talking," he says, avoiding my eye.

"Just talking?" I repeat, but he only nods. "Like maybe you'll talk later, too? Because I saw you get her number."

His arm is gone from my waist, his eyes not kind anymore. "That a problem?"

"I . . . well . . . ," I sputter. He was supposed to be caught. Supposed to be guilty.

"Look, maybe I wasn't totally clear with you about what's up with us," he says, leaning down so that his voice is in my ear. "I'm not a one-girl kind of guy."

"Oh," I say, my stomach bottoming out. He's saying

it so casually, like it's not a big deal. Like I have no right to be angry. Maybe I don't. I mean, I never did ask him if we were dating. I just let him do . . . well, basically whatever he wanted. As long as I got an Oxy first.

"I mean, that's cool, right?" Patrick says. "You didn't think that we were . . ."

"Yeah, no, yeah, I mean, duh," I say, all the words I didn't have for Gretchen coming out now, tripping over each other, not making sense. "I mean, whatever."

He nods. "Cool."

Sure, it's cool. Everything's cool. Everything is *awesome*. I walk back over to the girls and find my drink.

Chapter 61

Tress

Sophomore Year

My phone is ringing. At three in the morning. That can't be good.

"Hello?" I'm breathless after scrambling for it, the security light from the animal pens lighting up my room.

"Tress?"

There's a sob, a broken noise. It's Felicity. She's not okay.

"Where are you?" My heart is in my throat, and I'm up, pulling on shorts even though I'm not wearing underwear, throwing a sweatshirt on with no bra, rifling through the mess on the kitchen table for Cecil's keys.

I am coming. I will save you. Everything will be okay.

"He's seeing other girls," she says, her voice dull now.

"What?" I stop, watch an empty beer bottle roll off the table, breaking on the floor.

"Patrick," she says. "I slept with him, and I guess I thought, I don't know . . . I thought maybe he was, like, actually into me, or whatever."

"Where are you?" I ask again.

"What?" She sniffs. "I'm at home."

At home. In her house. On a nice street. With her family.

"Why are you calling me?" I ask, my voice hard as hell this time.

"What? I . . ." She trails off, confused.

"Why are you calling me?" I repeat.

"You said . . . you said your number was the same. You said call if I needed anything. You said call . . . anytime."

"If you need *drugs*, Felicity," I seethe into the phone. "Call me if you need drugs."

"Oh," she says, small and soft.

"Anytime," I say.

And hang up.

Chapter 62

Tress

"He's bad news," I tell Felicity, two years too late.

I should've said it on the path, I should've said it at the first party I saw him sniffing around her. I should've said it. I didn't. That's on me. And maybe her pill problem, too.

"You think?" she asks, the words slurred, the laughter that follows unhinged.

"I always thought . . ." My voice isn't strong, either, the thoughts slippery, the consonants and vowels needed to bring them out into the world something I can't conjure. "I always thought maybe you and Hugh . . ." I finally manage.

"Really?" Her voice brightens a second, like maybe it's an interesting topic. "I mean . . . I guess . . . I always thought . . . maybe *you* and Hugh."

Chapter 63

Felicity

Tress starts laughing, and there's an echoing answer from upstairs, weaker now. I don't know if it's because sounds have been going in and out for me in the past few minutes or if people are dropping off upstairs.

"No." She shakes her head, spinning the trowel in her good hand. The other one is turning purple, the tape she bound her wound with much too tight. "No," she repeats. "Not me and Hugh."

"Why not?" I argue. "I mean, he's cute, and if someone could convince him to drop the alpha act—"

"No," Tress interrupts me. "He can't. When the pack senses a weakness in their leader, they take him down. He knows that. I know that. You know that."

I guess I do, which is why I feel a little gut twinge of

joy whenever someone takes a cut at Gretchen, why I've got a couple of embarrassing pics of her on my phone, for whenever the day comes that I'm tired of her telling me what to do. If it comes. Following is easier than leading.

"You're both alphas," I say, understanding. "You and Hugh. It would never work."

She stops spinning the trowel, refocusing her thoughts.

"You finally ditch him?" she asks. "Patrick?"

"Yeah," I tell her, nodding. My head feels like a water balloon, too heavy. It rolls oddly, off to one side. I try to focus on the bricks, try to count them, see how high the rows are. I don't know, anymore. Higher than before, that's all I can say for sure. Math is hard when you've got a concussion and major blood loss plus are still slightly high and maybe a little drunk.

I open my eyes. What were we talking about? Oh yeah, Patrick.

"He went to college and majored in extracurricular activities," I tell Tress.

"Cheaters gonna cheat," Tress says. Her eyes have gone a little blank, and she's fixated on the floor, where her blood is starting to pool as it drips from the tips of her fingers.

Cheaters gonna cheat. . . .

Chapter 64

Tress

"Cheaters gonna cheat," I say. "Liars gonna lie. Haters gonna hate."

My mind is wandering, leaving the area as my blood leaks out, the point being lost. Lost like my parents. Lost like my dog.

Goldie-Dog.

I pull out my phone and show her the picture.

It's not the sign that got to me, when I spotted it on Brynn's phone. Or the smiling faces in front of it. It's Goldie-Dog. My dog, leaning into Felicity, her tongue lolling out, happy to see someone she knows. Someone she remembers. Someone she loves.

Chapter 65

Felicity

Cheaters gonna cheat. . . .

It's echoing in my head, bouncing off my skull, the hard truth of what I know needing to escape, find a new home inside Tress's mind. I can't focus, can't process what she's holding in front of me . . . a phone . . . a picture . . . I squint, wanting to do something right. Wanting to please Tress.

Shit.

I'd like to say I don't recognize that person, don't know who the girl is posing with Gretchen and David in front of Tress's trailer out in the middle of nowhere, cheeks red from drinking . . . but not as red as the words we'd sprayed on the sign behind us.

WHITE TRASH ZOO

And beside us, Goldie-Dog, my arm looped over her, her tongue out, happy.

There's nothing I can say, no defense for what happened. All I can do is be silent and take whatever punishment Tress feels is acceptable. I don't know how to explain that I was trying to find her again, trying to recapture the Tress I knew. But the Tress I remember is gone. The one I know now is standing before me, staring me down, a wild animal loose from its cage.

The Tress Montor I created.

Chapter 66

Tress

It's clear on Felicity's face—I just took everything from her. Any pretense of being a friend, or even a decent person. That's gone now.

It feels good. It's nice to be the one taking. There's a jolt of adrenaline in my veins, chemicals and fibers of duct tape and whatever is left of my blood all coursing through me, pushing me forward. To the inevitable end.

"Tell me how my dog died," I say, my parents now a faint echo, a memory from long before. Goldie's still fresh. I don't need to poke that wound to make it bleed.

"Tell me how the last thing from my old life was eaten by an alligator."

I put the phone in my pocket and reach for the mortar pail.

"Tell me what you did, Felicity."

Chapter 67

Felicity

Senior Year

Being in the passenger seat of your own car is weird. I don't think I've ever been here before. Where have I been, lately? Where was I tonight? Earlier?

I focus on the dash, the backlit numbers, trying to make sense of them. Two in the morning. It's two in the morning and I am incredibly fucked-up and David probably shouldn't be driving and Gretchen is in the back seat, her face pressed against the window, lipstick smearing on the glass.

"Why are you driving my car?" I ask David.

"Because you probably shouldn't be, babe," he says, his hand wandering over to my knee. I look at it for a second, study the long fingers and the knuckles. I brush it away. I don't like him. His hand isn't Hugh's hand.

"No, I mean, like, why are you driving my car?" I repeat, because he didn't understand that I'm not asking which of us is more fit right now. I'm asking why he can't just let me drive my own goddamn car, like Hugh does, putting the passenger seat far back enough to accommodate his bulk.

I had to adjust it when I got in, pulling it forward and smiling, thinking about the next time Hugh gets in and his knees will be up in the vents, his chin resting on them, and we'll laugh about it, and why isn't he here right now? And where are we going, anyway?

"Where are we going, anyway?" The last thought escapes my mind, leaks out through my mouth. This happens with the Oxy, sometimes. I should be more careful. Who knows what I could say, what might come out of me. Hugh is usually with me and he takes care of me when I'm this bad off, and why isn't he here right now?

"White Trash Zoo," David says in answer to my question, the one I spoke aloud.

"Fucking A," Gretchen says from the back seat, her words sloppy and slurred against the window. "Tressy Trash Montor." She tries again, lifting her head this time. "Trashy Tress Montor."

Shit. That's right. Hugh didn't want to come. Didn't want to do . . . whatever we're doing. We're going to do something to Tress. They are. Or I am. I don't know.

David cuts the lights, and the moon takes us the rest of the way, past the Usher house, like a huge tombstone in the night, the pond in front reflecting the glare of the moon. It's so bright, too bright, showing us everything, making me see. I don't know how we got out here. I don't want to be here, but I am here, and Gretchen has gained a second wind and is almost perky as she hands me something when we get out of the car.

A sack. A grocery sack. A dollar-store sack. The dollar store—the only place Tress can shop now—and why did we go there? Why would Felicity Turnado be in a dollar store?

"'Thank you,'" I say, reading the sack aloud, but Gretchen thinks I'm talking to her, and she laughs and reaches into the bag and pulls out a can of spray paint and it's red and she's shaking it and it makes a *click click click* because there's a little ball inside mixing the paint, like there's one inside my head right now mixing my thoughts and my words are going to come out like the paint, spraying out of my mouth, and I don't want these people to hear me because I don't know what I might say.

I don't know what will come out of me because I don't know what's inside me.

There's a smell, thick and heavy, with a sound, a hiss, and they are doing it, they are doing something bad. Something that will hurt Tress. Tress who was my friend, and these people are not my friends, and I know that but I am here with them now, anyway. And I feel something cold in my hand, and I look down and there is someone I know, an actual friend, looking back at me with a question.

"Goldie-Dog," I say, dropping to my knees. I wrap my arms around her neck, and she leans into me, and she smells like shit and animals and a dog, but it's not chemicals and it's not paint and it's not bad words. It's not a bad smell, just a smell, and I want to tell her that but I don't know how, so I just keep my arms around her and look deep into her eyes and hope she knows, hope she feels that I love her, right now. I loved her then and I love her now, and there's a flash and someone tells me to look somewhere and I do because I am a follower, and Goldie looks too and there's another flash.

Gretchen is laughing and she falls into David and her lips are red and the sign is red and now his lips will be red, too, and I don't want to watch this so I walk away. Goldie follows me, her nose pressing into my palm, then into my neck because I've fallen down and there is someone looking at me but it's not Gretchen or David. It's a nicer face. I crawl closer and there are hands on me, touching, and it's not a human. It's almost human, but not quite human, and that means it's better because being all human is not always good.

Almost human > Human

Human ≠ Good

And I'm touching it back, and it runs its hands down my arms and touches my hair, and there are bars between us, why are there bars between us? I am the dangerous one who should be inside, should be kept away. Should not be here. Goldie presses against me, and there is warmth from her and warmth from the hands and this is what Tress's life is like now, all animals no humans, and oh my God I want this for myself.

I want to know Tress now, new Tress, this animal life. I want to share it with her and feel her here in this place, and I'm on my feet and I'm going to the next thing, black and white stripes and big eyes that I'm lost in and wiry hair that I run my fingers through and a tap on my back, and there's a bird face and it's ugly and I love it and the wings unfurl and they are beautiful and I show my own arms and we talk like this now. Not words. Not words painted on a sign.

I didn't come here for that; I came here for this. I came to find Tress again and there's a path and maybe that's how I find her because she is also not human anymore she is an animal and she would be here, she would be with them and I will find her again. And I'm following and I'm walking where she has walked and I am running and our feet are the same and we are the same and we are together again and Goldie is tugging on my hand now pulling, because we don't use words now we do this and—

A snap. A flash.

And pain.

Not a flash of David's phone and not a snap of a picture being taken and not pain of words on a sign but real pain on my foot because it is not Tress's foot and we are not the same and I forgot that and now I am in water and I am drowning.

It's . . . familiar.

Why is that?

These are my thoughts and they are clear and cogent for the first time since forever, and I know that I have forgotten more than Tress. I have forgotten much more, but now there is Goldie and she is with me, and she has her mouth on my arm and she is gentle with not teeth and she is pulling me away from water and toward land but something else has teeth and it is coming and I try to tell her but how we talk now doesn't work anymore and I don't have words either and there is a *crack*.

And there is no more Goldie.

Chapter 68

Tress

"Yeah, that electric fence, it'll get you," I hear myself saying, an idiotic response to the story of how my dog died.

"Hurts, right?" I ask, digging into what Felicity just told me, doing the same thing she was, trying to find the scraps of what we still share.

Like being shocked by an electric fence.

Like knowing how something dies.

"I loved that dog," I say, and it's another dumb thing to say, but it's true, and like a lot of true things it's also incredibly sad.

I'm crying when I lay the next row.

Chapter 69

Felicity

Tress's hands shake a little as she lays the ninth row of bricks, drops of her blood mixing with the mortar. She doesn't speak as she does it, and I don't argue. There's nothing to say. I might have ranted and raved at her about the junior-class secretary thing, but I deserve the bricks she's laying right now.

I try to calculate, measure the distance that's left. But there's an echo in my head still, Tress's words not letting go of me.

Cheaters gonna cheat. . . .

Cheaters gonna cheat and I know how it feels to drown. These thoughts hold hands in my head, forming a chain leading back into the dark parts of my mind, the ones I threw shadows over, in order to forget.

But that's inside of me, and I need to concentrate on what's outside right now. The wall in front of me is past my thighs; the layer Tress is adding will bring it halfway up my body. There's still space between it and the ceiling, but the gap is closing. We're over halfway there. I exhale, the sharp smell of my own breath filtering up to my nose. What the fuck am I going to do?

My mom is an eternal optimist, always looking for the bright side of things, even if they do tend to verge on being incredibly shallow. *When life hands you lemons, put them in your hair for highlights* is one of her favorite sayings. Global warming means better tans. The flu that laid her low at the beginning of the week was doing her a favor by trimming off at least five pounds. Her immediate reaction to the doctor diagnosing my seizures had been to proclaim, "Well, at least it's not something with your face."

What would she have to say about this? I wonder.

You're going to die, but Tress Montor will still be a brunette.

I laugh a little, but it quickly descends into a sob, thinking of my mom. She's not going to be okay, if this ends the way I think it's going to.

"Something funny?" Tress asks. She puts the pail down, and rests on the chair, her skin sallow and sagging after the effort that went into adding the layer of bricks.

The truth is that nothing is funny, not a damn thing. I've been slipping in and out of consciousness, my mind hopping from the night her parents disappeared to this musty, dank hole I'm going to die in. I don't want to be in either place, and what I've remembered is not going to make Tress any happier. I'm chained to a wall, facing down a girl who wants to entomb me. And I have to tell her something that's going to kill her.

Then she'll kill me.

I guess that's fair.

"No," I say. "Nothing's funny." Upstairs, a roar of laughter contradicts me.

"Tress . . . ," I say, my words dry in my throat. "I need to tell you something."

She hears the weight in my words, looks up. "Yeah?"

"Your dad was cheating on your mom."

Her eyes, still blank, stare at me, and I think maybe I didn't say it. Maybe I've spent so much time not saying the important things that when I finally tried, the words didn't actually come out. Then she's up, one bare foot sliding in the pool of her own blood as she comes at me, pointing the trowel in my face.

"That's a fucking lie! You're a *fucking liar!*" she screams, voice cracking.

I shake my head. "No. No, Tress, I'm not."

I don't have the energy to be scared, or upset, or angry

in return. I don't have anything left, and it must show, because she backs off, the outrage in her eyes dying a little as she considers the possibility.

Tress might not have had her parents her whole life, but she also didn't have what I do—the experience of watching a marriage fall apart. She didn't get to see the big fights, the small digs, the knowing glances, the laden words said in conversational tones. Maybe the Montors were careful not to let her see, or maybe she never knew, and she's held on tight to just the good things, canonizing them in her memory.

Well . . . the Montors weren't saints. I can say that, for sure.

Wait . . . I can?

I pause, digging deep, wondering where that came from. "Tress . . . I think—"

"Shut up!" She whirls, throwing the trowel at me. "Shut the fuck up!"

I can't dodge it; can hardly move my head or keep my legs under me. Luckily, Tress is way too emotional to have good aim. The trowel bounces off the wall a foot from my head, ricocheting back at her to hit the lone light bulb. There's a flash of light, a pop, a yelp from Tress.

And then . . . it's utterly black.

Chapter 70

Tress

There's a blue halo in my vision, a burn on my eyes from looking at the bulb when it blew. I can't see anything, but I'm down on my hands and knees, feeling for my phone. I had it in my pocket, but it fell out, clattering to the floor when I jumped as the light exploded.

Shit, shit, shit.

My hand slides through my blood, already growing tacky in the coolness of the basement. I bump against the chair, and it screeches across the stone floor, unnaturally loud in the silence. Utter silence.

"Felicity?" I ask.

She doesn't say anything, and I'm scrambling now. I need that phone. Need the light. Need to . . . Shit, what do I even need to do? Fix everything? Go back in time and undo it all? My fingers brush against the phone and I grab it, relieved when it lights up, despite the crack across the screen. The streaming feed comes on, the viewer number still healthy.

"Can't get enough, can you?" I ask.

And from the darkness, comes my mother's voice, echoing me.

"Can't get enough, can you?"

Chapter 71

Felicity

Fifth Grade / The Night Of

"Can't get enough, can you?" Annabelle says, her mouth tight as she flips Lee's phone shut, putting it back in the cup holder.

"Do we have to do this right now?"

Lee turns in the driver's seat. I know he's looking back at me, can feel the weight of his gaze. But I've got my eyes squeezed tight, have made my body very small. It's what I do at home—pretend I'm not there.

"No—do *you* have to do *this* right now?" Annabelle says, her voice low and growling. "When your daughter has a friend over?"

"Jesus . . ."

I crack an eyelid. Lee's hands are tight on the steering wheel. His jaw muscles flicker.

"Just, seriously get a grip. You're being ridiculous."

"*I'm* the ridiculous one?" Annabelle asks. She fights like Mom; repeating what Dad said but making it sound stupid.

"Annabelle—"

"Yes." She cuts him off. "That's my name. That's who I am. Annabelle Montor. Your. Wife."

I don't know if she's not bothering to control her volume, or if my seizure is close. Her voice breaks higher, to a level I can't pretend to ignore. I jam my fingers in my ears, squeeze my eyes tighter. Pinwheels of color explode across black.

"First you were Annabelle Usher," Lee says. His words are quiet, and dark. Heavy pebbles that I can tell have been thrown before. I feel her rage, radiating to fill the car.

"And I'm supposed to be endlessly grateful?" she asks. "You lifted me up, and I'm supposed to look the other way now?"

"No, that's not—Shit, I missed her road. You made me miss the turn."

"Of course, you made a mistake . . . but it's my fault."

"Can you just shut up for one goddamn second?" Lee yells for the first time, his patience exhausted.

She falls silent, and I feel the car turn. I slide across the leather back seat, the fabric of my nightgown slick and sweaty. It rolls up, and I grab it, pushing it back down to cover my knees. I think I push down, but I might have pulled up. Directions are wrong, and time is thin, and I left Tress's house ten years ago and I'm still there. I'm slipping. I'm slipping. I'm . . .

"Lee, remember that bridge is out—"

This time Annabelle cuts herself short, and Lee slams on the brakes. I roll off the seat, land in the footwell, unable to catch myself. Warmth rushes down the side of my head, and blood trickles into my mouth, my lip already swelling where I bit it, too hard. Too much. Too fast. It's all here now, circling, getting ready to descend.

"Lee?" Now there's something new in Annabelle's voice—fear. And something new in the air, too. Lights. Bright lights, bouncing off the seats, into my eyes, into my head.

"Stay in the car," Lee says, and I hear his door open.

But Annabelle Montor (*Usher*) is not the kind of woman who stays in the car. Her door opens, too.

Words. Flashing. Like the lights.

papers

thief

stole

mine

yours

sister

don't

please

money

listen

But no one is listening, and I can't, either, because everything is fading and the door is opening and someone has grabbed me and I smell grass and earth and green things growing and Annabelle UsherMontor and different now I'm falling and the smell is wet and fish and river and dead leaves and—

I'm falling.

I'm falling.

I'm gone.

Chapter 72

Cat

I am very quiet
and very still.
Stone and silence.
The door was closed
once
But has not always been.
It was open when—
the swinging boy hoped someone would stop him.
(no one did.)
the sobbing woman hoped someone would hear her
and come.
(he did / he did not.)
The screaming baby had no thoughts
only need

and Mother did come.
(not everything ends badly.)
It was open then—
so I go there,
through time and space
and doorways.
Loose now.
In the place where humans
make their noises.

Chapter 73

Tress

"Felicity?" I'm shaking her, reaching over the wall that I've built, my panic rising. "Felicity!"

She moans, dangling by her wrists. She's unconscious, her legs like jelly. I let go of her to grab my backpack, and she falls forward completely, bells jingling, only held up by the manacles. She's bleeding freely, red channels running down her arms. It's a dark red in the light of my phone, her skin a horrid, sickly gray.

I drop my backpack on the ground, rifling through it with my good hand for the keys to release her. There's another roll of duct tape and pliers and a pack of gum— *Where the hell did that come from?* I think wildly. There's a bottle of Oxy and a baggie of weed and some cherry ChapStick, and I don't see the key.

"It's here," I say, then turn the light back on Felicity. "It's here, I'll find it. I'll get you out."

Get her out of where I put her. What I did to her.

I dump the contents of my backpack on the floor and hear a metallic *zing* . . . somewhere. I flash my phone around, looking for the glint of light on metal. I spot it and grab, with the wrong hand, pain lighting up my entire arm as I close my fingers around the key. The cat got something deep in there, his claw caught on tendon, or muscle.

I am not okay.

But Felicity is worse, and that's on me.

I can't hold the phone and undo the manacles with only one hand. I bite down on my phone, pieces of screen cracking off onto my lips, my tongue, tiny splinters digging into my soft parts, trying to hold the light just right. The first one comes unlocked, and Felicity leans into me, cold and clammy, smelling of blood and vomit.

"Mom?" she asks.

I can't answer, can't correct her with the phone in my mouth, and now half her weight is on me. I turn my head, and the light moves with it, as I work the second lock, tears of frustration running down my face. Some of them follow the curve of my cheek, find their way to my mouth, salt stinging the tiny cuts there.

The second lock lets go, and Felicity falls forward,

her head knocking into mine. My phone falls with a clatter at our feet, the light shining upward into my eyes as I lower her to the floor, my arm screaming with pain. I can't hold her, and she falls the rest of the way, slumping into a seated position on the other side of the wall, her head resting against the bricks I laid, one leg folded awkwardly underneath her.

"I can't carry you," I tell her, like that information will suddenly make her stand. "I don't think I can even get you over this wall. Not with my arm like this."

Nothing. No answer. No indication she hears me at all.

I lean over the wall, reach down, try to shake her again, the light from my phone practically blinding me.

"Carry me," Felicity says, her eyelids flickering. "Carry me."

"Felicity! Stay with me," I urge her. "Look at me!"

She opens her eyes, but her focus is not on me. It falls to the necklace that has slipped out of my hoodie, dangling now, flashing in the light.

"Oh . . . there it is," she says.

And she reaches up, closing her hand around half a heart pendant.

Chapter 74

Felicity

Fifth Grade / The Night Of

"Did you know Gretchen named her new puppy William Wilson? What a stupid name," I say, rolling my eyes. "Like, even her dog is kind of stuck-up."

Tress laughs, runs her hand down Goldie-Dog's nose. "You're not stuck-up, are you Goldie?" she asks, and Goldie farts in return, sending us both into peals of laughter.

"Girls . . ." Annabelle's voice comes from down the hall. "It's past midnight. You need to be thinking about sleep."

"Okay, Mom," Tress calls back. "We'll . . . think about it."

Which sets us off again but makes me feel a little bad. Tress's mom is cool.

"I don't want to make your mom mad," I whisper, my giggles making the whisper as loud as regular talking, which only makes Tress laugh more.

"Oh, wait . . . ," she says, something occurring to her. "Mom gave this to me." She gets up from the floor, going over to her dresser. She comes back with two necklaces, each of them with half a heart pendant hanging from them. One side reads *Best*. The other reads *Friends*. Tress holds them in front of me, swaying in the light from her bedside table.

"This used to be Mom's," she says. "I guess they were a thing once. Kinda cool, right?"

"Yeah," I say, reaching out. They're cheap, mostly brass, the chains corroded with age. My mom would die if she saw me wearing this. I'm okay with that. I close my hand around one, then pull back, questioning.

"Are you just showing me these, or . . . ?"

"Yeah, I'm totally just letting you know I have it. Obviously one is for Gretchen," she says.

"Oh my God," I say, giving her a shove. She falls backward, laughing.

"Girls!" Annabelle's voice again, sharper this time.

I take one of the necklaces and put mine on. "So . . . if this was your mom's, why does she have both pieces?" I ask.

"Huh?" Tress's hands are behind her neck, struggling

with the cheap clasp. I motion for her to turn around, and she does. I move her hair, latch the necklace for her.

"Who had the other part of your mom's necklace? And"—it feels super rude, but I'm curious—"why did they give it back?"

"I don't know," Tress says, shrugging, holding the charm and reading it upside down. "I didn't ask."

Chapter 75

Tress

Fifth Grade / The Night Of

"We're going to wear these forever, right?"

Chapter 76

Felicity

Senior Year

"Felicity? Hon? Do you have your box ready for the PTA rummage sale?"

Shit. No, I don't. But I need to clean out my closet like nobody's business. I grab the box Mom left in my room a week ago, open it, and jerk random things off hangers, grabbing shoes from the back of the closet, anything out of season. This rummage sale is going to be a gold mine for somebody.

Gold . . . I probably have some jewelry that can go, too. I crack open the box, laughing when I spot the pair of earrings that Brynn got me last year for Christmas—volleyballs, one that reads *Book*, the other one *Keeper*.

"A keeper, all right," I say, tucking them into a drawer to hold on to.

The smile fades when I spot a ring Patrick got me, an apology for something he did . . . again. It goes into the PTA box, falling among the piles of clothes without a sound. Something's jammed in the back, the charm pinched in the hinges, a cheap chain curled, greenish, lying on the bottom of my jewelry box like a snake.

I yank it free, my stomach dropping.

Rummage sale, here I come.

"Can she even afford to shop here?" Gretchen asks, glancing up from her phone.

"What?" I ask, shading my eyes. The sun is beating down on the school parking lot, the tables of clothes, toys, shoes, dishes—all the unwanted objects of Amontillado up for sale, the made-up moms of the PTA playing salesgirls.

"Tress Montor," Gretchen says, pointing. "She's like . . . here."

I follow Gretchen's finger to see Tress hovering over the jewelry table.

Shit.

Chapter 77

Tress

Senior Year

It hangs, dangling in the sun, too dirty to shine. The engraved word caked in neglect.

Around my neck, its mate, the answer. Under that, a patch of skin, always green now—because I've never taken it off.

The other half of my heart is on sale for a quarter.

Chapter 78

Felicity

Senior Year

"Seriously?" Gretchen's gum snaps in my ear.

"What?" I ask again, my back to her as I sort through children's clothes.

"Tress just took something off the jewelry table and walked away."

"Okay," I say. I fold clothes, adoring the symmetry in the squares I can make, the order under my hands.

"Do you remember when she stole your tampons? Klepto."

Chapter 79

Tress

She's got the heart in her hands, pulling down, pulling on my neck, pulling me over the wall.

"Felicity, you need to let me go. I can't lift you by myself. I've got to get Hugh."

"Where's mine?" she asks, her eyes on the necklace. "Where is my heart?"

"Here," I tell her, digging into my hoodie pocket. "It's here. I brought it for you. I thought . . ."

I don't know what I thought. That I would show it to her and she'd be overwhelmed by the grief of what we lost, pushed by her emotions to tell me what happened that night?

I don't know.

But I definitely didn't think I'd be putting it around

her neck, clasping the back through a bloodied knot of hair, lifting her chin because she can't raise her own head.

I didn't think I would kill her.

I reach past her legs, past a wet mess of all kinds of things, for my phone, turning the light away, out of my eyes.

"You've got it back now," I tell her. "You've got your half of the necklace."

It rests, lackluster, against her gray skin, next to a runnel of her blood.

Her half, the half that reads *Best*. Because that's the half she wanted. Of course she did. And maybe that's right. Maybe Felicity Turnado is better than Tress Montor, not because of her house or her car or her parents or her clothes. Maybe Felicity Turnado is better than Tress Montor because she never killed anyone.

"I'm going to get Hugh," I tell her. "Hey!" I clap my hands in front of her face, sending a massive jolt of pain up my arm. "Felicity—I'm getting Hugh. We're going to get you out of here."

"Hugh?" she asks. "Hugh didn't carry me."

"Okay," I tell her, agreeing with whatever she says. "I'm leaving you the phone, okay? I'm leaving you the light."

She doesn't answer, so I go, lost in pitch blackness

as soon as I turn my back, slipping in my own blood, finding the staircase by feel, pulling myself along the banister, one-handed, resting halfway up.

Jesus Christ. Neither one of us is going to make it.

I elbow the hook open, fall into the kitchen, sending bottles scattering. The glass rolls across the floor, making hollow music.

"Hugh!" I cry, not caring who finds me. Not caring who helps. Not caring about the questions. I just have to save my friend.

Chapter 80

Felicity

"Hugh didn't carry me."

My voice is strained, tired, a worn-out note.

But it's not wrong.

"Hugh didn't carry me," I say again, a little louder.

Something rests against my skin, something metal on my chest, something sticking in place. Something wet. Something smells something . . .

Chapter 81

Tress

I crawl on my elbows through the kitchen, black spots spraying my vision. I cry for Hugh, cry for help. I call for Brynn. I call for Maddie. I even call for Gretchen. No one comes.

I struggle to my feet, pulling myself up with a chair, and lurch to the door.

Chapter 82

Cat

The smell of the girl
is everywhere.
Red. Death.
Spots in the room
with the swinging boy
down these steps, a drop
I lick and taste
her last / best
Felicity / FELICITY
a puddle of her, in this room
with chairs
Felicity / FELICITY
a smear, by that door.
A beckoning, below.
Felicity / FELICITY

Chapter 83

Tress

Piles of people. Hands and arms and legs. Slick skin, pale faces. Hot breaths, warm and vacant, fill the air. There is no more laughter. All are silent.

Hugh, in his throne, suddenly small, bleary, barely there, a question not asked yet on his lips. Ribbit, naked, collapsed on the floor, the zigzag scar on the back of his calf bright and angry, fresh like only yesterday. The clock ticks, backward, the only thing moving in the room.

I'm down again, more blood out than in, crawling over people, but they are wrong, too small, hands and faces and feet, and the boy in the concert T-shirt is too young to be here, is only a child, who thought I was his mother in the stairwell; why are we all children again?

On the stairs, the clock stops.

Chapter 84

Felicity

Shadow. Shadow and light. Something in the dark. Something on my chest. Something is near me. Something is here.

Chapter 85

Cat

Another girl
different now
almost gone
her blood has spilled
mixed with my girl's
together they are
Fel—Tress—icity / FEL—TRESS—ICITY

Chapter 86

Felicity

My hair it floats tangles with Annabelle's we float bubbles from her mouth bubbles from Lee's nose eyes flat and dead and fish take a nibble there is a weight on my chest, half of a heart. I am pulled angry words (*no don't can't shouldn't won't LISTEN TO ME!*). Hair dangles swinging with my hair and the heart it tangles I am carried out of the water I am carried onto the bank I am carried I am dripping I am wet I am

carry me take care of me

not the raven flashing tattoo black it is an angry Z red slash of skin not healed stitches like small mouths held tightly shut hands on my face hands wanting me to be okay this boy always wanting to help always wanting to make it better always wanting to make up for the

thing that was so wrong Oh Tress oh Tress oh Tress
they are dead and I knew but I didn't know that I knew
and he KNOWS he KNOWS—not me. Oh Tress you
are in danger and you will not stop I know you and you
will know and I cannot help you I am going I am going
I am going

Chapter 87

Felicity

I am gone.

Chapter 88

Tress

I am helpless, and there is no one to help me. I will do it myself, like always. I grit my teeth, spit, come to my feet. Behind me, a shadow, some movement. I turn in time to see a black tail slip out the front door.

"Run," I tell it. "Go far."

Back to the kitchen, I unscrew a light bulb, propping myself against the table for a second to catch my breath, watching as a glimmer of sunlight reaches through the grime on the window.

"I'm coming, Felicity," I say, making my way to the door.

The steps are hard, my good hand clutching the light bulb, my bad one holding the rail as best it can. I follow the glow of my phone, find the empty socket, screw in the light bulb.

"I'm back," I tell Felicity.

She doesn't hear me.

Felicity is dead.

Chapter 89

Tress

There is no movement upstairs as I finish my work, the trowel heavy in my hand, the bricks impossible, but made possible, by dint of my will. I began something, I will finish it. Slowly, I entomb the body of Felicity Turnado.

My best friend.

Chapter 90

Tress

Upstairs again, my bad hand, purple and numb. I pick my way through the people, children no longer, my head clear now. Too clear. I know what I did.

I wake Ribbit, who smiles at me as soon as he opens his eyes. Naked. Trusting. A child. He sees my arm and wants to help, wants to fix it, wants to make everything better. I tell him it is unfixable, and he nods, still drunk, but seeming to understand the finality of *unfixable*.

We move through the yard, past what used to be William Wilson.

We put the Allan house behind us.

A house that will soon be torn to the ground.

Chapter 91

Felicity

I ask for the boy, as always.

"Hugh?"

His name bounces back to me. Echoed. Rejected.

"Hugh?"

There's no answer but my voice, saying the same thing. Again.

"Hugh?"

I reach for him, because he always reaches, too, and we touch, and then everything is okay. Because touching Hugh is how I know I'm back. But he's not here.

There's no one here.

I open my eyes to find him, but they are already open, and I cannot open them more.

There is nothing to see.
But I can feel.
And all I feel . . .
. . . is bricks.

Chapter 92

Cat

No metal no fence no bars
no girl no man no *Almost Human*
no old meat, only fresh,
many, many last / bests
and where once there was a house
and a boy swinging
and a woman sobbing
and a baby screaming
and the smell of my girl.
Those things are gone now.
And instead I hear, quietly,
under rock and dirt
The sound of crying.

ACKNOWLEDGMENTS

First, thanks as always goes to my agent, Adriann Ranta Zurhellen, who has yet to tell me that I've finally run off the rails. Secondly, to my editor, Ben Rosenthal, who probably assumes by now that I don't know how a calendar works or what the base ten number system is, but we both trust my copy editors to catch all my issues with logic and linear time.

There are so many people (and animals!) in a person's life that lend a hand in the writing of a book. I must thank fellow writer Kamerhe Lane for the stream of consciousness series of texts that she received from me over the course of a single day as I cooked this book and weighed the possibility that I couldn't deliver it, and trusted in her assurances that I could.

Kate Karyus Quinn and Demitria Lunetta are invaluable to me as sounding boards in both my professional and personal life, which I'm sure they may regret someday—if they haven't already. Thanks (as always) goes to Lydia Kang for not blocking my email yet, as I tend to send her fairly gruesome questions about just how much damage I can do to a fictional human while reasonably expecting them to stay alive. And finally, a big thank-you to Tiffany Ruhmer, my on-call zookeeper who was a tremendous help to me while writing this book.